Principles of Health Care Management
Compliance, Consumerism, and Accountability in the 21st Century

Seth B. Goldsmith, ScD, JD

Professor Emeritus
University of Massachusetts
School of Public Health and Health Sciences
Amherst, Massachusetts

JONES AND BARTLETT PUBLISHERS
Sudbury, Massachusetts
BOSTON   TORONTO   LONDON   SINGAPORE

World Headquarters

Jones and Bartlett Publishers	Jones and Bartlett Publishers	Jones and Bartlett Publishers
40 Tall Pine Drive	Canada	International
Sudbury, MA 01776	2406 Nikanna Road	Barb House, Barb Mews
978-443-5000	Mississauga, ON L5C 2W6	London W6 7PA
info@jbpub.com	CANADA	UK
www.jbpub.com		

Library of Congress Cataloging-in-Publication Data

Goldsmith, Seth B.
  Principles of health care management: compliance, consumerism, and accountability in the 21st century / Seth B. Goldsmith.
    p.; cm.
  Includes bibliographical references and index.
  ISBN 0-7637-3243-5 (pbk. : alk. paper)
  1. Health services administration—United States.   2. Health facilities—United States.
3. Compliance.   4. Consumer protection.   5. Liability (Law)
  [DNLM: 1. Health Services Administration—United States. W 84 AA1 G624p 2005]
I. Title: Principles of health care management.   II. Title.
  RA971.G573 2005
  362.1′068—dc22

                                                                    2004026714

Production Credits
Publisher: Michael Brown
Production Director: Amy Rose
Production Editor: Jeff Freeland
Editorial Assistant: Kylah Goodfellow McNeill
Marketing Manager: Marissa Hederson
Manufacturing Buyer: Amy Bacus
Composition: Roberta Landi
Cover Design: Diana Coe
Printing and Binding: Malloy, Inc.

Printed in the United States of America
09 08 07 06 05   10 9 8 7 6 5 4 3 2 1

Dedicated to

WENDY

My Ayshes Chayil

Acknowledgments

It is impossible to write a book of this scope without the direct and indirect assistance of countless individuals. Two long-time friends, Sol Goldner and Joel Dalva, have been especially helpful with their great assistance in the chapter on financial management. My numerous students over the past 32 years have assisted me by their perceptive comments and challenging ideas. In recent years the students who took the risk of taking my corporate compliance courses were particularly helpful in refining ideas. Others who deserve a special mention are my long-time colleague and friend Dr. Shlomo Barnoon, who always provided a wonderful and supportive sounding board for my ideas and experiences, and, of course, Michael Brown of Jones and Bartlett who has trusted my writing and judgment for 25 years.

Finally, I want to acknowledge the assistance of my wife, Wendy Benjamin Goldsmith, for her support and encouragement during the years of working on this project.

Table of Contents

About the Contributors

Joel Dalva, BS (accounting), MBA, CPA, is Senior Executive, Finance, Cambio Health Solutions. Previously, Mr. Dalva was Chief Financial Officer of Tenet St. Mary's Medical Center in West Palm Beach, Florida.

Solomon Goldner, MBA, MPH, is President of Premiere Healthcare Management, LLC, of North Hollywood, California, owner and operator of a chain of long-term care facilities. Previously, Mr. Goldner was Vice President and Chief Financial Officer of Golden Bear Health Centers, a chain of nursing homes; National Medical Enterprises, Hillhaven Division; and Coopers and Lybrand. His degrees in accounting and public health are both from Columbia University.

Introduction

The past several decades have been, to say the least, challenging for health care administrators, whether they are managing health systems, hospitals, nursing homes, assisted living centers, group practices, HMOs or other health care organizations. A medical center CEO summarized his recent experiences by simply saying, "It isn't fun anymore." While this book will not make management "fun," it will explain the critical changes and challenges that administrators must deal with as they go about practicing their profession and what students must learn as they begin their study of this vital field.

The source material for this book comes from several places. First, like all books, it comes from the experiences of its author. In my case, four decades in the field, over 30 years of writing and research, and years on the board of one of America's largest and most important for-profit health care businesses, a billion-dollar corporation that owns and manages nursing homes, home care services, and, in the recent past, hospitals, pharmacies, and related providers. Additionally, in 1998, I completed a 27-month stint as CEO of a multicomponent nonprofit health system with a budget of $70 million and a staff of almost 1100 people. Over the years in my various roles, I have had to deal with deficits, lawsuits, FBI investigations, labor strife, payrolls, ethical issues, good boards and bad ones—just for openers.

A second source is the literature of the field, including the extensive collection of government and legal material. I draw heavily on government and legal documents, the former because it represents some of the best realized and least known analyses of problems in the system, and the latter because the legal system is the main avenue for administrators to be held accountable.

The third source of material for this book is the experience of my many friends, former students, and colleagues in the field who have generously contributed their wisdom to this project. These people, who are living with the issues on a day-to-day basis, have been my sounding board for this book, and I trust their contributions will ensure its value to the "real world" of management.

This book's central theme is accountability, but the focus is effective management. I have organized the book into five sections with the goal of providing a useful text to both practitioners and students. The first section is essential foundation material on the U.S. health system. It is designed to give all readers a common understanding of the system within which management must occur.

The second section is a review of the essentials of health care management. In this review, I offer professionals an opportunity to reexamine how their own positions and performance stack up against what might be considered a theoretical model. For students, this section represents the health care spin on management, that is, how the principles of management apply in the field of health administration, where we operate with organizational structures that are not found in industrial organizations.

The third section examines the crucial area of corporate compliance. In the past decade, corporate compliance issues have changed the landscape of health care management. Not only have organizations been required to develop and implement compliance programs, but the federal and state governments also have actively pursued individuals and organizations that have failed to meet compliance requirements. Indeed, there is no other time in history when compliance violations have resulted in fines of more dollars for health care organizations and sentences of more jail time for health professionals. Perhaps no subject is more important to understand than corporate compliance for a health administrator's personal freedom!

In the fourth section, we look at how consumerism affects the health care organization. The consumer movement has not only had a major impact on American society but has, through a variety of legal and legislative mechanisms, also changed the way health care organizations must do business. And finally, we conclude with a model of accountable management that begins with a reconceptualization of strategic planning and ends with an analysis of the accountable organization.

Throughout this text, case studies are presented to illustrate the points that I am developing in that particular section or chapter. While some of the names and places in these cases are fictionalized, each one of them is based on an actual situation. If this book stimulates thinking, provokes discussion, or better yet, results in some positive changes, then its goal will be attained.

CHAPTER 1

An Overview of the U.S. Health System

A basic question that a health care manager should ask is: What is the nature of the system that I am being asked to manage? For most people who are not professionally engaged in organizing or delivering care, the health system means utilization, in other words, an occasional visit to a clinician or institution such as a clinic or HMO. To a manager, however, the health system should initially be analyzed in a variety of ways: in terms of expenditures, facilities, manpower, and patients, or perhaps in terms of the more marketing-oriented nomenclature of clients and consumers.

HEALTH EXPENDITURES

In the calendar year 2000, the total national expenditure for health for the 275 million people living in the United States was $1.3 trillion, or $4,637 per capita. This enormous amount of money represented 13.2% of the gross domestic product.[1] How was this $1.3 billion spent? By whom? For what? With what controls?

Most of the dollars (approximately 87% for the past decade) have been spent on personal health services. The bulk of these personal health dollars pay for hospital services, while other significant percentages are for physician services, nursing home care, drugs, and dental services. The nonpersonal health service expenditures are categorized as those associated with government public health activities, with prepayment and administration, and with research and medical facilities construction.

---

[1] U.S. Census Bureau, *Statistical Abstract of the United States, 2002*, Table 114, p. 92.

Hospitals consume by far the lion's share of the health dollars, but this has not always been the case. Prior to 1939, physician services were the largest single area of health care expenditures, followed closely by hospital services. Subsequent to World War II and up to the present time, hospital expenses have exceeded all other items by a significant degree. From 1928–1929, hospital care represented 18% of the total health expenditures. By 1939–1940, these expenditures represented 25%; by the pre-Medicare/Medicaid period of 1964–1965, this percentage had grown to almost 34%; and by 1980, the total had reached almost 47%. But, by 1990, as a result of pressure from the Medicare payment systems as well as innovations in therapy and ambulatory care, the hospitals' share of the national health expenditure pie had dropped to 37%, and by 2000 it was less than 34%.[2] During this same period, expenditures for physician services rose from 28% in 1928–1929 to 25% in 1939–1940 and to 34% in 1964–1965; by 1980, in the post-Medicare and Medicare world, physician and clinical services were slightly less than 21% of total personal health expenditures. By 1990, the figure was up to 23%, and in the year 2000 it hovered around 25% (ibid.).

What had occurred? Why have health expenditures escalated so dramatically, and why have the shifts in expenditure patterns been so great? Several explanations have been offered, including population growth, inflation, the cost of technology, and financing patterns.

Some of the dramatic increases in health expenditures simply are explained by the fact that there are considerably more Americans today than there were 10, 20, or 30 years ago. There are 75 million more people living in the United States today than there were in 1970. In conceptual terms this means that between 1970 and 2000 the United States annexed the equivalent of the entire populations of England, Scotland, Wales, Northern Ireland, Denmark, Norway, and Sweden. Or, on a more local level, the United States added the equivalent of the entire populations of Maine, New Hampshire, Vermont, Massachusetts, Rhode Island, Connecticut, New York, New Jersey, Pennsylvania, Maryland, Virginia, West Virginia, and North Carolina. More people means more demand, more services, and more expenditures.

Not only is the example of a 75-million-person growth in the population since 1970 an important explanatory variable in understanding why

---

[2]U.S. Census Bureau, *Statistical Abstract of the United States, 2002*, Table 114, p. 92.

health expenditures continue to increase, but the changing shape of the population is also a critically important variable. Most significantly, we have seen a dramatic growth in the senior population. For example, in 1970 we had a total of 20 million Americans over the age of 65, which represented 9.9% of the population. In 2000 we had 34.8 million people over 65, which represented 12.6% of the population. Within the senior population, the numbers are even more dramatic. We have seen a doubling of the 75- to 84-year-old group since 1970, from 6.1 million people to 12.3 million and close to a tripling of the over-85-year-old group, from 1.5 million to 4.3 million.[3] For the health system, more seniors translates into a greater demand for services such as doctor's visits and hospital days. In 2000, 23.7% of people over 65 visited their physicians more than 10 times, while only 12.2% of the population between 18 and 44 visited their doctors that often.[4] The trend lines are clear: The older we get as a society, the greater demands we make on virtually all components of the health system.

Another related dimension of costs is the increasing cost of managing complex diseases. HIV/AIDS is an example of a disease that did not have any impact on health care expenditures until the late 1970s and early 1980s. Similarly, SARS was an unknown disease until 2003, and its impact is still to be determined. We do know that in 2003 this one newly emerging disease wreaked havoc on the health system in Toronto, Canada, with cost implications that are still being calculated.

On a personal level, I can share that my late wife was a victim of ovarian cancer. Fortunately we had excellent health insurance and found superb physicians. She was able to obtain regular care at three outstanding medical centers: Brigham and Women's Hospital, Massachusetts General Hospital, and Baystate Medical Center. Additionally, she received useful consultations at Fox Chase Cancer Center and experimental care at the University of Texas Health Science Center in San Antonio. All told, between 1989 and 1995 my wife had more than 50 hospital admissions and 5½ years of care before she succumbed. The cost of this extraordinary care was in excess of $500,000.00.

One example of how technology has affected cost comes in the form of the drug Neupogen, which is a product of high-tech DNA synthesis. Its

---

[3]*Health, United States, 2002*, Table 1, p. 70.
[4]*Health, United States, 2002*, Table 72, p. 217.

value to cancer sufferers comes from its ability to stimulate the growth of white blood cells and thus reduce susceptibility to infection after chemotherapy. While Neupogen is an effective adjunct to chemotherapy, it is also quite expensive. When my wife first used the drug, she had a 10-dose cycle, later reduced to a 5-dose cycle. Each dose cost almost $1,000.00. Our co-payment was $10.00 per dose, the rest being paid by our health insurance. Today the cost is considerably lower, although still expensive: between $175.00 and $279.00 per dose depending on the dosage size.

During the long years of my wife's treatment I spent considerable effort searching out treatment options throughout the world. In one meeting with a senior official in Britain, I learned that the ovarian cancer protocols in that country were almost identical to those in the United States. Indeed, a good deal of their research had National Cancer Institute funding. Patients in the United Kingdom, however, did not have access to Neupogen. "Why?" I inquired. "Cost" was the straightforward answer. This official went on to say that it is simply cheaper to have patients isolate themselves during their days of highest vulnerability to infection than to give them an expensive drug.

Inflation—the increase in prices and cost with no particular change in value— is a second major factor in the trend toward increased expenditures. How much of the increase can be explained by inflation is debatable, but it is clear that a 1950 dollar is not the equivalent of a present dollar and that most bills must be paid in present-value currency. In one historical examination of the reasons for the increase in health expenditures, it was found that inflation accounted for 44% of the increase in health expenditures between 1950 and 1965, and 43% of the increased expenditures between 1971 and 1974.[5] A different report from that same period found that "52% of the $38.4 billion increase from fiscal year 1965 to fiscal year 1972 reflected a rise in prices." In explaining the remaining rise, the authors noted that "10% ($3.8 billion) was the result of population growth, and the remaining 38% ($14.7 billion) was attributable to greater utilization of services and the introduction of new medical techniques."[6] The inflation statistics on medical care pretty well tell

---

[5]R.M. Gibson and M.S. Mueller, "National Health Expenditures, Fiscal Year 1976," *Social Security Bulletin 40*(4) (April 1977), 14.
[6]B.S. Cooper and N.L. Worthington, "National Health Expenditures, 1929–1972," *Social Security Bulletin 36*(1) (January 1973), 13.

the story: Using 1982–1984 as the base period—that is, assuming an average price of medical care in that period of 100—by 1990 we are up to 162.8 and by 2000 we are up to 266.

Perhaps a more user-friendly way of considering inflation is thinking about the cost of gasoline today versus 20 years ago. The gallon is still a gallon and the gas is essentially the same, although more expensive (and to think it was about a quarter per gallon when I first started driving). Since the single largest component of any health care manager's budget is personnel, it is important to realize that higher wages and salaries are important variables in explaining the growth of national health expenditures. Not only do we have more people working in health care, but also the cost of employing them is greater. While few health care workers receive the minimum wage, that number does represent a base figure for calculating all wages. In 1967 the federal minimum wage was $1.40; in 1975 it increased to $2.10; by 1980 it was up to $3.10; in 1990 it was $3.80; and in 1997, with a few changes in between, it hit $5.15.

In a summary of analyses looking at the increasing costs for health care, Thorpe, Woodruff, and Ginsburg suggest that since 1998 the following factors explain the increases: "Growth in pharmaceutical expenses, expensive new technologies, aging of the population, increase in consumer demand, broader managed care networks, provider consolidation, health care labor pressure."[7] They go on to suggest that from 2002 through 2010 there will be additional increases in health care expenditure as follows: "Hospital care (21%); physician services (19%); outpatient prescription and over-the-counter drugs (21%); and nursing home and home health care (10%)."[8]

Not only has the use of the health care dollar changed, but the source of the revenue also has shifted. This shift has had and will continue to have a profound effect on management of health care organizations. The two most important shifts are related to the payer and the source of the revenue. In terms of the payer, direct patient payments have decreased, from 88.5% prior to 1929 to 27% in the fiscal 1980 period to 17.2% in 2000.

During that same period, third-party payments have increased to 82.9%, of which 34.6% comes from private health insurance, 5.0% from private funding such as philanthropy, and 43.3% from government.[9]

---

[7]Data retrieved (5/12/2002) from www.ahcpr.gov/news/ulp/ulpcosts1.htm.
[8]Ibid.
[9]*Health, United States, 2002*, Table 117, p. 293.

Indeed, Medicaid and Medicare, which did not come into existence until the mid-1960s, now account for 21% of all personal health expenditures. Government now not only pays 40% of the total health bill, but it also pays 55% of the hospital bill and 24% of the physician's bill.

Along with these increased payments from the government has come an increased control of the expenditures. For example, virtually every major health bill that has passed through Congress since the late 1960s has been supported on the basis that it would contain or reduce health care costs. Some initiatives, such as changing the system of paying hospitals for Medicare recipients from a cost-based retrospective payment system to the present case-based prospective system, have saved money nationwide. Other programs, such as health care fraud and abuse prevention, have saved the system money, but their actual implementation is so localized that there are clear cost savings differences from region to region. Illustrative of this is an analysis of the work of the U.S. attorney's office in Boston, which indicated that the aggressiveness of Boston lawyers as well as their colleagues in Philadelphia and Florida have made these offices the trendsetters in litigating fraud and abuse cases.[10] On the other hand, the United States is a large country, and one must wonder what is going on elsewhere that health care fraud and abuse cases are not being aggressively pursued.

Despite these massive expenditures, there is clearly a lack of equity in terms of access, cost, and quality in the U.S. health system. Many observers argue that this is inevitable, since our society is fundamentally inequitable; the health system simply reflects that. It should be recognized, however, that even some government programs institutionalize this inequity. For example, every state has considerable latitude in setting the level of eligibility for Medicaid, as well as the quantity, and to some extent the quality, of services that will be available. What this means in practice is easily seen in the long-term care industry. Medicaid per diem reimbursement rates for similar facilities ranged in 2003 from $99.25 in West Virginia to $171.17 in Delaware. For the individual institution, such differences in reimbursement rates translate into different staffing ratios and other services that result in a differing quantity and quality of care for residents.

A frequently mentioned aspect of the access equation is that of financial access to the system; that is, the ability to get through the front door

---

[10] *The Boston Globe*, May 13, 2003, vol. 263 (133), pp. A1, A5.

because of having health insurance. Current estimates are that approximately 40 million people are uninsured, although as many as 59 million people are uninsured at some time during the year. What is perhaps most interesting is that the typical uninsured person is not necessarily unemployed but rather is employed at a job that pays low wages and does not provide health insurance as a benefit. The fiscal crisis that beset states in 2003 is a cautionary tale about the interplay between the needs of society and money. A report from the National Conference of State Legislatures Health Policy Tracking Services underscored the equity issues in our society by pointing out that 19 states were contemplating significant cuts to their Medicaid recipients, including, in the case of Colorado, eliminating an entire group from eligibility (legal immigrants) and, in other states, cutting back on a range of services such as vision care, podiatry, and dental care.[11]

Perhaps the most interesting issue to contemplate is that even when the finances are in place through such programs as Medicare, which is the federal program primarily serving the elderly, equal access still does not exist. In a 2003 report by Gornick analyzing Medicare data, we learn that "in comparison with White beneficiaries, Black beneficiaries used fewer preventive and health promotion services . . . and underwent more of the types of procedures associated with poor management of chronic disease, such as partial or complete lower limb amputation."[12] Wennberg, the distinguished academic researcher from Dartmouth University who single-handedly called the nation's attention to the significant variations in medical care between regions,[13] also found that Medicare, the program designed to provide equal access and control costs, had major variations in spending and services.[14] Nationwide data also tell us that there are many variations in how categories of people use the health system, such as the poor and nonpoor,[15] or how people of different ages,[16]

---

[11]National Conference of State Legislatures, State Health Policy Brief 4, April 2003, p. 1.

[12]M.E. Gornick, "A Decade of Research in Medicare Utilization: Lessons for the Health and Health Care of Vulnerable Men," *American Journal of Public Health*, *93*(5), May 2003, p. 754.

[13]J.E. Wennberg and M.M. Cooper, eds., *The Dartmouth Atlas of Health Care 1998* (Chicago: American Health association Press, 1998).

[14]J.E. Wennberg, E.S. Fisher, and J.S. Skinner, data retrieved (February 13, 2002) from www.healthaffairs.org/WebExclusives/ Wennberg_Web_Excl_021302.htm.

[15]*Health, United States, 2002*, Table 72, p. 218.

[16]Ibid., p. 217.

ethnicities,[17] or from different parts of the country use health services.[18] Although some of these differences are related to the behavior of the population itself, there is another explanatory variable: the availability of resources. In the next section we shall examine some of the key resources of the United States' health system.

HOSPITALS

Since hospitals are so central to any understanding of the health system, and hospitals are also the largest employer in health care, it is worthwhile to briefly review their origins. The word *hospital* is derived from Medieval Latin, and meant "hospice" or "guesthouse" typically for weary pilgrims. The 1989 edition of the *Oxford English Dictionary* notes that the word finds its first usage in 1300 CE in reference to St. Thomas's in London: "Ther is nouth an hospital arerd of seint Thomas."[19]

The concept of a hospital dates from earlier times, indeed, hundreds of years before the beginning of the Common Era. For example, the Sinhalese claim that King Pandukabhaya established hospitals in Sri Lanka in the fourth century BCE.[20] Perhaps the most interesting account traces the idea of hospital chains to the time of the great Indian ruler King Asoka (273–232 BCE).

Legend has it that Asoka killed all rival claimants to the throne of the Indian Empire, most notably his 99 brothers. After his ascendancy he converted to Buddhism and became distinguished for promoting goodness and virtue throughout his kingdom, including the establishment of networks of medical facilities.[21] In what is probably the best and most comprehensive current history of hospitals, Risse describes the Greeks developing a temple culture in the ninth century BCE that included amongst their attributes health and healing.[22]

In biblical times we learn of hospitality from the great patriarch Abraham who, despite recovering from his own circumcision, invites

[17]Ibid.

[18]Ibid., p. 219.

[19]J.A. Simpson and E.S.C. Weiner, eds., *The Oxford English Dictionary*, 2nd Edition, vol. VII (Oxford: Clarendon Press, 1999), p. 414.

[20]Data retrieved (n.d.) from www.lankalibrary.com/geo/medicine.htm.

[21]J. Keay, *India: A History* (New York: Grove Press, 2000), pp. 90, 96, 99.

[22]G. Risse, *Mending Bodies, Saving Souls* (Oxford: Oxford University Press, 1999), p.24.

three strangers into his tent only to learn that the strangers are angels of God. Perhaps the single city that is most responsible for the growth of facilities to house and treat the weary and ill is Jerusalem, an important city for pilgrims. Hospices were vital to the city's landscape. In his discussion of Jerusalem, Risse notes, "Before the first century, the city already had a tradition of sponsoring Jewish hospices, and that tradition was taken on by Christians to house and serve their own pilgrims who began flocking to Jerusalem."[23] The Christian focus on Jerusalem began with its recognition by the Church and saw its height during the many years of the Crusades, when a visit to Jerusalem represented a step toward salvation.

The next thousand years or so coincided with the establishment of those Christian orders that took responsibility for the hospices. For example, there were the Hospitallers of St. John, founded in the eleventh century, the German Order of Hospital Knights, founded in 1199, and specialized orders such as the Knights of St. Lazar, who focused their energy on the care of lepers.[24] Although one hospital in Paris, Hotel Dieu, dates to 600 CE, it is not until the 13th and 14th centuries that we see the rapid development of institutions in western Europe, particularly Italy and France, that more resemble our present-day institutions.

American Hospitals (The Colonial Period to World War II)

As the American nation developed, so did its inventory of hospitals and related institutions. Each institution represented a specific response to the growth of the population, the needs of a specific community, the availability of philanthropy, and often the philosophy of an individual or religious group. The Pennsylvania Hospital, founded by Dr. Thomas Bond and Benjamin Franklin in 1751, is considered to be the oldest voluntary (that is, nonprofit) hospital in the United States. Like most of its successors, it was founded to take care of the sick poor; the more affluent were treated at home. When the hospital opened in 1756 it was utilized in the following way: "The ground floor of the east wing contained the cells for insane patients. The second floor was the men's ward. The third floor was

---

[23]Ibid., p. 138.
[24]Ibid., pp. 138–156.

the women's ward, and the space above was used as lodging for Hospital employees and patients who needed isolation."[25]

Other hospitals, such as Candler in Savannah, Georgia, also were developing in the same time period as the Pennsylvania Hospital.[26] Each of these institutions represented the growth of America. In its earliest days as a nation of seaport cities, growth came in the coastal towns and, as the nation expanded, so did its network of hospitals. For example, it was not until 1907 that Lawton, Oklahoma, saw its first hospital, the Turner and Lewis Private Hospital and Training School for Nursing. Today that small private hospital is a modern medical center, the Lawton Southwestern Medical Center.[27]

During the early 1900s, medical schools, teaching hospitals and a range of specialty hospitals for women, eyes, ears, nose, and throat developed. The nation also witnessed the growth of military and public health service hospitals, religious-oriented institutions, and thousands of community hospitals. A casual perusal of the Internet demonstrates the history and the pride in the history of many of these institutions.

World War II to the Present

Perhaps no event has had a greater impact on hospitals in the United States and elsewhere than World War II. For example, many observers link the establishment of the British National Health System to the devastating consequences of the war on the United Kingdom. In a different part of the world, the health system of Japan was essentially destroyed and subsequently rebuilt by the Allies.[28]

In the United States there was a long period during the war when wages and salaries were frozen. In order to get around this freeze, many employers looked to enhance their packages of fringe benefits, the most significant of which was hospital insurance. The development of hospital insurance and the subsequent rise of Blue Cross and Blue Shield to provide both hospital and medical care insurance put the pieces in place for the growth of the health care industry after the war.

---

[25]Data retrieved (n.d.) from www.uphs.upetm.edu/paharcltour2.Jrtml.

[26]Data retrieved (n.d.) from www.sjchs.orglbody.cfm?id=33.

[27]Data retrieved (n.d.) from www.swmconline.com.

[28]S.B. Goldsmith, *Theory Z Hospital Management: Lessons From Japan* (Rockville, MD: Aspen Publishers, 1984).

An interesting footnote is that for many years, until the federal government started scrutinizing the antitrust issues, Blue Cross and the American Hospital Association viewed themselves in partnership. This partnership even extended to sharing a building at 840 North Lake Shore Drive on Chicago's Gold Coast.

Post–World War II, the Hill-Burton Act passed in 1948, providing the funds and an impetus for the growth of hospitals and the building of scores of rural hospitals throughout the country. Many of these institutions remain today as the primary provider of both medical care and employment in their communities.

Comparing and contrasting hospitals of the World War II era and today is almost like comparing Lindberg's Spirit of St. Louis with a new 777 jetliner. They both fly and have wings, tails, and pilots, but that pretty much is where the similarity ends. The typical hospital of the postwar era, probably up to the late 1960s, was essentially a hospital without medical office buildings, ambulatory care facilities, nursing homes, or satellite operations. The hospital of the 1960s did not have one single computer or word processor. It did not have a CT scanner, an MRI, or ultrasound equipment. It may have had an operating suite for open heart surgery, equipment in the laboratories for multichannel blood testing, and its staff certainly had several peer committees for managing the quality of care. No one talked about marketing. (Indeed, in 1974, when the associate director of a hospital I had worked in attended a lecture on hospital marketing that I presented at Columbia University, he promptly and strongly castigated me for thinking of hospital services in marketing terms.)

From 1962–1963 I worked in a 300-bed teaching hospital where half of the beds were in eight- to ten-person wards. In that hospital not one single patient was covered under Medicare or Medicaid (the programs did not begin until 1965. Many procedures that today routinely occur both inside and outside of hospitals, such as ultrasonography or virtual colonoscopy, did not exist in 1962.

As noted earlier, hospitals take the lion's share of virtually every pie in the health system. Hospitals are usually categorized by ownership (governmental, nongovernmental, or proprietary/for-profit), and type of services offered (general medical and surgical, specialty, such as ear, nose, throat), or category of patient (children's hospital). From the early 1960s through the mid-1970s, the number of hospitals in the United States was fairly constant, although from 1953 through 1963 there had been an increase of over 1,000 institutions. But by the mid-1970s, the decline in facilities started. In 1975 there were 7,156 hospitals; three years later that number declined to 7,015; by 1990 the supply had fallen to 6,291 hospitals; and in 2000, the nation was down to 5,810. Not only has the number of facilities declined, but the number of beds available for patients has also diminished, from 1.4 million in 1975 to 983,628 in 2000,[29] all during a time when we have 75 million more people in this country. Of the 5810 hospitals in the United States, 245 belong to agencies of the federal government, primarily the Departments of Veterans Affairs and Defense, and 496 hospitals are for patients with psychiatric problems. The largest single grouping of hospitals are the 3003 nongovernmental, nonprofit facilities (your standard community hospital), and the second-largest grouping are those 1163 acute-care hospitals owned by state and local governments. Finally, investor-owned (that is, for-profit) hospitals account for 749 facilities, including close to 200 owned by the largest hospital chain, the Hospitals Corporation of America (HCA), and 114 owned by the second largest chain, Tenet Healthcare Corporation.[30]

During this same time period (1975–2000), the total number of hospital admissions declined slightly, from 36,157,000 to 34,891,000, and the number of births increased, from 3.09 million in 1975 to 3.94 million in 2000. Throughout this period, hospital personnel increased from 3.023 million people to 4.4 million, and outpatient visits more than doubled, from 254 million in 1975 to over 592 million in 2000.[31]

What is going on? What is behind all these numbers that at first glance do not seem to make any sense whatsoever? Fundamentally, what has occurred in the last 50 years has been an internal reorganization of bed utilization. For example, psychotropic drugs have allowed many persons to function outside of psychiatric hospitals, with the result being that the number of psychiatric beds has decreased from 620,000 in 1950 to 285,000 in 1977 to a mere 86,465 in 2000.

Other shifts in incidence and treatment of diseases have resulted in similar decreases, such as the decrease in the number of beds in tuberculosis and respiratory disease hospitals from 72,000 beds in 1950 to 3,315 in

---

[29] *Health, United States, 2002*, Table 107, p. 279.
[30] *Health Statistics 2002* (Chicago: Health Forum LLC, 2002). Table 1, pp. 2–5.
[31] Ibid.

1977 to 253 in 2000. However, it should also be recognized that some of these cases are also handled with dedicated services within traditional acute care settings.

The heart of the hospital system is the community hospital—the short-term, nonfederal hospital that provides a range of general medical and surgical services. In 2000 these 4,915 hospitals, which include in their classification the 3003 nongovernment, nonprofit hospitals, the 749 investor-owned, for-profit hospitals, and the 1163 state and local government-owned community hospitals, had a total of 824,000 beds.[32] While there is clearly a great variety within this group of hospitals, some basic data regarding the "average" community hospital can be identified. The average hospital in the United States has a total of 168 beds, with 21 states having average bed sizes greater than 168 and 29 smaller; indeed, 10 states have average bed sizes smaller than 100 beds.[33] National average length of stay in community hospitals is 5.8 days, ranging from 10.5 days in Montana and South Dakota to a low of 4.4 days in Oregon and 4.2 days in New Mexico.[34] We also see major variations in hospital occupancy rates. Thus, while the average occupancy rate in the country is 63.8%, New York's occupancy rate (78.4%) is dramatically higher than the rate in Kansas (52.6%) or Idaho (52.5%).[35]

AMBULATORY CARE

Ambulatory care is provided in a variety of locations: physicians' offices, hospital outpatient departments, hospital emergency rooms, and a range of other facilities such as surgical day centers, optometrists' offices, day-care centers, neighborhood health centers, substance abuse clinics, mental health centers, and pharmacies.

In 2000, 823 million visits were made to physician's offices; 83 million visits were made to hospital outpatient departments (many hospitals do not have outpatient facilities); and 108 million visits were made to hospital emergency rooms, 39 million of which were related to injuries

---

[32]K.O. Morgan and S. Morgan, eds., *Health Care State Rankings 2002* (Lawrence, KS: Morgan Quitno Press, 2002), p. 203.
[33]Ibid.
[34]Ibid., p. 207.
[35]Ibid., p. 438.

including occupational and motor vehicle accidents.[36] What is perhaps most noteworthy is that, although the hospital is still the center of complicated and high-tech care, the ambulatory care setting has increasingly become the site of choice for what used to occur in the hospital. For example, arthroscopic procedures on the knee have practically disappeared as an inpatient procedure; endoscopies have increasingly become an outpatient procedure; and hernia repairs are frequently done in ambulatory facilities. An interesting example of change is in the area of eye care. A Web page from a Massachusetts group promotes their day surgery services, and they note that their most frequently performed same-day procedures are "[c]ataract extraction with intraocular lens implantation, cornea transplants, laser surgery for treatment of glaucoma and retinal surgery."[37]

For a number of years, the federal government's National Center for Health Statistics has conducted an annual survey of ambulatory medical services provided by physicians in office-based practices. This study, the National Ambulatory Medical Care Survey (NAMCS), provides valuable insights into the practice of medicine. The following are some extracts from the data highlights section of their year 2000 report:

In 2000, 823.5 million visits were made to physician's offices—about 300.4 visits per 100 persons.

a. The visit rate for white persons (3.2 visits per person) was higher than for black persons (2.1 visits per person).

b. Approximately 30% of the visits were by health maintenance organization members.

c. Medicare or Medicaid was the expected source of payment in 28.3% of all visits.

d. General medical examination was the most frequently mentioned reason for visits, accounting for 7.8% of all office visits.

e. Complementary and alternative medical therapies were ordered or provided at 31.6 million physician's office visits, representing 3.8% of all visits.

f. Since 1997, there has been an increase in the percentage of office visits in which a cardiovascular-renal drug (by 21%), hormone (by

---

[36]*Health, United States, 2002*, Tables 83 and 84.
[37]Data retrieved (n.d.) from www.eyehealthservices.com.

25%), or metabolic/nutrient drug (by 49%) was ordered, supplied, administered or continued.[38]

The largest percentage of visits to physicians' offices are made to general or family practitioners (24.1%); 15.2% are made to internists, 12.6% to pediatricians, and 7.9% to obstetricians and gynecologists.[39] In 2000 the United States had 690,128 professionally active physicians, 525,691 of whom were graduates of U.S. medical schools; the remainder were international medical graduates. Of these 690,128 physicians, 631,431 were engaged in patient care, with 490,398 in office-based practice. The four largest specialty groups were the primary care specialties of general practice, internal medicine, obstetrics and gynecology, and pediatrics, which together account for 230,174 office-based physicians, or 47%.[40]

But the health system is not merely physicians and hospitals. Indeed, managers are primarily responsible for managing the human resources of the system, which includes 168,000 dentists, 2.2 million nurses, 97,000 nutritionists/dieticians, 55,000 occupational therapists, 29,500 optometrists, 208,000 pharmacists, 144,000 physical therapists, 10,300 podiatrists, 97,000 speech therapists, 47,200 chiropractors, and, in this generation, countless massage therapists and New Age healers.[41]

OTHER HEALTH CARE INSTITUTIONS AND PROVIDERS

The United States' health system includes scores of categories. For example, in the year 2000, 1.3 million people received services as home-care patients, 105,496 people were hospital patients, and over 1.5 million people were in nursing homes. Fully 80 million people obtained their care from health maintenance organizations.[42]

It is sometimes difficult to know the boundaries of the "health system." What should be included and excluded within a definition of health services, as opposed to other social services? For example, should the

---

[38]U.S. Government, Department of Health and Human Services, *Advance Data from Vital and Health Statistics, 328* (June 5, 2002), p. 2.

[39]Ibid., p. 3.

[40]*Health, United States, 2002*, Table 101.

[41]Ibid., Table 103.

[42]*Health, United States, 2002*, Tables 88, 97, 132, and 105.

definition include pharmacies that not only dispense prescription drugs but also sell billions of dollars of nonprescription, over-the-counter preparations that people use to self-medicate? Clearly, the corner drugstore for many is the source of primary care; thus, it is important to count it in a tally of health care resources. What about the range of nontraditional healers, such as herbalists and therapeutic masseurs? No doubt they help people. For the most part, however, they are excluded from the traditional health system in that they cannot utilize the system's major resources (such as hospitals) and often have only limited access to its insurance mechanisms. For the purposes of this review, they shall generally be excluded. However, the extent of their involvement in the health system should be recognized.

Sometimes the exclusion of practitioners is a matter of medical politics. For example, as part of my doctoral work I studied the history of midwifery in the United States. My research clearly demonstrated that during the early twentieth century there was a campaign of organized medical professionals, in particular professors of obstetrics in the major medical schools, against American midwives. This campaign was not based on sound scientific evidence but rather based on self-interest in establishing the new medical specialty of obstetrics and gynecology. Indeed, had the United States followed the lead of England at that time, this country would have had a totally different approach to obstetrical care—perhaps even a different health system.[43]

THE NEW ORGANIZATIONS IN TOWN

It sometimes appears that the past decade or two has spawned an entire generation of organizations whose prime concern is either regulating or redirecting the health system. Some of these organizations are not actually new, but are reincarnations of older and similar programs.

The regulators are likely to be on any manager's mind. There are literally hundreds of organizations involved in regulation in the health care field; others want to be. The Federal Trade Commission is interested in instigating some antitrust activity in the health field, and the Federal

---

[43]S.B. Goldsmith, "Physicians Attitudes toward Nurse-Midwives," Ph.D Dissertation (The Johns Hopkins University, 1970).

Communications Commission has expressed concern over the proliferation of sophisticated electronic medical equipment that is allegedly causing problems with certain communications equipment. At the federal level, in addition to the organizations fully involved with health—primarily large sections of the Department of Health and Human Services, including the Centers for Medicare and Medicaid Services (formerly the Health Care Financing Administration) and the Office of the Inspector General—other nonhealth-related executive branch departments, such as the Bureau of the Budget, the General Accounting Office, and the Office of the U.S. Attorney General, play critical roles in the health system.

State governments have similar structures: health departments that often have considerable regulatory power, and various related organizations, such as rate commissions and health planning departments. The local level also has a range of government or government-related health planning bodies and, again, some regulatory agencies, such as boards of health.

Organizations for personal professional development, special medical interest groups, and lobbying groups appear to be omnipresent. Virtually every health profession (or group of workers) has its own organization. Specific disease- or problem-oriented organizations are abundant, as are the lobbyists, some of whom tend to focus on organizations, such as the American Medical Association or the American Hospital Association, and some on fund-raising for activities to combat specific diseases, such as Alzheimer's disease, multiple sclerosis, alcoholism, mental retardation, AIDS, or mental illness.

The picture is one of an expensive, complex, and quite fragmented system. Clearly, the health system is not simply a group of well-defined and integrated components, all of which relate to a common goal. On the contrary, it is a system with considerable overlap, waste, and a multiplicity of goals.

CHAPTER 2

The U.S. Health System in Vivo

In the last chapter I presented a somewhat academic view of the health system with a fair amount of data about demographics, health expenditures, hospitals, ambulatory care, and other related subjects. In this chapter I will review the real world of health care by commenting on a sample of health-related newspaper articles that appeared in the year 2003. My focus in this chapter will be on technology and clinical developments, fraud and abuse, health systems and quality, and finances.

As a manager, it is imperative to be au courant with what the public knows and be able to respond to any board, staff, or public inquiries about these matters. For example, when I was CEO of a health system, one of the morning television shows presented a segment on automatic defibrillators. Several hours later a few of my board members (including the chairman) called to ask about these devices, inquiring about their cost, availability, and, of course, how many we owned. I immediately needed to be a "quick study" on the subject. Within weeks, I was also asked to set up demonstrations and was required to make a presentation to the board on whether we should purchase and install the devices throughout our facilities. The lesson here is simple: Not only must managers be on top of the professional literature (which often tends to be both academic and a trifle dated) but they also must be tuned into the popular media, particularly the major dailies and news magazines.

TECHNOLOGY AND CLINICAL DEVELOPMENTS

The health system and its components are both the beneficiaries and victims of technology. The benefits of technology are often obvious, such as safer and better drugs, procedures, or devices. The negatives are often less visible, such as when a drug or medical device passes through the Food and Drug Administration (FDA) process and is introduced, only to be found several years into use to have such negative side effects that it must be recalled and eliminated from the market. Consider the following seven articles and what they might mean for the health system, including those people receiving care, those providing the care, and those paying for the care.

1. Alzheimer's drug: On June 15, 2003, the *New York Times* reported that families with loved ones with Alzheimer's disease were turning to memantine, a drug not approved by the FDA in the United States but used in Europe, for treating the disease.[1] Like legions of people before them, these families were desperate because conventional treatment had failed. Similarly, in the world of cancer therapy, people have tried numerous alternative cures, the most famous of which is laetril. Inevitably, some of these therapies work, for reasons sometimes unknown. However, the issue the health system must contend with is still who should get these experimental, unapproved treatments and who should pay for them. The answer is that usually only the wealthy can afford to go outside the traditional system; rarely will insurance or governmental programs pay for these alternatives. Since 1992, the federal government has been trying to deal with many of these issues through its National Institute of Medicine–based National Center for Complementary and Alternative Medicine (NCCAM) (and its predecessor, the Office of Alternative Medicine) that, according to its website, is focused on "exploring complementary and alternative practices in the context of rigorous science, training complementary and alternative medicine researchers, and disseminating authoritative

---

[1]"Desperate families embrace unapproved Alzheimer drug," *The New York Times*, June 15, 2003, p. 1.

information to the public and professionals."[2] All of these goals were to be met in 2003 with a budget of $114,149,000, or less than 50 cents per American!

2. Sunscreen study: On June 3, 2003, the *Daily Hampshire Gazette*, my Northampton, Massachusetts hometown paper—and one of the oldest dailies in America—reported a *Los Angeles Times* article about Australian research finding that regular daily use of sunscreen, not just smearing it on oneself when going to the beach, will dramatically reduce the incidence of precancers of the skin.[3] The same study debunked the value of beta-carotene supplements to prevent skin precancers. Here we see an existing over-the-counter "supplement" that can help prevent a serious and expensive problem. This is an opportunity for the health system to utilize the tool of health education to save people the anguish and discomfort of skin cancers and also save the system the expense of dealing with the problem. Similarly, the system could educate people about the waste of money involved in using beta-carotene to stave off precancers (although it may have other important functions in a diet). Unfortunately, here as elsewhere, even though sunscreen may be an excellent form of preventive medicine for many consumers, I am unaware of any health insurance program that would pay for a sunscreen prescription.

3. Hormone therapy: A page 1 article in the May 28, 2003, issue of the *Boston Globe* reported that after years of study it was found that the risk of dementia doubled for women who took hormone replacement therapy.[4] For women going through menopause, the issue of whether to take replacement hormones has been a controversial and anxiety-ridden decision. Current research now contradicts earlier findings that suggested hormone replacement therapy not only had a dramatic effect on mitigating menopausal symptoms but also reduced the susceptibility to certain ailments such as heart disease. This new finding, though, indicates a slightly elevated risk of dementia associated with the drug. The dilemma is

---

[2]Data retrieved (n.d.) from www.nccam.nih.gov/about/.
[3]Study of sunscreen. *The Daily Hampshire Gazette*, June 3, 2003, p. C2.
[4]"Study ties hormone therapy to more risk," *The Boston Globe*, May 28, 2003, p. 1.

still in the hands of the consumer. She must make the final choice, often between what her physician may advise and her own limited knowledge. From a systems perspective, we have one final issue: The hormones prescribed by the physician will be covered by insurance (if there is a drug benefit); but any natural solutions, such as those found in the increasingly proliferating health food stores, or other self-care strategies, such as diet and exercise, will not have any subsidy through health insurance. Perhaps it is best to recognize that health insurance is primarily sickness insurance.

4. New delivery system for the flu vaccine: Building a better mouse-trap is often a good idea with significant benefits for everyone, except owners of the old traps. For most of us, taking a flu shot is a less-than-pleasant experience: Roll up the sleeve, turn your head, feel the alcohol swab, then the needle, and finally, we are done. When I was in the Navy, it was a regular assembly line with some type of compressed air gun delivering the shot. At last, as reported in the *New York Times*, a civilized approach developed in the 1960s will become widely available almost 40 years later. The system will simply be a mist sprayed up the nose, much like taking a nasal decongestant. The manufacturers expect to heavily promote this product, whose cost is estimated at $50–55 per dose compared with $10–25 per injection dose, by advertising in the pre-flu season.[5] For managers and consumers, the issue as demonstrated by the flu mist system is why is there such a time lag in getting new technology to the market. Several answers are suggested by this case. First, the FDA goes through its own process of scrutinizing new technology. In the case of the mist, the difference is not merely turning the vaccine into an aerosol but is the use of live vaccine compared with the dead viruses introduced into the system via the needle. Second, the live vaccines "have been engineered to survive in the cooler temperatures of the nose but not the warmer temperatures of the lungs. It provokes the immune system but does not cause serious disease."[6] So, to begin with, there are the technical and clinical issues that must be addressed. Next there are the financial issues that inevitably involve Wall Street. A major new

---

[5] "FDA backs flu vaccine given by mist not a needle," *The New York Times*, June 18, 2003, p. C4.
[6] Ibid.

product costs money in terms of production and marketing, and promoters of such a project need the backing of analysts and investors. In essence, then, it sometimes takes decades between the invention of the new mousetrap and its first sale.

5. Aspirin—Back to the basics: Although the idea of new technology certainly has its attractions, sometimes the older technology or drugs do just as good a job at a fraction of the cost. On June 11, 2003, the *Wall Street Journal* reported on a study published in the *Journal of the American Medical Association* that found that the relatively new high-tech drug ticlopine (at a cost of $100 per month) works no better than aspirin (at a cost of $10 per month) in preventing the recurrurence of strokes in African-Americans.[7] How is it that the health system allows the development of expensive new drugs or technology that are essentially a replacement for equally efficient older drugs or technology? A cynic would answer that it is all about profit. The companies see a market, make a slightly different product, and hope to capture the old market. A research scientist might say that his or her profession is always looking for a more efficient or elegant formulation to attack a significant problem and that the new product may indeed have special benefits, like reduced side effects or a better delivery system. For example, my favorite antibiotic is Zithromax, a drug similar to erythromycin but more expensive. I like the Zithromax because, unlike other antibiotics that require me to take the pill 4 times a day for 10 days, Zithromax has me taking 6 pills: 2 the first day and 1 every day thereafter. The Z-pak, as it is called, is more convenient and perhaps more effective because of higher compliance . . . but that remains to be studied.

6. Technology and unanticipated consequences: How many of us would choose to have surgery if we knew the consequences would be a brain injury? From a *New York Times* article of May 13, 2003, we learn about "pumpheads."[8] "Pumpheads" are the unfortunate people who suffer brain injury as a result of being put on a heart-lung machine during open-heart surgery. Although it is not exactly clear what the cause of the injuries are, some surgeons are responding by

---

[7]"Antistroke drug performs no better than aspirin, *The Wall Street Journal,* June 11, 2003, p. D6.
[8]"Heart pump and brain injury: A riddle deepens with time," *The New York Times,* May 13, 2002, p. D1.

doing the bypass surgery without using the heart-lung machine, a procedure known as off-pump surgery. Here we have an example of a problem (heart blockage); a solution (bypass surgery); the unanticipated consequence ("pumpheads"); and, finally, a search for an alternative route (off-pump surgery). Unfortunately, the last word will not be written on this issue until at least 2006, when the government will have completed a study comparing the two approaches. Once again, as in the case of treating prostate cancer, the consumers are left to making an uninformed decision guided only by their relatively uniformed practitioners, whose judgment is usually based on their own limited experience, and their equally uninformed (and arguably self-interested) insurance companies.

7. A new world of surgery: Minimally invasive surgery (MIS) is described in a *Boston Globe* article as such a significant breakthrough that "it constitutes a shift in practice so profound that its effect is akin to the arrival of anesthesia 150 years ago."[9] MIS is now used throughout the body system, including gynecological surgery, neurosurgery, cardiac surgery, and urologic surgery. The article points out that heart mitral valve repairs used to involve foot-long incisions followed by the breaking of the breastbone in order to access the heart valve. Hospital stays lasted 5–6 days with a 2-month recovery time. MIS for the same problem involves a 2-inch incision, use of miniature cameras and instruments, a 2-day hospital stay, and a 2-week recovery.[10] The brave new world of medicine is upon us, and for managers the changes will be enormous. As we learned in Chapter 1, we will need fewer beds for more people, more and better equipment, and certainly people with different training than before. For consumers, we will see a quicker return from the sick role and hopefully a better quality of life.

FRAUD AND ABUSE

Although the subject of fraud and abuse will be dealt with extensively in later chapters, I do want to introduce it here because it represents such an important new development in the health care field. Although sleaze has

[9]"As tools of surgery shrink, training expands," *The Boston Globe*, June 27, 2002, p. E1.
[10]Ibid.

always existed, the availability of huge reservoirs of insurance and government funds has taken corruption in the health field to a new level. The following articles and commentary provide a glimpse of this problem.

- Fighting fraud in Boston: The big picture about fraud in the health industry was presented in a page 1 *Boston Globe* article stating that amongst federal prosecutors, Boston lead the way on fighting fraud.[11] The statistical chart presented with the article illustrates that in 2000 the National Medical Corporation settled the government's suit against them for a variety of charges, including kickbacks and unnecessary tests and therapies for the sum of $486 million. Additionally, four executives were convicted of conspiracy to defraud the government. In 2001, the fraud unit settled with TAP Pharmaceutical for $855 million. In this instance TAP had been involved in illegal marketing and pricing of Lupron, a drug used for prostate cancer. In 2003, two drug giants, Bayer and GlaxoSmithKline, settled with the government for more than $350 million. In both instances they had intentionally overcharged the government for medications.

- Illegal marketing: Another drug giant, Parke-Davis, is in trouble with the government for the alleged illegal marketing activities of its epilepsy drug Neourontin.[12] In this case, the drug manufacturer allegedly provided illegal marketing trips and tickets to physicians under the guise of educational programs. The government's case will be based on the company's conduct, thought to be an illegal inducement to prescribe its drugs. Part of the problem with this activity is that the government says it was an inducement to use the drug for various ailments, such as bipolar disorder, rather than the ailment for which the drug was initially designed. Such so called "off-label" uses have a significantly positive impact on the drug company's bottom line. The line between aggressive and legal marketing and illegal marketing activities is still not clear, and until it gets well-defined we can anticipate many more similar government lawsuits.

- Faulty medical device for treating aneurysms: As reported in the June 13, 2003 edition of *USA Today*, a medical

---

[11]"Prosecutors here lead in health fraud cases," *The Boston Globe*, May 13, 2003, p. 1.
[12]"U.S. filing backs suit against drug firm," *The Boston Globe*, May 25, 2003, p. D1.

manufacturer, EndoVascular Technologies, agreed to pay a fine of $92.4 million and plead guilty to "covering up thousands of incidents in which the device malfunctioned and might have led to 12 deaths and 57 emergency surgeries nationwide."[13] In this instance, the company's balloon-like device had been approved by the FDA in 1999 and suspended in 2001 after some anonymous tips about problems. Aggressive marketing activities, including covering up the details of the problems, led to the criminal charges. Once again one must wonder whether less attention to sales goals and more attention to quality of the product would have been in the company's long-term interest. Additionally, one must raise the issue of surveillance systems for new medical devices—after all, but for the anonymous tips the defective products might still be on the market!

- Poor patient care leads to divestiture: An Albany, New York, nursing home company was required to divest itself of its eight nursing homes after state investigators found that it had falsified its business records and provided substandard care to the home's residents.[14] The owners are not only being forced to sell but also to pay over $1 million in fines and penalties. Nursing homes are among the most regulated sectors of the health system and, because of their large volume of Medicaid and Medicare business, come under both federal and state scrutiny. In recent years, many states have become increasingly aggressive in using significant penalties in order to change the behavior of nursing home owners and operators. As this case illustrates, the penalties can even include driving an owner out of business.

- Nonprofit medical center not exempt from problems: Even distinguished, world-famous institutions such as Massachusetts General Hospital (MGH) fall under scrutiny for fraud and abuse issues. For example, on June 19, 2003, it was reported by the *Boston Globe* that MGH would "pay the federal government $75,000 to settle allegations that it defrauded the Medicare program by billing for neurological services when no senior physician was present."[15] According to the article, there were instances where Medicare was billed for a

---

[13]"Medical firm fined $92M in coverup," *USA Today*, June 13–15, 2003, p. 1.

[14]"Operators must divest themselves of eight nursing homes," *Adirondack Daily Enterprise*, June 1, 2003, p. 2.

[15]"Hospital to pay $75,000 settlement," *The Boston Globe*, June 19, 2003, p. B2.

physician's services while the doctor was away in Bermuda. For a health care manager, this raises the simple question: How does this happen? Unfortunately, too often, personnel appear to be on automatic pilot and impute information when it is missing . . . and this is where the trouble begins. For example, I was once investigating a woman's complaint about the care her father was receiving in a nursing home. In reviewing the chart I noticed that the nurses were consistently reporting the same dietary intake and status each day despite the facts that the man had lost a significant amount of weight (also recorded) and the daughter stated he had no appetite. What was occurring was that the nurses, at the end of their shift and hurrying to leave, made similar entries on this man's records as well as on every other person's record on the unit. The lack of attention in this case lead to the man's hospitalization, as well as not only a subsequent change of staff on the unit but also a significant amount of in-service reeducation. If a lawsuit had been filed, those medical records would not have served the cause of the nursing home!

• Executives' problems: Two unrelated articles demonstrate the problems that both cause and result from the issues of fraud and abuse. In the first, a HealthSouth financial executive joined 11 other company executives in pleading guilty to a variety of charges about financial irregularities in the company.[16] The case itself, involving a chain of rehabilitation hospitals, began with investigation of illegal behavior in 1996 and by the summer of 2003 was far from resolved. The second article is equally troubling. Even though Jeffrey Barbakow was the executive who was brought in to clean up and run Tenet Healthcare in 1990 after it ran afoul of the government, he could not survive a new set of regulatory problems and subsequent loss of investor confidence.[17] This article reminds us that once an organization is stained by fraud and abuse, that stain has a way of affecting everyone, even the clean-up brigade. As will be shown in the chapters on corporate compliance, both an organization's reputation and the reputation of those that work there are best served by ethical and honest behavior.

---

[16]Former executive at HealthSouth pleads guilty [electronic version], *The New York Times*, (May 6, 2003) retrieved December 8, 2004.

[17]"Troubled Tenet Outs Chairman Barbakow," *The Boston Globe*, June 28, 2003, p. D2.

HEALTH SYSTEMS AND QUALITY

The standard model for examining quality in health care involves a three-part analysis: structure, process, and outcome. This model assumes that optimal care will be achieved when the proper structure exists. For example, to deliver quality radiology services it is necessary to have the right equipment, staff, and physical facilities. Process examines how that care is delivered. Were appropriate laboratory tests ordered for the likely problems? Were the tests done in a timely fashion? Were the results properly recorded and transmitted to the appropriate people? Were the tests properly done? Last, we have the true issue: outcomes. What were the expected clinical outcomes? Were they attained efficiently and effectively? We are now in a period of heavy government and foundation investigation into the area of outcomes research. This research is leading to clinical protocols and a potential standardization that could have some positive benefits. One issue that will likely be on the board for decades is inequity of care due to socioeconomic status. As one of the following articles indicates, the gap between the poor and wealthy is still with us.

- Quality of care: Perhaps one of the most significant articles on quality of care was a research report published in 2003 in the *New England Journal of Medicine*.[18] The authors of this study of the medical care of 6712 adults found that "participants received 54.9% of recommended care."[19] There was considerable variation, depending on both the mode of care and the condition. For example, if good-quality care dictated medication, then 68.6% of the people received that care. However, if good care recommended counseling or education, only 18.3% received that care.[20] The article also reported considerable variations with clinical conditions. If the condition was senility, cataracts, or breast cancer, the patients received the quality of care they should have approximately 75% of the time. On the other hand, many common conditions fell below 50%: diabetes mellitus (45.4%); urinary tract infection (40.7%); dyspepsia and peptic ulcer disease (32.7%); atrial fibrillation (24.7%); hip fracture

---

[18]E.A. McGlynn, et al., "The quality of health care delivered to adults in the United States," *New England Journal of Medicine, 348* (2002), 2635–2645.
[19]Ibid., p. 2641.
[20]Ibid., p. 2642.

(22.8%); and alcohol dependence (10.5%).[21] All of this suggests that there is considerable work to be done for both consumers and managers. The managerial responsibility is to ensure that the organization's staff provide the best quality care possible and that the organization has the resources to ensure that that quality is provided. While most organizations have internal quality control protocols such as "quality assurance committees," few organizations raise the bar to include the boards in quality discussion. Some years ago, as part of a program I was taking in England on the British health system, I visited one of the London teaching hospitals. In a discussion with a medical professor I raised the issue of quality review. My frame of reference was the United States' hospital quality review "system," consisting of a series of committees such as medical records, tissue, and credentials. The professor answered me by saying they had no need for such committees because of their continual daily oversight of each other. Frankly, I did not buy that answer then and still believe in the adage that foxes cannot guard chicken coops. As this article points out, despite the assumed best intentions of practitioners they do not deliver the best quality care in a significant percentage of the time. Management that sees its role as central to quality can make an impact on this problem.

- The burden of poverty: For those health professionals working with impoverished clients, there is a special challenge associated with the connection between economic status and health. This connection was highlighted in a Massachusetts Department of Public Health study reported upon in the *Boston Globe*. It found that two of Massachusetts's poorest communities, Lynn and Lowell, were dramatically less healthy than the affluent communities of Newton and Brookline.[22] The primary statistic used in this report was the premature death rate: Newton's was half that of Lynn. This finding is neither atypical nor unexpected. The poor have fewer dollars to spend on health care and generally have less access to that care. The clinical problems, behavioral issues, and other barriers that the less economically fortunate deal with make it imperative that the health

---

[21]Ibid., p. 2643.
[22]"Report underlines burden of poverty," *The Boston Globe*, May 28, 1903, p. B1.

system respond to these needs in a more efficient and effective way than it has done to this point. My own experiences with impoverished communities in New York and New Orleans, particularly prison inmates, suggest that we can and must do better![23]

- The pharmacist's role: The health system is certainly not merely about doctors, nurses, and administrators. In fact, billions of dollars are spent on self-medication. Everyone from massage therapists to faith healers and grandparents provide advice on health issues. Pharmacists are major-league providers of advice and dispensers of nonprescription remedies and, certainly, prescription drugs. In Hollywood, Florida, a local pharmacy tests for bone density, cholesterol, and hypertension. The pharmacist is well known for his suggestions on everything from snoring to menopause. He typically suggests a range of herbal remedies and usually has quite satisfied customers. With regard to presciption drugs he, like most pharmacists, is available for consultation, but the bulk of the information comes in the labeling. For example, a prescription medication from Walgreens comes with an information sheet that includes the medication, directions for use, ingredient name, common uses of the drug, information on how to use the drug, cautions, and side effects. In New York state, the role of the pharmacist has been taken to a new level. Rather than merely being required to ask a patient whether he or she has questions about a drug, they will now have to meet with every patient about a new presciption. In this counseling session they will "talk to every patient about the name, description and purpose of each drug. They will also discuss the dosage, any special precautions, techniques for self monitoring, storage requirements" and a host of other matters.[24] Fortunately for New Yorkers, a practice is now in place that will no doubt increase drug compliance and will likely result in better quality care. As this section illustrates, quality is a complex issue, and one that requires teamwork from all components of the system. The physician can write the prescription and usually give the patient a very short commentary on the medication. The pharmacist, though, is in the best position to

---

[23]S.B. Goldsmith, *Prison health: Travesty of justice* (New York: Prodist, 1973).
[24]"New rules for N.Y. pharmacists enacted," *Adirondack Daily Enterprise*, July 1, 2003, p. 9.

offer substantive information and help the patient in using the drug most effectively. It is unfortunate that the pressures on the health system are such that it requires state or federal regulations to get professionals to do what they have trained for.

- Medicaid and quality: On July 7, 2003, the *New York Times* reported on a U.S. General Accounting Office study that found that 11 of 15 states were operating suboptimal quality Medicaid programs with the funding and blessing of the federal government.[25] Quality assurance under the Medicaid program is a state responsibility that operates with federal rules and guidelines. Unfortunately, quality is something that happens at the grassroots level, and no level of inspection can ensure true quality. A quote from Professor Rosenbaum of George Washington University captures the essence of the quality dilemma: "States prepare good plans of care for Medicaid recipients, but there's no follow-through to see if people get the care. States assume that home and community care will save money, without realizing that it takes real money to monitor the quality of care."[26]

FINANCES

In Chapter 1, I provided an overview of health finances from a national perspective. In this section, a summary of articles will examine how money is affecting providers and beneficiaries of care. The inherent dilemma presented in these articles is that money is the fuel oil of the system and must come from somewhere, business or government. It is obviously easier to find the money in a good economy. But in a bad or uncertain economy, costs must be controlled, and health care expenditures are not sacred cows.

- Health costs slowing: In a page 1 article, the *Wall Street Journal* provided an analysis that suggested health care costs are slowing down because of a shift to generic drugs, increased substitution of outpatient surgery for inpatient (and, by definition, hospital) surgery, and decreased health benefits.[27] The article goes on to raise the most

---

[25]"Report criticizes federal oversight of state Medicaid," *The New York Times*, July 7, 2003, p. C8.
[26]Ibid.
[27]"Rate of increase for health costs may be slowing," *The Wall Street Journal*, June 11, 2002, p. 1.

common argument/analysis; that is, if people are responsible for their own health care costs through copayments and deductibles, they will be more careful about health expenditures. Perhaps the question to ask is: Why does the *Wall Street Journal* put health care finances on its front page? The answer is that health expenditures are a significant part of any organization's budget, and controlling expenditures is a prime function of management. In my CEO days I, too, was faced with the problem of health benefit expenditures. Although I would have loved to provide Lexus-level benefits to each employee, I had to compromise with the budget and provide Ford Escort level benefits (at least I avoided going to the used Yugo level).

• Hospitals in deep trouble: The first few years of the 21st century have not been kind to many large health care providers. For example, in the nursing home industry, five of the eight largest nursing home companies have filed for bankruptcy. HealthSouth, a large chain of rehabilitation hospitals, with various fiscal and regulatory problems, was another company heading toward bankruptcy in 2003.[28] The stain from these bankruptcies has spread throughout the health industry, eroding public confidence in investing in this sector of the economy, which further weakens the industry. Hospitals also have not fared well in this economy. The problems in Massachusetts were presented in an article reporting that many hospitals were in deepening financial straits because of both lower patient volume and poorer insurance coverage for treated patients.[29] One aspect of the problems for many hospitals nationwide is the fiscal problems that the states are facing. Inevitably, state budget cutters look to Medicaid payments to balance their accounts, and that balancing often takes a toll on nursing homes, hospitals, and clinical providers of care. Another aspect is simply that of disease. As the article stated, a hospital in the resort area of Cape Cod saw a decline in its revenues because of a mild flu season.[30] In a related piece, the *Boston Globe* reported that Waltham Hospital, after serving that

---

[28]"HealthSouth bankruptcy could come this summer," *The New York Times*, April 30, 2003, p. C2.
[29]"Weakening bottom lines worry hospitals," *The Boston Globe*, May 14, 2003, p. C1.
[30]Ibid., p. C6.

community for 117 years, was expected to close.[31] Unfortunately, a few months later, the hospital did close, and developers were in the process of using the land for housing and perhaps some type of medical office building and surgicenter. Although Waltham Hospital is one of hundreds of hospitals that have closed throughout the country, others have survived by downsizing or merging. Sometimes it takes years before a community knows what will happen to a closed institution. For example, in Miami Beach, St. Francis Hospital stood essentially vacant for years as discussions continued about turning the building into a geriatric facility, a medical office building, housing, and so forth. Eventually, close to a decade later, the hospital was razed to make way for an upscale housing development. In New York City, Mount Sinai Hospital was reported to be having its share of financial problems, with a 2002 deficit of $72.5 million.[32] By contrast, in 1997 the hospital had a profit of $30 million. A consultant's analysis of the problems at Mount Sinai found "flawed billing systems cost Mount Sinai tens of millions of dollars, even as it pursued ambitious expansion and building plans and paid its top executives salaries, detailed in tax records, that many experts say were unusually high for a struggling nonprofit institution."[33] Everything was complicated for Mount Sinai because of its relationship to its medical school and a merger with New York University's Medical Center. Finally, what is perhaps most disheartening about the Mount Sinai saga is that it was managed by some of the most talented executives in the country and had a board comprising many people who are considered the senior financial "geniuses" of New York City.

- Hospital desperation in troubled times: Calling an airline or hotel for a rate is a challenging experience. With the airlines, it's the 21-day advance, 14-day advance, 7-day advance, 3-day advance, restrictions, no restrictions, and so forth. At the hotel, it's the rack rate, then the discounts: AAA, AARP, corporate, government, frequent hotel user, and so forth. With hospitals we also have a discount structure, with

---

[31]"Waltham Hospital to be closed," *The Boston Globe*, May 14, 2003, p. C6.
[32]"How a venerable hospital helped undermine its own fiscal health," *The New York Times*, April 2, 2003, p. A19.
[33]Ibid.

bulk purchasers, usually HMOs, getting the best price. The fiscal problems facing hospitals has caused them to charge the uninsured a full price with no discount and then to aggressively pursue collecting those charges. This practice has come under increased public and governmental scrutiny and resulted in the hospital trade association, the American Hospital Association, urging its members to review their practices and "stop using harsh bill-collection tactics that reflect poorly on the industry."[34] Unfortunately, some of those who bear the greatest burden of the financial woes in the industry are employees who see their health benefits being constantly eroded. This area will be examined next.

- Employee health benefits and health costs: Health benefits are often an area of major payroll expenditures for any business. It is frequently said that the an automobile's manufacturing costs include more expenses for health benefits than for steel. This concept has industry reexamining the entirety of the health benefits and puts health benefits on center stage for any negotiations. At General Electric, the union declared victory when it was able to maintain the employee's contribution to health insurance at 18% for the first year of the contract rather than the 30% desired by management.[35] With estimated costs of $6,500 per employee, the difference is a contribution of $1170 per year versus $1950 per year. For the company, not getting its way involves a $13 million bottom-line expenditure that it had hoped to transfer to employees. A different strategy employed by industry is to promote healthy employees. One group of employers announced that they would fight obesity because, as the medical director of Ford Motor Corporation noted, it takes "an amazingly large portion of the $3 billion" that the company spends on health care.[36] National estimates by the director of health care management at Ford are that employers are spending $13 billion annually on weight-related problems, including disease and

---

[34]"Hospitals urged to end harsh tactics for billing uninsured," *The Wall Street Journal*, July 7, 2003, p. A9.

[35]"G.E. union cites deal to curb workers' share of health costs," *The New York Times*, June 18, 2003, p. A16.

[36]"Employers plan obesity fight citing $12 billion-a-year cost," *The New York Times*, June 18, 2003, p. C2.

lost productivity.[37] Another strategy used by industry is the limitation or elimination of health benefits for retirees or disabled employees. In Massachusetts, NStar, the energy public utility, cut back on health benefits to retirees as a strategy to eliminate some of its $20 million increase in its health care expenses.[38] In another Massachusetts situation, a lead article in the *Wall Street Journal* focused on the Polaroid Corporation's decision to fire employees who were on disability and thus save the costs of providing them health care.[39] What was perhaps most shocking about the article is that more than 50% of 723 large companies surveyed would fire an employee after some period on disability; indeed, 27% dismiss them immediately after they go on disability.[40]

In this chapter, as well as in Chapter 1, I have provided both a data-driven and a human-focused overview of the health system and its issues. It is now time to narrow the focus of this book on management and the health industry by examining in the next two chapters a managerial view of the health care industry and the beginning of all managerial efforts; that is, setting objectives for what we do.

---

[37]Ibid.
[38]"Healthcare for life, with exclusions," *The Boston Globe*, June 27, 2003, p. C1.
[39]"To save on health-care costs, firms fire disabled workers," *The Wall Street Journal*, July 14, 2003, p. 1.
[40]Ibid.

The Health Care Industry: A Managerial Model

Health care organizations can generally be classified into three basic groups, depending on their financial sponsorship: (1) for-profit, (2) non-profit, or not-for-profit, or (3) governmental. This classification results in a significant number of anatomical and physiological differences that to a great extent affect the organization's management processes.

THE PROFIT SECTOR

The for-profit sector encompasses a wide range of organizations. At one end of the spectrum, at least in terms of staff and revenues, are the independent practices of physicians, dentists, optometrists, chiropractors, and other providers' organizations such as independent pharmacies. In the past two decades these small businesses have reached a level of managerial sophistication rivaling that of larger organizations. Even the smallest practices have computerized appointment and billing systems, and many have payroll systems, accounts receivable and payable systems, and even marketing plans. Other practices find it more efficient to use the omnipresent consultant services to perform these functions. At the most sophisticated end of the range of for-profit direct care providers are large group practices, which are likely to be organized as partnerships, employ hundreds of professionals and nonprofessionals, and own real estate and a host of other business ventures (often under separate corporate entities).

Inpatient facilities are a more complex form of for-profit organization. The recent history of many of these large organizations, particularly in the areas of hospitals and nursing homes owned by large chains and publicly held corporations, has been quite interesting, albeit unstable. All of those activities that we have traditionally associated with big business we now see in the health industry: mergers, acquisitions, divestitures, leveraged buy-outs, and unfortunately bankruptcy. For example, one giant of the hospital field is HCA, formerly known as Hospital Corporation of America. This company started in Nashville, Tennessee as a single hospital by Dr. Thomas Frist, Sr. (father of U.S. Senator Bill Frist) and grew through a series of mergers and acquisitions to 465 hospitals in 1987. The company still remains a giant corporation. As of December 31, 2002, HCA owned and operated 171 hospitals with over 41,000 beds, 6 psychiatric hospitals with 1,925 beds, and a host of other organizations, including day surgery centers, therapy centers, and rehabilitation programs employing 178,000 staff (52,000 part-time).[1] The nursing home industry, once the darling of Wall Street investors, went through a period of enormous growth and integration that led to companies like Beverly, Manor Care, Kindred (previously Vencor), and Mariner. Changes in financing and reimbursement, the litigation environment, and general problems in the economy in the first few years of the 21st century resulted in a dramatic shake-up in the long-term care industry. For example, financial losses due to insurance costs and the litigious environment in Florida cost three of the big chains, Beverly, Extendicare, and Kindred, to sell their holdings in the "Sunshine State." On a national scale, between January 2002 and April 2003, the top 10 nursing home chains downsized almost 18%, from 338,684 beds to 277,960 beds.[2] Perhaps most important, in terms of loss of investor confidence, was that five of the largest publicly traded nursing home companies were forced into bankruptcy in order to restructure their organizations and debt.

Health maintenance organizations (HMOs) are one of the most recent and interesting organizational development in the health care industry. Although they have been around since the 1930s, their remarkable growth did not occur until the last two decades of the 20th century. In 1984 they cared for 15.1 million people, and by 2000 the number had grown to

---

[1]"Desperate families embrace unapproved Alzheimer drug," *The New York Times*, June 15, 2003, p. 1.
[2]"CMS Health Care Industry Market Update," *Nursing Facilities* (May 20, 2003), p. 6.

80 million.[3] Back when the HMO industry was in its relatively infantile stages with 10 million enrollees, 88% of enrollees were in nonprofit plans. Over the next two decades not only do we expect to see significant growth in addition to the 80 million of the year 2000 but we also expect to see a shift in ownership, with approximately 64% of enrollees now in for-profit plans. Equally important is that many of these for-profit plans started their life as nonprofit organizations. In their analysis, the organizational model of a for-profit enterprise provided significant advantages over the nonprofit model. For example, it was argued that for-profits had easier access to capital markets and tended to manage themselves more efficiently and effectively.

A final group of for-profit organizations that are often forgotten, although they are clearly forces for development and change in the health care field and offer a wealth of managerial challenges, are the commercial firms. Examples are chain pharmacies, drug manufacturers, clinical laboratories, investment bankers, and insurance companies. It is tempting to include in this group virtually any organization that employs a large number of people and thus is obligated to expend significant resources on health benefits. For example, as noted in Chapter 2, General Electric's stake in health care is so large that it is focusing on obesity in its workforce as one strategy for controlling its health expenditures.

THE NONPROFIT SECTOR

The nonprofit organizations are those most often associated with the health field. Nonprofit does not literally mean that the organization should not make a profit but rather that any surplus of revenue over expenses should not inure or be passed on to any group of stockholders or owners. Rather, all "profit" should be reinvested in the organization for its growth and development. Such organizations are classified by the Internal Revenue Service as 501(c)(3), which means nonprofit and tax-exempt. They can be the recipients of tax-deductible contributions and usually do not pay sales or real estate taxes (although there are many challenges to the real estate tax exemption). The significance of this 501(c)(3) exemption should not be understated. Nonprofit hospitals, for example,

---

[3]"CMS Trends and Indicators in Changing Health Care Marketplace," *2002-Chartbook*, Table 1.18.

often sit on prime real estate that would generate significant dollars for a community, which still must provide the organization with community services such as fire and police protection. The sales tax exemption is also real dollars. The organization I headed spent about $21 million per year that was not taxed at the regular 6% rate, saving the organization $1.2 million per year, which the community had to find in other ways (or cut services). Most community hospitals, health system agencies, hospital councils, and voluntary health-related organizations, such as the American Cancer Society, MS Society, or the Association for Voluntary Sterilization, are in the nonprofit category, as are 90% of the Blue Cross and Blue Shield Plans throughout the United States.

The mixed for-profit and nonprofit situation of some organizations within this framework is somewhat confusing. Kaiser presents one of the simplest examples. The nonprofit Kaiser hospitals work hand in glove with for-profit Permanente medical groups. A different example can be observed within a community hospital, where a snack bar or gift shop is run on a for-profit basis and the surplus from this unit is used to subsidize the operations of other parts of the institution. In some instances, such as when an organization has a highly visible business spun off from the original nonprofit, the subsidiary may be a for-profit venture. This typically occurs when a hospital or health system has a for-profit consulting business or thrift shop. The idea is that the for-profit organizational vehicle is more flexible and less likely to run into regulatory constraints, and if the subsidiary corporation does make a profit, it will be returned to the parent nonprofit.

GOVERNMENT

The federal government, state governments, and even local governments own and operate a staggering array of facilities and programs. At the Department of Veterans Affairs (VA) there are 138 hospitals with 45,000 beds, a size rivaling that of the large private chains such as Beverly, Quorom, or Tenet. Theoretically the average size VA hospital is 326 beds, which happens to be the exact bed count at the VA in the Bronx. Obviously there are larger VA hospitals, but also far smaller ones, such as the 60-bed facility in White River Junction, Vermont. The Department of Defense operates 18 Navy hospitals, 18 Air Force hospitals, and 25 Army hospitals. Some, such as the Army's Tripler Army Medical Center in

Hawaii, have a moderate number of beds (209) but huge outpatient loads (in excess of 596,000 visits per year). Another federally funded hospital and health care operation is the U.S. Public Health Service's 50 Indian Health service hospitals with a total of 2062 beds and active ambulatory clinics. Official health agencies such as health departments or the U.S. Department of Health and Human Services (HHS), the Center for Disease Control, and state and local health departments are also important organizational components of the health systems. The importance of governmental health agencies was well demonstrated in 2003 during the SARS outbreak in China and Toronto. Finally, there is a range of state health-related or programs that often do not belong to official "health" agencies, such as family planning services, Medicaid management programs, and health care in prisons and jails.

MANAGERIAL MATRIX

The managerial matrix is a way of considering the issues in this chapter. Across the horizontal axis of the matrix are the three previously discussed classifications: for-profit, nonprofit, and government. The vertical axis lists a range of managerial functions and structural elements that relate to a manager's ability to organize and direct an organization.

Organizational Function

Delivery of Services

The first question considered in this matrix is that of primary function: What is it that the organization is supposed to do? One function is the delivery of services to individuals, which clearly can and does occur in all three organizational forms. Abortion services are perhaps a simple illustration. An individual desiring such a service can usually find it in a non-profit hospital, a for-profit abortion clinic, and in some states a government-owned hospital. Whether potential customers recognize the particular financial status of the organization they are dealing with is a matter of conjecture, as are some of the implications of the organizational form. In some cases, however, it is an important distinction. For example, a for-profit organization that is responsible to stockholders may refuse to accept the patient who is unwilling (or whose insurer is unwilling) to pay the bill. On the other hand, if the deliverer of care is a governmental agency or nonprofit organization, it might view its responsibilities in such a way as to essentially require the delivery of care to the uninsured patient.

The blurring of distinctions between organizations is well illustrated in the hospital field. Decades ago, the federal government owned and ran hospitals for the indigent or for specific beneficiaries such as the military and their dependents. The nonprofits tended to be the community hospitals, which took a share of the indigent as well as the insured. In this group of community institutions we also found the teaching hospitals, with their internship and residency programs, and medical school hospitals. The private hospitals were oftentimes the "Doctors' Hospitals" and were used primarily by practitioners for their privately paying patients. For example, in 1929 two brothers established the for-profit 59-bed maternity and pediatric Madison Park Hospital on Kings Highway in Brooklyn, New York. In 1972, because of financial problems, the hospital converted its ownership form to nonprofit. Today, the hospital, now known as New York Community and part of the 11-hospital New York-Presbyterian Healthcare System, is a 125-bed general medical and surgical hospital that no longer offers maternity or pediatric services. In discussing the management of this facility, Lin Mo, its president and CEO, suggests that in many ways it has to be run like a bottom-line-oriented business: "[T]here is a constant and continuing process of striking the right balance between providing the best patient care we can afford to give; meet the regulations and not loose our shirt in the process through unnecessary services such as an MRI that may not be required or unnecessary overtime. This is a constant balancing act that requires continual attention to our budget and education of staff and physicians."[4]

While the conversion of proprietary to nonprofits has blurred one line, there has also been a blurring due to the conversion of traditional community hospitals into components of private chains. Illustrative of this state of affairs is St. Mary's Hospital in West Palm Beach, Florida and Good Samaritan Hospital in Palm Beach, Florida. These hospitals, formerly part of the nonsectarian Intracoastal System, were sold to Tenet Healthcare in 2001 for $244 million. The sale was precipitated by losses during the previous years, including a $40 million loss in 2000. As of

---

[4]Interview with Lin Mo, July 25, 2003.

2003, Tenet has been able to manage the hospital in a profitable manner while continuing to provide the same level of charitable care that was given by its nonprofit predecessors. (This was also a condition of sale.) How have they been able to do it? First, they are careful in their admitting process, ensuring that uninsured patients have properly applied for either Medicaid or county support. As part of this admission system, they aggressively collect copayments and deductibles. Finally, they engage in intensive organizational management practices, such as careful shift staffing management and inventory control. In the simplest terms, they have introduced a level of careful bottom-line management heretofore unknown.

The buying and selling of these institutions and the movement between for-profit and nonprofit status has one additional dimension. For example, when a for-profit hospital less than a mile from New York Community was sold to be part of a different system, the owners were able to get an asking price in excess of $40 million. But, it also goes the other way. The Intracoastal Hospitals were sold to Tenet for a price of $244 million, with an apparent net proceeds of $50 million going to the establishment of the Palm Healthcare Foundation. This foundation generously provides in excess of $2 million each year to improve health care in Palm Beach County.

Planning

In the context of this discussion, I am referring to community planning for health services rather than individual organizational planning. The issue, then, is to what extent is an organization responsible for the planning of health services on a community basis? Most community planning in the United States is carried out by governmental and nonprofit organizations. Indeed, to some extent, government defines a major role for itself as that of planning. For example, the state of Florida, like most states, has a comprehensive health plan with clear implications for the providers of care. Goals such as "Enhance and improve the Emergency Medical Services (EMS) system," or "Increase the availability of health care in underserved areas" clearly affect the size and shape of the system. How government uses various points of leverage to achieve the desired outcome is essentially a political decision. Some years ago, Massachusetts decided to do something about health care cost, quality, and access by passing a balance billing law that made it illegal for physicians to bill Medicare patients for more than their approved coverage. The law was also expanded to cover other groups such as state employees and Blue Cross and Blue Shield subscribers. What is most interesting is that the power to enforce this law came through the licensure system; that is, as a condition of obtaining a license to practice medicine in Massachusetts, a physician must agree not to balance bill. Another Massachusetts example comes from the General Laws of the State, which give considerable planning and management power to the board of registration in medicine. Two quotations from the General Laws illustrate this point:

> The board is hereby authorized and directed to develop and implement, without cost to the commonwealth, a plan for a remediation program designed to improve physicians' clinical and communication skills.

> There shall also be established within the board of registration in medicine a risk management unit. Said risk management unit shall provide technical assistance and quality assurance programs designed to reduce or stabilize the frequency, amount and costs of claims against physicians and hospitals licensed or registered in the commonwealth. The board shall promulgate regulations requiring physicians to participate in risk management programs as a condition of licensure; provided that such regulations shall provide for an exemption from such requirements for physicians who are participating in pre-existing risk management programs that have been approved by the board.[5]

Clearly, government, because of its power of licensure and control over vast sums of money, has the greatest potential leverage in planning health services. Private firms do enter the world of planning, but usually as consultants to voluntary and government agencies that have the responsibility and authority for planning.

Some states have the power of "Certificate of Need"; that is, they can approve or disapprove any major project through a governmental review process. Failure to receive a certificate effectively blocks financial reimbursement for the project. For example, in Virginia, the state Department of Health has a Division of Certificate of Public Need, and that Division is part of the Center for Quality Health Care and Consumer Protection. The preface to its 2002 annual report to the governor and General Assembly of Virginia on the Certificate of Public Need (COPN) provides a useful statement about such programs:

---

[5]ALM GL ch. 112§ 5 (2003).

The COPN is a regulatory program administered by the Virginia Department of Health (VDH). The program was established in 1973. The law states the objectives of the program are (i) promoting comprehensive health planning to meet the needs of the public; (ii) promoting the highest quality of care at the lowest possible cost; (iii) avoiding unnecessary duplication of medical care facilities; and (iv) providing an orderly procedure for resolving questions concerning the need to construct or modify medical care facilities. In essence, the program seeks to contain health care costs while ensuring financial and geographic access to quality health care for Virginia citizens at a reasonable cost. . . .

During FY02 . . . [t]he Commissioner issued 103 decisions. . . . [N]inety-six of these requests were approved or conditionally approved, for a total authorized capital expenditure of $629,138,592. Seven requests were denied. These seven denied projects had a proposed total capital expenditure of $54,370,371.[6]

It would be a mistake to assume that because so few projects were disapproved that such programs were not successful. The political reality is that in many instances projects are simply not submitted because proponents know that they will not fare well. In the case of Virginia, the state received letters of intent for 27 other projects, but for various reasons they never got to the level of a COPN decision.

Monitoring and Evaluation

A third broad function is related to the monitoring and evaluation of health services. Although this is a function that all organizations perform, the question really is whether this is a primary function of the organization. Does the organization in part exist in order to monitor and evaluate other health care organizations? The function is typically a governmental responsibility that may be handled directly by government or delegated to a nongovernmental organization. When delegation occurs, the agent of government is typically a nonprofit but may also be a for-profit organization. Its organization form is less significant than its clearly delegated and delineated function.

Consider this example from the field of criminal justice. Since 1983, the Corrections Corporation of America (CCA), a for-profit company that is traded on the New York Stock Exchange, has been empowered to

---

[6]Commonwealth of Virginia, Annual Report on the Status of Virginia's Medical Care Facilities Certificate of Public Need Program Fiscal Year Ending June 30, 2002, pp. 1–2.

manage 60 jails and prisons in the United States that house approximately 55,000 inmates.[7] This company, which also owns 40 prisons, contracts with governmental agencies to house prisoners who have been sentenced by the government. While obviously the inmates must received medical treatment and the prison run within a variety of governmental guidelines, we see here a significant blurring of the traditional lines between the role of government and the role of the private sector. And so it is in health care!

Thus, while the function of monitoring and evaluating health care is usually considered governmental in nature, it sometimes is taken on in quasi-governmental organizations or voluntary organizations that receive most (if not all) of their funding from the government and thus are in one way or another accountable to government. Professional review organizations (PROs) are an example of non-governmental organizations that contract with the federal government, and sometimes state governments, for the purpose of reviewing Medicare and Medicaid medical claims as well as state health insurance programs for the medically indigent. In Massachusetts the PRO, known as MassPRO, is a "wholly owned subsidiary of the Massachusetts Medical Society . . . [and] is a nonprofit organization governed by a Board of Directors comprised of physicians, health care administrators, researchers, academicians, and consumers."[8]

There are many instances in which proprietary organizations, particularly consulting firms, get into the business of monitoring and evaluating health services. Recently, many of the large public accounting firms and management consulting firms have developed significant capabilities in the areas of health services. No longer do these firms limit themselves to the roles of auditor and occasional advisor, but bid on requests for proposals from Washington or any state capital. Indeed, many of these firms have developed a remarkably strong record of excellent evaluations of health services.

Regulation

A fourth broad function is that of regulation. Government at the local, state, or national level has maintained essential control; it could even be argued that this control can never be totally delegated or transferred. To a limited extent, however, governmental agencies do transfer or allow

---

[7]Data retrieved (July 30, 2003) from www/correctionscorp.com/main/media.html.
[8]Data retrieved (July 23, 2003) from www.masspro.org.

voluntary agencies to "regulate." With Medicaid, for example, one level of government subcontracts with another level. This is illustrated by the fact that the auditing of the performance of nursing homes is handled by state inspectors operating under the direction of federal regulations. At the national level, the federal government has also essentially transferred one of its major control devices for Medicare to the Joint Commission on Accreditation of Healthcare Organizations (JCAHO, pronounced "Jayco"). If a hospital chooses to be inspected by JCAHO and passes, it receives a "deemed status." This deemed status means that the organization has met the federal Medicare standards and the government will accept that JACHO inspection as a certification. (In a small number of cases the government will go in to verify the survey.) Medicare-certified home health agencies and hospices can also go the voluntary survey route of JCAHO rather than the federal inspection route. Other JCAHO inspections, such as for nursing homes, do not result in deemed status and do not preclude the state surveyors from visiting. This pattern of cooperation among various levels of government and voluntary agencies appears to function as an organizational analogue of professional self-policing, and for the most part abuses have been limited.

Proprietary, voluntary, and governmental organizations all pay for services, but each approaches payment with a rather different philosophy. The largest group of payers are the commercial insurance companies, whose primary responsibility is to their stockholders. This "bottom line" approach, which takes into account the fact that insurance coverage is not marketed solely as a social good but also as a means for a commercial organization to make a profit, results in a somewhat hands-off attitude toward the health system and its consumers. The insurance company is duty bound to charge premiums in accordance with likely risks; if the costs of doing business go up, so do the premiums.

In the past several decades, the health insurance industry has gone through many changes. For example, to most outsiders, it appears that the big payer for health services is the Blue Cross Blue Shield organization. The "Blues" were originally all nonprofit organizations, very much tied into the hospital industry. A significant number of the remaining 43 Blue Cross and Blue Shield plans today are nonprofit entities who compete with other commercial insurers and HMOs for the health insurance dollar. For-profit Blue Cross organizations currently exist in numerous states, including California, Georgia, Missouri, Wisconsin, Indiana, Kentucky, Ohio,

Connecticut, New Hampshire, Colorado, Nevada, Maine, and Virginia. Many insurers are also in the business of being fiscal intermediaries for the government. According to the Blue's trade association, "In 2002, Blue Cross and Blue Shield Medicare contractors processed more than 90% of the claims from hospitals and other providers (Part A) and nearly 67% of the claims from physicians and other health care practitioners (Part B)."[9]

GOAL CLARITY

Another basic question is: How clear or diffuse are goals for organizations under these three classifications? In the for-profit organization, regardless of its function, the goal clearly is to make a profit. While it is evident that a for-profit organization may have "lines" that do not make a profit but serve a public good, the organization's overall viability is quite clearly related to its ability to generate profits. A proprietary hospital or group practice cannot continue in existence if its income is less than its costs; further, it will have significant difficulties if it cannot offer a balance sheet or profit-and-loss statement attractive enough to bring in additional capital.

The nonprofit organization has goals that are somewhat less clear. If asked what the goals of the hospital are, a typical teaching hospital administrator is likely to respond, "We have a threefold mission—teaching, research, and service." These days, administrators talk of fiscal integrity, return on investments, and market penetration, but there is also the possibility of fundraising, endowment incomes, and the often not-very-remunerative goals of teaching and research

At another point on the spectrum of clear to diffuse goals are those of government health care organizations. These organizations are partly constrained (or facilitated) because they are governmental agencies and must to a great extent be responsive to an elusive constituency; additionally, they are constrained as public health organizations by the myriad problems that health care organizations of all types encounter.

In operational terms, these differences can be seen in the staffing ratios of proprietary hospitals versus those of government institutions. For example, in New York City in the mid-1970s, municipal hospitals had a ratio of seven staff to each bed (7.5), which was more than 100% higher than

---

[9]Data retrieved (July 30, 2003) from www.onlinepressroom.net/bcbsa.

that of comparable proprietary or voluntary institutions. Analyses of the functioning of these institutions did not reveal any significant differences in patient mix or intensity of service; they did reveal lower productivity in the public sector, less control of productivity, more politically motivated appointments, and, finally, the anathema of all government programs— civil service, or what some view as the protection of incompetent or unnecessary staff. Return on investment decisions were not made on any basis other than political expediency. Another way of viewing this was offered by a former director of a government hospital when he referred to his institution as an employer of last resort in the community.

Revenues

How do these organizations earn or acquire their operating and capital funds? Proprietary organizations have only one significant source of operating capital: those who utilize their services. Fundamentally, these organizations become directly responsible to consumers, who, in classical market terms, vote with their dollars. Here it is necessary to recognize the clear imperfections of the medical care marketplace, in that effective demand is for the most part determined by the providers, since consumers have quite limited knowledge of the costs and benefits of the various options. A group practice that is poorly located or offers services at inconvenient times may find itself out of business simply because it depends on clients for revenue and has no opportunity to generate revenue from nonclient sources.

Capital funds are a somewhat different matter, since proprietary organizations can readily avail themselves of a range of private investors who willingly offer capital if they envision a good return on their investment. Perhaps the best example of this are health care stocks and bonds. Despite the vagaries of the stock market, health care companies still rank as reasonable investments and bond offerings still tend to be in the investment range.

Nonprofit organizations derive their operating funds from two major sources: consumers and philanthropy. In a very real sense, they, too, must satisfy their constituency; otherwise, their major source of operating income could be jeopardized. They have important ways of supplementing their accounts, however, such as fund-raising and gifts of various sorts. Such donations are rarely made to a proprietary organization, partly because these organizations do not solicit donations and partly because such a gift not only has no tax benefits for the donor but is also considered taxable income for the recipient. Further, few charitable organizations will provide money to for-profit organizations, since such gifts could jeopardize their own charitable status.

Capital sources for nonprofits are fourfold. First, like all organizations, they can attempt to have surplus revenues and then invest those funds for future capital projects. Second, because of their tax-exempt status, they can actively solicit donations from individuals and foundations for building projects. Third, they can go into the bond market and offer tax-exempt bonds, which typically sell at lower rates than corporate bonds offered by for-profit companies. The quality of their bond offering is a function of their balance sheet, so it is imperative that even the most community-minded nonprofit organizations be managed almost as if they are for-profit entities. Finally, they can attempt to borrow money from any number of lenders. The issue for the lender, once again, will be the strength of the organization's balance sheet.

A third source of income is really not income at all but is essentially a bonus to nonprofit organizations, and this is the often debated tax exemption. Depending on location and quality of facility, a small community hospital may be worth millions of dollars. What would that amount to in terms of real estate tax? What about sales tax? A hospital or health system typically will save millions of dollars each year as a result of their tax exempt status.

Government organizations and, to some extent, quasi-governmental organizations, acquire their money from three primary sources: consumers, philanthropy, and taxes. A state health department, for example, does not have to generate any funds itself (although some enrich their operations by seeking additional project money from foundation or governmental funding); its dollars flow from the state budget, which is in turn related to taxes. Many government-funded programs, including those that are direct service programs, are removed from direct responsibility for generating their budgets. The conceptual notion of a service responsibility predominates, although even in government programs, accountability is required; but this accountability is usually upward to a field or regional office as opposed to downward to the consumer.

A related question with regard to resources is: To what extent can managers affect the flow of resources into an organization? In other words, how much freedom does a manager have in developing programs to attract new clients or new dollars? Despite the range of controls exercised on health organizations, there is some degree of freedom; the extent varies between the three major types of organizations.

Managers in for-profit operations probably have the greatest flexibility within their organizations for expanding revenue sources, since the clear mission of these organizations is related to their ability to generate adequate (and increased) revenues. Nonprofit organizations have certain constraints, the most significant of which is (as was noted earlier) their tax-exempt status. While this is fundamentally a benefit, it is also a potential problem in that it may preclude the development of new and profitable services. This is not to suggest that nonprofit organizations cannot or do not go out and market their services; indeed, they do in a variety of ways. Perhaps the major conceptual constraint is related to the somewhat more diffuse mission of the nonprofit organization. A nonprofit organization might knowingly develop a program that is clearly unlikely to be self-supporting simply because there is a community need for it or because it is viewed as part of the organization's service responsibility. Rarely is such benevolent behavior seen in for-profit organizations.

Government organizations are usually much more constrained than either of the two other types of organizations. Government organizations may be prevented by law or custom from offering services to "non-eligible" recipients. To put it another way, the programs in which they are engaged are developed solely to satisfy certain clearly defined constituencies. To go beyond those constituencies is an encroachment on someone else's territory and may be beyond their scope of responsibilities and likely reimbursement. If an organization does go beyond its jurisdiction, there are often disincentives to provide the service. It is interesting to note how many municipal hospitals that had limited themselves to indigent patients decided to open their doors to insured or privately paying patients when faced with budget crises. As President Clinton was fond of saying, "It's the economy, stupid."

Expenses

While resources are one managerial headache, costs are no doubt the major headache of managers of all health care organizations. The question of concern here is: To what extent can managers in these various organizations control costs? To address this question properly, it must be recognized that the typical health care organization has two types of costs: fixed and variable. The fixed costs are those that, for the most part, are beyond the scope of the organization's, or at least the manager's, ability to control, and may be considered overhead. Of course, even this concept is a bit illusory, since there is a certain latitude within fixed costs; for example, energy costs might be considered fixed, and yet through careful analysis of alternative systems a manager might find satisfactory substitutes. The variable costs are simply those attached to each specific patient visit. As an illustration, a family planning clinic has fixed costs for its land and building (mortgages and interest), regardless of the number of visits of patients per week, month, or year; however, each visit generates other costs directly related to the visits, such as supplies that are consumed.

The single largest item in virtually any health care budget is salaries, typically running upwards of 60% in a hospital or nursing home. How can a manager affect that item? In a for-profit enterprise, the traditional solution is careful attention to productivity and hiring. Control of this critical section of the budget has been more difficult, however, in government and voluntary agencies, where hiring has historically been used to provide a safety valve for unemployment.

Community organizations, simply because of their "closeness" with the community, must be more circumspect in how they deal with this issue of staffing. Perhaps one of the best examples is the Hunterdon Medical Center in Flemington, NJ. In the mid-1970s, in response to a declining census, the hospital closed off beds that logically would have dictated laying off workers. Yet, as one of its largest community employers, the company felt a responsibility to the community and decided not to lay off workers, hence putting itself into a difficult financial situation. Would a for-profit company have acted in such a way?

Some years ago, one of the nation's largest tire manufacturers negotiated a 50 cents per hour pay decrease with its union so that the plant would not follow other companies that moved to the Sun Belt and abandoned workers in the "decaying" industrial East. Could this happen in the health care field? How can the Health and Hospitals Corporation of New York close hospitals or hospital beds without losing jobs? Many managers admit that their health care organizations are overstaffed, but what can they do about it? In the for-profit organization, the answers seem simpler, perhaps because the self-interest of the organization is more clearly identified than the amorphous "public interest" that the government or voluntary organization must serve.

Feedback and Action

Assuming that the problem has been diagnosed, what can be done? This is perhaps one of the most perplexing problems facing the line manager. In the context of the matrix, this is termed the feedback loop and action. To what extent will data and analysis result in some type of corrective action? Assume that a particular program area is not achieving its goals because an individual worker is simply and blatantly unproductive. Attempts at assisting the worker have been to no avail, and the manager has come to the distasteful conclusion that the worker must be fired. In the for-profit organization, it is usually the manager's prerogative to discharge the worker; if justification is required, it is to a higher-level manager or perhaps a union. In the voluntary agency, additional constraints may be imposed because of community pressure; discharging an informal community leader may bring unacceptable consequences. In government, the obvious problem is the civil service, a system that was designed to protect the worker from arbitrary and capricious "bosses" and that now functions, in part, to protect arbitrary and capricious workers from the reasonable and often difficult economic decisions of management.

Many other examples can be used to illustrate the differences among these three major organizational types when they are faced with data and information. In New York City, the president of the Health and Hospitals Corporation "buried" a report on one of his hospitals because he felt the community would be outraged if it was known that "their" hospital was threatened with closing. A for-profit management company "cleaned house" at one New York voluntary hospital by laying off hundreds of employees and thus brought a measure of fiscal stability to that institution. Is it possible that the former hospital director, one of the nation's most thoughtful and knowledgeable professionals, had simply not been aware of the solution? Hardly! Rather, as the agent of a charitable organization, he was not empowered to make the "hard-nosed" business decisions that were acceptable under the regime of a proprietary business firm.

Action, then, is in large part related to the number of constituencies and constraints that must be satisfied. Certain organizations have fewer constituencies than others, and the goals of some are sharper than others. Action for the for-profit organization relates to the bottom line, either today or in the foreseeable future. At the other extreme, action in government relates to an unclear and oft-debated public good, as well as to the prospect of reappointment or reelection.

A final example: During the time I was a CEO of a nonprofit, I decided for a number of legitimate reasons to discharge a senior staff person. I offered him the option of resigning or being fired. He selected the option of an immediate resignation. Later that day I was discussing this with my brother, who was then the dean of a major medical school. At the other end of the phone line I heard his astonishment and perhaps envy. He, too, wanted to fire some staff and faculty, but organizational rules and tenure made such personnel actions time consuming and not always possible. In this case, each organization operated with different constraints, and the university's constraint of tenure represented a major stumbling block to change.

MANAGERIAL TIME FRAME

The time frame in which management must act may differ in these various organizational arrangements. In for-profit and voluntary organizations, it is postulated that both top and middle management have and can afford a time frame long enough to plan and implement properly. In essence, they can emulate the model of private industry, such as the automobile industry, in which up to a decade may pass from the time of a new model's inception to the time of its introduction. Both top and middle management have a sense of stability that allows them to plan, develop, and, in some cases, test alternatives. They simply do not have to make a "splash" to survive the next political purge or election.

For the middle manager in government, who is often protected by civil service, the time frame may also be long. On the other hand, top management in governmental agencies and programs are continually asked to produce results by absurd deadlines. A governor is elected in November and asked to produce a multibillion dollar budget in January. A member of Congress complains, and a secretary or commissioner is asked to solve a complicated social problem within a few days.

The press both facilitates and complicates these public management positions. Most people cannot name the heads of the Fortune 500 companies but can easily identify senior government officials. Why? Because these officials are always in the spotlight and, in many senses, are being asked for "action." A government agency must act in order to develop a constituency both within and outside of government and thus ensure its own managerial well-being. Because they have their own resources, private and voluntary organizations can afford more independence in both planning and action.

The reward structure for management is rather diffuse and sometimes confusing. In the private and nonprofit organizations, income, benefits, and privileges are usually directly related to the quality and quantity of work, or, to put it another way, to the value or esteem in which the organization holds a person. A top manager in one of these two organizational types has considerable latitude in how or when people are rewarded; sometimes a day off, a small bonus, or a new title can be given. For top management in the government organizations, however, degrees of freedom are severely limited, particularly with nonprofessional staff. With so little latitude, managers may find themselves not only unable to motivate employees but also unable to prevent them from being dissatisfied because of those tremendous trivialities that so often irritate employees and prevent them from doing a reasonable day's work.

THE MANAGEMENT ROLE

In both private and voluntary organizations, individuals become managers and remain managers because of their loyalty and performance. Most organizations want people who are loyal to their ideas, concepts, and goals. Loyalty is not enough, however. The manager must have needed skills, which can range from being a financially technocratic whiz to being a skilled negotiator. Organizations have natural histories and needs for different types of people at different times. The manager's skills must contribute to the organization, and the possessor must be recognized as the integral implementer of the skills.

In a theoretical sense, it could be argued that effective health administrators are those who have an understanding of the health system within which they have to operate, the skills to manage it, and the knowledge to apply those skills judiciously. Some, on the other hand, argue that "management is management" and is a totally transferable skill. Others say that "management is a bunch of crap" and that what a manager really needs is to know something about how health services are organized and to have a feel for the "people."

The most costly and possibly most unfortunate natural experiment on this issue has been the New York City Health and Hospitals Corporation.

In 1978, for example, the newly appointed president of this billion-dollar corporation was described by the mayor as a man with top-flight management skills gleaned from his experiences as the number-two man in the New York City Police Department. The official health establishment in New York City mumbled under its breath and did nothing. Who did this management expert replace? A former Catholic priest and college chaplain who, by a series of accidents, became president of the corporation with less than five years in health administration (not one day of which amounted to anything approximating hospital administration). Who had he replaced? An outspoken activist physician without a day's worth of hospital administration experience, who in turn had replaced a psychiatrist with federal government experience but no hospital administration experience.

In this natural experiment, it has been demonstrated that the road to the top in government has nothing to do with a logical model of managerial competency and experience but only political expediency. Those appointed for such reasons are obligated to those with the appointment power. Thus, in order to stay on the top in a political position, those appointed must pay extremely careful attention to constituencies, not only their own, but, perhaps more importantly, those of the individuals who have the power to appoint (and no doubt) remove them.

CONCLUSION

Each of the three types of organizations appeals to different constituencies, has different possibilities to offer to the public, and, in this author's opinion, has an appropriate role in the health system. Ideologues would claim that the poor can be served properly only in the public general hospital because that is the institution where there is accountability. How has this accountability been brought into play? Certainly not in the accessibility, availability, or even quality of services. If there is accountability in these institutions, it appears to be related more to the workers than to the patients. Private health care organizations are criticized for "skimming the cream" of the system; however, they have also reacted much more rapidly and in some respects more sensitively to public needs. When laws were passed legalizing abortion, for example, where were the public clinics and voluntary agencies? The "Medicaid mill" is criticized—but who else is willing to go into Washington Heights or the South Bronx and provide care?

Finally, voluntary organizations are criticized for virtually everything, but it must be remembered that they have made major contributions to progress in clinical medicine and to the advancement of health care.

In sum, the United States has a pluralistic system that has many edges and angles that disturb and perturb. But, before we throw it out, it behooves us to understand it and make it work in the most effective way for the special needs of our society.

Case Study 3-1
THE CABINET MEETING

Every Tuesday and Thursday morning, the senior management of the Central Valley Medical Center, a 411-bed hospital, meet to discuss a broad range of managerial issues. A major subject of concern for the past several weeks has been the declining Medicare census, and discussions have revolved around strategies to increase the census. At today's meeting, the following conversation takes place:

CEO: Any progress on the census initiatives?

COO: One new thing we are exploring is a telemedicine initiative that may develop better relationships with practitioners in rural areas and result in their sending us patients.

CFO: Have you costed the project yet?

COO: No, but we are working on it. Besides, if it smells viable I am going over to development and seeing if they can get some state, federal, or foundation money to pay for the deal.

CEO: Anything else?

COO: Yes, I've been approached by the Revere brothers, who are interested in doing a deal with us.

CFO: Who are they?

(continues)

Case Study 3-1

COO: They are two guys who own and run two private nursing homes with a total of 500 beds, mostly Medicare. Anyway, they want to work a deal whereby we would be their only referral hospital. I suspect they could put between 10 and 20 patients a day into the hospital.

CEO: Sounds good, but what's the deal?

COO: They want a guaranteed $75,000 per year for the referrals.

CFO: It's certainly worth it, but we don't want to run afoul of the Medicare regs. Maybe we could give them a job or responsibilities for the money?

CEO: Right! See if they would be interested in being Chief of Gerontology.

COO: I doubt if they want to do anything, but I'll talk to them.

CEO: Great!

DISCUSSION QUESTIONS

1.   What is wrong with this picture?

2.   What type of moral and intellectual leadership is being offered by the CEO?

3.   What do you suspect will be the likely scenarios in this case?

CHAPTER 4

Setting Objectives in the Health Care Industry

As noted in Chapter 3, different types of health care organizations have different fundamental goals or objectives, and these differing objectives can strongly affect the managerial activities of the organization. In order to put these objectives into the perspective of the health system, it is necessary to establish a definition of system. Several historical ones are quite useful. For example, a system has variously been defined as: "an organization of interrelated and interdependent parts that form a unity,"[1] "a set of parts coordinated to accomplish a set of goals,"[2] and "an organized or complex whole: an assemblage or combination of things or parts forming a complex or unitary whole."[3]

A good illustration of the concept of systems is a sound system. I was recently in the market for such a system and learned that I would have to begin by purchasing a number of components, including an AM-FM digital receiver, a turntable (I still own records), speakers, and a compact disc player. Do these items make a system? Not yet! They are the components of a system. They become a system only when the wires connecting all the components are set into place and the set is plugged into a power source. Within the system, some components are considerably more important

---

[1]G.A. Theodorson and A.G. Theodorson, *Modern dictionary of sociology* (New York: Cromwell, 1969), p. 431.
[2]C.W. Churchman, *The systems approach* (New York: Delacorte Press, 1968), p. 29.
[3]R.A. Johnson, F.E. Kast, and J.E. Rosenzweig, *The theory and management of systems*, 2nd ed. (New York: McGraw-Hill, 1967), p. 4.

than others; for example, although the breakdown of one speaker will affect the quality of sound, as long as the other speaker continues to function, a total system collapse will be avoided.

On the other hand, if the power transformer in the receiver blows out, the rest of the system becomes mute. In the system of the human body, it can also be seen how the breakdown of one leading component, such as the heart or brain, can result in a total shutdown. The breakdown of other components, such as sight, however, can be compensated for, to an extent, by the remainder of the system. In short, then, systems are comprised of interrelated components that must function together in order to achieve a desired outcome.

A useful analysis of the U.S. health system developed by the American Public Health Association postulates three major components: (1) the personal component, that is, individuals who need or demand health services; (2) the professional component, meaning the range of people who provide the health services; and (3) the social component, which is the range of organizational arrangements for delivering the care.[4] Each of these components is quite complex, and what occurs within the boundaries of the component has a profound impact on the system overall. For example, if one were developing a system for low vision screening and rehabilitation services in a community and that community was primarily comprised of young families, the service would be designed differently than if the population were primarily elderly.

Similarly, an economically impoverished community might need a different mix of services than an affluent community.[5] Consider the community of Kotzebue, Alaska, located just above the Arctic circle. Between 1996 and 1998, this community's major ethnic population of Eskimos had death rates that were often dramatically different than that of the rest of the U.S. population. The death rate from heart disease, lung cancer, and chronic obstructive pulmonary disease was close to 50% lower than for the rest of the U.S. population. On the other hand, deaths from suicide were six times greater than in the rest of the United States, and deaths from alcohol-related causes were five times greater. This data illustrates

---

[4]American Public Health Association, *A guide to medical care administration Vol. I, Concepts and principles* (1964), p. 15.

[5]L.M. Rosenstock, "Why people use health services," *Milbank Memorial Fund Quarterly,* *XLIV*(3, 94) (1966), p.-124.

the significance of understanding the epidemiology of a community before developing preventive and delivery services.

The system is also impacted by the quality and range of skills available by the professionals in a community. As noted in an earlier chapter, there is considerable variation communities in the care provided by ostensibly similarly trained professionals. Whether it is community custom, resources, or other factors, we do know that services offered are very often provider driven.[6,7]

Finally, we have the social component. To a major extent these days, this is where the rubber hits the road. Whether a person has health insurance and what type of insurance is of enormous importance in terms of the services received and oftentimes where that service is available. My own insurance only covered 50% of the cost of an outstanding physical exam at the Mayo Clinic. Do I think it would be valuable to have such a physical on an annual basis? You bet! Am I willing to again pay out of my pocket several thousand dollars a year? No. Do I think everyone should get such terrific exams? Absolutely . . . but few individuals and employers are willing to pay the price.

Another dimension of this component is simply accessibility and availability. If you live in Chicago, Boston, Seattle, or virtually any large metropolitan area, you have the potential to tap into some of the best doctors and hospitals in the country on a 24/7 basis. But what about the more remote sections of the country where a hospital might be 75 miles away and that hospital is small with limited services? If you happen to be living in the city of Kotzebue, with its service area population of 7200 people and a 17-bed hospital, your access to the entire range of medical center–based specialists and technology will be somewhat limited. Indeed, you don't need to be in Alaska; limited access is also an issue in rural Massachusetts or Montana. The point is that for some people obstacles to the system may result from physical availability (or the lack thereof) and for others obstacles may be a question of physical, psychological, or financial access.

---

[6]S.W. Bloom, *The doctor and his patient* (New York: Free Press, 1963).
[7]M. Shain and M. Roemer, "Hospital costs relate to supply of beds," *Modern Hospital, 92* (1959), p. 71.

REAL AND STATED GOALS

As I write this chapter, the Boston Red Sox are once again fighting for a post-season spot, hopefully a shot at the pennant, and finally the ever-elusive goal of a World Series championship! Fortunately, in the time between the writing and publishing of this book the "Curse of the Bambino" was broken and the Red Sox won the 2004 championship! This annual ritual going on throughout the country reminds all of us of the different perspectives on this "game." For fans, the point is winning. For players, it's winning, ego satisfaction, and, no doubt, bigger contracts. For owners, it's all of the above but also returns on investment. Consider the case of the Florida Marlins. What happened immediately after they won the World Series in 1997? The owners sold off the best players and then sold the team! The following year the Marlins were back to being a losing team. Consider the following hypothetical: Assume a team had a great home run slugger like Barry Bonds or Sammy Sosa. After a careful analysis they learned that the team played better and won more games when the star slugger was out of the line-up, but that attendance was significantly better when the slugger was scheduled to play. What would drive the line-up—attendance or winning?

With that sports preamble, we can address a fundamental question: What is the objective of the health system and its organizational components such as hospitals, ambulatory care centers, and even physicians' offices? Is its objective to raise the health status of an individual or a community, or simply to deal with symptomatic problems? An answer to that question must begin with the realization that goals can be both real and stated. For example, oftentimes one can hear administrators of health care facilities and programs say that they have three goals: teaching, research, and service. But what are the real goals? What do they actually mean when they say teaching, research, and service? What is behind such a goal?

The somewhat murky history of obstetrical care in the United States might illustrate this point. A controversy about poor quality obstetrical care and the use of midwives raged in the United States and Great Britain in the late 1800s and early 1900s. What was behind the stated goals of the physician leaders of this profession? The solution developed in Great Britain was to educate, license, and upgrade midwives so that they had the role and responsibility in the medical system of providing normal obstetrical care. On the other hand, the controversy over responsibility and authority for delivering normal obstetrical care continued in the United States for decades.

This controversy pitted those physicians trained in the new specialty of obstetrics against the rather disorganized group of traditional providers, that is, midwives. Even the American Medical Association had a surprising position on this issue. In 1912, its president, Dr. Abraham Jacobi (for whom a major teaching hospital in the Bronx is named), pointed out in his inaugural address that the current view of midwives as dirty and sloppy women was based not on fact but rather conjecture and that, if clinical facts surrounding obstetrical care were examined, physicians, not midwives, would be eliminated.[8]

What, then, motivated distinguished professors (primarily from Johns Hopkins University) to work so assiduously to eliminate midwives? Was it simply that the midwife provided poorer quality medical care? According to some sources, the goal was to eliminate midwives in order to provide the appropriate volume of patients for fledgling physicians to practice their new skills. Further, once these skills were learned, midwives had to be eliminated if physicians were to build a practice to support themselves. Others, however, have argued that midwifery died because the new immigrants considered seeing a physician to be the "modern way," while midwifery was considered "old-fashioned."[9]

Regardless of the reason, it is obvious that midwifery essentially passed from the scene for decades, even though there was no clearly defined medical care objective in its elimination. More recently, other public policy decisions in health care have been made with almost the same lack of clear objectives. A case in point might be house calls.[10] As a matter of public and private policy, the house call has been eliminated. Was this a deliberate objective of the health system? Indeed, was it in the best interests of the health status of the individual and community, or rather in the best interests of the providers and/or the organized arrangements for delivering the services?

---

[8]A. Jacobi, "The best means of combating infant mortality," *Journal of the American Medical Association, 58*(23) (1912), pp. 1735–1744.

[9]F.E. Korbin, 1966. "The American midwife controversy: A crisis of professionalization." *Bulletin of the History of Medicine, XL*(4), (1966), pp. 350–363.

[10]S.B. Goldsmith. "House calls: Anachronism or advent?" *Public Health Reports, 94*(4), (1979), pp. 299–304.

The concept of prisons, a subject of my own research and writing, can also be used to illustrate the problem faced in determining real versus stated goals. Many wardens, sheriffs, or court officers state that prison is a place for rehabilitation; others say that it is a place where offenders go to "pay their debt to society" or, to put it another way, that it is a place for punishment. Essential to all of these stated goals is the real goal; a prison is an institution organized by society to segregate people from "free" society for some period of time. Although never overtly stated, one of the clearest goals of any prison or jail is that of keeping certain people locked up.[11]

GOAL SETTING

It is useful to remember that goals are set in a variety of ways and that organizations often have multiple and sometimes conflicting goals. Indeed, the manager is frequently charged with resolving the most serious of these conflicts.

In general, goals are set as a result of four major factors: (1) politics, (2) economics, (3) constituencies, and (4) organizational personalities. Politics are local, national, regional, and environmental, or internal. For example, the sheriff and the mayor of a southern city realized that the health and medical conditions of a prison, which had already resulted in a federal lawsuit,would prove an embarrassing political issue during a forthcoming election unless the situation were "cleaned up." Further, they envisioned the possibility of amassing some political capital from developing a model health system. Internally—that is, within the prison—the feeling was that the system was simply out of control and the warden and sheriff were being used for the political purposes of the medical department. Thus, to some extent, a desire for change was dictated as a convergence of local political needs.

Always an important factor, economics is becoming an even stronger element in the setting of organizational goals. In a small northeastern town, two competing hospitals are now attempting to resolve their

---

[11]For a more detailed discussion and analysis of prison health, see L.F. Novick and M.S. Al Ibrahim, *Health problems in the prison setting* (Springfield, IL: Charles C. Thomas, 1977); and S.B. Goldsmith, *Prison health* (New York: Prodist, 1975).

differences so that a merger can be consummated. Why is there even an interest in this merger between hospitals that have traditionally been competitors and have somewhat different social orientations? The answer appears to be related to the difficulty of surviving economically in an increasingly regulated environment. Although neither institution is weak enough to be "picked off," neither has enough clout in the state capital to obtain a certificate of need or a rate increase. Merged, they would move up a few notches in the hierarchy of institutions and could afford to take advantage of certain strategies that individually they cannot afford, such as the use of expensive (and thought-to-be) effective consultants and more sophisticated financial planning. Finally, they believe that their combined organizations will allow for better sharing of services and a generally more efficient operation.

The conventional wisdom in health care is that the demand for services comes from inside, not from outside. The patient walks in, states a complaint and symptoms, and goes through the usual examination. Despite what the consumer may think or feel, it is the health professional who "turns on" the effective demand of the system. The physician orders the laboratory tests, X-rays, a back brace, or whatever. The only demand actually generated by the patient is through drugstores, herbalists, and such. To a large extent, this theory has been correct. In the past few years, however, there has been a slight change, and perhaps newer changes are in the offing. Organized patient constituencies are demanding services. An interesting historic example is that of abortion services. With the legalization of first trimester abortions, the patient walks into the medical facility and demands a specific service. She does not discuss a symptom and say "help me," but rather states in unequivocal language what medical procedure she wishes to obtain.

Community groups have grown more vocal about their desires, and sometimes these desires, which are wrapped in the mantle of medical care, are masking something else. For example, are the goals of neighborhood health centers to provide medical care or to provide jobs? In recent years pharmaceutical manufacturers have spent fortunes on promoting their prescription drugs directly to the public in hopes of having formerly docile patients walking into the doctors' offices and demanding a particular drug. The range and depth of information available on the Internet has also turned a certain segment of the population into knowledgeable and discerning consumers.

Finally, it is imperative to recognize the importance of the individual in setting organizational goals. At the national level, a president can restate and reorganize national priorities. One person in a leadership position can have power and choose to exercise it. A case in point is a VA Medical Center that I studied, where a new director was able to shift the goal of that seemingly highly controlled organization from that of being a self-sufficient non-community-oriented organization into that of being an organization that is an integral part of the economic and professional life of a community. Examples abound in the managerial literature about the role individuals can and do play in the leadership and management of organizations.

The most typical story, and one that I have seen quite often, is that of a CEO or board president who has clear organizational goals but whose goals are rarely articulated to the organization as a whole. Whether it's the leader's brilliance, insight, or merely dumb luck, the organization becomes successful for a number of years. Then trouble hits. But the leader, much like Idi Amin or Robert Mugabe, has secured total power over the organization and no one who likes working or being on the board dares to challenge him.

It may be only total financial disaster or the leader's death that brings change. One consulting client of mine provides an excellent case study of these phenomena. In this situation, a new chief financial officer decided to do a careful audit and learned, amongst other things, that the financial health of the organization was dramatically worse than the board president was presenting to the board and the public. The CFO documented his findings and offered a belt-tightening and revenue-generating solution for the future. By acknowledging the accuracy of the CFO's analysis, however, the president would be admitting that he had for years been steering the organization off course. So instead of making the called-for changes he simply fired the CFO and installed a "yes-man" as the top finance person. The organization eventually went into financial extremis. Indeed, this management tale is an echo of the Hans Christian Andersen story *The Emperor's New Clothes*. In the fairy tale, the emperor's ministers are afraid to call a spade a spade out of fear for their own positions. The emperor himself fears acknowledging what is before his eyes, that is, he is parading through the streets in his underwear. Only the naive child speaks up and tells it as it is. Unfortunately, fairy tales and management have too much in common!

IDENTIFICATION OF ORGANIZATIONAL GOALS

Skeptics like to point out that the goals of most organizations predate the manager, often by that manager's lifetime, so why bother identifying organizational goals? There is really only one reason: It gives the new manager the necessary bearings to chart a suitable personal course in the organization. The identification of goals has value to the organization in three major ways: orientation, legitimization, and measurement.

Orientation

Goal identification provides an organization with a certain direction, or orientation, that can and does help in the shaping of planning and policy directions. In practice, however, most organizations, particularly health care ones it sometimes seems, have such general goals that they can and do fit into their plans whatever makes sense at a given time. To be less charitable, it could be said that most of these organizations are simply responding as typical economic opportunists.

One health services research center began its career with a clear goal and orientation toward community health needs; even its name indicated a commitment to the community. In the early years of the research center, a great deal of effort and many dollars were funneled into identifying community needs and developing research projects that would meet those needs. Its goals during these early years were clearly very community oriented; because of initially secure funding from foundations that shared its goals, the center was able to pursue its community direction. As the initial grant funds were exhausted, however, the research center began searching for funds simply to pay staff and rent. Over time the orientation shifted from the community needs for which there were no funds to a variety of national problems for which funds were available. More recently, in response to the fact that private foundation funds are again available, the nature of the problems to be researched in this center has again shifted.

In practice, then, a major orientation of most organizations is simply survival; organizations do not commit suicide. Years ago, when the March of Dimes met its goal of contributing to the conquest of polio, it did not close down its operation. Rather, it shifted its focus to a new "goal:" battling birth defects.

Orientation should not be belittled. It has an important influence on the resources that are attracted to an organization. Managers who seek positions are or should be interested in the goals of the organization with which they are likely to be associated. Is there a shared orientation or general value system, and, if so, how important is that issue? It might be of major consequence for an organization's viability. For example, an excellent small rural hospital interested basically in maintaining its special niche as an excellent small rural hospital hired a director who misunderstood the goals of the hospital, or perhaps the hospital misunderstood its own goals when he was hired. With an evangelical burst of energy, the new director began to transform the institution into a national model of rural medicine. After less than a year, he was forced to resign; his goals and the institution's had become irreconcilable. Had he known that the hospital was not interested in the "big time," he would not have considered the position. Maybe the hospital did not understand what the "big time" meant before the new director's regime. In another example, a new hospital director was hired with the clear understanding that he would have carte blanche to restructure the hospital's board and bring in his own management team. The honeymoon that began with a great deal of fanfare ended when he began to implement his plan. His restructuring efforts were simply goring too many sacred cows, and because of that, his contract was terminated early.

Legitimization

Goals, both stated and unstated, have a way of providing their own legitimacy for an organization's or individual's activities. If a voluntary organization has a goal of providing health services to home-bound individuals, it can, with great ease, legitimately extend its boundaries of operation to include a gamut of activities that are not thought of as traditional health services.

Perhaps the most dramatic example of this, which has already passed into the folklore of American medical care, is the work of Dr. Jack Geiger at the Delta Health Care Center in Mound Bayou, Mississippi. When he and his team arrived in that depressed area to set up a health center funded by the Office of Economic Opportunity, they found the social and economic problems to be considerably more pressing than the health problems. Their solution was not simply to prescribe drugs but to prescribe other necessities—most notably, food. Within the context of the general goals of those programs, what Geiger and his group did was unique, but it was also within the legitimate goals of the program.

On the other hand, with no goals or only the vaguest, it is difficult to win support for virtually anything and even more difficult to sustain support. Simply stated, why buy a pig in a poke?

Measurement

One of the most common reasons for setting goals is measurement. Most people have been socialized from early childhood to achieve in one way or another. Growth charts, scales, reports, and myriad other types of documentation make it clear that some predetermined goals should be met. The underlying problem in all of this is that most people also have a natural tendency to set goals that can be measured, even though those measurable goals may have little to do with what is to be achieved. Perhaps it is my age or my experience as a naval officer from 1963 through 1968, but to me the worst example in American history was the body count mentality of the military during the Vietnam War. Our daily papers were filled with data on how the United States was "winning," and "winning" was defined as the number of people killed and tons of bombs dropped.

The ideal of "winning hearts and minds" was somehow translated into something much more measurable. Perhaps this explains our interest, bordering on fascination, with such health care data as occupancy rates, average lengths of stay, and cost per day. Clearly, it is convenient to have something easily measurable.

Some years ago, these problems of measurement led me to engage in a research project to develop a single "consumer price index" of health. The idea was to find an easily understandable measure of the changes in an individual's and a community's health status. In the sense of developing or discovering such an index, the project was a failure. What it did demonstrate were the complexities of finding a clear measure when a goal was diffuse. It is difficult indeed to measure progress toward a goal when that goal is unclear, unidentified, or controversial.

An analogy might be made with a ship proceeding at great speed on a cruise to nowhere or a jet traveling eastward at 500 miles per hour with everyone (passengers, pilot, navigator, stockholders, and air controllers) disagreeing or uncertain as to where the plane should go. Great progress, but to what end? In our health system, the current goals are cost containment, increased access, and better quality. But how do these goals relate to the individual's or community's health status?

CONSTRAINTS ON HEALTH SYSTEM GOALS

A consideration of the stated and real goals of the health system is important to management, since so much of managerial behavior is related to an organization's goal. No system operates in a vacuum, however, and it must be recognized that the health system has significant constraints on its goals.

Legal Constraints

One major and increasingly important constraint is the legal one. Court-rendered definitions of health have profound operational implications; a court's interpretation of health can grant or deny jurisdiction to a health department or agency, deny or award claims for insurance and injuries, close down businesses, and enforce warranty provisions. In 1852, for example, the North Carolina Supreme Court noted in *Bell v. Jeffreys* that: "In its ordinary usage, *healthy* means free from disease or bodily ailment, or a state of the system peculiarly susceptible or liable to disease or bodily ailment." But the court said that when the word *sound* is added to the word *healthy*, it means "whole, right, nothing the matter with it, [and] free of any defect." In this case, the plaintiff was attempting to recover damages that he had sustained through the purchase of a female slave who was supposed to be "sound and healthy" but was myopic. The nearsightedness, the plaintiff claimed, precluded the slave from performing "the common and ordinary business in the house or field, which slaves are taught and expected to perform and which is usually required of them."[12]

The issue of health again came before the North Carolina Supreme Court in 1857 when a person, after buying a slave who was warranted to be "sound in mind and body," found that the slave had a "contraction of the little finger of each hand." The contraction, the owner argued, made the slave less than healthy and justified the awarding of damages to the

---

[12]*Bell v. Jeffreys.* 35 N.C. 356 (1852).

plaintiff. After three pages of opinion that interpreted *health, healthy,* and *sound* by quoting from a variety of regular and medical dictionaries, the court decided that, although the contracted fingers did make the slave somewhat less than useful and therefore somewhat less than healthy, the basic warranty was not broken.[13]

The modern legal definition was first stated in 1928 by the West Virginia Supreme Court of Appeals in *Venerable v. Gulf Taxi Line*.[14] The court said, "Health means the state of being hale, sound or whole in body, mind, soul or well-being." This legal definition is not very far removed from the North Carolina court's definition of the 1850s or the World Health Organization's definition in the twentieth century: "Health is a state of complete physical, mental, and social well-being, and not merely the absence of diseases and infirmity."[15]

Political Constraints

The political process can and does shape or even distort goals. Several years ago I queried state legislators in Louisiana about the significance of various health status indicators on their budgetary decisions. In general, the indicators that were important to these politicians were those that are most commonly heard, although not necessarily understood, such as infant mortality rates. Perhaps of greater interest than the statistics from the study are excerpts from some unpublished letters I received from these Louisiana legislators:

> I support health services with specifics—I leave this to the experts; in other words, I supply dollars. How they are parceled out and what the priorities are is not my decision to make.

> Aside from local health problems with which I am familiar, the Louisiana health programs are presented to the Legislature on recommendation by the Governor. Only vague generalizations are used to support needed appropriations. Maybe the budget committee sees such statistics, but I haven't.

> To be quite candid, none of these particular points [health indicators] were instrumental in making my decision and I have serious doubts that they were in the minds of practically any other member of the

---

[13]*Harrell v. Norvil.* 50 N.C. 29 (1857).

[14]*Venerable v. Gulf Taxi Line.* 141 S.E. 622 (1928).

[15]*World Health Organization: The first ten years of the World Health Organization* (Geneva: WHO, 1958), p. 459.

Legislature. In the short time we had, the entire Legislature was generally guided by the Governor's suggestions, the amount of allocations received during the past years, and on general advice from people such as Senator [X], a good friend of mine whom I personally relied upon. This is not the best way to handle these matters . . . but we have no assistance . . . and this system just does not allow for detailed study.

It is my belief that each person has the responsibility of providing the means to pay for his own health care. It seems unjust to me that the people of this State are taxed in order to pay for the health care of others. . . . I believe that the factors listed in your questionnaire . . . are the proper concern of professionals who practice in the health field and that they are not the proper concerns of politicians. State legislators have no more business trying to run the health care business than they would in trying to run the grocery business.

Professional Constraints

The role of professionals in setting goals for health care organizations cannot be minimized. To conceptualize this point, it is necessary to understand something about the ritual that physicians, the group with whom most managers have to work most closely, have passed through en route to their medical degree. This ritual of an extended educational experience, the acquisition of technical and social skills, and a value system that is the exclusive property of the profession results in a professional philosophy that holds as almost sacrosanct the idea of autonomy. Only members of the profession are qualified to evaluate or discipline other members. The loyalty of most professionals is to their profession, not to the organization for which they work. Their goal orientation, then, is toward professional goals; in medicine, for example, these goals might be technical excellence rather than an organizational goal. Conflict comes when the profession's goals diverge from that of the organization.

Before the advent of diagnostic related groups (DRGs) (or perhaps two decades ago) and the pressure on hospitals to discharge patients as soon as possible, a typical case in point might be a well-insured consumer with a low back pain problem. The orthopedist would examine the patient and feel that the most appropriate treatment would be 10 days of complete bed rest. The physician would say, "You have two choices: 7 to 10 days at the Community Hospital or 7 to 10 days at home."

The patient would ask, "What will happen at the hospital that couldn't occur at home?"

The physician would respond, "Essentially nothing of note—the nurses will bring you muscle relaxant medication, we'll do a few more lab tests, take a series of X-rays, and we'll know for certain that you've been on complete bed rest."

Because of the health insurance in those pre-DRG or pre-HMO proliferation days, there would have been little direct costs to the consumer for the hospitalization. There were the costs involved in time lost from work and the costs of home care, although the latter would usually seem minimal when the family was intact. For the physician, hospitalization made patient management more certain, since patient compliance was likely to be higher in the hospital than at home; in addition, a bill for the equivalent of one or two visits made while the patient was hospitalized would appear appropriate. In all likelihood, the hospital utilization review committee would not balk at this hospitalization, which was usually considered reasonable and conservative treatment of a common problem. For the health system, however, the costs were dramatic: seven days in the hospital at the-then cost of $200 per day versus seven days at home or even the Ritz with room service. It could be argued that the diagnostic imaging was not available at the Ritz, but a hospitalization was hardly justified simply for X-rays or perhaps even for patient compliance. On the other hand, the health system was not set up to handle many of the "walking wounded."

Today's decision process is significantly different because there is a clear conflict between the needs of the hospital and those of the professional. The hospital's interest lies in moving patients through the system as quickly as possible, thus taking advantage of the financial incentives associated with being paid for the totality of care for a given case regardless of the resources expended. The physician, on the other hand, is paid by the visit, and his economic efficiency as well as the quality of care he can provide may be enhanced by hospitalization. Even today the professional has choices, such as managing a coronary case through medication or surgery. There are other examples: choices of medications, lab tests, ordering an MRI, or simply waiting a few days and seeing whether a problem resolves itself. In essence, then, what we do see is that any given problem can result in a range of "demands" on the health system, and many factors can be variables in predicting these demands.

PRISON HEALTH SYSTEM: CONFLICTING GOALS AND OBJECTIVES

As has been discussed, the objectives or goals of an organization are of profound importance, not only to the organization itself but also to the various constituencies it serves. The goals themselves set a legitimate direction and allow measurement of progress toward the attainment of the goal. Under the best of circumstances, objectives are clear, understandable by those who must work in the organization as well as by those outside the organization, and measurable in the sense that there is a reasonably direct way of analyzing how well the total organization is performing vis-à-vis the goals and to what extent each component contributes toward the goal.

How this works in practice is pointedly illustrated by considering the objectives of the consumers, professionals, and provider organizations in delivering health care to prison inmates. To begin with, the organization has an overriding goal of custody; no warden, sheriff, or guard is going to maintain his or her job and no prison is going to maintain its budget allocation without keeping the inmates in custody. Although this goal at first seems obvious and indeed simplistic, it is in fact crucial to an understanding of prison health problems. A second and related organizational goal is control, which translates into "keeping the place quiet." The positive goal of rehabilitation is often mentioned, but the attitude that prisons are not the place for rehabilitation but rather for punishment is becoming more prevalent. For example, some states, such as Utah, have an indeterminate sentencing system, whereby offenders are sentenced to a range of prison time (such as 1–15 years) under the theory that when they are "ready," that is, behaving properly in prison, becoming "rehabilitated," and showing proper remorse, they are then released. Other states, such as New York, have recently (1998) eliminated the indeterminate sentence, yet these "determininate" sentences also have ranges, formulas, and post-release supervision.

A few and often forgotten goals of prisons relate to their role in a community's political affairs. In some instances, they are sources of political patronage jobs, although this is no longer very common; in other cases, they are led by elected officials who must be reelected or who have an interest in higher political office. From the organization's perspective, then, the goals of its medical service must be related to the general organizational goals. Thus, medical care might be delayed or denied because no guard is available to escort an ailing inmate, or tranquilizers might be heavily prescribed in order to keep the prison quiet—behavior that would be considered inappropriate in a "free" health system.

Consumers also approach the health system differently inside prison, in large measure because they are forced to by circumstances. For example, a consumer in the "free world" has access to considerable medical information and a range of different opportunities and incentives with regard to the health system. "Free world" persons are encouraged to take care of themselves (to an extent) via health education programs and commercial advertisements, and pharmacies are fully stocked with over-the-counter medications that can seemingly cure anything. Rare is the house without some aspirin, Vaseline, or Band-Aids. In many penal institutions, however, even these basics are denied. Inmates with a headache therefore are often required to seek medical attention simply to get what would be readily available if they were not incarcerated. So an inmate obtaining medical care within a prison may be attempting to attain a different objective than is a person in the outside world. An inmate, locked in a cell for a majority of the hours in a day, may want to go to the medical department simply to alleviate boredom. Who in the "free world" visits a physician out of boredom?

If the physician prescribes a medication, that medication usually has an economic value in the prison. Almost any medication, but particularly anti-anxiety drugs, can be sold to another inmate for money, sex, or sometimes personal security. Most people outside of prisons do not visit a physician in order to get a prescription for subsequent resale, but some consumers within penal institutions do. This is thus an additional demand on the system.

Another set of objectives or goals from this group of consumers is escape. As noted earlier, one type is escape from boredom. There are two other types of escape: escape from work and escape from prison itself. Escape from work is usually conditional, based on some kind of extenuating circumstances. One of the most reasonable circumstances is an illness that precludes a person from working. In this situation, the health system plays the role of "legitimizer" of a person's health status. Thus, inmates who want to avoid a day in the laundry or at the license plate–stamping machine have to convince the medical staff that they are in no condition to work. They cannot simply call in sick and have it charged to their sick leave or annual leave; they cannot simply fail to show up. It should be noted that there are some similarities to this situation in the general workforce. For example, some organizations have a rule that after three days of sick leave a person must bring in a physician's note. In view of the difficulty of getting an appointment with a physician, this perhaps explains some of the emergency room crush.

A final type of escape is the classic one. Although going to a prison's medical department per se does not increase an inmate's chance of escape, it might be important if it is determined that the inmate requires secondary or tertiary care in a hospital without a prison ward (which is almost all of them). In such a situation, the inmate may be guarded by a hospital or prison security staff; within the confines of a hospital, however, there are few backup security systems or even a custody-oriented attitude. Thus, a determined inmate, particularly with help from friends, would have a much simpler time escaping from a hospital than from a penal institution. But the medical department sits in judgment about who shall go to the hospital and who shall receive treatment inside the walls.

The difficulty of coordinating these goals in practice can be seen in the case of an aged, acutely ill patient who was delayed in a county jail about 30 minutes while a security crew was rounded up for this almost comatose patient. Clearly, the custody goal reigned supreme over the care goals.

The third group of goals in this example are those of the professionals: the physicians, nurses, and paraprofessionals who deliver the care. Their primary professional goal is the provision of high-quality clinical care in an efficient and effective manner. However, the prison health system also requires them to be traffic cops and triage the sick from the malingerers. It also asks them to utilize their skills to assist in the custodial functions: "Be liberal with the tranquilizers; it's better to have a bunch of quiet zonked inmates than anxious obstreperous ones." While this might be less-than-optimum medical care, it is effective "wardening." Thus, the medical department is, for the most part through no fault of its own, placed in a most uncomfortable position. It knows what it wants to do, but the demands made by the organization and consumer require behavior that, while unpleasant and at the margins of professional acceptability, is quite clearly necessary for survival.

Finally, constraining all of this is a host of political variables, such as the political ambitions of sheriffs or mayors, the economic realities of government (this is one area that the free enterprise system has avoided), and philosophies; for example, does the country at large really care about those persons who are incarcerated? Since most people do not consider themselves vulnerable on that account, they can easily avoid this issue in their complicated lives.

In this chapter, we have been concerned about exploring the concept of goals in management. We shall revisit the concept of goals through the managerial function of strategic planning in a later chapter. In the private sector, it is often heard that goals boil down to the "bottom line," but translating this into an operational objective becomes difficult. It is appropriate to close this chapter by recounting Lynn Townsend's experience at AVIS Car Rentals, where it took six months for his firm to come up with its business objective of "renting and leasing vehicles without drivers."[16]

The delineation and acceptance of this goal had profound implications; it caused AVIS to get or stay out of the hotel business, tour bus business, and so forth. While it is acknowledged that the goal setting challenge in health care, particularly the nonprofit sector, is far more complex than merely the "bottom line," we should also learn from AVIS and others. Clear goals and objectives are hard to come by, but once obtained they allow a concentration of effort that results in a more efficient and effective organization.

Case Study 4-1
THE MERGER

On November 9, 1918, two days before Armistice Day ending World War I, the small western New England community of Oriole celebrated the opening of the 36-bed St. Anne's Hospital. Largely funded by Raymond McGee, a wealthy textile mill owner, the hospital was gifted to the Little Daughters of Perpetual Compassion, a Catholic order based in the state capital. The Little Daughters not only

(continues)

---

[16]R. Townsend, *Up the organization* (Greenwich, CT: Fawcett, 1970), pp. 111–112.

Case Study 4-1

held the ownership of the hospital but also ran the institution for the next 80 years. The fortune of St. Anne's was in large measure a reflection of the fortunes of the Oriole community. As it struggled through the Depression, the hospital managed to stay afloat through the generosity of several wealthy Catholic families and some assistance from the Daughters of Perpetual Compassion. World War II brought considerable business to Oriole's four textile mills and tool making shops. With that prosperity and subsequent increase in population, the hospital was expanded to 100 beds. Unfortunately, the end of the war, as well as threats of unionization, caused the mills to leave for North Carolina, and the town went into an economic tailspin from which it never recovered. By the late 1990s, the hospital had closed half of its beds, was running at 50% occupancy, and was flirting with bankruptcy.

Meanwhile, on the other side of the Oriole River, a mere 7 miles to the east lay the town of Hawes. Since the end of World War II, Hawes had followed the course of retail and commercial development, eventually becoming the site of the state's first and largest Wal-Mart. In the early 1950s the town's mayor, a former state representative, was able to convince the government to route the interstate highway just east of the town, with two exits leading into Hawes. Several motels and restaurants were able to develop as a result. The most recent boost for the Hawes economy was the opening of the state regional office for motor vehicle licenses and registration. Overall, the local hospital in Hawes has done well, both because of the economy and aggressive leadership, which resulted in the hospital having one of the first general hospital-based inpatient psychiatric units in the state. By the late 1990s, the Hawes hospital was licensed for 190 beds, had an 80% occupancy rate, and usually ran in the black with the help of a modest endowment.

(continues)

Case Study 4-1

There was generally little overlap between the two medi-cal staffs of Hawes and Oriole. In the last few years; the Hawes hospital has become closely affiliated with the regional medical school as a strategy for upgrading its staff and services. Because the two hospitals are in the same county and relatively physically close, there has often been talk of merger, particularly during the years when federally funded health planning agencies were active.

Once again, at the outset of the 21st century, there is new talk of a merger because of Oriole's difficult financial situation. The perspective of the Hawes board is that the merger will be good for the hospital and medical staff. The extra 20 inpatients per day would help build a solid finan-cial situation for Hawes and, although the Oriole medical staff is generally not of the Hawes caliber, most of them are on the verge of retirement. Additionally, the Hawes prop-erty could be converted into a health center, perhaps some type of long-term care facility. While the Little Daughters of Perpetual Compassion are interested in relieving them-selves of the financial burden of the hospital, they are deeply concerned about two issues. First, they are con-cerned about the legacy of St. Anne's in a subsumed orga-nization, where there is a good chance that their name will be lost. Second, they are concerned that abortions are per-formed at Hawes Hospital and that there is an active fam-ily planning center.

DISCUSSION QUESTIONS

1. What are the exact objectives that each organization is seeking to attain in the merger?

2. Is there a way to accommodate their conflicting objectives?

3. How will the history of similar mergers affect their decision making?

4. What is likely to be more powerful, economics or ideology?

5. What do you anticipate is the likely outcome of this situation?

CHAPTER 5

Management in Industry and Health Care

At some point, virtually every textbook dealing with management offers the reader a definition of the subject. For example, in 1947 Cornell answered the question by noting:

> The work of management is to plan, direct and control the organization and to weave together its various parts so that all factors will function properly and all persons cooperate—that is, work together efficiently for a common purpose.[1]

In perhaps one of the grandest understatements, Drucker, in his best-selling book *Management*, suggests, "management is tasks, discipline, people and practice."[2] In a more recent work, Drucker modified his definition by stating: "Management is about human beings. Its task is to make people capable of joint performance, to make their strengths effective and their weaknesses irrelevant."[3] Two "to do" books suggest slightly different definitions. One defines the job of management as follows: "Most managers need to supervise the work of more junior employees and to ensure that the staff function effectively."[4] The second, *Management for Dummies,* defines management as "making something planned

---

[1]W.B. Cornell, *Organization and management in industry and business* (New York: Ronald Press, 1947), p. 46.

[2]P. Drucker, *Management*. (New York: Harper & Row, 1973), p. xiii.

[3]P. Drucker. (2002). *The essential Drucker*. New York: HarperCollins, p. 10.

[4]R. Heller and T. Hindle, *DK essential manager's manual* (New York: DK Publishing, 1998), p. 10.

happen within a specific area through the use of available resources."[5] Finally, I am impelled to offer that management is running the team. In the American League 2003 playoff season, tens of millions of Americans and all of Boston saw what happens when management does not do its job. In this instance, manager Grady Little allowed a tired pitcher, Pedro Martinez, to pitch beyond his physical but not ego capacity, and once again the Boston Red Sox suffered under the curse of the Bambino. What happened was simple. Little, seeing Martinez faltering, went and asked if he wanted to continue. Martinez said yes and then went from being the brilliant pitcher of seven innings to the screwing-up pitcher of the eighth inning. Why didn't Little remove him? Depending on what account you believe, it was either that Little had no one better in the bullpen or that Martinez needed to be treated with kid gloves and Little was always deferential to him. The morning after this fiasco I was getting my usual cup of coffee at the Broadway Market, a few blocks from where I lived in Cambridge, when I saw Richard, the market's manager, who was in a foul mood over the game. I asked him his opinion and heard the following: "Little violated the first principle of management—you cannot let the inmates run the asylum!" The end of the story was simple: Grady Little's contract was not renewed.

Management might best be viewed as both an art and a science. On the one hand, it deals with sharply defined areas such as productivity and efficiency, areas best exemplified by the operations research/management science approach to problem solving. On the other hand, it also deals in more diffuse areas such as leadership and motivation.

This sets up a challenge for the manager. How does he or she construct or reconstruct organizations so that they maximize efficiency and effectiveness to their various external constituencies and simultaneously minimize stress, disaffection, and unhappiness to their internal constituencies? It should be recognized that this problem or challenge is a value-laden statement, as are most definitions of management and concepts of the manager's role. The emphasis in this statement is on satisfying external constituencies, performing efficiently in economic and financial terms, being effective, and, finally, respecting the human dignity of workers. If,

---

[5]B. Nelson and P. Economy. (2003). *Management for dummies* (New York: Wiley Publishing, 2003), pp. 9–10.

for example, workers are considered drones, peasants, or simply inputs for a resource system, this challenge might be restated to eliminate concern with the disaffected workers. Indeed, the manager's concept of the meaning of work can dramatically shift his or her perspective.

A management approach based on a value system, as they all are to some degree, must examine that system if it is to be responsive and continue to function as a mechanism for achieving organizational goals.

THE FUNCTIONS OF MANAGEMENT

The specific activity a manager may be involved in is likely to vary from one organization to another, as well as between periods within the same organization. The sum total of management in an organization tends to be relatively stable, however. The same managerial functions are carried out, although circumstances, organizational needs, and personalities dictate which of these functions predominates at any given time. The most oft-cited of these functions are planning, organizing, staffing, directing, controlling, coordinating, and representing.

Planning

Planning involves those activities associated with objective setting, policy making, and developing strategies for attaining objectives within the organizational policy framework. As noted earlier, it is considerably more difficult to identify objectives, particularly in the health field, than it appears at first glance. Organizational objective setting is a process that requires global vision, diplomatic skill, and considerable good fortune. Planning normally results in an output; that is, a written plan. Such a document can cover periods of time that vary from rather short periods, such as six months or a year, to longer periods, such as several years. An effective plan results in a positive outcome for the organization; a bad plan is likely to be worse than no plan because of the tendency to honor the written word. Sometimes even the best plans have to be scrapped because of changing circumstances, either fiscally or personnel-wise.

I am reminded of my early days at the University of Massachusetts at Amherst. A year after I arrived, a new chancellor was appointed, who proceeded to develop a major planning initiative. Perhaps because I was peripherally involved and also admired the new leader, I was rather excited about the new plan. The day it was finally announced, I had a chance encounter with a senior faculty member outside my office building and expressed my excitement about the new plan. She quickly dampened my enthusiasm by stating that the university library was stocked full with plans for restructuring, reorganizing, and reinvigorating the university, and they were all gathering dust. "This will be different," I naïvely replied. But within six months the chancellor had resigned and moved to Arizona. By the time I left the university 25 years later, we had gone through countless plans, over a dozen chancellors and provosts, and several serious financial crises.

Individuals who serve as planners in organizations may seem to take that responsibility off the shoulders of management, but this is an illusion. Management never totally delegates this responsibility or authority. A plan is the organizational control device. With a plan, management can continually identify expectations; that is, goals for people, programs, or projects, and measure the progress and the rate of progress being made toward these goals. Some managers prefer to utilize the lack of a plan as a control device for their organizations; the only plan is what is in the manager's head. In this way, the manager maintains total control and great flexibility but reigns over a situation that may often be close to disaster.

Two final points on planning. First, for any plan to be successful, it must be grounded in the reality of the organization's situation: its strengths, weaknesses, opportunities, and threats. It simply cannot live in a managerial/organizational fantasy world. For many years I kept a set of Head 360 skis in my office. Students would often come in and wonder about this item, which would result in the following story: In the mid-1960s, the Head Ski Company was the dominant manufacturer in the industry. Their model 360 was clearly the gold standard. It was a metal ski developed by Howard Head and incorporated the best available technology. It came in one color: black with yellow bottoms. The company was so focused on its own technology that it ignored and dismissed the developments of other companies that were using fiberglass as the prime material for skis. By the early 1970s, Head was practically out of business. Its previously superior products were now being outsold by a range of colorful and high-quality fiberglass skis. The message is clear: To be successful, organizations have to be flexible enough to constantly learn from their environments and reinvent themselves for the future.

Second, for any planning process to be successful, it must include all the key people, both staff and board, who will be required to implement the process. In my CEO days I worked hard to develop a strategic plan for my organization. I circulated drafts, held retreats, developed data, drafted new plans, got feedback, revised, and held meetings ad nauseum. In the end we had an excellent plan that senior and middle management agreed upon. However, there was one problem: The board and its chairman were totally disinterested in the plan. At the outset of the planning process, the board chairman had clearly indicated his lack of support for a plan, yet those of us in senior management felt that if we could produce a first-class plan we would change his mind. We were wrong. In retrospect I realized that, if the board endorsed the plan, it must also transfer power to management to follow the plan. By not endorsing a plan, the board kept its options open for the ad hoc planning approach that the organization had followed in the past.

Organizing

Organizing is a second function commonly associated with management. This is the function of determining what activities shall be carried out in the organization, how these activities should be grouped, and who shall have the authority and responsibility for carrying out these activities. The control device for this function is the organizational structure. In practical terms, this may explain why some organizations seem to be in a continual state of reorganization: Managers are trying to gain control through this managerial function.

There are considerable constraints, however, on the value of the organizing function and the manager's use of it. For example, a new organization chart on which mediocre staff members are shifted to new "boxes" may simply be an illusion of progress. Occasionally, such a shake-up has a positive effect, but in the health field, where a significant number of people are in the public sector (government of one level or another), change through reorganization may be viewed as another temporary and feeble attempt of management to control the organization. One cannot help but wonder whether all the changes in government post–9/11, such as the reshuffling that established the Department of Homeland Security, have done more than generate enormous confusion, countless office changes, and power exercises for senior administrators. Has there been any substantive program change that could not have been accomplished without the reorganization?

Legal and fiscal constraints, such as third-party reimbursement requirements, dictate certain elements of organizational structure in the health field. Tradition and the reality of staffing generate other structural requirements. Could pathologists be recruited if the organizational structure were such that they reported to a non-physician laboratory manager? The conflict engendered by having registered nurses report to non-physician, non-nurse ward managers must also be considered. Professionalism of all types is deeply ingrained in the health field and is a force to be reckoned with in the organizing function.

Staffing

Staffing is perhaps the most obvious, most useful, and most critical of management functions. Basically, this involves getting the right people for the jobs and then developing their skills. Theoretical control devices for this function are personnel management tools, such as job descriptions, job specifications, and, of course, the budget. The exercise of these control devices might be illustrated by three examples from the world of academia. In one instance, a new university president was hired, and he made his first priority that of building a high-quality faculty, a difficult task in a university with more than its share of marginal faculty. His strategy was to use the management functions of staffing and budget. He personally reviewed every candidate for a faculty position and refused to sign the papers authorizing the hiring of anyone who did not meet his standards.

In a different university, with an equally marginal faculty, it was decided to build a new department. Two options were presented: (a) draw faculty from related departments, or (b) acquire a whole new staff for the department. Although option (a) was quite attractive because it could cut the time frame from inception to optimal operation by years, perhaps a decade, it also represented a commitment to the qualitative status quo. Option (b) was selected, and within 10 years the new department became the leader in its field, despite the overall reputation of the university.

The third example involves a distinguished university that was awarded a one-time grant of $2 million to start a research center. Here again, two options were considered: (a) spend the money to attract a limited number of senior researchers and hope their work would generate funds in the future to keep the operation viable, or (b) build a high-quality support system of junior staff, such as research assistants and secretaries, and hardware, such as computers, and hope that some of these people developed into researchers able to generate funds and/or that the support systems attracted the senior researchers. In this case, option (b) was selected. Within five years, no senior researchers had been attracted, the junior researchers had produced little, and the research center was forced out of business.

These illustrations point up the critical nature of the staffing function in management. Staff make or break an organization, and people develop other people. Although a resource-consuming and often discouraging activity, staffing either will bring healthy blood into an organization or will create a potentially debilitating influence.

It is interesting to consider how often industry utilizes "headhunters" and how reluctant health care organizations are to undertake careful executive searches. For example, in one hospital that I am familiar with, a physician was hired, over the protest of the full-time medical director, at a significant salary although he was not board-eligible or certified in his specialty. His primary "credentials" were that an influential member of the staff liked him and he was willing to provide services at no charge to several key members of the board.

It must be noted that although the costs of utilizing headhunters are significant (sometimes as much as a third of a year's salary), they do add value to the managerial equation. For example, many firms have former health care executives as some of their partners, who begin the search process by developing an understanding of the organization, the key personnel, and the job for which they will recruit. Only by doing this background work carefully can they be in a position to search for the right candidates. Their next job is developing a pool of acceptable candidates, followed by prescreening them, and finally presenting them to the organization's search committee. My experiences have included the full range of the search process: I have been the accepted as well as the rejected candidate; I have participated and chaired internal search committees that have run searches themselves and hired headhunters to run searches. And as a consultant I have been hired for the purpose of searching for a CEO. These experiences have taught me that using an experienced and competent search firm or consultant is worth the expense. Why is this the case? Generally, search firms, because of their extensive contact network as well as their chutzpah (such as calling up the best people in the field and trying to entice them into considering a move), are able to put together a higher quality pool of candidates than the organization is likely to find on its own.

Additionally, they save wear and tear on the organization because they are simply the outsiders who have taken on a time-consuming and often potentially politically sensitive project, thus sparing the emotional resources of the organization. From a short-term perspective, search firms are expensive. However, in the long term the cost is paltry if a firm brings the organization the right person.

Dr. Daniel A. Kane, the former president of New Jersey's Englewood Hospital and Medical Center, supports the use of search consultants for senior positions. In his experiences, these consultants have offered his organization candidates for positions who simply would not have responded to traditional newspaper and journal advertisements. For example, his senior vice president for finance had been a vice president for finance at another institution and was not actively searching for a position when the search firm approached him with the opportunity at Englewood. Kane also suggests that a long-term relationship be developed with a firm or firms so that the search firms have a good understanding of the organization, its culture, and key staff. He rightly suggests that this understanding makes it more likely that a search firm will find candidates who "fit" the organization properly.

Directing

Directing is the function most often associated with management. Many people view managers as sitting in their offices, no doubt quite removed from any part of the operation, barking out orders to a compliant group of employees. Except in rare cases, this is a fantasy. Managers may like to view themselves as captains of ships, but their word is no longer the law. They must use their position to guide, persuade, or coach subordinates. The control device is less the organizational position itself than the ability to lead and motivate. Even in highly bureaucratic organizations, such as universities or hospitals, management is by consensus, and the effective manager must shepherd that consensus to meet goals.

Health care managers should always remember that few physicians, no matter how low they are on the organizational totem pole, ever walk into the director's office and think they are going to the "boss." During my tenure as a CEO I often wanted to simply say, "Just do it!" The question is whether that autocratic approach—something akin to "Father Knows Best"—is indeed the best approach. Probably not, particularly in light of the complexity of these organizations.

If there is an organizational analogy, it is perhaps the orchestra. For years I have been a devotee of the Boston Symphony and have often watched them rehearse their performances, sometimes with their conductor and other times with guest conductors, including Sir Colin Davis, the late Leonard Bernstein, and the late Eugene Ormandy. Two things have struck me while watching these rehearsals. First, the conductor knows precisely what sound he or she wants to get from the orchestra; that is, he or she knows the music perfectly and how the music should sound. Second, he or she is listening very carefully to the performances of each of his musicians and is able to pinpoint problems and request changes in tempo, sound, and timing. And so it is in health care management. Managers at all organizational levels must know what the music should sound like; that is, what their mission is, and then they must use their personal and financial resources to get the job done.

The best resources for directing often are a person's intellect and personality. A case in point: One day a woman walked into my office complaining about the care her father was receiving at one of our nursing homes. I listened to a sad tale about a man who had once been a pillar of the community and now was elderly and confined to a nursing home with a host of problems. Her complaint was that the staff were not paying proper attention to his health situation and that lack of attention had resulted in a recent hospitalization with some painful treatments, including an amputation. I immediately asked my assistant to get a full report from the nursing home's director about this gentleman's care. Within a day I heard back that the information that I had received from the daughter was correct with regard to his health status and hospitalization, but the nursing home staff had treated him properly, everything was well documented, and the daughter had a reputation for being a chronic complainer. I thought about these two divergent views and decided to review the records myself. Six inches of records arrived on my desk, and for three hours I read and made notes about the care that this man had received. The next day I scheduled a meeting with the senior nursing, dietary, administrative, and activities staff of the nursing home. I presented them with my detailed analysis of the records that clearly showed that a lack of communication among disciplines, lack of attention to trends in the patient's health status, and too much robotlike charting had resulted in an unfortunate and avoidable outcome. No formal discipline was meted out, but it became clear that I would not accept pat answers and that I expected from all concerned a much higher quality of care to those the nursing home was serving. Did everything change overnight? I doubt it, but the "directing" message was sent out across the organization.

Controlling

Controlling, a fifth function, is concerned with the measurement of performance against some predetermined standard. Two elements must come together if the manager's control is to be effective: (1) there must be standards; and (2) there must be information systems to indicate the progress that is being made toward attaining those standards.

One example of an effective control device is the budget and its companion budgeting process. For example, an organization may have a clear budgeting process that not only projects revenues and expenses but also requires targets and reviews. In accepting a given department's budget and holding it accountable for its projections, the manager is controlling the department's activities. If ambulatory care projected expenses of $5 million for the fiscal year and seven-eighths of the way through the year came to the manager with a request for more money to hire a new staff person, the manager could use the controlling function via the budget to direct the organization. Money and ego are probably two of the most potent controlling mechanisms, ego being the more difficult to deal with since there are few "performance standards" and information systems about egos are limited, at best.

The fundamental problem in controlling is that of metrics; that is, finding the right measurement tools. The grossest measure in personnel is turnover, but that number may mask a host of other problems. For example, if organizational leadership has a push to eliminate turnover, poor quality performance may be accepted in order to avoid turnover. One illustration of this could be the problems of "pool nurses," temporary nursing staff who are hired because of unanticipated shortages due do sickness, vacations, or simply the inability to hire regular staff. The limitation of pool nurses is both their dramatically higher costs and their unfamiliarity with the hiring organization and their patients or residents. Most health professionals would like to avoid using pool nurses whenever possible. However, if an organization makes this too strong a goal, it is possible, although not necessarily inevitable, that the bar will be lowered with staff nurses in order to avoid the pool problem. A marginally performing nurse might be retained in order to avoid the pool; but that also eliminates the possibility of hiring a better quality nurse if the marginal nurse is terminated. Unfortunately, this happens in many organizations, including academia, where faculty are granted tenure as a strategy for a department to avoid losing the position during tight financial times.

Coordinating

Coordinating is a sixth function and, in some senses, one of the weakest. Traditionally, a coordinator has plenty of responsibility and little authority, analogous to the carpenter who is given wood and nails but no hammer. It appears that the most successful coordinators are those with real or apparent authority, a total commitment to the program, or extraordinary skills as a persuader. To put it differently, important managerial problems are too complex both in terms of the problem itself and the system that has generated the problem to be "coordinated." They must be "managed" in an affirmative manner.

Representing

The seventh traditional function is representing, or being the spokesperson for the unit, organization, or industry on the outside. A department head represents the department and its case on the division level, and the director represents the organization to the government, a foundation, or even the board.

Representation is a critical managerial function. Those on top of each component usually represent the component to those on the next higher level. This is a time- and energy-consuming function that requires a political sensitivity to the needs of a constituency (or unit) and a similar sensitivity to the needs of those to whom the constituency is being represented. The skills of presentation, debate, analysis, and articulation are critical, since they are weighed in the minds of those who are listening to the presentation. Many of the skills necessary to be effective in this function can be learned.

In many senses, the representation function has two dimensions: substance and theatre. The substance component is obvious—the manager must know what he or she is talking about. For example, if a lawyer is arguing a point of law in front of a judge and cites a particular case, it behooves that lawyer to know the cited case quite well. Without the knowledge of the case, he or she is treading in dangerous water should the judge start asking questions about the case. Not only will he or she lose the legal argument, but his or her credibility on the case, as well. To top it off, his or her reputation will be damaged. So it is in management. Credibility and reputation are always on the table.

The theatrical dimension is more elusive and, in my judgment, ensures that the message is clearly heard without unnecessary distractions. At one extreme, assume the CEO of an organization walks into a formal meeting of the board in torn jeans and a Bart Simpson T-shirt. What exactly would be the mood of the board members when he began his director's report? What would be the response of the community to an executive who mumbled her way through a presentation? It is imperative that an executive have something the U.S. Navy calls "command presence." In the simplest terms, this means that the executive must look and sound like an executive. If this is a problem, there are myriad consultants who will assist a person in everything from writing and delivering as speech to clothes and hair styling. But it is essential to remember this is style, not substance. The style's value is getting the substance listened to.

A final confession: When I agreed to take the CEO position, I had a full-blown academic wardrobe: one suit and lots of sport coats, blazers, and maybe one corduroy jacket (no patches, though). One of the first things I did was buy several conservative business suits—I needed to dress for the new part!

WHO IS A MANAGER?

A traditionalist would say "anyone who gets things done through other people" is a manager, which portrays the manager as the grand puppeteer. Perhaps a less offensive approach might be to say that a manager is anyone who is not personally involved in the direct implementation of the work. A manager, then, is someone who is involved in a range of activities, but a manager's responsibility stops short of personal implementation of these activities. A manager might be someone involved in creating an innovative ambulatory care program, putting it together so that it becomes a reality, or evaluating it for further nurturing or retrenching.

Particularly in health care, it seems that managers expend a great deal of their time "fighting fires," chasing solutions for small problems. These problems are part of a larger system and context, a point often overlooked in dealing with the specific fire.

In general, managers can be classified into two groups: staff and line. In contrast to the staff or supportive function manager, the line manager is generally thought to be directly involved in the production functions of the organization. The line of distinction is blurred, however, when certain functions are discussed as line and others as staff. For example, human resource departments are usually regarded as staff, but what about the director of human resources who has 35 employees reporting to him or her?

As a generality (which is certainly open to challenge), line managers appear to thrive when dealing with action-oriented problems. Scores of telephone calls and appointments seem to fan the fire of their psychic systems. On the other hand, staff managers appear to be more deliberative, attempt to analyze all the angles, and, in the words of one executive "headhunter," take fewer risks. Line managers are sometimes criticized for "shooting from the hip," a charge that may be based on form rather than substance. Rapid information processing based on experience and expertise often appears to be "hip shooting," but may in fact be effective management. Indeed, it is an example of the critical information processing thread that is common to all the activities of management. Managers must transmit, receive, and interpret verbal, nonverbal, and written information.

The transmission mechanisms include one-to-one and one-to-group communications, memos, newsletters, press releases, letters, facial expression, tone of voice, and selected words. By choice of the medium and method of delivery, the manager is making a statement, such as "I am the boss," "Let's share as equals," or "Your work or being means nothing to me." As a recipient of information, a similar process occurs in reverse.

Interpretation of information received is probably one of the most critical activities associated with processing. An effective manager does not simply react to what is said but rather attempts to understand what is meant by what is said. Such skill in communication can be developed and is invaluable to a manager.

EXPECTATIONS FROM MANAGERS

What should be expected from a manager? In answering this question, two dimensions must be considered: behavior and values. Both fiction and reality have presented a picture of managers as "organization men and women." Their loyalty is to the organization, and the most important professional person in their lives is their boss. The image (and reality, to a great extent) is of a tight hierarchical structure and operations that respond to that structure. Regardless of the theoretical "flatness" of the organization, there is always someone on the top who has the authority and responsibility to represent the organization and negotiate for its well-being, or at least that person's concept of its well-being.

A clear example of this is the case of the attempted takeover of the McGraw-Hill publishing company by American Express. McGraw-Hill's chairman, Harold McGraw, Jr., viewed this takeover as anathema. Because of his personal view, he waged a relentless and successful campaign against the invasion. He stated in a letter to the chief executive officer of American Express that American Express lacked "integrity, corporate morality and sensitivity to professional responsibility."[6] He then went on to criticize the management and behavior of American Express. All of this was carried out with the express approval of stockholders, many of who clearly stood to gain by such a merger.

A different perspective on management is presented by Michael Blumenthal. During his tenure as Secretary of the Treasury, he prepared an article for *Fortune* titled "Candid Reflections of a Businessman in Washington."[7] In it, he contrasted his experiences as a senior government official in charge of an agency employing 120,000 people with his position as chairman and chief executive officer of the Bendix Corporation. Control, he suggests, is related to the ability to "hire and fire." He identified his problem in government: "Out of 120,000 people in the Treasury, I was able to select twenty-five maybe. The other 119,975 are outside my control."

It was noted earlier that top management is involved in setting goals and organizing activities that allow the goals to be attained. Blumenthal's noting that the senior executives in industry can control who is and is not involved in policy development and implementation highlighted the contrast between the private and public sector, but because of the plethora of official and nonofficial interest groups in government, many of whom have influence and power, the policy process is considerably more complex.

---

[6]In the news. *Fortune*. February 12, 1979, p. 16.
[7]Candid reflections of a businessman in Washington. *Fortune*. January 29, 1979, pp. 36–49.

A final point is that management in industry does most of its business in private. Government executives, however, must function under the spotlight of the press. Shortly after I asked for and received the resignation of a senior medical executive, I was on the phone with my brother who was then the dean of a major medical school. I was discussing the resignation, and he listened and lamented the fact that the tenure system at his university handcuffed him and prevented the organization from ridding itself of senior staff that had become unproductive.

How, then, do the expectations of the health care manager differ from those of the industrial manager? Probably not much. To be successful, managers need to develop a positive attitude toward the organization and the job, be joiners and innovators, accept the organization's goals as their own, and invest their spiritual and physical energy in building an organization.

The two dimensions that are no doubt of the greatest importance in management are technical skills and the ability to recruit and retain able subordinates. Technical skills are often underemphasized, but they are a major element in a manager's credibility and value to an organization. For example, can the manager accurately forecast the utilization of services, and is that forecast based on a high quality assessment of needs, likely demands, and competition? Can the manager develop an appropriate strategic plan or budget for the organization? This does not mean that the manager must write the budget personally, but that he or she must plan, organize, and review the budget before it is placed in the hands of the board. Mistakes, conceptual or mechanical, indicate a careless or technically unskilled manager, particularly at the beginning of a career.

If there is one shortcoming of new managers it may be an over-reliance on the importance of their image as managers and an under-reliance on the technical substance that is expected from them.

Since few managers—even workaholics—have the time and ability to do everything themselves, they must rely on subordinates for their success. Their ability to find people who will be supportive and who will complement their own skills is crucial. Some managers view high-quality subordinates as threats and hire sycophants. These people typically are only marginally productive and often eventually have to be replaced. Another group of managers view subordinates as "tools" to carry out unpleasant jobs and hire "hatchet men." It is always so pleasant when the wheels of the gods finally turn, and poetic justice is meted out with the firing of these people. A third group, and the one I like to think I belong in, view subordinates as key colleagues. This group attempts to surround themselves with the "best and brightest" and work toward encouraging their growth and development, with the full knowledge that someday they may leave to accept more challenging positions. When I look back to my accomplishments as a CEO, I think they are all about the people I brought aboard and their professional development.

VALUES AND ETHICS IN MANAGEMENT

Unfortunately, the first decade of the 21st century will probably be remembered for the host of industrial scandals in which corporate and personal greed hit a new low: Tyco, Enron, HealthSouth, and numerous other organizations, including mutual funds, and, perhaps the worst of all, the Catholic Church, where pedophile priests were protected by senior administrators.

It should also be recognized that these problems have been with us for decades. In the 1970s, a dean of a school of public health was forced to resign after he was indicted (and subsequently convicted) by a federal court of conspiracy to defraud the government; a nationally prominent hospital administrator lost his job when his organization discovered that he was double-billing for his travel; a professor and chair of a department of health administration lost his job and ended up in jail after serious wrongdoings were discerned; and seemingly countless nursing home administrators were indicted and prosecuted for a range of offenses.

These, as well as numerous other examples, suggest several alternative hypotheses regarding the ethics of health administrators: (1) the pressure on health administrators is getting so great that the ethical fiber is breaking down at an increasing rate; (2) the low-level ethics of health administrators is finally being discovered and exposed; or, perhaps, (3) health administrators are simply devoid of any sense of ethics. I personally reject hypotheses (2) and (3) but find hypothesis (1) quite plausible because I have seen it on countless occasions. Indeed, a number of years ago, when I was on the faculty of Columbia University, I was so concerned about this subject that I undertook a study about the ethical problems facing three different groups of health administrators. All three groups were asked the same four questions:

1. What was the most difficult ethical decision you had to make in the past year?

2. What did you see as the major alternative decisions that could have been made?

3. What was your decision?

4. What do you see as the major implications of your decision?

Clearly, such open-ended questions were not developed to give definitive answers to the problems plaguing health administrators, but rather to set some realistic parameters on the type of ethical issues they face. Forty-two responses from four different groups of administrators were analyzed: 12 hospital administrators, 12 drug program administrators, 10 nursing home administrators, and 8 nursing home administrators who were department heads at long-term care facilities. Of the 12 hospital administrators, 6 were chief executives and 6 were at associate levels. Although all 12 administrators were associated with similar institutions in somewhat similar communities, no two problems identified by the administrators were similar. However, 5 of the 6 chief operating executives identified problems that could be classified as medical staff problems:

- Oppose facility expansion desired by medical staff
- Oppose employment of new physician who was needed but whose recommendations were less than satisfactory
- Oppose the medical staff's position on malpractice
- Integrate (racially) medical staff and trustees
- Fire a senior-level physician
- Shorten utilization

In those pre-DRG days, this sixth problem, shortening utilization, had profound implications for the hospital's income and, potentially, for the individual physician's income.

Associate administrator level respondents, not surprisingly in view of the scope of their responsibility, tended to identify problems that were more operationally oriented:

- Accept part-time self-serving position with potential purveyor
- Support chief operating executive when personal position was contrary

- Terminate a nonprofessional employee with cause but without due process
- Become a complainant against a medical staff member
- Reprimand medical staff

Even the reprimanding of a physician was viewed as an ethical problem. The associate director felt that the physician deserved a reprimand, but it clearly was not the decision of the hospital's board, trustees, or administration that this physician be reprimanded.

The alternatives in most instances were black and white—either do it or do not do it. In the 12 cases reviewed, the administrators found some compromise position in three instances, did what they felt they should do in seven instances, and in the remaining two cases they did or allowed something to occur that they did not support.

The second group surveyed were 18 nursing home administrators: 10 individuals in line administration who held positions such as administrator or assistant administrator, and 8 persons who were in department or other supportive roles, such as social workers or dietitians.

The decision list generated by the line administrators is heavily weighted in the area of what might be classified as basic personnel management:

- Order staff to come to work on time
- Fire a mentally retarded worker
- Reassign a team of workers
- Evaluate a nurse's work
- Allow an employee to leave work a half-hour early
- Fire a poor-quality employee
- Hire an employee of another faith for a religious nursing home
- Resign from a facility that is violating the law
- Accept a more difficult job
- Accept employment in a field (nursing home administration) that was tainted

A review of the problems identified by this group does not suggest that any momentous issues were considered. For example, one assistant administrator wrote the following:

> An employee, RN, came to me last week and asked if she could take off from work 1/2 hour earlier because her son was going to sing in a church

choir and she wanted to be with him. I decided that I would let her go with 1/2 hour docked off her pay.

Three of the problems were seemingly highly personal, in that they involved the administrators' future. Two of those responses suggest that the authors actually went through some sort of personal crisis or soul-searching:

Should I stay, leave, or try to convince top management of reasons why the organization should eliminate violations?

Am I jeopardizing "my reputation as an upstanding citizen" by entering this Field?

Although the third response was a job change decision, no ethical considerations were evident.

The staff and department administrators in nursing homes presented a range of problems that were generally dissimilar from those seen with the other administrators:

- Advocate a patient's position, which is in opposition to the institution's position
- Voice concern about a suspicious patient injury
- Investigate a patient's complaint about inadequate medications
- Place Christmas trees on all floors of a kosher, nonsectarian nursing home
- Maintain state health code standards
- Expose serious operating deficiencies in another department
- Create a harmonious work environment for staff
- Enter into a relationship between a nonprofit and for-profit organization

Three of these problems were patient-oriented; two were almost classic conflict of interest situations; and the remaining three were general organizational problems. Perhaps this can be explained by the fact that, while many of these people see themselves as administrators, they usually function as social workers or dietitians. These are roles that are traditionally quite close physically and spiritually to patients.

The final 12 respondents were administrators of drug programs, all of whom had a background in social work and were employed in operational programs that involved the treatment of drug addicts on both an inpatient and outpatient basis. The range of problems that they identified comprised predominantly staff personnel matters or general policy matters:

- Start termination action against a chronically ill employee
- Act in a consistent manner with regard to personnel policies of time, attendance, etc.
- Release an employee because of age
- Hire staff primarily because of their ethnic background
- Select employees for layoff
- Transfer to a better job in another department with a different philosophy
- Debate an administrative edict
- Implement a personally unacceptable course of action
- Implement a patient treatment plan that was unacceptable to the next higher level of management
- Cooperate with a state investigating group

Rather surprisingly, there were few patient-oriented problems. For example, four administrators identified a hiring/firing problem as their most difficult ethical decision of the past year, and two of the three patient-related problems were general and related to a specific patient, such as the issue of whether an administrator should cooperate with a state investigating group.

This modest study suggested at the time that administrators have few serious ethical problems. Could this be the case? I would argue that, even in those days, they simply did not know what an ethical problem was. Perhaps this explanation is too harsh or too simplistic, but it should be obvious that a significant percentage of "ethical" problems identified were fairly typical administrative problems, usually involving personnel management. It appears that both then and now the broader issues of conflicts between personal values, organizational values, and the myriad requirements of corporate compliance (to be discussed in later chapters) are simply not being identified by top health care management. Perhaps this is because administrators have lulled themselves into believing that the administrative decision process is value-free. It is not, however, and it is imperative that these values be identified and analyzed. Obviously, this is not yet taking place, or we would not be so busy with matters of corporate compliance.

The antidote I suggest is a constant focus on ethical issues and a tone set by the senior executives that is exemplified by their personal behavior. While the key is the action that people take—that is, acting in an ethically correct way—a major step is an ethics policy that is sensible, intelligent, and enforced. In Britain this is being addressed by a code of conduct for National Health System managers. In a letter of May 23, 2002 the chief executive of the system laid out the draft of this Code, two aspects of which are:

- be honest and act with integrity.
- accept accountability for your own work, the performance of those you manage, and of your own organization.[8]

In a related document, the Royal Surrey County Hospital Trust in Guilford, England, has a corporate governance RSCH code of conduct that defines their touchstone values of accountability, probity, and openness. Accountability focuses on the need for the organization to stand up to examination by all levels of government, as well as the professions and the public. Openness suggests that the operations and processes should be "transparent" to all concerned about the organization, including patients. Probity is perhaps the most powerful statement, and one that could well be important across the great pond, that is the Atlantic Ocean. In discussing probity, the Royal Surrey document states: "there should be an absolute standard of honesty in dealing with the assets of the NHS; integrity should be the hallmark of all personal conduct in decisions affecting patients, staff and suppliers, and in the use of information acquired in the course of NHS duties."[9]

Virtually every health care organization today has something akin to a code of conduct and certainly a corporate compliance effort. Tenet's "Standards of Conduct," easily found on their website, runs some 25 pages and covers their values, expected conduct, including an interesting set of examples in the form of illustrative questions and answers, and useful courses of action for staff to take in given situations.[10] For example, in one illustration they deal with the secretary who is asked to submit an expense report for a boss who may be submitting excessive expenses; another deals with a staff member who thinks the doctor is not doing the required training. Other scenarios involve competitive bidding, conflicts of interest, gifts, vendor relationships, and so forth. Another useful example comes

---

[8]Data retrieved (n.d.) from www.doh.gov.uk/codeofconductconsultation/index/htm.

[9]Data retrieved (n.d.) from www.royalsurrey.nhs.uk/internet/Royal-Surr/Freedom-of/2--Who-we-/.

[10]Data retrieved (n.d.) from www.tenethealth.com.

from the nonprofit Texas-based Memorial Hermann Healthcare System.[11] In 19 clearly written pages, the system covers similar ground to Tenet. While both documents are explicit in their goals, the Memorial Hermann standards contain far more detail; indeed, it almost appears as an operating manual for various departments, such as accounting, where it states: "Regularly review our records for patient credit balances and promptly refund any overpayments. . . . Not routinely waive insurance co-payments or deductibles."[11] As an essential element in any effective standards or compliance policy, the documents also present the reader with key compliance contact people. In my judgment, this documentation suggests that these three organizations are demonstrating a commitment to ethical behavior on the part of the staff and boards as well as a structure and processes for ensuring the ethical behavior.

A final and key component of making any policy effective is the person responsible for implementing the policy. Some organizations, most notably Tenet Healthcare, are going so far as to employ full-time compliance officers in their facilities. Others appoint a staff member as a "point person" compliance officer. Depending on the person and the organization's seriousness about compliance, the "point person" is either effective or merely a dupe. In one hospital that I consulted with, a corrupt board forced the hospital director to appoint a close personal friend of the board president to the compliance officer position. Obviously this person did not have the trust of the staff and did not have the integrity of a compliance officer—but did serve the needs of this corrupt board.

ENTERING MANAGEMENT

In his text *Management*, Drucker identifies six common mistakes in designing managerial jobs. These mistakes are (1) designing "the job so small that a good man cannot grow"; (2) having a job that is not really a job; (3) having a job that does not combine work with managing; (4) having jobs that require "continuous meetings, continuous cooperation and coordination"; (5) giving out titles rather than jobs; and (6) creating jobs that are simply impossible to do.[12]

---

[11]Data retrieved (n.d.) from www.mhhs.org/aboutusStandardsofConduct060103.doc
[12]P. Drucker, *Management* (New York: Harper & Row, 1973), pp. 405–410..

Drucker's presentation is particularly useful for a chief executive officer who must establish or reorganize an organization. However, his statements are also useful for a manager who must decide whether to accept a new position. So with apologies and acknowledgment to Drucker, the following is a list of my six ideas to consider when entering or shifting positions on the managerial ladder.

1. Take a job in which you can grow. In the field of health administration, growth is both a function of the job as well as the organization. Hospitals were once the fast track for new managers; however, because of decreasing facilities, increased numbers of graduates of health administration programs, and economic controls, hospitals have become a much slower and more slippery track. Specific organizations as well as types of organizations are born and die. In the 21st century, good positions are available in all levels of government, regulatory and review organizations, health maintenance organizations, insurance companies, group practices, ambulatory care programs, foundations, nursing homes, and all manner of community-based programs. What is perhaps most encouraging today, as opposed to previous decades, is the breaking down of the prejudices concerning the transferability of skills between programs and even the proprietary and nonprofit segment of the industry. Time was that if you went to work in the for-profit sector, you were branded with a scarlet letter that prevented reentry into the nonprofit world. No longer. Today, experience is experience, and expertise is expertise.

2. Do not be a "go for" for another person. Nonjobs are particularly common in the health industry and are well described by Drucker as those positions in which the title is "assistant to." An individual's performance should be observable by the total organization, and the position should not be dependent on the goodwill of one person. In small health care organizations, particularly at the entry levels, this is a difficult pitfall to avoid. Some managers attempt to avoid this by continually defining and redefining their positions in writing (via a series of memos). If there is goodwill and if those higher in the organization feel secure, there are few problems with this method. If the junior manager is simply another tool in the senior manager's bag, all the memos in the organization are

insignificant compared with the opinion of the "boss." To the extent possible, then, the job should represent a commitment from the organization, not from a single person at the next level up in the chain of command.

3. Take a job in which you work and manage. No one can suggest that management is not hard work, but quite clearly there is a tendency for young managers to ensconce themselves in pleasant offices and deal only with those who seek them out, respond to those higher on the hierarchy, and "play the manager role." Periodically, however, managers should get their hands dirty. For the physician manager, this is easily translated into seeing patients occasionally. For the nonphysician manager, it may mean such things as handling special projects or observing certain operations. Managers must continue to develop their own competencies and periodically test these competencies by "working." Such tests and development have positive effects, in terms of both personal self-esteem and respect from colleagues and subordinates. An analogy with academia might clarify this concept further: A dean should not only administer the school but should also teach and do research.

4. Avoid a position with a great deal of nonproductive time. Most people are measured by their output or the outcome of what they do, not the process used to attain these goals. While process is critical for reaching goals, it is easy to forget that the process is not, in fact, the outcome. For example, meetings become more important than the decisions and implementing the decisions reached at the meetings. All positions have some of this nonproductive time, but new managers must look for positions in which this is either minimized or in which they can exert some control over nonproductive time. Many new managers have found they spent much of their first few years as managers in meetings, and as a result accomplished little. The organization in its evaluation wants the bases touched but also wants the runs scored.

5. Get your objectives straight: What do you really want? This is extremely difficult, because there is a strong current impelling managers toward accepting the objectives of the organization as

their own. Soul searching is often a tiring and time-consuming process, but it is necessary if managers are to understand what they really want from their position. Is it power, prestige, security, glamour, intellectual stimulation, money, or a combination of these and other factors? A person who has come to grips with these personal objectives is in a much stronger position to make career choices. Without addressing these personal objectives (which may be subconscious), managers may generate unnecessary and possibly debilitating anxiety in their lives.

6. When in doubt, maximize your potential for success by taking proven jobs. Managers should not risk their future on what Drucker calls a widow-maker job, a job that others have tried and failed. The payoff for being a hero is high, but when other qualified people could not handle the job, new managers must be careful not to slip on their egos. A clearer and proven path is more sensible and less fraught with uncertainties and danger. Here, again, objectives come into play; some people find the proven ladder less appealing than the greased flagpole.

ON BECOMING THE CEO

The goal of most young managers is to someday become the CEO. This is a worthy and honorable goal if the reasoning behind it is that by being the organizational leader you can run, develop, and implement programs and services that will be positive for both the organization and its constituencies. A bad reason for wanting the job is greed and self-aggrandizement! Yes, the job of CEO does often come with a large salary and "perks." But, as a good friend of mine who was CEO of a billion-dollar company told me, "When someone pays you a great deal of money, they also want a great deal of your soul." So, in a nutshell that is the trade—you get the money, the power, and the office, but you also get the headaches and possibly the ulcer. Indeed, one of the best students I ever had decided early in his career that he did not wish to ever be a CEO and would be content to always play a minor role in the enterprise. Today, 20 years later, he has had a very good career as a manager of a clinical support department where he is responsible for a $20 million budget and over 200 employees. His salary is a third of that of the CEO, yet he is also quite comfortable, enjoys his job, his leisure time, and his family, and views himself as a valuable contributing member of a major medical center.

Based on my own experiences, as well as those of other CEOs and former CEOs, I would offer the following advice about taking CEO jobs:

- Do your own organizational due diligence. Typically, an executive search firm manages the CEO search, and their focus is to find the right person for the job. They will often be quite helpful in providing information about the organization and its key players. But it is imperative that a job aspirant uses his or her own network to learn about the organization. It is also imperative to believe organizational history. If an organization has a history of turning over CEOs, do not assume that your tenure will be any different. If an organization has a history of being corrupt, don't assume that your being a person of integrity will change everything. Unfortunately, decay is often quite deep and covered over by a thin veneer. In practical terms, this means examine the organization's books (and, if necessary, hire your own experts). Talk to people. Do not become so enamored of the CEO job that you forget to ask the right questions.

- Forget the oral tradition. Too often, a potential CEO will negotiate a job based on meetings and discussions with headhunters or boards. It is imperative to reduce important points to writing. These points are usually not found in employment contracts but can find their ways into a memorandum of understanding. This comes directly from my own experience when I took the CEO job. Before agreeing to take the job, I had several meetings with key board members about various subjects, one of which was the size, structure, and functioning of the board. They all solemnly nodded their heads in agreement when I told them that the 200-person board was too large and the 54-person executive board was also cumbersome and there was a need for more focused and decision-oriented board meetings. But my mistake was not to commit that discussion to writing with some agreement to change, because when the time came to implement changes, I simply had no support or leverage.

- Get a contract and/or generous severance package. Never take a CEO job without a contract with at least several years' tenure or at the minimum a generous severance package. CEO jobs are high profile and high risk, and it is imperative that the CEO be protected, both personally and professionally. A contract and/or severance package ensures that the organization will not treat the CEO as an employee at will. In essence, this means that the CEO will have the time to develop and implement his or her agenda for the future.

- If you have the responsibility, make sure you have the explicit authority. A friend of mine who was CEO of an organization in New England assumed that he "ran" the show. When his first winter came around, he sought bids for snow plowing. He was about to award a contract when he received a call from an irate board member, demanding to know why "Jim Brown" was not being given the contract as he had been for the last 10 years. The CEO explained that Brown's bid was $3500 more than the lowest bidder and, in checking around, he had found that the lowest bidder had an excellent reputation and Brown's work in the past decade had become barely satisfactory. The board member dismissed the complaints and insisted that Brown be rehired. A few minutes later, the board president called the CEO and tried to smooth things over between the CEO and the board member by saying that the board member was a bit of a "hot head" but really cared about the organization. In the end, though, he urged that "Brown" be hired just to calm down the board member, who was said to be a very generous donor. The CEO gave in and hired Brown, who did a lousy job. The staff lost some respect for the CEO, who they thought was coming in to change things around; and the board member's donation never came close to compensating the organization for the extra money paid out for plowing. Also, the CEO never found out why a snowplowing contract was so important to these board members.

- Obviously, there are always areas where a CEO should negotiate and compromise with the board. But it is imperative that if the CEO is expected to run the organization, he or she should have the authority to do the job. In my own experience, the good news was I was immediately given authority to spend up to $25,000 without board approval. The bad news, though, was that the board had many more sacred cows than I had anticipated and when I tried to reshape the organization through terminations, reassignments, or reorganizations I immediately learned why I had been warned away from this organization: the micromanagement of its board. My favorite example was that of "Pete" the baker. Pete had worked in the kitchen of one of the constituent corporations for more than three decades and was earning almost as much as the department head. Pete was a nice man, well past retirement age, and if he collected his pension he would make about the same as if he were working. By way of work, Pete would only bake Danish pastries from frozen packages. Because of various deficits, Pete's name came up on the proposals for cutbacks. I saw no harm in Pete being terminated since his departure would mean a considerable savings to the department, he personally would not suffer economically, and others could easily accomplish the Danish baking. When word got out that Pete might be involuntarily retired, the board president, who was fond of Pete for a variety of reasons, told me that he would rather fire me than Pete. So, there it was, a sacred baker and a CEO without the authority to reduce expenses but with the responsibility of bringing the organization into fiscal balance. It can't be done!

ON UNEMPLOYMENT

An unfortunate risk of being in management is that of being unemployed. As noted earlier, a manager can try to mitigate the damage of unemployment through a contract or severance package, but rarely will anyone other than the most senior managers be able to negotiate such organizational commitments. In the last several years I have met more and more senior executives who have become unemployed and stayed that way for extended periods of time. Based on these experiences, I think those who have the most success in finding their next jobs have followed the following strategies.

First, several people I know smelled the unemployment coming and immediately got busy, not trying to politic to keep their job but rather finding a new job. They recognized the old maxim that it is easiest to find a job when you have a job, not when you are unemployed. These people did not get into the frame of thinking that three months off with a severance package makes for a great paid vacation. Rather, they immediately started networking with professional colleagues and exploring job options that often did not pay as well as the job they were leaving. In one case, a senior finance person found a job that paid 15% less than the job he was losing, with considerably fewer fringe benefits. He took it and within two years had passed his previous salary and was in line for a major promotion. On the other hand, a well-paid experienced senior hospital executive held out for a job and salary at his current level and three years later was still unemployed, forced to sell his house, and considering personal bankruptcy.

Another strategy some have chosen is to consider related and alternative careers, such as sales in the health industry. For example, one former CEO now works as a sales representative for a nursing temp agency. According to his reports, it's a great job with good earning potential and without the pressures of being a CEO.

Going into business for oneself is a different, perhaps risky, and sometimes quite rewarding option. One friend pursued that option by opening a health care case management business for seniors. Despite good marketing and reasonable capitalization, however, the operation was simply not able to become financially viable. Another friend bought an executive search franchise, focused his efforts on the health field, and retired at the age of 60 as a wealthy man. A third friend opened a consulting business, promoted his operation on the Internet, and is well on his way to financial independence and professional success. These vignettes suggest that unemployment or the threat of unemployment will definitely be a challenge that managers may face in their personal lives, but it is a challenge that, if met, may well be the opportunity of a lifetime.

CONCLUSION

This chapter provides the framework for thinking about management in the health care sector. My goal in this chapter was to examine management from a variety of perspectives and in that examination offer the reader a variety of perspectives. The final part of this chapter is a case study that is based on an actual incident. It illustrates the real-world managerial, ethical, and political problems managers face on a daily basis. I trust that wrestling with this problem and the discussion questions after it will prove useful.

Case Study 5-1
TROUBLE AT TRIANGLE

Dr. John Porter is one of 50 full-time physicians employed at Triangle Hospital, a 600-bed university teaching hospital in Metroplex. Porter's specialty is gastroenterology, and he is generally regarded as a competent physician. Indeed, in the 14 years that he has been at Triangle, not a single complaint has ever been lodged against him. He is clearly one of the informal social leaders of the medical staff. For example, he plays viola in a chamber music group that he founded nine years ago, and he has numerous friends on the medical staff. Also, he has been happy to use his political connections (his father was once mayor of Metroplex) to benefit the hospital and its staff. Three years ago, Porter went through a traumatic divorce, in which he lost a bitter custody fight over his children.

Last year, a housekeeper making a routine Sunday evening check of the physicians' offices found Porter's office in disarray. She straightened it up and on Monday reported this unusual situation to the executive housekeeper. The following Sunday evening, the office was again in disarray, but this time an empty needle and syringe were found in the wastepaper basket. The housekeeper reported her findings to the executive housekeeper, who brought the situation to the attention of the assistant director and CEO of Triangle. After a few minutes of discussion, the executive housekeeper was told to have the housekeeper retrieve the needle and syringe if it happened again. Also, the hospital CEO asked for the emergency room roster for the past two weekends and asked the medical records department for a run-down on Porter's cases for the past two weeks. Both sources indicated that he had not seen patients over the weekend. On a hunch that Porter may have seen a private patient during that period, he checked with Porter's business office, but that turned up nothing.

(continues)

Case Study 5-1

During the next week, the CEO casually asked Porter's colleagues about his general state of health, both physical and mental. Responses from the staff indicated no problems. The following Monday, another report was delivered about a "messed-up office," but this time the syringe and needle were retrieved. It was clearly a used preloaded morphine syringe. For confirmation the CEO sent the items to the laboratory for examination. The CEO then briefed the hospital's chief of medical staff on the entire situation. The chief said he would talk to Porter. The following is the transcript of the conversation:

Chief: John, how are you feeling?
Porter: Fine, why do you ask?
Chief: Well, you look tired lately, maybe even a bit depressed.
Porter: Yes, I'm tired, but that's because I've been working my butt off. Just this week alone I had 10 colonoscopies.
Chief: Are you depressed?
Porter: No, why? What are you getting at?
Chief: O.K. I won't beat around the bush. The housekeepers found a morphine syringe in your office wastebasket during the weekend and your office has been messed up. What's going on?
Porter: Oh, well, my pet golden retriever, you know, Lassie, has terminal cancer, so I've been giving her morphine to ease the pain. I apologize for not disposing of the syringe properly.
Chief: Is that all?
Porter: Yes.

The chief went back to the CEO with Porter's story, adding that, in his opinion, Porter was not telling the truth.

(continues)

Case Study 5-1

The CEO and chief decided to put Porter under close sur-
veillance for the next few weeks in order to see how he was
dealing with his patients. No major problems were
observed, although reports from the nursing staff indicated
that he was more short-tempered than usual and, despite
what he told the chief about being very busy, the business
office indicated that his patient load seemed to be slowly
decreasing. His appearance was generally neat, although he
did come to the hospital on a few occasions without a shave
and in badly wrinkled clothes. Only once during this four-
week period was another used morphine syringe found in
his office. During this time, however, the housekeeper
reported that Porter had personally installed another lock
on the inside of the door.

The chief and CEO met again and decided that Porter
represented too great a threat and that he needed a sabbatical to straighten out his problem. The CEO called
Porter in.

CEO: John, how are you feeling?
Porter: Fine, but why the hell all this interest in my
         health here?
CEO: John, I'm concerned about you. Are you into
         drugs?
Porter: No!
CEO: So why morphine syringes in your office? Look,
         we want to help you.
Porter: I told the chief my dog is dying of cancer, and
         you can help by just leaving me alone.
CEO: Look, John, the chief and I think you need a rest.
         We want you to take a two-month sabbatical with
         pay and get yourself together.
Porter: I am together.

(*continues*)

Case Study 5-1

CEO: We don't want a big hassle here. If you want to stay at Triangle, we want you to take a sabbatical and see a psychiatrist during that time.

Porter: Do I have a choice?

CEO: Not really.

Porter: I'll go.

After Porter left, the CEO and chief reviewed the situation. They both felt that Porter was involved with drugs, and their solution was reasonable. Two months later, the director received Porter's letter of resignation from the medical staff. Dr. Porter provided no explanation for his resignation.

A year later, a letter came from a hospital in another state asking for a recommendation from the CEO and chief of the medical staff for "Dr. John Porter, whom we wish to appoint as Chief of Gastroenterology at our hospital."

DISCUSSION QUESTIONS

1. What alternatives could the chief and CEO have pursued?

2. What are the implications of these alternatives?

3. What should be the response of the chief and the CEO to the request for a recommendation?

Case Study 5-2

DEATH AT BONDVILLE

On a cold Tuesday morning in January, probably between the hours of midnight and 3 A.M., Max Morse, a resident of the Bondville Geriatric Center, left his room, went outside the center, and died of exposure in the frigid night air. Mr. Morse's body was found between 8:00 and 8:30 A.M., after the morning shift discovered that Mr. Morse was missing.

On the Monday evening before this incident, at approximately 5:30 P.M., Richard Albertson, the center's administrator, left work after checking with the evening supervisor on the overnight (11:00 to 7:00) staffing pattern, which called for a total of two aides and one nurse for the 200 residents in the three-story building. At approximately midnight, one of the aides put Max Morse to bed. The nurse's records indicated that the side rails on Morse's bed were put up and that he was checked every two hours and passed an uneventful night.

DISCUSSION QUESTIONS

1. With regard to Max Morse's safety, what was the duty of the night supervisor? Of the administrator?

2. How could this incident have been prevented?

3. Was there any staff negligence?

4. Was there any criminal behavior involved in this case?

CHAPTER 6

The Board
of Directors

Boards of directors are a fact of life for managers of corporations, both health care and otherwise. State statutes usually set some requirements for corporate boards, such as age or number of members on the board. These same statutes then enfranchise the board with the legal responsibility and authority for the operation of the enterprise. The board, in turn, normally delegates significant amounts of their powers to a full-time managerial staff headed by a chief executive officer.

Although problems with boards are not a new issue, the last few years have seen considerable controversy over the role and functioning of boards of both for-profit and nonprofit corporations in and out of the health sector. This controversy has led to an increasing literature about boards, CEOs, and governmental oversight, including the passage of the Sarbanes-Oxley Act of 2002, a landmark piece of corporate reform legislation directed at the accountability of public corporations. In this chapter I shall be examining a variety of board issues, including their role and responsibilities, relationships with management, their required knowledge base, and how to most effectively develop a board.

I am relying not only on the published literature but also on my own experiences as a health care executive, researcher, academic, and, most significantly, board member. Over the past 35 years, I have served on the boards of various organizations including hospitals, nursing homes, community organizations, and a public corporation. These experiences range from the privilege of serving on outstanding boards, that is, with fellow board members who were dedicated, knowledgeable, and hardworking, to the depressing experience of being on a board with people who were lazy, unprepared, and self-serving. Managers usually work with the board they find in place when they are hired. This chapter is designed to assist managers in the noble task of reshaping and energizing their boards.

BOARD ROLE AND RESPONSIBILITIES

Boards are the legal entity responsible for governing the corporation. Although they delegate a good deal of their responsibility to a managerial group headed by a CEO, they do still retain the ultimate authority and responsibility for the enterprise. In the world of public corporations, the board's focus is usually increasing shareholder value. In the nonprofit world, its concern is more related to ensuring that the corporation fulfills its "trust" obligations to the community. Regardless of these broad differences, directors of all corporations must be concerned about the long-run mission and solvency of the enterprise. What should they do? Paul Brountas, in his book *Boardroom Excellence,* states: "The board is responsible for overseeing management's efforts to enhance stockholder value. In that capacity, a director serves as monitor, counselor, protagonist and critic."[1] What this translates to is a role with responsibilities that initially are defined by those governmental agencies, typically the office of the state attorney general, that have the ultimate legal authority over the charter of the nonprofit organization.

In Oregon, the attorney general provides a guide for board members of nonprofit organizations. It states: "[T]he principle role for the board member is stewardship. The directors of the corporation are ultimately responsible for the affairs of the charity . . . [they] must insure that the organization is operated for a charitable/public purpose . . . the resources and efforts focused on the charity's mission." The guide goes on to say that the board should not be engaged in the daily operational management of the organization but rather hire and periodically evaluate the activities of a chief executive. In Massachusetts, the attorney general identifies the role as follows: "[Y]ou and your fellow board members are responsible for governing the charity as it carries out its charitable mission."

---

[1] P. Brountas, *Boardroom Excellence* (Boston: Hale and Dorr, 2003), p. 22.

In practice, what does this mean for an organization's board? The first role is that of establishing or at least affirming the mission of the organization. Boards must periodically reexamine their mission and make either significant or minor modifications. This often occurs in public corporations after negative financial results. In the nonprofit sector, finances and competition will frequently result in a similar reexamination. For example, in Pennsylvania, a large teaching hospital that was supported by a religious community was sold to another hospital, and the net proceeds of the sale were used to establish a community foundation focused on the health care needs of the religious community. Only a board can make such a decision, and such a decision requires the rethinking of an organization's mission.

The second crucial task of the directors is to select senior management, typically the CEO and possibly the COO or the CFO. Some people will say that the board should turn over the reins of the organization to the CEO and step aside. I have rarely seen this in the nonprofit health sector. The board, usually through some type of committee structure, is involved in many senior management decisions. In my own experience, I had several board members participate with me in the selection of a chief medical officer and a chief financial officer. My role as CEO was essentially to bring forth my candidate to them. I only proposed people who I was comfortable with, and I even vetoed several candidates who were proposed to me by various board members. For example, when I was searching for a CFO, an important board member asked me to meet with someone who was interested in the job. It turned out that this person was an accountant from another state looking to relocate to our city; he had no health care experience other than a few hospital audit engagements years earlier, but he was a fraternity brother of this board member. I vetoed his choice, stuck to my guns, and the process proceeded until the board approved my first choice. This example also illustrates that the board and management must work together if both are to be successful.

A third job of the board is to evaluate the CEO or senior management team. Like most activities on the board, this is a committee project and should occur in a proscribed time and manner. An ad hoc approach to job evaluation is certainly not fair to management and represents a flaw in board performance, which also must be evaluated on a periodic basis. Both evaluations benefit from clear guidelines. In the case of management, these guidelines should be part of the initial understanding when senior staff is hired. If the charge to the CEO is to create new programs, cut the deficit, or increase the endowment, for example, these are the parameters that he or she should be measured upon, not some newly designed criteria that will either bolster or diminish the manager. Academia is famous for its floating standards for promotion and tenure. While often stated as "teaching, research, and service," it frequently occurs that these standards vary by person, and thus each year, at the end of tenure review season, we have a spate of lawsuits against colleges and universities.

A fourth board function is program evaluation. While the board should never be involved in managing any organizational programs (except perhaps its own self-education), it should certainly approve and periodically evaluate new programs. Here it is imperative to both draw some lines and allow some managerial flexibility. For example, if a CEO wanted to implement a new employee recruitment program, I would suggest that the board executive group needs merely a short report on the program's design and a periodic informational update on its functioning. On the other hand, when an organization is considering the acquisition of a new facility or the expansion of its range of services, then board involvement is absolutely necessary. Disaster is often on the horizon when a board remains uninformed or mute about such matters. For example, in Pittsfield, Massachusetts, the Berkshire Medical Center narrowly avoided a disaster after its CEO, with little board involvement, began a multistate expansion into long-term care, with the apparent explanation that nursing homes would support the deficit-prone main medical center. Perhaps if the board had been more alert, concerned, or less intimidated by management, they would have approved neither the expansions nor the CEO's personal benefit package, which was also quite out of line. In another example, various boards at Tulane University allowed a professor, who later became dean of the school of public health, to develop a broad range of family planning programs that brought positive publicity, community relations, and money to the university. However, a lack of oversight eventually led to federal indictments and convictions that sent the dean and other staff to the federal penitentiary and gave the medical center a black eye—including a vice-chancellor, who was an unindicted coconspirator. In simplest terms, boards are not permitted the luxury of saying, "Officer, we were all sitting in the back seat."

In the nonprofit sector, a board frequently has the job of raising money. That sometimes involves giving of their own money and at other times giving of their time to raise money. A friend of mine who is a professional fund-raiser in Boston once gave me the rundown on the Boston "arts scene" and what each board "cost." Some boards expected significant annual donations for membership, while others were satisfied just to get members. My board chairman in Florida was a master at raising money. Indeed, he was the ultimate boutique marketer. Years ago he intuitively recognized that many wealthy elderly people were moving to South Florida and that a significant number of them were looking for familial-like connections to community. His organizations provided these connections. Periodic dinners, recognitions, parties, luncheons, volunteer activities, and events became for many of these people their "lives." And in return, they provided charitable donations. Some of these people had no close relatives; in those instances, the organization became the major beneficiary of their estates. My director of development, Norma Orovitz, summarized it nicely when she said, "Fund-raising is really friend-raising." In this instance in Florida, the chairman of the board was a world-class friend-raiser, and many people in South Florida viewed him as a good friend simply because for them he was indeed a very good friend.

However, the role of fund-raiser (and friend-raiser) is not limited to the board officers. Generally, all board members are expected to give the time to raise money, either directly, such as by running a charity golf tournament, or indirectly, such as by being an ambassador or simply lending one's name and credibility to a fund-raising effort. The job of fund-raising, discussed elsewhere in this book, is both a managerial function through the development department and a board function.

Although it is technically not fund-raising, a related job for all board members is representing the organization to the greater public. All organizations are judged by their board members, and that is why the myriad solicitations most of us get in the mail frequently have well-known public figures on the boards or as honorary chairs. The representation of the board to the public may be on a formal basis, that is, when a board member is asked to sit on a committee or in a meeting as a representative from the nonprofit organization, or on an informal basis, such as at a social gathering, where someone might mention that they had poor service at the community hospital and "Joan over there is on the board, you should talk to her." It is thus imperative that management works closely on initially orienting all new board members and later updating them, so that when they do represent the organization, the board members know what they are talking about.

Overseeing the fiscal operation of the organization is a central role of the board. This is typically carried out by an audit committee. Post Sarbanes-Oxley, the audit committee's role is in the spotlight in the public sector. This spotlight has yet to refocus on the nonprofit sector, although such a shift is likely in the future. A recent article said it all in its title, "Next On The Griddle: Nonprofit Boards," and in its summary sidebar: "Corporate reformers and the IRS are circling, and the big donors want to be doubly sure how their money is spent. These days, directors of charitable foundations and the like need more than a big heart."[2] Regardless, the board is the steward or trustee for the community, and it must continually examine the organization's fiscal operations, including the annual approval of an operating and capital budget. An excellent board will receive detailed financial statements on a regular basis, and a significant portion of the board meeting will focus on the financial health of the organization, including its cash flow, income, expenses, and balance sheet. In poor board situations the board is simply uninformed, and in the worst does not care to be informed. Disaster is always around the corner!

Just as the board needs to review and approve the annual budget, it must also periodically review the organization's strategic plan. This plan provides the direction for the organization and in many senses drives major decisions. One of my consulting clients was a large nonprofit health care organization where the board chairman did not believe in strategic planning or strategic plans. A CEO's attempt to develop a plan was met with resentment and indifference by the board chairman, who much preferred his own ad hoc approach to planning. This approach had worked successfully in his own personal business but certainly is a poor idea in a large nonprofit corporation.

Board renewal is another responsibility of the board membership. This renewal has two dimensions. First, self-renewal means that the board must continually stay abreast of what is happening in the industry and what is going on in their own organizations. Generally, good CEOs make

[2]J. Connelly, "Next on the griddle: Nonprofit boards," *Corporate Governance* (Nov.–Dec., 2003), p. 79.

it their job to have an educated board and will ensure that a steady stream of information flows to the board. For example, the CEO of EXTENDI-CARE regularly sends board members a packet of industry-relevant articles, thus keeping the board up-to-date on current issues and trends.

A second aspect of renewal is activism in retiring board members and selecting new ones. The key here is simply a board recognizing that appointments should not be for life and that at different times in the history and development of an organization different people are necessary to represent the community and move the organization forward in a relevant way. Failure to recognize these changes may doom an organization, as was the case of a large hospital in Brooklyn, where a failure in board leadership led to its eventual closure. In one board that I served on, former board presidents were automatically given a board appointment for life. By the time I was elected to the 18-person board, 9 of the members were former presidents. Because they had been together for so long, they thought of themselves as controlling the organization and simply viewed the 9 other members as insignificant. Unfortunately, they also started to meet privately about board activities and at one point made a major decision for the organization. When this was learned about by the other members, a holy war resulted between the ex-presidents and the other members, with the other members finally prevailing. This illustration suggests that turnover is necessary and healthy. Without turnover, many organizations start functioning as inefficient and nonresponsive family businesses—which is not in the best interests of a community.

A final function is evaluation of the board, management, and the interactions between these two groups. The board must periodically go through a process of self-evaluation to ensure that it is structurally sound, that is, that its committees are functioning properly and that it has the right number of people with the right mix of backgrounds. It must examine its processes, or how business is conducted within the board, to make sure that issues are fully and fairly vented. In evaluating the CEO, the board is also making a broader evaluation of the organization's performance. How well is the CEO leading the organization toward its previously determined goals? Finally, the board should take a hard look at how well the board and management is working together. The bottom line is simple: Are management and the board an effective team? In all organizations, particularly in the nonprofit sector, teamwork is essential for the organization's long-term success.

BOARD EFFECTIVENESS

While some of these functions are irrelevant for nonprofit health care organizations, most of the responsibilities are appropriate for the board member of a health care organization.

The problem of board effectiveness and involvement is common to all organizations. Whether we look back decades to the "honor roll" of business bankruptcies of W.T. Grant, Lockheed, Eastern Airlines, or the Penn Central Railroad or more recently to the debacles of Enron, K-Mart, United Airlines, Health South, or World Com—who claimed to be uninformed? The board! Does it seem possible that board members of major industrial concerns, the elite of America's business establishment, could be so unaware? History suggests that we should not be surprised.

For example, Drucker, in *Management,* titles a chapter "Needed: An Effective Board." He argues that boards are programmed for failure by their very nature, ambiguity of mission, and divergence of interest.[3] A common experience in health care is that of finding executives whose performance is excellent in business but who cannot function effectively on the board of a nonprofit organization. This can be understood in part if the composition of boards, whether health care or industrial, is considered. Data from a Hedrick and Struggles study of directors indicate that most board members are well into middle age (the average age being 57), that most people are selected for their personal or professional stature, that a person's functional area of expertise is a second but significantly less important reason for selection, and that availability is a considerably less important reason in selection.[4] An illustration of this is the membership on the board of HealthSouth, a troubled publicly owned health care company, whose nine board members are all men, have an average age of 63 with four over 70, and none of them are health professionals (except the CEO). Essentially, it appears that, apart from the CEO who also sits on the board, they are all private investors and represent people whose primary interest is making more money. While this is a perfectly acceptable goal, there also needs to be a health care component in the board dialog, which is likely not significantly present at such a roundtable. Imagine the typical meeting, at which the board simply does not understand the

---

[3]P. Drucker, *Management* (New York: Harper & Row, 1973), pp. 627–636.
[4]Heidrick & Struggles, Inc. "The Changing Board" (Author: 1975), p. 5.

services the company is delivering and is thus totally dependent on managerial representations. They would obviously only focus on what they know, most likely the short-term bottom line. It would indeed be surprising if such a board could ask the "hard questions" of management.

Even when a representation is mandated, it often does not happen. Health systems agencies (HSAs), for example, are organizations that operate under strict federal guidelines calling for a membership that is "broadly representative" of the communities being served. During the heyday of government-mandated HSAs and mandated representative boards, a 1978 study of 134 boards found that 65% of the board members were classified in professional and managerial positions, 10% in the remaining occupational categories (e.g., clerical), and 22% were not in the civilian labor force (e.g., persons formerly employed who were housewives, disabled, and so on). For executive committees, the figures for these categories were 75%, 7%, and 17% respectively. In contrast, 1970 Census data indicated that 13% of the experienced civilian labor force were in professional and managerial occupations, 45% in the remaining occupational categories, and 42% were classified as not in the civilian labor force. Thus, the higher-status occupational groups were extremely over-represented, while persons of lower-status occupational groups and not in the civilian labor force were extremely under-represented. This under-representation was even greater for the executive committees.[5]

This pattern is seen almost universally in the health care field. A review of a typical board membership (with the exclusion of community-based programs such as a neighborhood health center) is like reading the "Who's Who" of an area. Boards are not generally representative of any group other than the upper middle class of the community. The justification for this skewed representation is that such a group is likely to bring greater financial and intellectual resources to the organization. The good old days were described nicely by Connelly as follows: "The formula for becoming a member of a philanthropic board used to be simple. You had to give money (personally) or get money (from someone else)."[6] Today, with philanthropic money diminishing in significance, other factors may be more important, such as legislative savvy, financial oversight expertise,

---

[5]U.S. Department of Health, Education and Welfare, Project Summary, Board and Staff Composition of Health Planning agencies, HRA Pub. No. 78-609, 1978, p.10.
[6]J. Connelly, p. 78.

professional experience, availability, enthusiasm, or community connections. At one point I had the opportunity to review the membership of the board of one of New York's most prestigious medical centers. What struck me was that they were the cream of New York society. What also struck me was that a number of the board members had a notation next to their name that they did not wish to receive mail from the medical center. Such behavior is simply no longer acceptable in today's complex and challenging world.

BOARD/MANAGEMENT RELATIONS

For the manager, the fundamental question is: How can a manager have an effective relationship with a board? At one extreme, the manager must cope with what some perceive as a necessary evil; at another, the manager is able to utilize the resources that a board can offer. Many managers view their relationship with the board as somewhat adversarial. This was well articulated by J. Peter Grace, the chief executive of the multibillion-dollar W.R. Grace conglomerate, when he said, "Do you mean to tell me that if I work 100 hours a week for 4.3 weeks a month on average so that I'm working 430 hours a month, some guy is going to come in and in three or four hours outsmart me? I mean that's crazy! No matter how smart you are, if I work 100 times harder than you on a given subject you have no way of catching me."[7] Reflecting this perspective, Grace's boardroom does not have the traditional conference table but is arranged more like a college classroom. In dealing with his board, Grace states that he keeps them fully informed; for example, for one month's meeting he provided them with a report that was over 400 pages long.

Is this typical? In the Heidrick and Struggles study, it appeared that most companies provided their directors with only the minutes of previous meetings, some financial data, and an agenda before board meetings. In most cases, no summaries of board committee meetings subsequent to the last board meetings, marketing data, or data to support agenda items were provided. It can be concluded that only those board members who are involved with committees, which is usually the group making critical decisions, or those who are extremely well informed about agenda items

---

[7]"Peter Grace's Love-Hate Relationship with His Board," *Forbes*, May 15, 1976, p. 76.

can offer much of worth at a given meeting. In the Grace example, it must be recognized that without an independent staff or a major investment of their own time, board members would find it impossible to digest or evaluate critically the 400-page report. Management, then, through its de facto control of information to the board, has a major impact on the board's effectiveness and value.

In my experience, even well-meaning boards and managers often have difficulty managing their information. For example, I once served on a board of a foundation grant program. Our 15-person board was responsible for allocating $30 million to community hospitals that were developing hospital-based group practices. Our job involved reviewing scores of complex applications plus staff-written field visit reports about the applicants. The typical package per applicant was an inch thick. At any given board meeting, we reviewed 7–10 applications, and those documents usually arrived at the board member's offices about three days before the meeting. Frankly, I doubt if all the members carefully reviewed the hundreds of pages presented to them. I suspect most of them instead turned to the executive summary and listened to the staff presentations and recommendations at the board meeting. In the course of the three years of this program, not one staff recommendation was disapproved. Although we did have a top-flight staff, it must also be acknowledged that the essential decision-making power truly resided with staff because they were in control of the information.

Effective relationships are of major concern in health care organizations. On the one hand, the board is necessary for fund-raising and community contacts, while on the other hand, the board can rarely match the professional expertise or time invested in the organization by its professionals. From a managerial perspective, boards become problematic in a variety of ways. First, they simply do not do their homework. If a manager sends out material for a board to review prior to a meeting, he or she expects the board member to review the material and be able to discuss the subject intelligently. As a board member and CEO, I have too often attended meetings where one or more board members were sitting reviewing the material while the discussion was in progress and would then ask questions that were profoundly stupid. A second problem is the board members whose success in one industry gives them the sense that they could run the health facility or programs with their eyes closed. This board arrogance often translates into disrespect for the management and the second-guessing of managerial decisions. My favorite example is of a board member who owned a pizza franchise and wasted 30 minutes at a board meeting over a managerial decision to hire a new snow removal company to clear the hospital grounds. A third problem involves board members who directly or indirectly use their positions for personal gain. When this occurs, the manager is often put into the position of walking on eggshells. Over the years, I have seen board members insist on jobs for their family members, use institutional monies for essentially private parties, promote their businesses through the institution, insist that the institution use their companies as a primary purveyor, hire the board members for professional services, or use suppliers that would benefit a board member. For example, at one medical center the owner of a large restaurant was also treasurer of the board. He demanded that certain food service suppliers be used by the medical center, the same ones he used for his restaurant, who then provided him with much better prices because of the deal he could deliver with the medical center.

The question is the following: Why does management go along with a board that cannot behave in a professional manner? The answer is probably ego and job security. In my own experience as CEO, I found that I had a board that, while personally quite congenial, was also quite dysfunctional. When I joined the organization there were 200 people on my board. Most of them liked being on the board, but few had any clue as to their responsibility or authority. When I was hired it was agreed that I could reshape the board into a smaller, more effective group, that the long-time chairman would retire, and that we would have a board with a rotating executive group.

In the first few months of my tenure, I learned that all board meetings were essentially Sunday morning breakfasts with 60-minute show-and-tell reports that were scripted by the public relations department. The social nature of these board meetings was emphasized by the tradition of bringing family and friends to the breakfasts and the total lack of any financial reporting. Occasionally a vote on an issue was taken, and all of those votes were unanimous. Hundreds of bagels, Danish, omelets, cups of coffee, and pounds of halvah later, the meeting was over and no real business was transacted. All of the major decisions were made in smaller meetings of the board chairman, board president, and a handful of trusted advisors.

My ego told me that I could change this system. So shortly after I arrived I began "educating" the board with mailings about current issues, including various reports about board functioning from the American Hospital Association. I also made myself available to board members for meetings on a variety of subjects. Finally, I made it a point to attend all of the meetings of the various board committees. I thought that I could change a 40-year-old system by the power of education and my personality. I, like many other CEOs, found that it is not very easy to change what are essentially the board habits of a lifetime. In this case it was a board that had learned to go to the party and neither pay the bill nor clean up afterward. They as a group had long ago ceded their power to an inner circle, and now they were coasting. It did not take long before I went from the white knight to the intruder; the next step was for me to leave. While there were a few board members who wanted to see the organization change, they were clearly in the minority and were unwilling to speak up in public for even the simplest of changes, such as board reports on the organization's finances.

Clearly, many managers continue to work for years with less-than-optimal boards. Some do it simply for the money; a job is a job and most boards are problematic, so why trade the devil you know for the devil you don't know? Others persist with a spirit of hope for the future. Over the course of years, the fortunate few are able to influence the selection of board members with whom they can work successfully, while others live with the vagaries of the board selection process. In one midwestern city I met with the CEO of a nonprofit geriatric system, who was pleased with his new board chairman. I had lunch with the chairman, a young self-made millionaire, and concluded that his arrogance and lack of respect for nonprofit organizational managers boded poorly for this CEO. Within a year he was out of a job. If there is an analogy, management board relationships are like boating: The wind, the currents, and unexpected weather all affect the outcome at the end of the day. The smart manager realizes that board management relationships change constantly and that the most that he or she can do is act professionally and competently and offer his or her best judgments on the issues of the day.

A final thought: A medical center CEO I am friendly with is an avid golfer. I once asked him whether he was a member of the country club in his community. He told me that it was a perquisite available to him with the job but he hadn't joined. He preferred to play at the local municipal course because that way he never confused himself; that is, he reminded himself that he was an employee of the medical center. Despite the high salaries, perks, and titles, the board does not forget that management works for them.

BOARD DEVELOPMENT

Ideally, boards are valuable assets for a health care organization, but they must be properly selected and nurtured. The process must start with the organizational by-laws that call for terms of appointment, including a maximum period of service. Without such a structure the board will simply become stagnant. The second part of the structure is that of a nominating committee that develops a pool of candidates for a board position and screens the pool. In the best of circumstances, the committee will develop some criteria for the new board member, such as expertise in a particular area or connections to a particular community, and then solicit nominees who typically come from other board members and management. Following interviews, the nominees should be presented to the board, which usually ratifies the recommendation of the nominating committee.

Organizations should approach the selection of directors with considerable seriousness and select only those people who enhance the value of the organization because of their expertise, availability, and, yes, in some cases, personal stature. What should be considered in this decision is the question: If time and effort are invested in this person, will there be a return on that investment? A negative answer suggests that the search process should be continued.

Having selected the right people, the organization must then make an investment. This investment has several dimensions. First, the manager should learn as much as possible about the new director and that director's home organization, experience, or profession. This includes assessing areas of strength and weakness. Doing this diagnostic workup demonstrates an interest in the board member's professional and personal development, while simultaneously permitting an evaluation of how and where the new director can fit into the organizational scheme. I always urge my CEO clients to make these assessments at the new director's workplace. What you can learn about someone from visiting him or her at the office is invaluable. In one instance, I learned that a new board member, who most other members thought was a senior executive, was in fact the office manager of the company and was a pretty nasty person in his interpersonal relations at the job. Second, the board member must be educated in the major issues and problems facing the health industry in general and the particular component specifically. In doing this, it is not as necessary to focus on detail as it is to look at issues and options. Finally, the board member must keep informed. The strategy of overwhelming the board, as Grace does, is not likely to result in an interested, involved, and supportive board. On the other hand, a board that is tuned in to an organization can be invaluable for both the organization's and the manager's success.

PAYING THE BOARD

During a consulting project with the board of a nonprofit geriatric system several years ago, I learned that the board was paid. My initial reaction was that of great surprise because, while board members of for-profit companies typically are paid, it is rare for nonprofit board members to receive any fees. The fees that this board was paid were not enormous: $2000 per year for each of the 12 members and $10,000 per year for the chair. Additionally, the chair had another $15,000 available to him for use on an institutionally based pet project.

In summary, boards are a fact of life for management. The challenge for all managers is to develop and maintain a healthy and respectful relationship with the board, one based on the best interests of the organization, not on the best interests of individuals. If such a trusting relationship is developed, then the winners will be the organization and the community, and there will simply be no losers.

Case Study 6-1
FIRING THE CEO

On the morning of November 1st, Paul Blackman, administrator of the Crescent City Nursing Center for the past 23 months, received a call from Roger Johnson, former president of the nursing home's board, who told him that, on behalf of the other former presidents of the board, Johnson was asking for Blackman's resignation by the end of the year.

(continues)

Case Study 6-1

Blackman was stunned by this call and immediately telephoned Angela Fisher, the home's board president, and received assurances from her that, despite the fact that he had no employment contract, his job was secure.

The Crescent City Nursing Center is a 250-bed skilled nursing home that has a reputation for being the finest in the region. Since its founding shortly after World War II, the home has been under the direction of a 24-member self-perpetuating board of trustees. The original board comprised a number of people who were instrumental in the founding of the home, including members of the Johnson family, who were not only involved in the home's founding but also provided close to $3,000,000 of the home's total $5,000,000 endowment. The most important of the Johnson family members were two brothers, Roger and William. The 24 members of the present board consist of seven former presidents and at least 10 other people who have been involved with the home for over 15 years. The board is now dominated by Roger's son Kenneth and William's son John. In addition, five other Johnson family members are on the board, along with several board members who have significant business involvement with the Johnson family.

Since the home opened, there have been three administrators. The first administrator also served as director of nursing and held the job until 1965, when she was replaced by Mac Davidson, who administered the home for the next 30 years. Davidson's training was in social work, and he came to the home at a crucial time in its evolution. He was responsible for its growth from a 100-bed old-age home to the high-quality home it is today. Davidson and his wife Leslie were intimately involved in all of its functionings. Although Leslie was only a part-time receptionist, she made her presence felt throughout the home by being there a significant part of each day, visiting the residents daily, participating in the various resident shows, and socializing

(continues)

Case Study 6-1

with many of the volunteers and board members. Mac Davidson also kept a very high profile in the home through various means, including early morning rounds of all the resident units, close contact with family members, and an active series of social engagements with many of the board members, especially the Johnson clan. In contrast, Paul Blackman has spent more time in his office and less time visiting with residents or socializing with the board. Mrs. Blackman, who is an accountant with a certified public accounting firm, has also been quite uninvolved with the home, in sharp contrast to Leslie Davidson.

The last few years of Davidson's tenure were both professionally and personally difficult for him. On the professional side, he faced a broad range of challenges, including an attempted unionization at the nursing home, a decrease in the home's ability to raise funds, and a decrease in income from residents due to a declining private pay census as well as Medicaid cutbacks. On the personal side, Davidson had a series of medical problems, including a heart attack, bypass surgery, and a bout with prostate cancer. After enduring these problems for three years, the board prevailed upon Davidson to retire. Because of Davidson's health problems, he retired in January and his long-time assistant, Alvin Jones, who for 27 years was the home's personnel manager, took over as the acting administrator.

The board recognized Jones's limitations and agreed among themselves to increase their supervision of the home, particularly in the area of finances. The increased supervision provided the board with some unexpected and unpleasant information about the facility's fiscal health, such as an undisclosed (by management) deficit of close to $1,000,000. They also learned that the home was overstaffed and that its salary and benefit structure was exceedingly problematic.

The board decided to find a new CEO to solve the problems and bring the home's finances into line. After a

(continues)

Case Study 6-1

six-month search, they hired Paul Blackman, a 39-year-old experienced nursing home administrator with an MBA in health administration. On January 1st of the previous year, Blackman took over the job and set about identifying and rectifying the problems. The first of these involved low morale among the staff, largely due to Davidson's long history of favoritism, which had resulted in inequitable pay and fringe benefits. For example, in the food service department, a cook with 20 years of seniority was paid less than another cook who had been with the home only 7 years. Also, the 20-year veteran was only entitled to three weeks of paid vacation, whereas Davidson had negotiated a four-week vacation package for the new cook after 5 years of service. The food service example was not an isolated case. There were numerous inequities throughout the organization, many of which apparently resulted from Davidson's desire to control staff through a series of private negotiations. The individual staff member would thus become beholden to Davidson because he had bent the personnel rules to accommodate the employee's desires.

Other problems included the huge deficit resulting from overstaffing and state Medicaid cutbacks. Blackman dealt with these problems by undertaking a thorough review of personnel policies and actions as well as staffing levels. In addition, Blackman decided to replace a number of senior management personnel with people loyal to him. In one conversation with Angela Fisher, he stated that the home was still full of Davidson loyalists who ran to him with every complaint or controversy. A further problem was that many of those who were likely to lose from Blackman's policies had cordial relationships with the board. This was another legacy of the Davidson years, when the CEO often hired people at the suggestion of board members, particularly the Johnson family.

(continues)

Case Study 6-1

In pursuing his policies, Blackman felt considerable pressure to get things in order as soon as possible. He also felt that every change he made reflected poorly on his predecessor, and that frequently either Davidson or one of his friends on the board would react to a proposed change with the question, "How come we never had this problem when Mac ran the home?"

Blackman's analysis of the situation was that Mac Davidson was an out-of-touch and manipulative manager who ran the home by keeping the board in the dark and that the board was complicit by choosing to stay in the dark. John and Kenneth Johnson, both former board presidents, viewed Blackman as the key problem. From their perspective, Blackman was doing a respectable job of dealing with the home's fiscal problems but was making a mess of the staff situation. Specifically, they believed he was wrong to fire or force into retirement so many top management staff, including the director of nursing, the director of the physical plant, the food service director, the personnel manager, and the purchasing agent. In addition, while they applauded his efforts at developing a more equitable system of wages and benefits, they were concerned about its costs as well as its potential for labor strife. Other matters that concerned these board members included Blackman's active participation on the state nursing home association's board of trustees and his lack of time to socialize with the residents.

Angela Fisher found herself in the middle of this dispute. On the one hand, she personally liked Paul Blackman and respected what he was trying to accomplish. On the other hand, she felt that he should probably spend more time at the home and perhaps be more diplomatic about board relationships.

Her main concern, however, was how to deal with the powerful group of former board presidents who had announced that they were firing Paul Blackman.

CHAPTER 7

Motivation

If Monty Python were a management consultant, his search for the Holy Grail would be an endless journey toward the understanding of motivation. No other subject has been so important and elusive. Emblematic of that sad search is an experience I had several decades ago in Baltimore at the headquarters of the McCormick Spice Company. This company was one of the pioneers in participative management, which is the art and science of involving all levels of employees in decision making so that they commit themselves to the future of the organization. McCormick Spice itself credited its survival through the Depression to this type of participation.[1] My extraordinary opportunity involved a tour of the Baltimore factory with the company's CEO, Charles McCormick. After taking me on a walk through the main plant, during which he greeted a number of long-time employees by first names and exchanged pleasantries about their families, he said to me in a rather somber tone that it seemed that the workforce was changing in a most unsatisfactory way. He felt that people in the past had really been concerned about job security and about being part of a company at which top management was concerned about their welfare. Today, he noted, the workforce seemed more interested in a paycheck and less interested in security. He could not understand, for example, why young people were willing to quit jobs after only a few weeks. In his mind, a job was analogous to a career.

What was going on at McCormick? Why the high turnover? Why the problems with motivation? On the one hand, the organization's environment was impressive. This was perhaps best exemplified by the personnel department, which was called the Department of Human Relations, and

---

[1]C.P. McCormick. *The power of people* (Baltimore, MD: Penguin Books, 1949).

its motto, displayed in foot-high letters at the intersection of the walls and ceiling: "Know all ye that enter here have faith not fear." Clearly, the executives had a genuine interest and commitment to the theory and practice of participative management. On the other hand, it was clear that there was a generation gap in their workforce. The old-time employees were people of the Depression to whom their brand of participative management was important, while the new workforce was composed of high school graduates, most of whom had been born after World War II. It appeared that major social events, plus changing demographics and economics in Baltimore, certainly not the good intentions of the company, were affecting a carefully developed strategy for employee motivation that had been successful for a number of years.

Theoretically, roles should be very clear in for-profit organizations such as department stores, where the owners or their designated managers are at the top of the organization, and each member of that organization works toward the "bottom line" goals of the store, which are spelled out. Because each person is not an individual entrepreneur but part of a team, effort is toward goal achievement, and that achievement is measurable. Large elements of the workforce are interchangeable and dispensable, since only limited training and experience are required for the job. Finally, the workforce is generally nonprofessional and responds to organizational rather than professional needs as motivation. This, though, is merely theoretical! A friend of mine, who is president of a department store, has as many problems motivating his large workforce as most health care managers.

However, the typical health care administrator is likely to have even greater problems motivating staff. Consider the case of the typical hospital. Employees of such an organization are a rather heterogeneous group, ranging from physicians to janitors. Education, social class, and age differences are significant, and job functions vary from those that require a great deal of education and are rather intellectual to those that require practically no education but are physically demanding. This situation is complicated by the continual interaction and interdependence of these people and the somewhat unclear bottom line of a hospital's activities. Further, the key personnel, community physicians, are independent contractors who utilize the facility and its resources to enrich themselves intellectually and economically but do not reimburse the institution for its support of their activities; rather, the costs are simply transferred directly to the consumer, in this case, the patient. Adding further complexity is the range of ethnic and language backgrounds found in the typical organization. For example, in one medical center, the CEO made it a practice to issue all important staff memos in three languages: English, Spanish, and Creole.

The complexity of the hospital situation is well illustrated in the operating room. The procedure is performed by a surgeon, probably a white male who is a private practitioner and is billing the patient privately for the procedure. The operating room clothes he wears, the instruments he uses, the facility, and other supplies utilized all belong to the hospital. An anesthesiologist, who is also billing the patient privately, is likewise a private entrepreneur who utilizes hospital-owned equipment, which is likely to have been purchased at his request. The scrub nurse, the circulating nurses, the surgical technologists, and the other supportive personnel in the operating room are hospital employees. The nurses are likely to be female graduates of a two-, three-, or four-year nursing program with some on-the-job training for their specialized duties in the operating room. The surgical technologists are graduates of 10-month training programs. The physicians are all college and medical school graduates and have completed extensive 3-, 4-, or 5-year postgraduate surgical training programs. If a specimen, such as a frozen section, has to be analyzed during the procedure or an X-ray taken and read, another group of people are needed: the technicians in the laboratory or X-ray department plus the pathologists and radiologists. This last group of physicians may have a complex financial arrangement with the institution in which their salaries are related to a percentage of the revenues generated by their respective departments. Again, the facility provides the lion's share of the resources necessary for the department to generate its revenues.

Between cases, the operating room is scrubbed clean by a group of housekeeping employees. These are likely to be high-school graduates with minimal education; in most cases, they are from a considerably lower socioeconomic class than the physicians and nurses. Scheduling for operating room time is handled by either a hospital-employed clerk or nurse under the general direction of the administration.

What motivates the operating room crew? Is the surgeon motivated in the same way as the anesthesiologist, the nurse, the operating room supervisor, and the housekeeping employee? The central dilemma in terms of motivation is that a heterogeneous group is likely to have different needs and aspirations. The managerial goal must be to set a tone in the managerial environment whereby people can simultaneously meet their personal aspirations while satisfying organizational objectives.

This goal is extremely difficult to attain for two major reasons. First, organizations are fundamentally impersonal; jobs in organizations are designed to fit the organization's formal wear. The sleeves are raised a bit and the trousers shortened; the next week the trousers are lengthened and the waist taken in a bit. Rarely do large organizations go out of business because someone leaves or dies. Second, from the organization's perspective, jobs have to be designed, structured, and assigned. Work has to be done on a structured basis and in an orderly manner. The housekeeping employees cannot scrub down the operating room when it fits into their schedules, and the food service employees cannot deliver the meals at their convenience. Thus, somewhere within the hospital organization, priorities must be set, and these priorities dictate the resources, human and nonhuman, necessary to meet these goals.

Conflict is inherent in the process of simultaneously meeting both personal and organizational goals, since personal needs are inevitably made subordinate to major organizational goals. For example, the hospital or nursing home must function 24 hours per day. Who should staff the institution on the least desirable shifts? Although the organization can provide extra financial compensation for working on Thanksgiving or Christmas, is the extra money a satisfactory substitute for time?

ATTITUDE AND BEHAVIOR

Attitude and behavior are not synonymous terms, and a person's attitude toward something, or even his or her beliefs, are not necessarily reliable predictors of that person's behavior. An attitude refers to a person's feelings, perhaps interests, not to an overt act, which is behavior. Much research lately has been done in the area of factors that have an impact on work satisfaction. The importance of this research lies in the assumption that a more satisfied worker is likely to be a "better" worker, which usually means a more efficient and effective worker.

Such an association between satisfaction and performance has not always been observed in the research on the relationship between attitude and behavior. The classic example of this difference is in the 1934 work of LaPierre, who undertook an inquiry about the attitude and behavior of

Americans toward the Japanese and demonstrated the lack of congruence between attitude and behavior.[2] He had Japanese-Americans attempt to get service at hotels and restaurants while he hid in the background and observed the generally negative reactions to these requests for service. Next he questioned the innkeepers about their attitudes toward the Japanese-Americans. The results were startling: They felt positively toward the visitors but acted negatively. Subsequent research suggests that attitude may be only one of many intervening variables that are related to behavior, and that the association is not necessarily direct.[3] Managers must carefully examine not only the attitudes but also the behavior of their staff. In the process, they must examine their own attitudes and behavior concerning their job, their staff, and the goals to be achieved, since all of these factors are likely to have an impact on the managerial processes used to reach goals as well as the final outcomes.

FAVORITE THEORIES OF MOTIVATION

There is no shortage of theories of motivation, and few provide a totally adequate explanation for what happens in the real world. Further, based on hundreds of discussion with real-world managers, I have yet to meet one who operated with a "theory." Most manage by conviction; that is, they believe that certain people behave in certain ways because _____ (fill in the blank). Stereotypes abound, as does misinformation. So what value is there to theories? It is my judgment that some theories are valuable because they assist all of us in organizing our thinking and perhaps developing our own understanding and sensitivity toward motivational issues. On the next few pages I present those theories that have assisted me in my thinking and that I have found somewhat valuable in the practice of management.

Favorite Theory #1: Maslow's Hierarchy of Needs

One of the most important conceptual contributions to our understanding of motivation was made by Dr. Abraham Maslow when he presented his theory on the hierarchy of needs. He assumed that people's needs are

---

[2]R.T. LaPierre, "Attitudes vs. actions," *Social Forces, 13* (1934), 230–237.

[3]L.G. Warner and M.E. DeFleur, "Attitude as an interactional concept: Social constraint and social distance as intervening variables between attitudes and action," *American Sociological Review, 34*(2((1969), 153–169.

hierarchical in nature and are met on a stepwise basis. Thus, the lowest level need must be met before an individual can move on to the need at the next step, and so forth. While his assumptions have been frequently commented upon and criticized, the basic categorization of needs has been widely acknowledged and often accepted.[4,5]

Maslow postulated that the lowest level of need was physiological: the need for bread and water. When a person is deprived of the means to meet this need, nothing else appears to be important. This need is not usually a concern of managers, since the general attitude is that most people have "enough" to fulfill their basic physiological needs. These needs have a tendency to shift as expectations grow higher, however. One person's castle is another's shack; an acceptable standard of living for one person is too low for another. Government officials are notorious for resigning from what most of us think are well-paying positions because they say they cannot afford to live on that salary. While many of us might find their salaries a considerable improvement on our own, these government officials have a different perspective on how their taxpayer-supported incomes are meeting their "needs."

Maslow's second-level need is that for security and safety. Managers have commonly perceived this to mean that people need to know that no physical or psychological harm will result from their work. This concept has within it the notion of equity or fairness; if workers feel that they are being treated fairly, their needs are being met. In my interpretation, it also refers to a person's feeling of insulation against the stress of transitions. This is particularly significant in the health field because of the widespread use of government monies to fund delivery programs. Those working in the health industry at almost any level need to know the probable impact of growth, development, or winding down on their future. Unfortunately, those individuals with the least mobility are likely to be the ones to feel the greatest impact of any program change.

The third level has been defined as social, sometimes "love." An individual has a need to belong to and identify with a group and an organization. The recruiting techniques of the Marine Corps in the 1970s were based on this need. With the assistance of the J. Walter Thompson marketing firm, they advertised for "A Few Good Men." Belong to a select

---

[4]A. Maslow, *Motivation and personality* (New York: Harper & Row, 1954), pp. 80–106.
[5]A. Maslow, *Eupsychian management* (Homewood, IL: Irwin-Dorsey, 1965).

group—belong! An interesting example of this in the health field involved a hospital in Brooklyn, New York. At the suggestion of the chairman of the board of trustees, all hospital staff were required to wear white coats. Despite the expense of clothing hundreds of employees and the burden on the laundry of keeping the coats clean, it gave the staff an unusual sense of belonging as well as professionalism, at least superficially.

The fourth level on Maslow's hierarchy is that of esteem. People must be recognized by their peers and supervisors as important contributors to the organization. They also need self-recognition, a rather complicated issue, since numerous perfectly competent people lack confidence (and, occasionally, quite confident people lack competence, which is a different sort of problem). Some people in organizations simply cannot recognize their self-worth, despite external acknowledgment. Because of the rigid educational barriers to "advancement" in health care organizations, there are often problems with satisfying an individual's need for esteem. For example, state and federal laws prevent the upgrading of the world's best nursing aide to a licensed practical nurse or registered nurse without further training. The world's finest nurse-midwife is stymied in advancement without a medical degree.

The highest level of need, Maslow suggests, is that of "self-actualization." In today's parlance this means that people are truly "turned on" by what they do. In a sense, they have become totally integrated; they have interlaced their personal and work lives and are thoroughly "enjoying" both. Examples most often used when talking of self-actualized persons are dead artists and musicians such as Beethoven or van Gogh. Rarely has anyone suggested that a bolt-tightener on the Ford assembly line was self-actualized, or the foreman, or even the supervisor. Perhaps the plant manager was self-actualized. Certainly Henry Ford was!

As noted earlier, an underlying assumption of Maslow's was that self-actualization is impossible before these other hurdles are cleared. Consider the example of a friend who was health commissioner of a major city. He took the job after getting a leave from a tenured university professorship. He loved being commissioner but after three years resigned to return to academia and a job that he truly did not enjoy as much. Why? The public service job offered little security—a new mayor meant a new commissioner. The university job not only represented security but also the opportunity to earn far more money than from consulting. His obligations to his family took precedence over his professional satisfaction. This example suggests that the levels are useful handles when various discrete reasons for motivation are considered, but they may not always interact as postulated.

Finally, certain of these needs appear to be more critical than others. For example, many people work in jobs that do not satisfy their ego for the security that they offer. In addition, certain of Maslow's defined needs require satisfaction only at a minimal level. Occasionally, however, specific needs predominate. In times of personal stress, for example, an individual may find it most important to be in a low-risk, high-security job. At other times, the high-risk, potentially high-payoff job may be more appealing.

Needs are not static. As a person ages, needs shift, become more intense, or change completely. Often, after having attained security, a person no longer values it. Many professional colleagues have resigned once they were granted tenure. The competition and challenge turned them on, not the prize. As a young academic I was shocked when my former departmental chairman resigned to take a nonacademic job. It took me 20 years to understand that academia can also lose its charms!

Favorite Theory #2: Herzberg's Motivation-Hygiene Theory

The second major theory of motivation, and perhaps my favorite, is Herzberg's motivation-hygiene theory.[6] Herzberg suggests that certain job factors serve a motivating function by providing job satisfaction. He notes that "motivation factors that are intrinsic to the job are: achievement, recognition for achievement, the work itself, responsibility and growth, and advancement." On the other hand, Herzberg suggests that job dissatisfaction "or hygiene factors that are extrinsic to the job include: company policy and administration, supervision, interpersonal relationships, working conditions, salary, status and security."

According to Herzberg's theory, when people are not dissatisfied, they are not necessarily satisfied; they may be simply not dissatisfied. For example, salary is listed as a hygiene factor. A level of salary does not really motivate a person but simply prevents that person from being dissatisfied. On the other hand, a sense of being an integral and highly valued person in an organization may produce a highly motivated person.

---

[6]F. Herzberg, "One more time—how do you motivate employees?" *Harvard Business Review,* 46(1) (1968), 53–82.

The validity of this theory can be demonstrated with a simple example. Assume there are two assistant administrators, both on the same organizational level, and both earning the same amount of money—for the sake of the example, $50,000. At the end of the year they are both evaluated similarly and administrator #1 receives a bonus of $50,000. How can you get administrator #1 to resign? I suggest the answer is simple: Give administrator #2 a bonus of $75,000. Real money is not as important as the perception of what the money means!

Favorite Theory #3: The Alphabet Theories: X, Y, and Z

A different and perhaps the most popular concept of motivation was provided by McGregor when he offered his Theory X and Theory Y.[7] Theory X is based on the notion that workers are lazy, indolent, and undisciplined or, in today's language, "rip-off artists." To get such people to achieve, a manager must use a reward and punishment approach. For the Theory X manager, a carrot and stick are the two major management tools. Theory Y assumes a different type of worker, one who is mature, responsible, and genuinely interested in doing a fair day's work for a fair day's pay. In this instance, the manager sets a tone and direction for the environment within which the worker achieves.

On the face of it, X appears repugnant, while Y is quite attractive. Indeed, the issue resembles the open classroom/closed classroom debates: One is highly structured, rigid, lacking flexibility and enrichment; the other is open, creative, flexible, and enriched. The problem in all of this is clarity of expectations. Theory Y appears to put a great deal of trust in the worker's ability to set goals and achieve those goals without direction from management. Is this possible? Perhaps it is possible in a high-achieving organization populated by mature, experienced, self-actuated people. However, Drucker points out that disaster that occurred at one major university when a Theory Y-oriented official attempted to use Theory Y management as a vehicle for a revolution in quality at the university. It did not work![8]

Some structure is necessary, and it is useful to the manager and the workers if the goals are clear. This is not to suggest that goals, the inputs

---

[7]D. McGregor, "The human side of enterprise" in *Management of human resources*, P. Pigois, C.A. Myers, and F.T. Maim, eds. (New York: McGraw-Hill, 1964).pp. 55–61.

[8]P.F. Drucker, *Management* (New York: Harper &. Row, 1974). p. 233.

needed to achieve those goals, or even the processes of combining those inputs are not negotiable or open to review. But an organization or component without direction is simply confusing itself, everyone around it, and complicating the motivational task of the manager as well as the workers' self-motivational tasks.

Over the past two decades, a number of scholars have advanced other theories of motivation based on observation and research. Many of the newer approaches take a view that motivation is contingent on a number of interacting factors, some within the control of managers, but others clearly outside their purview.

Circumstances do play an important part in a person's need for motivational stimuli and the power of various stimuli. In one organization that I studied, a young man who was a department manager "loved" his job. Each morning he reported bright and eager for the day's events, which were heavily developmental in nature. He enjoyed putting the management systems into place and watching them function as he expected. He thrived on contributing to the senior-level policy meetings in which decisions that affected his department were made. He tackled staff recruiting with a passion. In his third year, he was bored. He could barely drag himself into the office, and the pettiest problems irritated him. He became overbearing with the staff and started shifting his management practices from Theory Y to Theory X.

What was going on? Seemingly, everything was functioning in the way he wanted it to function. The systems he developed worked, and the staff he recruited were excellent. When the organization was stable, however, he was no longer challenged. The tumult of a developing organization excited and motivated him; an ongoing operation represented little personal challenge. Thus, while our limits of understanding motivation can be viewed as an exoneration of anything a manager does, it should be emphasized that understanding human behavior, while a complex task, is indeed the keystone of management. In this example, the organization's director called me in order to find candidates for an innovative senior-level post. The idea of recruiting the young man who had already demonstrated his skills had not been considered; he was seemingly content since he was not complaining.

Theory Z is the term used to describe the Japanese approach to management. This was so intriguing to me that I spent several years studying it in the United States and Japan and subsequently wrote a book on it. The next chapter will consider Theory Z in some detail. Suffice it to say now that Theory Z is an approach to management that recognizes the critical contribution of the human resource in the success of the corporate endeavor. In recognition of this importance, employees are invested in through orientation programs, lifetime employment, and other managerial actions. However, there are dimensions of Theory Z that are neither appropriate or relevant in the American context, and these will be examined in Chapter 8.

In the health care field, the task of motivation is exacerbated both because of the nature of the economic relationship between those using the system and the system itself (physicians, patients, and hospitals) and because of the heterogeneity of the workforce that must be managed. Typically, health care managers are dealing with professionals, semi-professionals, and nonprofessionals, and do not have line or direct authority over all these people. How does a manager motivate a prima-donna surgeon whose behavior is continually fouling up the operating room schedule but whose patient load is an important asset to the institution and who has a strong relationship with the trustees (the manager's boss)? How does a manager get a private practice anesthesiologist on the institution's staff to accept the responsibility for obstetrical anesthesia?

There are no clear-cut solutions to these questions, but they do point out that those in health administration are in the business of motivating key people over whom they have little economic or social control. The two groups affected most are physicians and nurses. A third general group might include the other emerging professionals in the health care organization. To deal more effectively with these groups, it is necessary to understand more about professionalism and the socialization process that these groups undergo.

PROFESSIONALS

In 1933, Carr-Saunders and Wilson identified the three major characteristics of a profession:

1. A lengthy and specialized training that results in the rendering of specialized services to a community;

2. An approach to using the specialized techniques that emphasizes the competence and honor of the individuals using the techniques;
3. A mechanism for quality control within the profession.[9]

In court decisions, a definition of *profession* has been enunciated that defines it by the following four parameters:

1. Prolonged training;
2. Work that is predominantly intellectual and varied in character;
3. Work that requires the exercise of individual discretion;
4. Work that cannot be standardized in relation to a given period of time.[10]

In looking at the physician, Bloom notes in his classic work that "at the core remains the two primary characteristics: (a) a prolonged specialized training in a body of abstract knowledge, and (b) a service orientation."[11] American medicine thus can be defined as a high-status occupation that is supposed to be directed toward a social good, theoretically learned, privy to special knowledge and skills, adhering to high ethical standards, and autonomous.

High status is perhaps a result of the other elements. People who possess specialized and important knowledge, as well as skills valued by society, are often "awarded" high status. This status in turn attracts other people to make the "sacrifices" necessary to obtain the knowledge and skill necessary to become a similar professional.

The three traditional professional areas of medicine, law, and the clergy all have a common element: They meet a societal need for specialized intermediaries. The medical profession acts as an intermediary between man and the environment and, to an extent, between man and himself. The legal profession functions as the intermediary between man and man or man and society. Finally, the clergy functions as the intermediary between man and the supernatural. Each of these professions in recent years has lost a good deal of status due to self-serving behavior, which has included taking advantage of their privileges. The Catholic priests who

---

[9]A.M. Carr-Sanders and P.A. Wilson, *The professions* (Oxford: Clarendon Press 1933), p. 284.
[10]*Aulen v. Triumph Explosive*, D.C. Md. 58 F. Supp. 4.
[11]S. Bloom, *The doctor and his patient* (New York: The Free Press, 1965), p. 89.

have violated their sacred calling by inappropriate sexual behavior, the physicians who have violated the law through fraud and abuse, the lawyers who have misappropriated client's funds, not only do they bring disgrace and dishonor upon themselves, but they also impugn their entire professions.

Nevertheless, every work group wants to be a "profession." It appears that new professions are legitimized when society needs people to interface with some component of society that cannot be handled routinely by the average person. The concept involves control. When people lose or feel unable to establish control over important elements in society, special status and privileges are granted to those individuals who will act for the societal good as controllers of the elements in question.

This concept of controllers can be recognized in the fact that professionals must expend considerable time and effort to acquire the knowledge and skills to practice their professions. Clearly, if the knowledge and skill of any profession could be acquired easily, there would be no reason whatsoever for singling out members of the profession for special status.

Because of their special knowledge and skills, professionals have a contract with society. In the case of medicine, society says, "You practice your skills to the best of your ability, and we will give you special privileges." These privileges range from parking a car anywhere to probing the innermost parts of the human body, cutting it up with knives, and injecting a variety of substances into it. Each privilege of a profession is specific. Thus, what is appropriate in the interactions between a lawyer and client differs from what is appropriate between a physician and patient. A final clause of this contract is that society admits that it cannot properly evaluate the quality of the profession's work and therefore the profession itself must take on the major responsibility for evaluating its own functioning. In essence, a profession in the United States effectively controls itself.

Professional Control

The central, and one of the most important, channels through which the health profession exercises its control is undergraduate medical education. Such authors as Hyde and the staff of the *Yale Law Journal* have noted that the American Medical Association's Council on Medical Education in fact controls the nation's medical schools. For many years, it has been the actual authority for the licensing of medical schools, although the nominal power rests with the state.[12] The result, Kessel contends, is a natural or franchised monopoly that allows American medicine to regulate its own production.[13]

The second channel of control for the profession is postgraduate medical education. In many states, a one-year internship must be taken after graduation from medical school before new physicians are eligible for licensure. Physicians often desire additional training beyond internships. Although this training is usually taken with a hospital, it is still subject to approval by one of the review committees of the Council on Medical Education. Licensure, professional status, and privileges rest on an approved internship or residency.

Licensure, the legal sanction to practice provided to a physician by the state through its medical practice act, denotes general and sometimes specific qualifications. Prior to the medical licensure acts, individual medical schools or preceptors gave new physicians their "license" to practice medicine. Present licensure, although a state function, is in fact controlled by the medical profession through the state board of medical examiners, the agency that tests and licenses physicians. These boards are composed primarily of physicians, who most often are recommended for their positions by organized medical associations.

Professional status and subsequent privileges, such as entree into the hospital, the main arena of practice, are firmly predicated upon an approved education and postgraduate training. A physician must be trained by profession-approved institutions, in profession-prescribed programs, and must pass profession-designed, profession-administered, and profession-graded examinations. Ultimately, the board of trustees of a hospital grants a physician privileges, but not until the medical board sanctions the appointment: In essence, the board acts as a rubber stamp for the medical staff in these decisions.

In summary then, the medical profession controls itself from the beginning (medical education) to the end (privileges). It is a natural monopoly, although the profession's hold might be loosened if there were appropriate alternatives.

---

[12]D.R. Hyde, et al., "The American Medical Association: Power, Purpose, and Politics in Organized Medicine," *Yale Law Journal, 63*(7) (1954), 937–1022.

[13]R.A. Kessel, "Price discrimination in medicine," *Journal of Law and Economics, I*(2) (1958), 20–53.

Some would argue that chiropractors, osteopaths, or even midwives compete with physicians in the health care field. It is well recognized, however, that competitors do not account for a great percentage of the medical care delivered.

Further, such competitors are generally kept outside the medical care system by the medical profession through its privileged societal position as gatekeeper to the system. Physicians sit on the boards of examiners of competing professions, which sometimes include little or no representation from the profession being licensed. Additionally, through their involvement in Blue Cross and Blue Shield and government reimbursement programs, physicians have made it difficult, if not impossible, for competing professions to obtain third-party payment for services, preventing a large pool of potential patients from economically using alternative services.

Perhaps most importantly, the physicians are in the dominant position in the utilization of the health facilities of a community. Not only do they control the entrance of their peers into the institutions, they also control the entrance of others. For example, midwives or chiropractors can seldom avail themselves of hospital equipment or technology. A facility owned by and operated for the community is controlled in essence by a small group to the exclusion of any possible competition.

Central to management's concerns about motivation of the physician is an understanding of their professional value system, which, it can be argued, largely determines their likely behavior. What was learned during those early years of training shapes their motivation and attitudes toward their own practice and the activities of other health providers that they must interact with in the health system.

The basic theoretical framework for this was set out by Parsons. He suggests that the physician's role can be explained in terms of four pattern variables, or choices that relate to specific motivational and value orientations.[14] Their role, Parsons suggests, is functionally specific; their work relates only to medicine, and technical competence is the keystone of status. In effect, he says that physicians should be and should always strive to remain technically competent. A second attribute is that of neutrality, meaning that physicians should behave in an objective, evaluative, and, in a sense, unemotional manner. The third variable is identified by Parsons as

---

[14]T. Parsons, *The social system* (Glencoe, IL: The Free Press, 1961), pp. 428–460.

collective orientation. He notes that "the ideology of the profession lays great emphasis on the obligation of the physician to put the welfare of the patient above his personal interest." The final attribute is universalism; physicians must abide by the overall rules of the profession as approved in the specific relationships between them and their patients. In discussing this, Bloom uses the example of euthanasia: "the professional rule about it is the MD's guidepost to his behavior in treating painful terminal illness."

It can be seen that the motivation of professionals requires skills in negotiation and politics, not simply directing. For example, appeals to generalized notions of quality, technical competence, professional standards, and the general well-being of a class of patients are likely to produce more action than economic or political threats (either overt or masked).

SEMIPROFESSIONALS AND EMERGING PROFESSIONALS

Large numbers of people working in health organizations may be classified as semiprofessionals or emerging professionals. In many respects, what they do has some of the flavor of a profession: the work is cerebral in nature, the training takes several years after high school, and, in many respects, it is difficult for someone not in the particular field to judge the quality of a person's output. The way our system has been structured, however, these people are not autonomous and must function as part of an organization.

An interesting example of this is the nurse-midwife, a person who has had college and nursing training, postbaccalaureate education, specialized training of one to two years, and probably considerable experience. In many countries, including most of Western Europe, she (in most cases, the nurse-midwife is a woman) functions as independently as a physician. In the United States, however, she must function under the supervision of a physician and in all but a few instances as part of a larger organization, such as a hospital or clinic, where her role is in large measure defined by the organization.

A cynic could make a convincing argument that the health system teases people with the notion of professionalism. In fact, it may be a way of keeping people in line when, because of the tight structure of the system, there is no way for an individual to advance. Physician's assistants are a case in point.

The professional and emerging professional groups are composed of individuals who, for the most part, have trained in and around the health system and whose jobs, for the most part, are restricted to the health system. For example, the jobs outside of the health system for a nurse, physician, or X-ray technician are quite limited. Others who work in the health system, such as an accountant or housekeeper, could just as easily be working in other parts of the public or private sector. Since their interest and commitment to the health system may be somewhat different from those whose careers are dependent on the system, what interests or motivates them may also be different.

MANAGERIAL APPROACHES TO MOTIVATION

There are several specific managerial approaches to motivation. Fear is perhaps the most widely used (or at least considered) approach. Joseph Heller's statement in his book *Something Happened* should become a classic:

> In the office in which I work there are five people of whom I am afraid. Each of these five people is afraid of four people (excluding overlaps), for a total of twenty, and each of these twenty people is afraid of six people, making a total of one hundred and twenty people who are feared by at least one person. Each of these one hundred and twenty people is afraid of another one hundred and nineteen, and all of these one hundred and forty-five people are afraid of the twelve men at the top who helped found and build the company and now own and direct it.[15]

Fear perhaps derives from the child-adult conflict many people feel. The boss is the adult; the worker, the child. Workers look to the person in authority for recognition and advancement and, to a large measure, find themselves being defined by the job they have, the organization they work for, and the evaluation they receive from their superior. An interesting and all-too-prevalent conflicting (and conflicted) managerial type is what Einstein Associates, an executive recruiting firm, labeled years ago as the *counterfeit executive*: a person who kicks the people below while simultaneously caressing the people above.

---

[15]J. Heller, *Something happened* (New York: Ballantine, 1975), p. 9.

Fear certainly works in certain situations, but as a long-run strategy, it is likely to attract and hold the wrong people in an organization. Although tension can be a creative force in the organization, the source of the tension should not be fear but instead a person's motivation to achieve and excel through a positive set of incentives.

Herzberg makes a strong case for job enrichment as a way of motivating people. Job enrichment, he suggests, loads a job vertically, not horizontally. Horizontal loading "merely enlarges the meaninglessness of the job." He suggests that making 20,000 bolts a day rather than 10,000 or doing two meaningless tasks rather than one is simply of little value. Vertical loading (or enrichment) makes the job more meaningful by giving the employee greater control over its processes and inputs. For example, he suggests "removing some controls while retaining accountability" as one mechanism of motivating people through their own sense of personal responsibility and achievement.

A second mechanism Herzberg suggests is shortening the evaluation and feedback loops by "making periodic reports directly available to the worker himself rather than to the supervisor." This is one way of providing internal recognition. Herzberg clearly states that it is management's responsibility to develop the job enrichment scheme and that the value of employee participation in the development phases is limited. He notes that "it is the content that will produce the motivation, not attitudes about being involved or the challenge inherent in setting up a job." Some jobs in health care lend themselves to job enrichment activities, but others are excluded as candidates for enrichment because of technical or legal requirements.

A different, perhaps related, approach is that of active, effective, or dynamic listening. This is an idea that is found in management communication as well as child development literature. The notion is deceivingly simple: Listen to what people really mean when they talk. The problem is that most people communicate in a coded form; to be most responsive, the listener must break through the code. Motivating another requires a true understanding of what that person is saying and feeling. Thus, the spoken message must be examined on a variety of levels and responded to at the most useful level.

There are also a great many nonverbal messages to which the active listener can respond, such as low productivity, absenteeism, poor quality work, and other indicators of a person's distress. Many managers want to be able to rectify these situations with a quick stroke of the pen or a few words; oftentimes, however, a significantly greater investment is necessary before there can be any return.

ORGANIZATIONAL MOTIVATION

A related question is: What motivates this impersonal entity called an organization? For example, why would a hospital decide to develop an innovative ambulatory care program? What does such a development mean to management and those people potentially involved with such a program? A hospital usually involves itself in a new ambulatory care program for several reasons. There may be a declining census ("If we had a new ambulatory care program, we could assure ourselves of a flow of patients") and a companion problem of finances, which could be helped if a new service were developed to utilize ancillary services. Another problem might be competition from a hospital across the street or across town. The most likely reason for involvement in new programs, however, is some difficulty with existing facilities and programs. Typically, the traffic in the emergency room has increased dramatically with non-emergency patients, staffing is not optimal, follow-up is poor, and the hospital views itself as extremely vulnerable to lawsuits, poor public relations, and poor medical care unless it does something. The something then becomes a new program or a major reorganization.

Other factors that generate a demand for innovation and change include a perceived patient demand for services, which is often verified through a statistical analysis; the need of an institution to fulfill its "destiny" to become a community or comprehensive institution; and, finally, the need of people within the organization to get their own adrenaline flowing through planning and developing new programs.

Assuming that a community hospital has decided to develop an ambulatory care program, what kind of people should it hire for its management and delivery staff? Who should be the medical director, manager, physicians, nurses, and so forth? Should they be certain kinds of people, or will virtually anyone do? It is argued here that, although the motivation of the people who are engaged to begin this project is critical to its initial success, the project's viability over the long run may be related to either the development of the original team or its replacement. Just as football teams have found that they can be most successful with offensive and defensive teams, organizations may have to learn that there are certain people who need the excitement of working in young and developing programs, while others prefer to work in older, more established ones.

What is needed initially is a group of hardy people who thrive on the excitement of moving into uncharted areas and who can stand up to the pressure of a medical staff that is likely to be less than enthusiastic, perhaps even hostile. These people should love the excitement of change and debate and are skilled enough to reach desired outcomes. In some ways, they are the gourmet cooks of the management field. They love trying something new and different; they are very skillful, but the fun is in the cooking (once) and not in the eating. Such persons are motivated by challenge, responsibility, autonomy, and recognition. They are not turned on by security or personal survival.

The organization's time frame and interests go on significantly longer than those of the people involved in developing the program. While the innovators are interested in starting a new and exciting program, the hospital must be concerned about the program's existence in 10 years. To keep that first team interested may require continual changes in the new program, which may be unnecessary or even unacceptable to the hospital. For example, a community hospital develops a hospital-based ambulatory care group practice with four physicians and a manager. It takes two very exciting years to establish this practice, and by the middle of the third year it is running smoothly and breaking even financially. Everyone gives much credit for the success of the program to the group's medical director and manager, who have been involved since the program's inception and have nurtured it since its infancy. The founding fathers are bound together because of the internal developmental problems as well as the external threats they have faced. Listening to them over coffee is like overhearing Vietnam veterans on Friday night at the VFW post. Three years later, the practice has become routine, and the old war horses are ready for some new challenges.

The question for the institution is whether these challenges should come from inside the practice or outside the practice. Is change necessary for the practice itself or for keeping the staff motivated? Is it time for the developmental team to move on and be replaced by others whose motivation is different? The answers are related to what the organization wants to do with that program. If the organization does not wish to take an active stand, then a new round of developments, such as program expansion or

facility and staff changes, can be expected. These will inevitably be justified on the basis of patient demand, but, in large part, they may be generated by the developers' desires to feed their own motivational needs.

LEADERSHIP AND MANAGEMENT

Motivation requires leadership—but is there something called leadership,
or is it simply a euphemism for good management? Management literature is replete with articles on leadership, both formal and informal, and
the role that leaders play in organizations. The military and other large
organizations often provide training in leadership; yet there is controversy
over the very existence of leadership types and management types.
Presidential primaries and races are often about leadership. No candidates
suggest, "I will be the person who can manage the country better than the
other candidate." Rather, what fills the airwaves are promises of a "new
leadership." Some of the controversy is related to academic interventions,
suggesting that leadership can be taught, much like financial techniques.
In fact, there is an ongoing debate in the field of health administration
over who shall train the leaders and who shall train the managers. All of
this is rather value laden, in that leaders are considered the top-level group
and managers are at least a rung or two down.

In a superb article on the subject, Zalesnick argues that managers and
leaders are different types of people.[16] It is recognized, of course, that certain people are leaders by virtue of their positions, such as the director of
a community mental health center or a hospital. At a different level, there
can be a certain degree of leadership from a department head or supervisor. The critical point that Zalesnick raises concerns the difference in
personality traits between a leader and a manager. He suggests that managers and leaders differ in attitudes toward goals, conceptions of work,
behavior toward risk taking, relations with others, and their sense of self.
In his view, leaders are active in terms of setting goals and tend to per-
sonalize them, that is, they see goals as an extension of themselves.
Managers' views of goals, on the other hand, are rather impersonal and
are directed by organizational needs. It is suggested that managers
respond to goals; they do not initiate them. Their goals do not become

---

[16]A. Zalesnick, "Managers and leaders: Are they different?" *Harvard Business Review,* 55(3)
(1977), 67–78.

the organization's; rather, the organization's goals become theirs. In terms of conceptions of work, leaders are characterized by Zalesnick as movers and shakers, artists who are very much integrated into their own work. They are, he suggests, visionaries, people who excite others with their own vision of what could or should happen. Managers are the doers, those who, through their skills, can make things happen. Everyone has known people who had great ideas but were simply unable to implement them.

This dichotomy, according to Zalesnick, leads to a different type of risk behavior on the part of the two types. Leaders like to gamble and take risks; they get excited about the possible return on their enormous investment. Managers are considerably more conservative; they tend to be survival-oriented and are much more calculating, perhaps far more reality-oriented. A leader's concept of reality may be more global and is certainly more challenging than a manager's.

In terms of working with others, Zalesnick clearly characterizes managers as people who have a need to work with others but in a somewhat orchestrated way. He suggests that managers are role players who might say to themselves, "If I am a manager, what should I do?" Much of their time and effort is spent in conflict resolution, which requires them to wear various masks. This might lead people to ask about a manager: "I wonder what kind of person he really is?" Leaders seem to have more highly charged relationships with others, perhaps love-hate relationships. When they get involved, they get deeply involved. It sometimes appears that leaders have no gray areas in their relationships; they are either on or off.

A final area considered by Zalesnick is that of self-concept. He suggests that leaders feel very much a part of a global community, not simply a part of an organization. Although managers derive a major portion of their identity from the organization that employs them, a leader's identity is very much supraorganizational.

Based on my own research in an ambulatory care organization, in which a few dozen of these developing and established programs were studied, it appears that such personality types do indeed exist and are important to organizations. For example, several years ago, a 400-bed hospital located in a major metropolitan area received a modest grant from a private foundation to start a hospital-based ambulatory care unit. It engaged as its program director a 40-year-old physician who was trained as a surgeon but who wished to work full-time for the institution in order to start this program and to organize all of their ambulatory care facilities. He was an exciting and attractive person who seemed to inspire strong feelings (both positive and negative) on the part of those he met. His vision of ambulatory care was very much in concert with that of the foundation, the hospital director, and the board, but quite contrary to that of the hospital medical staff. Over the first year of the new program, he spent much of his time sharing his vision and convincing the medical staff of its accuracy. He was interested only in the broad outlines of making the program functional, not the details. His friends and adversaries described him as a charmer and a diplomat, and as someone who shoots from the hip. His ideas and plans were rarely carefully detailed but always exciting. His personnel decisions tended to be made quickly, seemingly by instinct. For example, a young physician in the program had been with this man only a few minutes when he was offered the job. The director liked him and that was enough.

Managing the program was a 30-year-old business school graduate. Rarely was he involved in generating major new concepts for change, but he was, in a sense, the leader's simultaneous translator, taking his ideas and visions, perhaps putting a bit of his own personal twist on them, and then translating these concepts into a workable plan. The manager enjoyed understanding which buttons to push to make the program function and then pushing the buttons.

Both of these people were most excited by the idea of working in a new, innovative, and somewhat glamorous program. As the program started to age, however, each became a bit disenchanted, not by the program, but by the lack of managerial challenge for one and the lack of leadership challenge for the other. The leader went off to take on new tasks and become more involved in activities outside of the hospital. The manager, on the other hand, looked within the job for more challenges and eventually began searching for a new and more exciting managerial position.

In this example, the two people recognized themselves and each other as a manager and a leader, and they were pleased to play their respective roles. They enjoyed each other's professional company and respected each other, although they were totally uninvolved socially and knew little about each other's lives outside of the institution. They were in every sense of the word a team that worked. While it was important for the manager to recognize and not be threatened by the presence of a strong leader, it was equally important for the leader to recognize that his ideas and programs would be so much hot air unless a manager translated them into action and programs. The hospital administrators had not planned this strategy of organization, but, having observed its functioning, they have become extremely sensitized to its value.

How does an organization recognize people who are motivated in one way or another? This is a chemistry problem, since how people react and function in one organization may not indicate how they will behave in another situation. Universities are often confronted by applicants who have poor undergraduate records and now want to go to graduate school. They always say that they were not motivated before. What has happened between 18 and 21 that might have turned a mediocre undergraduate student into a star graduate student? The answer, it would appear, has to do with the chemistry of maturity and ambition—the person is now "turned on." While one clear indicator of probable success is a person's track record, others might be evident to someone who is listening carefully to an applicant. The challenge, then, to management is not only to recognize obvious talent but also to "turn on" latent talent.

Case Study 7-1
HOSPITAL HOUSEKEEPING CARE

The housekeeping department at the 330-bed Jewish Hospital of Philadelphia is managed by Mrs. Ethel Greenburg, a 55-year-old widow who is a Russian immigrant. Prior to working at this hospital, Mrs. Greenburg spent eight years as the assistant executive housekeeper at Central General Hospital in Philadelphia, a 550-bed government hospital. Mrs. Greenburg's background includes one year of nurse's training in Moscow and graduation from a two-year post-high-school training program at the Soviet National School of Hotel Management in Moscow. In the Soviet Union, Mrs. Greenburg worked in various administrative capacities in different hotels. Prior to leaving her country, she was one of four assistant managers at a 300-room modern "intercontinental" hotel. Since arriving in the United States 10 years ago, Mrs. Greenburg has been active in hospital housekeeping circles, attending seminars and professional meetings.

(continues)

Case Study 7-1

In Mrs. Greenburg's present assignment as executive housekeeper of Jewish Hospital of Philadelphia, she is responsible for a staff of 20 men and 25 women, as well as for the administration of a budget of close to two million dollars. Approximately half of the employees in the department are Hispanic, and the other half are black, including several from Haiti. The department is organized with Mrs. Greenburg as the head and Mr. Iglesiada, a Puerto Rican, as assistant head. All staff assignments are approved by Mrs. Greenburg weekly after Mr. Iglesiada submits to her a schedule of activities for each cleaner, maid, and janitor. Both Mrs. Greenburg and Mr. Iglesiada interview each prospective employee. Mr. Iglesiada has been at the hospital for nine years and has worked his way up from janitor to assistant department head. Prior to Mrs. Greenburg's arrival, he functioned adequately as acting department head for three months after the previous department head retired from the position after 37 years at the hospital. He was generally well regarded by the employees but viewed as unprofessional and a poor manager by the management.

Since Mrs. Greenburg's arrival, the quality of housekeeping in the institution has improved slightly. Relations between the department heads of housekeeping, dietary, laundry, maintenance, and nursing have become markedly better, but the morale among the staff has deteriorated. Turnover and absenteeism have increased dramatically, and it appears that union activity has increased in this unit.

The assistant administrator has discussed the morale problem with Mrs. Greenburg, who feels that Mr. Iglesiada is undermining her efforts to professionalize the housekeeping service. Mr. Iglesiada, she contends, is making it difficult to install new mechanized cleaning equipment, develop more efficient work schedules, and run an effective

(continues)

Case Study 7-1

inservice training program. Mrs. Greenburg's analysis is that the department had been loosely run and that treatment based on favoritism had been the norm under the previous department head.

Mr. Iglesiada argues that Mrs. Greenburg was a bad choice for the job because she is insensitive to the needs of the workers and is only interested in "her own ego trip," not in the best interests of the hospital. Mr. Iglesiada has threatened to quit unless Mrs. Greenburg is dismissed, and he says that half the department will leave if he does.

The assistant administrator thinks that about 10 or 15 employees might quit if Mr. Iglesiada left. Although he believes that he did an adequate job as acting department head, he does not think that Mr. Iglesiada has the managerial experience and perhaps the potential (although there is uncertainty about this) to be the department head.

DISCUSSION QUESTIONS

1. What are the probable points of conflict between Mrs. Greenburg and Mr. Iglesiada? Between Mrs. Greenburg and the staff?

2. What options are available for resolution? What might be the costs and benefits of these possible resolutions?

Theory Z:
An Alternative
Approach

This chapter will present an extensive review and analysis of Theory Z, the Japanese approach, because American managers and students of management periodically look abroad for solutions to their managerial problems. Not too many years ago, it was the factories of Sweden and at times the British and the Germans who were considered to have the answers. Indeed, we can track this phenomenon by our level of interest in various autos: Volvo and Saab, Rolls Royce, BMW, or Mercedes. Today, it's a Lexus for the rich and a Honda for the thrifty. Who knows—the future may be the Kia and Hyundai! But for the past few decades, the focus of managerial attention has been on Japan. According to a number of commentators, the Japanese have a magic formula that, when applied to ailing American industry and government, will solve the problems of alienation, turnover, and productivity.[1,2,3]

THE MAGIC POTION OF
JAPANESE MANAGERIAL SUCCESS

The "magic potion" that has become popularized in the United States boils down to the following elements: lifetime employment; a company concern for its employees' total well-being; consensus decision making;

---

[1]E.P. Vogel, *Japan as number 1* (New York: Harper Colophon,1980).
[2]P.P. Drucker, "What we can learn from Japanese management," *Harvard Business Review, 59* (3) (1971), 110–122.
[3]P. Patton, "Bringing the Japanese work ethic to the U.S.A," *Pan Am Clipper* (May 1982), p. 43.

the development of company-oriented generalist managers rather than professionally oriented specialists; a steady, but by American standards slow, system of promotions with little formal evaluation; and an organizational orientation toward the long run.[4,5,6] Some observers credit the great successes of the Japanese to their managerial approach and point out that its history dates back to the samurai and Confucius.[7,8] Of course, they do not explain why these approaches, now credited with a tightly organized and productive industrial machine producing first-rate goods, also gave the world poor quality and technologically unsophisticated merchandise during an earlier period. It is suggested that using historical antecedents as explanations for the present day successes, Japan is akin to invoking the Puritan ethic in America: full of nostalgia but hardly enlightening.

STEREOTYPING JAPANESE INDUSTRY

This chapter will examine the concepts that appear to be the bulwark of Japanese management. However, before examining them, we must recognize some important facts about Japanese industry, the literature on Japanese management, and about ourselves. The Tofflers, long-time observers and analysts of Japan, note that Americans tend to view Japan in a stereotypical fashion, seeing a nation of 115,000,000 as docile, dedicated, and highly motivated workers smoothly managed by a few giant paternalistic corporations whose top leaders work hand in glove with an understanding government."[9] This simplistic characterization of the Japanese, they note, is a dangerous building block for racism. Indeed, in the wake of the difficult economic times in the United States and the

---

[4]W. Ouchi, *Theory z* (Reading, MA: Addison-Wesley, 1981).

[5]R.T. Pascale and A.G. Athos, *The art of Japanese management* (New York: Simon & Schuster, 1981).

[6]R. Hayes, "Why Japanese factories work," *Harvard Business Review, 59*(4) (1981), 57–66.

[7]M. Musabi, *The book of five rings: The real art of Japanese management*, trans. Nibon Services Corporation (New York: Bantam Books, 1982).

[8]R. Yates, "Japan's business excellence goes to the roots of its culture," *Chicago Tribune,* April 15, 1982, Section 2, p. 3.

[9]A. Toffter and H. Toffter, "Sifting facts from fiction about number 1," *Japan Times Weekly,*. March 7, 1981.

apparently healthy economy in Japan, a number of articles have indicated the development of an anti-Japanese sentiment, in part making the case that Japan is an exploiter, rather than an excellent manager, of its labor resources.[10,11,12]

JAPAN, INC.: DOES IT EXIST?

The literature that told the story of the amazing success of "Japan, Inc.," focused on the largest industries in Japan, often the world-wide trading companies. The examples offered were the Sony Corporation, Toyota, Mitsui, Panasonic, or Mitsubishi companies. In fact, Japanese industry is primarily made up of smaller business organizations. In discussing this aspect of Japanese business the Japan Press Center noted that "smaller business establishments account for 99.7% of all Japanese companies . . . [and] in 1999 they accounted for 51.7% of all shipments by manufacturing industries, 62.3% of sales by wholesale businesses, and 73.3% of retail sales."[13] For classification purposes, a small business is one with fewer than 50 employees if retail; 100 employees if the business is service or wholesale; and 300 employees if in the rest of the economy such as manufacturing.[14]

These points concerning the size of Japanese industry become increasingly important when one realizes that the magic of Japanese management is not evenly diffused throughout the system. For example, quality circles are most likely to be found in the largest corporations and, as Woronoff, a well-known commentator on the Japanese scene, notes, productivity increases appear to be a function of size, with the largest companies doing considerably better than the smaller ones. He further notes that there was a decline in productivity in the service sector of the economy between 1970 and 1978.[15]

[10]S. Roberts, "In Ohio, the enemy is Japan," *New York Times*, April 25, 1982, p. F-8.

[11]J. Matthews, "Japanese as 'sneaky little yellow people,'" *Japan Times*, May 19, 1982, p. 16.

[12]S. Kamata, *Japan in the passing lane* (New York: Pantheon, 1982).

[13]Japanese Prime Minster's Office, *81 Japan* (Tokyo: Statistics Bureau,1981).

[14]Ibid., p. 31.

[15]J. Woronoff, *Japan's wasted workers* (Tokyo: Lotus Press, 1981), pp. 14–17.

THE JAPANESE LABOR SCENE

Unionization

Unions play an interesting and important role in the full spectrum of Japanese organizations, including the health care industry. While there has been a decline in union membership from 28.9% of the labor force in 1985 to 21.3% of the labor force in 2001, there are sectors of the economy with strong union penetration, such as government with 62.8% union membership; finance and insurance with 40.6% union membership, and transport and communication with 38.2% union membership.[16,17,18]

Enterprise Unions

Perhaps what is most interesting about Japanese unions is their tradition of enterprise unions. The enterprise union is basically a company-specific union that evolved after World War II. As Cole defines it, the enterprise union has members from both the blue- and white-collar workforce as well as temporary and regular employees. Membership is automatic upon joining the company. Union officers are elected by the membership and paid their salary by the union, but always retain their company employee status. This, Cole suggests, results in union officials seeing "their union activities as an opportunity to provide service to the company and a means of enhancing their promotion opportunities."[19] Evidence of this assertion is found in an information bulletin from the Ministry of Foreign Affairs, which points out that in a survey of large corporations, 16.2% of the executives were former union leaders.[20]

But it should be noted that the Japanese labor relations situation is not without its ups and downs. In the year 2000 there were 958 labor disputes affecting 1.1 million employees. This led to a total of 118 strikes (of a half day or more) involving 15,000 employees. There were a total of 35,000 lost days of work with 45% of these occurring in the transport and com-

---

[16]"Figuring out Japan," *Japan Times*, May 5, 1982, p. 1.
[17]"Japanese labor unions and 'shunto'." *Focus Japan*, JSA, JSB, March 1982.
[18]R. Cole, "Enterprise unions," in *Business and society in Japan*, B.M. Richarson and Taizo Ueda, eds. (New York: Praeger, 1981), pp. 36–37.
[19]Ibid., p. 41.
[20]Ministry of Foreign Affairs, Public Information and Cultural Affairs Bureau,"Unions are pools for future executives," Japanese *Information Bulletin, 29*(1) (January 15, 1982).

munication industry and 37% in the manufacturing industry. The Ministry of Health, Labor, and Welfare reported 1,279 labor disputes in the year 2000 with almost 70% of these disputes related to wages and another 20% related to business and personnel administration. Perhaps what is most interesting are the statistics about the methods used to settle these disputes: 38% were settled by conciliation provided through the labor relations commission while 42% were settled through a third party.

So, in thinking about Japan, we must factor into our equation the information that 80% of the workforce is not unionized and, in some sense, not protected by collective bargaining agreements, and that the union has a company-wide, as opposed to an industry-wide, focus, which causes the union to identify strongly with the success of the organization.

A Homogeneous Workforce

A second crucial point to consider is that the Japanese are, for the most part, dealing with an ethnically homogeneous work force. The Japanese work force is almost entirely Japanese, virtually every member having been born in Japan, having had a similar standardized primary school education and having been socialized to the values, attitudes, and beliefs of the Japanese society and family. Consider the implications of the following data: Between 1972 and 1980 Japan's divorce rate was under 1%—one of the lowest in the developed world, by 1983 it had climbed to 1.51 per 1,000 persons and by 1997 to 1.78 per 1,000 persons. By comparison, in 2002 the United States rate is estimated to be 4.0 per 1,000 persons.[21,22] Thus for the Japanese youngster, who eventually becomes the Japanese worker, the years of childhood will likely be with an intact family and an employed father and, more likely than not, the full-time attention of a mother. The Japanese also share their Buddhist or Shinto religions as well as their range of secular holidays. All of this is in sharp contrast to the United States, where the production workforces, and to some extent the managerial workforces, particularly in hospitals, come from all social classes, ethnic backgrounds, and frequently, foreign countries. The mosaic society of America is reflected in its workforce and the managerial problems that are encountered. For example, of the 1,100

---

[21]"Divorce in Japan," *Japan Times,*" December 14, 1981.
[22]U.S. Department of Commerce, *Statistical Abstract of the United States,* 102nd ed. (Table 124, Marriages and Divorces, 1950–1979), 1981, p. 80.

employees in the health system that I managed we had three major language groups and employees from over a dozen countries. Clearly, the mosaic society of America is reflected in its work force and the managerial problems that are encountered.

Some Japanese companies recently have gained first-hand experience with the problems of a heterogeneous workforce because they have opened production facilities in the United States. They have encountered a range of difficulties as the two cultures have come into contact with one another. In some instances, the Japanese branch manager has difficulty making the home office understand the American way of relating to employees, and in other instances, the Japanese manager must make significant stylistic adjustments in order to manage in the United States. It is suggested that the task of managing people with a shared socialization and value system is easier (and certainly less challenging) than the task of managing a work group comprising people from different social classes. For an evening of entertainment and enlightenment on this point I suggest watching the movie, *Gung Ho*, starring Michael Keaton. It is a well done story about a community that is trying to save itself by bringing a Japanese auto manufacturer into town and the ensuing culture clashes.

A third point is that Japan, Inc. doesn't exist. The idea that government and industry are happily marching down the street together, both holding hands with labor, is a simplistic overstatement. As Drucker points out, the Japanese government has not been able to get the computer manufacturers to pool their resources, and there is considerable competition in Japan for both the domestic and foreign markets.[23] Put simply, whether it is cars or computers, Japan is not one big happy family.

THE ELEMENTS OF JAPANESE MANAGERIAL SUCCESS

Now we shall turn our attention to the five elements that are allegedly the secret of Japanese managerial success.

---

[23]P. Drucker, "Behind Japan's success," *Harvard Business Review*, *59*,(1) (1981), 83-90.

Lifetime Employment

The first of these elements is lifetime or permanent employment. To begin, it is clear from the literature and interviews that the Japanese company hires most of its staff with the intention that those hired will be permanent employees. However, this concept, as most westerners understand it, is grossly oversimplified. For example, lifetime employment defines *lifetime* fairly narrowly, normally from the time of first hiring (somewhere between ages 18 and 24) to the retirement age of 55. In actual practice, we are usually talking about a 30-year contract, the most productive 30 years of one's life.[24] After 55, in most cases, workers receive a lump sum payment, usually equal to one month's pay for each year of service, and are sent off on their own. With life expectancies in excess of 70 for males and 75 for females, there is still plenty of life that the company isn't concerning itself with. But to one important commentator, Tadashi Hanami, professor of law and dean of the School of Law at Sophia University, lifetime employment is a powerful force. It ensures "strong loyalty to and identification with their enterprise. Since they stay in the same enterprise for their entire working lives, their fate and well-being depend almost entirely on the prosperity of the enterprise."[25]

A second point of significance is that the Japanese workforce is divided into two groups: permanent employees and temporary employees. The latter group, representing an estimated 20% of the workforce, does not have lifetime employment status. Women, as a category of worker, are also usually excluded from the permanent employee category. All of this does not preclude a company from discharging temporary employees and temporarily laying off permanent employees or shifting them to other parts of the firm. There are numerous stories in the literature describing how companies have sent their production workers into the field to sell the companies' products to stimulate demand or how top executives' salaries were cut to save the jobs of workers.

Another aspect of the lifetime employment question is from the perspective of the potential employee. In a study of graduating male college seniors, the Nippon Recruit Center found that 69.4% of those surveyed expected to work for the same company until retirement; 8.6% thought

---

[24]R. Clark, *The Japanese company* (New Haven: Yale University Press, 1979), p. 174.
[25]T. Hanarni, *Labor relations in Japan* (Tokyo: Kodansha, 1979), p. 28.

they would change employers; and 21.7% thought that eventually they would go into business for themselves.[26] In short, lifetime employment in Japan is a situation in which both employers and employees expect a long-term commitment to the organization and can act on that commitment in making personal and personnel investments.

Economic imperatives are also changing these traditions. There has been a rising percentage of the workforce over 55 years of age: in 1975 there were 15.1% of workers over 55 years of age and in 2000 the percentage had risen to 23.4%. In response to this, the government has been urging industry to raise its retirement age. Simultaneously many corporations have had to deal with restructuring as well as global ownership (Nissan is now controlled by the French company Renault), which has resulted in early retirement packages. Another strategy to deal with economic uncertainty includes the use of temporary contract workers: in 1986 corporations used 86,000 people by 2000 the number was up to 1.39 million staff. Finally, in Japan there is a new category of workers called "freeter" possibly derived from the word *free*. These are young people who are stringing together several part time positions that allow them to manage their own time and pursue other options in life such as music and art. In 1997 it was estimated that there were 1.5 million "freeters."[27]

Holistic Concern for the Employee

The second element of Japanese managerial success is a concern for the total welfare of the employee. This concern is evidenced by the provision of company housing and a wide range of social programs for employees, including sports and cultural clubs, health benefits, retirement programs, vacation resorts, and almost anything else that can be conjured up. In discussing this attitude of holism, Chie Nakane wrote in her seminal work that new employees "were trained by the company not only technically but also morally. In Japan it has always been believed that individual moral and mental attitudes have an important bearing on productive power."[28] For those of us who have spent any number of years in the

---

[26]Japan's job hunting season. *Focus Japan*, October, 1981, pp. JSA, JSB.
[27]*Japan: A Pocket Guide*, 2002 edition, pp. 70–71.
[28]C. Nakane, *Japanese society* (New York: Penguin, 1970), p. 17.

armed forces, particularly on remote foreign duty stations, the holistic approach of the Japanese company is strikingly familiar.

The folklore of Japanese management is full of stories about corporations inducting new employees into the firm with the parents of the new employees essentially turning their children over to the company as locum parentis. While I did not observe any such dramatic activity in hospitals, this text will show the strength of the commitment made to the new employee, as evidenced by programs such as the intensive orientation periods. Is this typical in the United States? Again, the military analogy is apt: Think of the drama of the commissioning, promotion, or awards ceremonies or the "birthday parties" held each year for the services or even the units in the services. For example, there is the tradition of the annual MSC birthday party in the Navy, where hundreds of officers share an evening of celebration, ostensibly to celebrate the birthday of the founding of the medical service corps.

Worker Orientation Periods

One important development of this holistic concern is the general practice among Japanese companies of hiring employees once a year and providing an orientation, often in the neighborhood of 10 days, to the entire group. This practice accomplishes three purposes: It develops "team" spirit; it builds a support network among all new employees who begin their working careers at the same time; and it allows the company to invest more heavily in orientation because it occurs only once a year.

Orientation serves many purposes. It is a mechanism for fostering loyalty as well as a means for establishing the ranking of the various staff within the organization. By the end of the orientation period, each new employee clearly knows the pecking order, which is a very important factor if one is to function both effectively and politely in the Japanese organization. The net result of this total involvement of the company in the life of the employee is a significantly different relationship between Japanese workers and supervisors than between their American counterparts.

Attitudes of American versus Japanese Factory Workers

Perhaps the clearest illustration of this difference in attitudes was demonstrated in the research project of Takezawa and Whitehill, in which they compared the attitudes and opinions of Japanese and American factory workers.[29] In one question, workers were asked if they thought their supervisor should be involved in their marriage plans. Of the U.S. workers, 74% thought the supervisor should not be involved in the plans; in contrast, only 5% of the Japanese workers thought the supervisor should not be involved.[30] Another question in the survey asked whether an employee who is not feeling well should offer his or her seat to an immediate supervisor who boards the same bus. Thirty-two percent of the Japanese workers, but only 5% of the American workers, replied affirmatively.[31] In a question about the company providing subsidized housing, 47% of the Japanese workers but only 7% of the American workers agreed that this was something the company should provide.[32] A final question touched on the issue of extracurricular activities: "With reference to baseball games, picnics or overnight excursions for workers, it is best for the company to plan such activities for workers, but leave participation strictly voluntary." Sixty-one percent of the American workers but only 14% of the Japanese workers agreed with this statement.[33] This research, as well as other studies, reveals fundamental differences in how the worker perceives the role of the company and how the behavior of the company reveals fundamental differences in its concept of how it relates to, and invests in, its employees.[34,35]

Consensus Decision Making

A third element in the formula of Japanese managerial success is collective or consensus decision making, or, in Japanese, *ringi-seido*. This, as Gibney points out, is the "bottom-up initiative as opposed to the top-down direction."[36] In reviewing this approach, Gibney describes the slow process of a document passing through various organizational layers, being reviewed

---

[29]S. Takezawa and A. Whitehill, *Work ways: Japan and America* (Tokyo: Japan Institute of Labor, 1981).

[30]Ibid., pp. 117–121.

[31]Ibid., pp. 122–125.

[32]Ibid., pp. 157–163.

[33]Ibid., pp. 165–171.

[34]R. Dore, *British factory—Japanese factory* (Berkeley: University of California Press, 1973).

[35]R. Cole, *Work, mobility and participation* (Berkeley: University of California Press, 1979).

[36]F. Gibney, *Japan: The fragile superpower* (Tokyo: Tuttle, 1979), p. 215.

and commented upon and eventually passing, with modification and approval, to the next organizational level, so that by the time it reaches the president, "all that is needed is his seal." The net result of this process is a series of commitments at lower levels through involvement in the decision-making process; clarification of the human and material resources necessary to effect the process; and assurances that the pieces are in place before the president signs off. The Japanese manager is depicted as a person more concerned with discussing and organizing the details of a decision than the American manager, whose focus appears to be on making the decision and leaving details of its implementation to others. It is as if American managers are most interested in expediency, while Japanese managers are more concerned with the effectiveness of implementation.

This approach was well illustrated to me over a pizza in a Tokyo restaurant. Toward the end of one of my trips, I was discussing hospital administration education with a professor from a Japanese university. I had reviewed several curriculums and had what I thought to be a series of reasonable suggestions for change. After I offered my ideas, with appropriate politeness and caveats, the discussion moved away from the merit of those ideas to the fundamental issues of implementation. I wished to talk about the value of my conceptualizations; my luncheon partner wanted to talk about the details of implementation. As the discussion evolved, my suggestions were shown to have a limited value because of the realistic details of implementation.

Another analogy: As a young naval officer I found that even my most brilliant ideas had to be approved by the lieutenant who supervised me, the commander who supervised him, and the captain who supervised all of us. In turn, the corpsmen who worked for me required my "chop" on most things before they could move them up the line, despite my being a wet-behind-the-ears ensign. The system dictated the decision process, rather than the people in it, who were essentially interchangeable.

The Generalist Approach

The next element in the formula is the generalist as opposed to the specialist approach. The idea here is that Japanese managers spend their careers rotating through the various components of the organization, developing their expertise in the organization itself, but not necessarily in a particular part of the organization. Thus, someone might work three years in personnel, then be shifted into domestic marketing, and then into finance, and so on. The advantages of such a system are clear: Management personnel acquire a broad view of the organization, and when decisions are considered, they have the experience to see the possible impact from a number of vantage points. It also means that all staff are tuned into the total system of the corporation. As is often pointed out, when you call a Japanese business and get the wrong department, the person at the other end of the line often knows the answer to your question because that person worked in the other department at some time in his or her career. All of this is somewhat reminiscent of the family unit, where people have a good idea of what is happening in one another's lives and sometimes even know each other's schedules.

Amae: *Holding It All Together*

The glue holding all of this together is the concept of *amae,* popularized by the Japanese psychiatrist Takeo Doi in his oft-quoted book, *The Anatomy of Dependence.*[37] *Amae* is defined by Doi as "an emotion which partakes of the nature of a drive and with something instinctive at its base."[38] He has further defined it as the psychological craving a newborn has for its mother and "the desire to deny the fact of separation that is an inevitable part of human existence, and to obliterate the pain that this separation involves."[39] One observer has defined *amae* as "indulgent love" and suggests that it is the central concept in Japanese relationships.[40] According to Gibney, *amae* means literally "to presume on the affections of someone close to you."[41] Further, he notes that "the *amae* syndrome is pervasive in Japan. It is a mark of this collective society that most of its members expect in some way to be taken care of. The minority who do not expect this have a stern and relatively unprotected role in Japanese life, although to put it mildly, an essential one."[42]

The concept of *amae* takes on great significance in the organizational setting, in that the worker is a dependent of the supervisor. In practice, it

[37]Takeo Doi, *The Anatomy of Dependence* (Tokyo: Kodansha, 1973).

[38]Ibid., p. 166.

[39]Ibid., p. 167.

[40]B. DeMente, *The Japanese way of doing business* (Englewood Cliffs, NJ: Prentice-Hall, 1981), pp. 13–17.

[41]F. Gibney *Japan: The fragile superpower* (Tokyo: Tuttle, 1979), p. 119.

[42]Ibid., p. 120.

means that if an employee fails to get promoted, the supervisor views himself as a failure. In America we would simply say, "That's too bad, but it's not my problem," rather than the Japanese style of saying the supervisor "owns the problem." The mutual interdependency that one sees in Japan is sorely lacking in the United States.

DISADVANTAGES OF THE JAPANESE SYSTEM

Little is usually said about the disadvantages of the Japanese managerial system. First, however, it precludes anyone from developing depth in any given area. As will be seen in the public corporation case study, the rotation of managers involves the staff in a process of continually learning a new routine and, just when they are at the point of developing some expertise, moving on to another post. Second, from an American perspective it increases the strain on the employee, since the constant job shifting often involves relocation. In the United States, we are in the midst of a revolution among management staff concerning relocation. Third, from the managers' perspective, it makes them captive to the corporation. After 10 or 15 years with a given corporation, all that managers have learned is their company's approach to dealing with a range of issues and problems; they have not developed depth in an arena that might be valued at another company. Thus the system has the somewhat insidious effect of keeping the employee beholden to the corporation. Contrast this with the American system, where, with the exception of some executive training programs, the young manager goes straight into marketing, personnel, or another specialty and begins to develop expertise in that area. That expertise is readily transferable and marketable to other firms.

PROFESSIONAL VERSUS GROUP IDENTITY

Americans appear more concerned with professional identity, which is, to some extent, an extension of individuality. Although this is a broad generalization, the Japanese appear more interested, workwise, in group identity. The often-cited experience of asking a Japanese worker what he or she does and hearing a reply such as "I work at Mitsui" is a reflection of this group identity. An American's response is invariably "I am a . . . ," reflecting the American striving for a personal or perhaps group identity within a profession but not within an organization.

RISING THROUGH THE JAPANESE CORPORATION

The final element to be discussed in this chapter is the issue of slow promotions and evaluation. This has often been described as the escalator approach. Basically, Japanese managers get on an escalator when they join the firm and slowly move up the line. At some point (at about age 45) they will be reviewed by the top management, and a decision will be made whether to track them into top management or into the level below. If selected for top management, the mandatory retirement age of 55 is waived. If not selected for top management, their career with the company will come to an end within the next decade. The literature tells us that the decision is based on a series of informal evaluations made by superiors over a span of years.

All of this again reminds one of an example involving the American military: the promotion of military officers. If you do an outstanding job, you are promoted from ensign to lieutenant (junior grade) in a year and a half. If you do a barely adequate job, you are promoted in 18 months. Moving up to the next rank also involves a specific time spent in rank. Thereafter, time is still a factor but merit becomes increasingly important. The difference between the military, with its structured promotions, job rotation, permanent employment, and regulated retirement ages, and the Japanese organization is the feedback provided by the evaluation schemes. The American military and most American organizations put much emphasis on the need for regular evaluation and feedback to staff about their evaluations. Conversely, Japanese managers may spend most of their career without any direct feedback concerning their performance. They will have to pick up on and correctly interpret subtle clues to know how they are doing. Sometimes, as Drucker points out, a mentor is assigned and the mentor will provide advice and guidance.[43] But without a mentor, man-

---

[43]P. Drucker, "What we can learn from the Japanese," *Harvard Business Review, 49*(2) (1971), 120–121.

agers, essentially bound to their company, may not know where they stand. Some observers say this is why managers spend so much time at the workplace or socializing with colleagues, often skipping vacations or taking them with the "boys," all in an effort to develop and maintain relationships that are important to a cordial work environment and a secure future.

IMPLICATIONS OF THE JAPANESE SYSTEM

Training and Educating Managers

The implications of all of this are important. For example, each company must be essentially responsible for the training and education of its own managers. Sasaki notes that management training at Toyota consists "of on the job training, off the job programmed education and human relations activities."[44] Sasaki goes on to label this approach as *confined management development*, "a situation where the manager becomes so organizational specific that he or she is of limited value to the greater marketplace."[45] In Japan, the graduate-level degree in management is not the entry ticket into the corporation. Rather it is the college degree from the right college, which is more important than the major, since the corporation will provide the essential training. Second, as noted earlier, personal relationships are crucial with both colleagues and superiors. Relationships with colleagues are significant because of the family-like atmosphere, and the relationships with superiors are critical if one wishes to advance one's ideas or have a chance for a slot at the top.

Corporate Stability

A third implication is that the corporation is essentially stable. Turnover is low; predictability is high. One knows the chain of command; surprises are few. What this means is that long-range planning can go on in an atmosphere of some certainty and commitment, in sharp contrast to many American organizations. An example of this is an American state university where a new chancellor embarked on an 18-month effort to

---

[44]N. Sasaki, *Management and industrial structure in Japan* (Oxford: Pergamon Press, 1981), pp. 40–41.
[45]Ibid., p. 47.

develop a long-range plan. Tens of thousands of dollars and countless hours were invested in his plan, which resulted in a several-hundred-page document. He announced his resignation shortly after its release. The acting chancellor then essentially scrapped the plan in favor of his own version, which was dramatically shorter. Several months later a new chancellor was appointed, who decided to take another look himself.

The Japanese organization allows people to invest of themselves with some assurance of stability. By the same token, the Japanese organization invests in its people, because it knows that it is dealing with a stable resource and that the payoff will result in long-term gains. Compare this with the American manager, who often seems permanently available for a new job, or the American corporation, permanently available to hire a new manager from the outside, ready to shift directions.

APPLICATION TO HEALTH CARE ORGANIZATIONS

The bottom line question is whether anything that is learned from studying how the Japanese organize and manage their health care facilities has any application to American health care organizations. During my years in Japan and intensive study of three different Japanese hospital/health systems I came away with several ideas, which over the ensuing years, I have had a chance to suggest to organizations during consultations and implement myself during the late 1990s when I was CEO of a health system. The last section of this chapter will be devoted to a review of these ideas.

RECRUITMENT AND ORIENTATION

Virtually all health care organizations in the United States recruit employees 250 days a year. Indeed, with the popularity of the Internet it may be fair to say that recruiting goes on twenty-four hours a day and seven days a week. This level of recruiting is a function of the noncontractual nature of employment relationships in the business environment. In fact most employers desire an employee-at-will situation meaning employees can be terminated at the will of the employer with limited exceptions. Thus the employment environment is simply one where the expectations of both employers and employees are, that given better opportunities, the employee will leave. Job openings through retirement, resignation, or perhaps organizational change and expansion simply do not operate on a defined time schedule with the single exception of interns and residents who almost always commence their employment on July 1st.

Despite the issues surrounding recruitment, all organizations could do themselves a favor by developing higher-quality orientation programs. The best I observed was at St. Luke's International Hospital in Tokyo. The first day included a 90-minute talk from the hospital director on the history and philosophy of the institution. Following this were several more presentations from senior management on hospital organization, the nursing program, and the chaplaincy program. Following a catered lunch the employees spent the afternoon on the wide range of personnel management issues, including the chores of filling out various forms. The next day the new employees introduced themselves and spent several hours discussing a book that they had previously received on the history of St. Luke's. The second afternoon was devoted to discussions about the attitudes of personnel to one another and to patients, plus a presentation on fire safety and security.

The third day began with an overview of the hospital's administration followed by instruction and role-playing on telephone usage. After lunch the new staff were taken on a two-hour guided tour of the hospital followed by discussions on attitude and courtesy.

The last day of orientation began with more discussions about attitudes, followed by a presentation about the employee health service. Lunch on this final day was a special event, with employees going to lunch with their new supervisor. Following this meal, a distinguished person was brought in for a closing and presumably inspiring lecture.

While the contrast in investment, time-wise, financially and spiritually made by St. Luke's with the typical American health care organization is huge there is also a basic reason for the difference, that is, the Japanese organization has essentially one starting day per year and thus one orientation period per year. The American organization with its continuous recruitment, would have trouble mounting such an orientation program every few days. My suggestion is simple: In place of the daily or weekly orientation programs, have monthly programs. The value of monthly programs is twofold: financial and organizational commitment. From a financial perspective the organization, in some instances, can save some money by delaying the commencement of employment until the orientation. From a commitment perspective the monthly orientation allows for larger groups to be educated together and potentially develop a team spirit. Additionally, the monthly orientation, now less burdensome for the organization, can become more comprehensive and in some ways try to follow the St. Luke's model.

This idea was implemented in my organization. We went from a weekly to a twice monthly and then finally to a new staff orientation every three weeks. Because of the new schedule, I, as CEO, was able to participate in almost every new staff member's orientation, at least 15 people attended each session, and the orientation went from less than a day to two days. All of us involved felt that the change was useful but, like most operating organizations, we simply never measured it in an appropriate quantitative manner. I will say that over the years I had more contact with the employees and in my judgment meeting with them that first day set the tone of a relationship with management and the organization that was quite positive.

PERMANENT EMPLOYMENT

On one hand, my thirty-two year career as an academic has made me somewhat skeptical about this idea of permanent employment, that is, unconditional tenure. On the other hand there is a point where dedicated, competent, and loyal workers should be rewarded with some sense of permanency about their jobs. By providing such a reward to selected staff, the organization is more likely to insure its own stability as well as clarify its organizational development investments.

A second potential value of such a system is in terms of quality assurance. An effective organization that is devoted to enhancing quality must be certain that every team member is committed to quality and is not intimidated by others who are perceived to be more powerful. Recent incidents in Boston where, in one case, a surgeon took a break from the operating room to go to the bank and another where a surgeon reported for a case while inebriated demonstrate how important it is that staff have the ability and security to speak up where a patient or an institution is in jeopardy. Maslow, in his hierarchy of needs discussion, lists safety and security as the basic needs of all individuals and the conditions that must precede any further development and growth. Assuming that Maslow's ideas are valid then the idea of a sense of permanency about a job is crucial to the health and well being of all staff.

However, one should not be naïve about this concept. Permanency must also come with conditions such as a continual record of satisfactory evaluations and continued professional growth. What must be avoided is the stagnant behavior that one periodically sees with those in tenured positions.

HOLISM AND PATERNALISM

In the 1950s interns received a salary of $125 per month, plus room and board. The first level of competition for house staff was always on the basis of the quality of the medical education, but the second level of competition often revolved around housing. In one hospital where I worked, the salary was raised during the early 1960s to a "living wage" of $400 per month, but food privileges (first for the families and later, the house staff) were taken away. So, we thought, ends paternalism.

Many health care organizations provide generous fringe benefits including medical care, pensions, subsidized meals, subsidized housing, and even theater tickets. But many of the benefits that are of particular importance to the typical salaried worker only find their way to the highest-paid executives. For example, during my years as CEO I received a six-figure salary, a car with all expenses, a generous travel allowance, an unlimited business expense allowance, a housing allowance, and a pension that would have vested if I had stayed the required five years. I recall hearing of the head of a medical department, another medical center tell me how he received an allowance from the hospital for his daughter's tuition. In other instances senior executives receive interest-free loans to purchase homes. But what about the nurses trying to send their teenagers to college? Where are their tuition packages? Or their interest-free loans?

There is no easy solution to the problem of demonstrating care and concern for the employee. However, the trend, primarily in industry, of offering the employee a smorgasbord of possible benefits and then helping him or her choose an appropriate package is certainly a step in the right direction. Setting up in-house counseling services for the alcoholic employee, day care centers for children of employees, and crisis counseling programs are also steps in the right direction. Perhaps the health care organization could even pick up the older children of staff at local schools and provide them with a supervised after-school play program. Financial or technical assistance in securing mortgage loans should also be considered in the range of possible benefits. Career counseling services for employees and their families, in-service education, and tuition assistance are all programs that indicate a concern about the staff member's growth and development. Finally, the managers and middle managers must take the time, and the organization must support their efforts, to get to know their staff as people. Getting together for a relaxed lunch or supper will return psychological as well as organizational dividends; the annual Christmas party is simply not enough. Nor is it enough for these meals to go on during business hours or solely in the hospital cafeteria, where the manager's sense of territoriality is well protected.

Communications

Many organizations publish a weekly calendar of events. In order to save money they often distribute several copies to each department, one to each administrator, and one to each clinician. What's the message? There are those who count, and those who don't count. While the interest in hospital marketing is a positive trend, I propose that more effort be expended on internal marketing. All staff members want and need to be kept informed. In several Japanese hospitals there is a 15-minute morning assembly where polite greetings are exchanged, followed by a report on the present status of the hospital, for example, occupancy, number of admissions and discharges, and any particularly noteworthy events. Everyone is told about the broken steam pipe and the AIDS conference at three o'clock. In the typical American hospital, there is only the grapevine.

In one hospital where I worked, free coffee was served in the dining room from 10:00 A.M. to 11 :00 A.M., and the custom was for the nursing staff, the administrators, and the entire medical staff to stop by during those hours. Informal communication worked well there, but a new administrator put a stop to that practice; he chose to save $100 a week instead. We need to examine our communications networks and plug in those who were never connected. It's hard to be a member of the team when you don't get the information.

In one medical center that I consulted with in Kansas City the CEO complained to me that his staff felt uninformed and unappreciated. I told him that I was not surprised in light of my experience that cold and snowy morning. I had arrived at the medical center and was guided to a spot in the doctors' lot adjacent to the main hospital building. I walked through a covered walkway into the building where, upon entering, I found a credenza with a computer on it. I was told that all physicians and executives logged themselves in on the computer and was then given a demonstration. The screens instantly welcomed the person by name, told them of upcoming appointments and meetings, and in the case of physicians, the status of their patients. Curious now to see how the other half lived I walked over to the employees' entrance and found that it was two blocks from the closest parking lot; was stark to say the least; had three time clocks and racks of time cards on the wall; and an expressionless security guard standing watch over the clocks. Later I learned that bulletins were distributed as noted earlier. Why was the administrator surprised to find an alienated work staff? The challenge in this situation was to turn the work environment around!

PAYOFFS AND RISKS

Would following this agenda payoff in dollars? The direct payoff, it is proposed, would be in terms of reduced alienation, which should lead to a more efficient and effective work force.

A second measurable payoff should be reduced turnover and, hence, reduced personnel expenses for training and redevelopment. Additionally, it means that personnel development investments can be planned on a long-term basis.

But there are risks. The first risk relates to implementing the plan and then finding out that turnover has not decreased, production is the same, and alienation is just as high. Also, the organization is stuck with a large number of permanent employees who act just like they always have. The social pressures that induce people to leave in Japan are not likely to have the same effect here. One response, as suggested earlier, might be to limit people and positions eligible for permanent employment. A second response might be to give it time. The importance and impact of most significant changes, getting married, having children, or obtaining tenure, for example, are not immediately obvious. If, after implementation and waiting, there is still no difference, the costs of the risks are probably not so high as to outweigh the second risk.

This second risk is that of doing nothing, that is, simply allowing the organization to continue as it has for decades, absorbing the financial drain of alienated staff with high turnover and the emotional drain of a staff in turmoil.

It is suggested here that one of the few organizational levels most managers have to work with is staffing. Most choose to operate on a management-by-exception basis, but this leaves too much vital activity unmanaged. Managers must learn to anticipate problems and their solutions and to adapt the innovative ideas of their Japanese colleagues. In the long run the payoff will be for the staff, the patients, and the community.

Case Study 8-1
THE CONSULTATION

The international consulting firm of AB&C has recently finished an engagement for Rolatel, a publicly owned (NASDAQ) chain of 130 nursing homes headquartered in California, with facilities in California, Arizona, Oregon, and Washington. For the past five years, the chain has been plagued with problems of high labor turnover, particularly with administrators, nursing directors, and nurse's aides. In some years this turnover has reached in excess of 50%. These problems generally have been more pronounced in central and southern California and Arizona, where 80% of the homes are located. Turnover is minimal in Washington and Oregon, and in northern California, turnover is in the 30% range.

The study by AB&C has confirmed what Rolatel's senior management has long suspected: High turnover is affecting the bottom line through increased labor costs as well as increased regulatory problems. The study concluded

(*continues*)

Case Study 8-1

that the staff at all levels were "alienated" from "corporate" and that they did not feel invested in the individual facilities or in the organization. The major suggestion from the consultants was that Rolatel move toward a more Japanese-style organization.

DISCUSSION QUESTIONS

1. Based on Chapter 8, what options might Rolatel consider?

2. What would be the advantages and disadvantages of such changes?

3. Is there a better alternative to reach the goals of reduced turnover, more employee buy-in, and better quality of care?

4. Can Rolatel implement a Japanese-style change in just the regions where there are problems, leaving alone areas such as Washington and Oregon?

CHAPTER 9

Machiavelli and Health Care Management

The essential element in the practice of health administration is politics. The notion that a health administrator's job is political strikes some as abhorrent, but it is simply realistic. Managers are simultaneously called upon to allocate scarce resources among competing factions and maintain something akin to an equilibrium in the organization. To do this requires the political skills of persuasion, knowledge, and empathy, as well as being relatively secure in what they are doing and clear as to their goals.

Perhaps the single greatest text written on politics was the early sixteenth-century work by Niccolo Machiavelli, which can certainly offer numerous lessons for health administrators. Machiavelli wrote *The Prince* as a gift for Lorenzo de Medici in order to help the Florentine ruler understand the politics of management and leadership.[1] Machiavelli viewed management and leadership in an almost amoral way, and his purpose in preparing his text was to curry favor with those in power so that he could reattain a governmental position from which he had been dismissed after an apparently successful career as a senior-level official.

PHASE I: THE MANAGEMENT HONEYMOON

One of the first sections in *The Prince* is titled "Composite Principalities." In that chapter Machiavelli writes of the problems likely to be experienced

[1] N. Machiavelli, *The prince* (New York: Penguin, 1975).

by a new monarch. He begins by noting the fickleness of people; he suggests that, because people's expectations are not usually met, they are always willing to accept a different leader. Other points that Machiavelli makes include the importance of obtaining and maintaining the goodwill of the people in the new country and identifying allies and potential enemies, such as members of the deposed family. In this, as well as elsewhere, Machiavelli suggests that those who oppose must be eliminated.

A few of his major points have particular relevance to health administration, since administrators are often taking someone else's job (or at least it is perceived that way). Sometimes the person who is being replaced has voluntarily resigned and is leaving with all good thoughts on everyone's part; other times the resignation has been requested and there is ill will throughout the organization. The former incumbent has supporters and detractors. The supporters feel they lost; the detractors smell a victory. The new administrator has probably not been involved in the battles but is immediately asked to choose sides.

This phenomenon was illustrated at a rural New Jersey hospital where, within a few weeks of his arrival, a new chief executive officer was challenged by the medical staff on a basic issue that related to the special organization of this institution (it was a closed-staff, fee-for-service institution). His response, however justified, re-created the tension that had been smoldering since the resignation of the former chief executive officer and redrew the battle lines that had existed. This fight, while inevitable, came at a most inopportune time for the new administrator: before he was able to identify his allies and likely protagonists, and before he was able to establish his own power base. In essence, he had to do battle without the proper support lines, and the net result was that he was forced to resign within a few months.

Machiavelli suggests that it is critical that the new "ruler" establish his territoriality. He must let everyone know that he is in fact the new ruler, by words and deeds. At the simplest and most superficial level, he must move into his new office and make that office state that he is there and that it is his. When one manager accepted an important position at a large teaching hospital, part of the agreement with the institution was that he could be away two days a week on consulting work. For the three years he was there, his office always looked vacant: a big desk, a table and chairs, and bookshelves. It looked almost like a Madison Avenue showroom rather than a line manager's office. This manager was sending messages to those around him that his heart and soul were elsewhere. This diminished his effectiveness because, although most people he encountered admired his intelligence and judgment, none took him seriously and thus they easily stonewalled his programs. Even his supporters were reluctant to pit themselves against his detractors; after all, they reasoned, he would not be there in a year or two to take the heat. And they were right.

A good example of how managers establish territoriality can be found in the military. During the five years that I was a naval officer, I served under five commanding officers, and each one of them held an inspection on Friday mornings. The inspection was usually rather informal, but virtually every nook and cranny of the hospital was inspected by the commanding officer and his entourage. These inspections also included verbal interchanges (usually pleasant) between the commanding officer and whomever was present, including patients on the ward. Most of the commanding officers used the time to see for themselves what was going on and to make themselves accessible to the staff. For example, one always had his scribe keep a list of the problems that had been identified on inspection. On subsequent inspections, he would follow up to ascertain the problems' resolutions. On the psychological level, the commanding officer was saying that he was indeed responsible for (and to a degree had the authority to change) what was going on in the institution.

When I accepted a CEO position in the late 1990s, one of the conditions of my employment was the rebuilding of my office suite. My predecessor, who had left two years earlier, had been using an office that had been designed by a previous director from the early 1980s. The office was huge and cavernous, dark and dingy, with broken bookcases and stained rugs. Once the renovation was completed, the office was considerably smaller and brighter, with new furniture, wooden floors, and an adjacent small conference room—all within the original space. Perhaps symbolically, when the dropped acoustic ceiling tiles were being replaced, the workmen found dead rats in the overhead space. The results of this were that, first, I had a pleasant environment for my workspace and numerous meetings and, second, it said in no uncertain terms that there was "a new sheriff in town."

It is interesting to note how few executives personally make their presence felt in an institution. In many ways, it is more secure and certainly easier to stay in an office. This even happens in university administration. For example, there was a professor at a school of public health who, in over a year, had never met the new dean. After four years in office, a vice chancellor had never visited one of the three constituent schools of his chancellorship, despite the fact that the school was less than a block away and his relationship with its staff was positive.

When Machiavelli suggests that "one of the best, most effective expedients would be for the conqueror to go to live there in person," he is giving important advice on establishing territoriality and managerial presence, another thing accomplished by my commanding officers' weekly inspections. Such a presence allows subordinates to feel comfortable in the knowledge (or at least belief) that there is someone at a higher level who is capable of making decisions, and it allows for maintenance of the organization. As Machiavelli notes:

> Being on the spot, one can detect trouble at the start and deal with it immediately; if one is absent, it is discerned only when it has grown serious, and it is then too late. And besides, this policy prevents the conquered territory from being plundered by one's officials. The subjects are satisfied because they have direct recourse to the prince.

Being there and being accessible, then, are two points of importance. The military inspection can be translated into administrative rounds, and presence into literally being there. In other words, managers should take one job, not two. They should work for one organization, not two. They should be evaluated by one boss, not two. A novel way one hospital administrator handles the presence issue is through a "zone defense." He does this by assigning each of the front-office subordinates to a physically different section of the hospital. In this way, virtually everyone in the institution has easy access to a front-office administrator and, according to the hospital director, problems are spotted early and resolved before they get out of hand.

The final advice from Machiavelli in his third chapter is that the prince must be a wise planner:

> [T]he Romans did what all wise rulers must: cope not only with present troubles but with ones likely to arise in the future, and assiduously forestall them. When trouble is sensed well in advance it can be easily remedied; if you wait for it to show itself any medicine will be too late because the disease will become incurable.

The wise manager, Machiavelli would suggest, is a wise planner. He organizes and husbands his time and resources and waits for the right moment. A former senior executive in government once said that, when he was in Washington, he had a file drawer full of future plans and that his effectiveness was in large part related to the quality of his plans, coupled with the correctness of his timing. Effectiveness, he suggested, was having the right plan or solution available at the right time.

PHASE II: CONSOLIDATION

In Chapter 4, in which he discusses why the kingdom of Darius conquered by Alexander did not rebel against his successors after his death, and Chapter 5, which discusses how cities or principalities that lived under their own laws should be administered after being conquered, Machiavelli suggests alternative managerial approaches. Using the Turkish and French empires as examples, he contrasts centralized and decentralized power. He suggests that a kingdom, such as Turkey, with a centralized power system in which everyone is responsible to the king and all authority is exercised by him or his agents at his direction, would be difficult to conquer. Once conquered, however, it would be easy to administer because one strong man would be substituted for another, and people were used to obeying a central authority. This is contrasted with the decentralized form in France where there was "a long established order of nobles, who are acknowledged in France by their own subjects and are loved by them. They have their prerogatives; the king cannot take these away from them except at his own peril."

In Chapter 5, Machiavelli reiterates his advice concerning what the conqueror should do in order to maintain his new kingdom:

> When states newly acquired, as I said, have been accustomed to living freely under their own laws, there are three ways to hold them securely: first, by devastating them; next, by going and living there in person; thirdly, by letting them keep their own laws, exacting tribute, and setting up an oligarchy which will keep the state friendly to you.

Clearly, Machiavelli came down on the side of options three and two, and was not in favor of option one.

His arguments for centralization and decentralization in a sense strike at the core issue of power. To what degree can management feel secure if people who are essentially subordinates have independent power? The centralized mode is quite clearly a replication of the paternalistic (or maternalistic) family: One person is effectively a benevolent dictator. Decentralization seems to have not only the greatest dispersion of power but also the most stable power base.

In health care organizations, two phenomena can often be observed: (1) an uncontrollable decentralization of power and authority to the professional staff, and (2) a high labor turnover at the top and bottom levels of the organization and great stability in the middle. For example, in one large municipal hospital in the South, top management was totally immersed in state health care (and other) politics and was certainly not attending to the problems of this large teaching hospital. The operation managed to still function because there had been a significant decentralization of authority and responsibility, which had resulted in a strong and solid middle management capable of carrying on despite the climate at the top. In my own organization, this point was always evident at the annual recognition party, where senior staff were the ones getting the 5-year pins and the hardworking aides, nurses, and housekeepers were getting the recognition for 15 or 20 years of service.

PHASE III: LOYALTY AND INNOVATION

To Machiavelli, loyalty is one of the key elements in the success of a new manager or leader. Loyalty that runs deep would more likely be generated by Theory Y behavior and attitudes than those of Theory X, as Machiavelli suggests that loyalty is earned. Care must be taken not to confuse acquiescence for loyalty. Perhaps one of the most difficult jobs of a manager, particularly one new to a job, is to avoid the clever sycophant.

As noted earlier, one of the important strategies that management can adopt is that of innovation, both fostering it and being innovative oneself. On the subject of innovation, Machiavelli notes in Chapter 6 ("New Principalities Acquired by One's Own Arms and Prowess"):

> The innovator makes enemies of all those who prospered under the old order, and only lukewarm support is forthcoming from those who would prosper under the new. Their support is lukewarm partly from fear of their adversaries, who have the existing laws on their side and partly because men are generally incredulous, never really trusting new things unless they have tested them by experience. In consequence, whenever those who oppose the changes can do so, they attack vigorously, and the defense made by the others is only lukewarm. So both the innovator and his friends are

endangered together . . . all armed prophets have conquered and unarmed protests have come to grief . . . the populace is by nature fickle; it is easy to persuade them of something, but difficult to confirm them in that persuasion.

Throughout *The Prince*, Machiavelli appears to admire change, but in this chapter he notes its danger: inertia and fear of change in those people likely to be affected by the change. Managers, particularly a manager who is new to an organization, are often tempted to use change either as a way of learning how the organization functions, much as a chemist in a laboratory uses tracer elements, or as a way of establishing their territoriality. Both of these are less-than-optimal approaches to change. It is postulated that any organization can absorb innovation at some (not quite clearly determined) rate, and that, when this rate is exceeded, stress in the organization becomes greater than the potential benefit of the innovation. This is somewhat analogous to the capacity of a body of land to retain water; when the absorption rate is exceeded, there are puddles, then pools, and finally a flood.

Another organizational response, equally unsatisfying, occurs when innovations become so commonplace that the workers become inured to them and stonewall them by noncompliance. Since the innovations come so frequently, it is almost impossible to follow up. One hospital administrator commented, "Be careful not to offer more than one new idea a week." A former commissioner in the New York City Department of Hospitals wryly noted one day that he could have the best idea in the world but some "damn grade-two clerk is simply not going to implement it, and that's the end of my great idea."

Certain types of health care organizations, such as hospitals, are continually bombarded by technical innovations; other types, particularly in the federal government, are always being streamlined by organizational innovations. Innovations, while extremely important, extract a price from any staff, and a staff must be sold on the importance of an innovation before it is likely to cooperate willingly. Machiavelli's description of "armed and unarmed prophets" may be a managerial metaphor for people who have thoroughly researched their ideas and have developed a sound strategy for innovation, as opposed to those who come in with half-baked ideas. Since there is a limited absorption rate, managers must take care not to use their innovation bullets carelessly. The unemployment line is filled with former executives who pushed their organizations too fast through the barrier of change. Change is a process that requires intelligence, maturity, and, the most difficult ingredient for an active and fertile innovator, patience.

PHASE IV: DEALING WITH CHALLENGES

In Chapter 6 and in the following three chapters, Machiavelli advises courses of action for those who come to power in different ways: (1) by means of their own strength and wits, (2) with the aid of wealthy and powerful friends, (3) by crime, and (4) by constitutional principles. Analogies can be found in the field of health care management. A new health care administrator may have acquired the position as a result of the death or retirement of the previous beloved administrator. Or, the previous administrator may have been forced to resign by the board after they somewhat reluctantly concluded that he was not terribly competent, although everyone agreed that he was a wonderful person. A third scenario might be that of an administrator who was quite good but was fired because of hostility from the medical staff.

In the first instance, Machiavelli would advise that "a prudent man should always follow in the footsteps of great men and imitate those who have been outstanding." The rationale here apparently is that, if the new administrator can establish linkages to a beloved predecessor, the latter's reservoir of goodwill can be transferred to the new administrator. The director of a large metropolitan teaching hospital had an 18" × 20" color photograph of the previous administrator on his office wall opposite the couch, where most visitors were likely to sit. The picture was inscribed, "Best personal regards and wishes for success." When asked why he had that, since in private he had made somewhat disparaging comments about his predecessor's ability, the new administrator replied that the man had been helpful to his career and had been much loved in the medical center. Obviously, the photograph was a symbolic link to the past to benefit the present and, perhaps, the future. The problem for the administrator in this situation is to acquire the loyalty and devotion of the first one.

The second case is a somewhat more complicated situation, since the group in power has recognized the incompetence of the administrator but has not acknowledged it publicly. It will be difficult for the new administrator to point out the shortcomings of the well-liked former administrator without offending those in power, who have avoided doing that themselves, or offending those who supported the former administrator. The problem, Machiavelli would suggest, is that the new administrator has no strong roots in the organization, nor are the roots that are available worthy of transfer: "Governments set up overnight, like everything in nature whose growth is forced, lack strong roots and ramifications. So they are destroyed in the first bad spell." A second and related point that Machiavelli makes is that new administrators do not have any loyalists, that is, people who can be counted on to do the job. It is thus imperative that a new administrator approach the job judiciously, taking time to learn about the organization and to understand its history and the nature of the relationships in the organization. Only then will the new administrator become effective in designing and implementing programs and begin to earn loyalty and develop a power base for subsequent operations. The new administrator could eventually be accepted as the organizational choice for the management and leadership position. The payoff in such situations, as Machiavelli describes it, is most attractive:

> A prince who builds his power on the people, one who can command and is a man of courage, who does not despair in adversity, who does not fail to take precautions, and who wins general allegiance by his personal qualities and the institutions he establishes, he will never be let down by the people; and he will be found to have established his power securely.

Unfortunately, this did not happen for a friend of mine. He was hired by the board after it realized that the previous administrator had taken the organization to the brink of financial disaster. The previous administrator was retired with numerous accolades because he was a beloved figure in the community. On a personal level, many of the board members socialized with him and his family and were genuinely fond of him. To compound the problem, the former director lived in the community and was quite defensive about everything that he had done over the prior 30 years. As the new administrator started to implement the changes necessary to correct the problems, he not only had to deal with the stress within the organization, but he also had to deal with a board that was constantly listening to the former administrator telling them how the new guy was destroying the organization. And since no one wanted to confront their friend and former director with the "truth," the new man was constantly being undermined by segments of the board. In the end, the stress was unbearable all around and the CEO resigned.

In the final example, an administrator who has been enfranchised after the overthrow of the previous one by the power bloc of the medical staff has some obvious problems. The new administrator is to some extent beholden to the medical staff, who are now feeling their power. To put it another way, the new administrator must appear to be acceptable to this group. The second problem is that many people in the organization may have loyalties to the previous administrator, feel that this person was done a grave injustice, and see the new administrator as the manifestation of that injustice. Machiavelli would probably consider this type of situation as the acquisition of power through the crime of others. Although not a participant, the new administrator is certainly its beneficiary. The advantage in this situation is that, since some blood has been spilled, it is relatively easy to identify the factions and who is likely to be in which camp.

Machiavelli's advice in this instance has earned him his tainted reputation:

> So it should be noted that when he seizes a state the new ruler ought to determine all the injuries that he will need to inflict. He should inflict them once for all, and not have to renew them every day, and in that way he will be able to set men's minds at rest and win them over to him when he confers benefits. Whoever acts otherwise either through timidity or bad advice is always forced to have the knife ready in his hand and he can never depend on his subjects because they, suffering fresh and continuous violence, can never feel secure with regard to him. Violence should be inflicted once for all; people will then forget what it tastes like and so be less resentful. Benefits should be conferred gradually and in that way they will taste better. Above all, a prince should live with his subjects in such a way that no development, either favourable or adverse, makes him vary his conduct. For, when adversity brings the need for it, there is no time to inflict harm; and the favours he may confer are profitless, because they are seen as being forced, and so they earn no thanks.

While this may seem a bit cruel, it does make some pragmatic sense for the new administrator. Firing those people who have to be fired as rapidly as possible is not only politically expedient but also allows the new administrator to build a loyal team. In government, it has long been accepted that when an administration becomes a lame duck, either by losing an election or by declaring an intention not to run, those on the staff are immediately on the market. Machiavelli is certainly a believer in the notion that to the victor belongs the spoils. Management may not be a warlike situation, but it is clearly often a politically active situation, and administrators cannot have people in their camp who are attempting to undermine them or their efforts. In terms of doling out favors, be they programs, money, or stature in the organization, Machiavelli would suggest that the administrator would be wise to dispense favors slowly and deliberately. Again, politicians can be observed doing this; they are servicing their accounts, using whatever authority they have to build a strong constituency for their programs. In essence, politicians and administrators are in similar positions; both are in part dependent on quid pro quo relationships for their power.

The most profound mistake that I made when I accepted the CEO's post was not cleaning house of the incumbent executives although I knew that at least one of them had lobbied for the CEO position himself. My reasoning was simple (or perhaps simple-minded): I knew the people, I liked them personally, they had experience with the organization, discharging them would not be enthusiastically supported by the staff and board—and most importantly, I naively thought that I could get them to be loyal to me. In reality, all of the above situations happened. Some became fiercely loyal to me; some couldn't stand my way of managing and quit; some were fired; a few hung on, stayed disloyal and undermined my efforts. In retrospect, I would have cleaned house and would have that in writing as a condition of employment: The new director has the authority to terminate anyone's employment. In my own case I was told that I had that authority, but when I tried to exercise it three months after I arrived, I was vetoed by the board chairman and president.

PHASE V: STRATEGIC PLANNING

Strategic planning is a continuous thread of Machiavelli's philosophy and is of critical importance to any administrator. In Chapter 14 ("How a Prince Should Organize His Militia"), Machiavelli notes that "a wise prince should observe these rules: he should never take things easy in times of peace, but rather use the latter assiduously, in order to be able to reap the profit in time of adversity. Then when his fortunes change he will be found ready to resist adversity." Such notions of planning can be found in a great deal of literature beyond contemporary management texts; for example, in the Bible, Joseph advises Pharaoh about the years of a bountiful harvest and the years of famine.

Health administrators spend so much of their energy fighting the crisis of the day that it almost seems as if there are never times of peace. There are, but it is sometimes hard to recognize them when the organization and the manager's personal energy system constantly are geared up for full battle. Machiavelli's words could be translated for our purposes by saying that managers must attempt to organize their time so that there are times of peace even in the middle of adversity. Thinking and planning time are precious commodities. People with administrative inclinations are easily seduced into almost hyperactive behavior. Rarely is there a sense of calmness and tranquility in a manager's office; phones are ringing, people popping in and out, intercoms buzzing, and schedules that begin early in the morning go late into the evening. It is indeed very ego-satisfying to be "desired" by so many people, but the question remains: What kind of planning or thinking time is available, and to what extent is such an executive developing the means to prevent executive burnout?

Fire fighting is the present; strategic planning is the future, and most of what happens to an organization will happen in the future. Good planning will, over time, minimize the fire fighting and certainly mitigate its potential destructiveness. A commitment for administrators to allow themselves the private time for planning and reflection is too often viewed as a luxury rather than a necessity, however.

In Chapter 17 of *The Prince*, Machiavelli talks of cruelty and compassion, and whether it is better to be loved or feared. He proposes that a prince should want to have "a reputation for compassion rather than cruelty; nonetheless, he should be careful that he does not make bad use of compassion." He goes on to distinguish between different degrees of compassion, arguing that too much compassion results in anarchy, which works to the detriment of the entire community, while appropriate compassion occasionally affects individuals negatively but has an overall positive effect on the community.

The administrator who wants to be loved and says "yes" to everyone about everything is assuming that this is the path to credibility and respect. Indeed, it is actually a path in the opposite direction. Administrators are paid to make tough resource allocation decisions. In a fair percentage of these decisions, the administrator has considerable latitude, and this is where compassion can and should be exercised.

Sometimes, a decision may be "cruel" to an individual and yet compassionate in terms of the work community. For example, what should be done with an offensive and obnoxious worker who is disrupting the work of others and who obviously has serious psychological problems? The most compassionate solution for the individual may be the least compassionate for the group. Balancing these conflicting needs, as well as the administrator's personal needs, is a difficult process with no clear-cut and totally satisfactory solutions.

In the next chapter of the book ("How Princes Should Honor Their Words"), Machiavelli provides considerable food for thought. Basically, he makes the case that the means justify the ends, that situational ethics prevail, and that image is at least as important (and maybe more so) as substance:

> Princes who have achieved great things have been those who have given their word lightly, who have known how to trick men with their cunning, and who, in the end, have overcome those abiding by honest principles . . . a prudent ruler cannot, and should not, honour his word when it places him at a disadvantage and when the reasons for which he has made his promise no longer exist. If all men were good, this precept would not be good; but because men are wretched creatures who would not keep their word to you, you need not keep your word to them.

Obviously, Machiavelli is a Theory X man. He does not trust people and views them as fickle, at best. "Men are so simple, and so much creatures of circumstance, that the deceiver will always find someone ready to be deceived."

In discussing image and substance, Machiavelli points out that to those "seeing and hearing [the prince] he should appear a man of compassion, a man of good faith, a man of integrity, a kind and religious man. . . ." Machiavelli then offers this advice, "So let a prince set about the task of conquering and maintaining his state; his methods will always be judged honourable and will be universally praised. The common people are always impressed by appearances and results." Like the emperor in the fairy tale, "The Emperor's New Clothes," the prince can always be assured that those around him and those dependent on his goodwill (and good humor) will not want to be the messenger with the bad news. Indeed, recent studies of the presidency have shown numerous examples of senior staff and even cabinet-level administrators who have skewed their observations and analyses to please the president and distort reality.

The issue of means and ends is a very sensitive one in the health care establishment, in part because of the large number of voluntary boards that have considerable authority but limited involvement in implementation. In one case, the chairman of a hospital's board had a reputation in philanthropic and business circles as an unethical person and, for that reason, had found it difficult to get on a hospital board. The one that did accept him promptly elevated him to a very high position because of small gifts and the promise of larger ones. Is it appropriate for an institution to honor someone who is less than honorable? Is the legitimacy of the institution and its board for sale? Do we judge Lyndon Johnson for the Civil Rights Act, the Vietnam War, or his sleazy relationship with the oil and gas barons? Do we judge Martha Stewart for her contributions to style or her inappropriate stock transactions? Do we judge George W. Bush for a shaky economy, the quagmire of Iraq, or capturing a ruthless dictator? Obviously, in 2004 the electorate made its judgment in his favor.

Machiavelli would argue that the benefits would clearly outweigh the costs. In the aforementioned board example, it should be pointed out that the involvement of this person in an important post on the board probably repelled others, some of whom may have been of more value in various ways. This person never gave the hospital any sizable amount of money, and he used the hospital as a means of dealing with his own personal and business frustrations. For example, when the hospital was in the early stages of unionization, he directed an all-out offensive against the union, which included physical violence. Why this response? A large part of the reason seems to have been that his own business, and he himself in the bargain, had been brought to their knees on several occasions by a powerful union. In his own factory, he was continually waging a losing battle with the union; in fact, the National Labor Relations Board had made decisions against him and his firm for serious unfair labor practices.

Under this man's influence, the hospital's response to its union was not related to the issues but rather to its board chairman's overall anger. Obviously, he lived his life, as the institution and its management did, with the notion that the ends justified the means. Thus, the price paid by the hospital may have far exceeded any immediate or potential long-range benefit of having this person as chair of their board. Regardless, the ethical fiber of the institution was clearly weakened by his presence. Ironically enough, the hospital won the unionization battle but five years later lost another election and today is a stronghold of unionization in the health industry.

In the next two chapters of *The Prince* ("The Need to Avoid Contempt and Hatred" and "Whether Fortresses and Many Other Present Day Expedients to Which Princes Have Recourse Are Useful or Not"), Machiavelli suggests some interesting concepts about interpersonal relationships. He begins by noting that, if people are angry with or hate the prince, he must always be afraid of everything and everyone. On the other hand, he suggests that "well organized states and wise princes have always taken great pains not to make nobles despair, and to satisfy the people and keep them content."

To effect this, Machiavelli suggests several strategies. First, unpopular acts should be delegated to others, while the prince should always be the one who passes out favors. Some administrators, however, seem to thrive on tension and adversity. Indeed, one successful executive took great pleasure in searching for assistant administrators who had what he described as the "killer instinct." These people could do the dirty work while allowing the administrator to maintain his "good guy" image.

A second problem Machiavelli identifies is that of satisfying multiple (and in many cases irreconcilable) constituencies. He uses the example of a new ruler trying simultaneously to appease war-loving soldiers and the peace-loving populace. The administrator of a health care organization must recognize that perhaps dozens of constituencies must be dealt with, each one motivated in a different way. Sometimes meeting the demands of one constituency will offend another. The solution, according to Machiavelli, is to "strive assiduously to escape the hatred of the most powerful classes." Good advice, but sometimes it is difficult to tell which group is most powerful, which group will become most powerful later, and, finally, how power and correctness can be reconciled on a given issue.

Next, Machiavelli returns to the importance of image. He suggests that the downfall of one Roman ruler was related to an image problem: "He forgot his dignity, often descended into the amphitheaters to fight with the gladiators, and did other ignoble things hardly worthy of the imperial majesty; as a result the soldiers came to despise him."

This leads Machiavelli to a prescription for success. First, he notes that the prince must build a staff loyal to himself; this is in part accomplished by arming people: "Those who were suspect become loyal, and those who were loyal not only remain so but are changed from being merely your subjects to being your partisans." Then he suggests having these people engage in a few "battles" where their victory is assured to build a sense of confidence and esprit de corps. Finally, he proposes that the prince must keep his people busy with worthwhile projects. Machiavelli seems to agree with the saying that "idle hands are the devil's workshop."

Machiavelli's proposals here appear to make considerable sense in health administration. Invest in people, develop them, and they will provide a good return on that investment. Keep them busy on serious and worthwhile projects, praise them in public, damn them in private, help people feel confident about themselves. The philosophy expressed in these sections of Machiavelli is similar to that of the great management guru Peter Drucker, who emphasizes the importance of management development.[2]

The next two chapters of *The Prince* ("A Prince's Personal Staff" and "How Flatterers Must Be Shunned") are really the key to Machiavelli's thinking. They are written out of Machiavelli's self-interest, of course, because he wished to ingratiate himself with Lorenzo and thereby earn a position in his administration. In them he points out that the most important decisions are those made about the prince's senior staff:

> The first opinion that is formed of a ruler's intelligence is based on the quality of the men he has around him. When they are competent and loyal he can always be considered wise, because he has been able to recognize their competence and keep them loyal. But when they are otherwise, the prince is always open to adverse criticism, because his first mistake has been in his choice of ministers.

Machiavelli advises looking for deputies who can "understand things for itself." A second-level person would be one who "appreciates what others can understand." To be avoided is someone with little capacity for understanding.

A caution he raises is one noted earlier about sycophants; he suggests that top aides should understand that the prince values the "truth," but that the prince sets the time and tone of the truth. In essence, he argues that universal access to the prince denigrates his role and power. The prince should select who shall talk to him on what matters, but the staff must know that the prince expects and values truth.

---

[2]P.F. Drucker, *Management* (New York: Harper & Row, 1974), pp. 419–429.

These final lessons about senior staff are quite relevant in the health industry, where recruiting decisions are often made in a most thoughtless and cavalier way. While most organizations can carry out a competent executive search without consultants, it is nevertheless interesting to note how poorly recruiting is done in large segments of the health field. Indeed, as Machiavelli suggests, the most important decisions to be made are those about recruiting; they have ramifications that could make or break an organization or program. After my own years as a CEO, I would periodically muse about my own successes and failures. At the top of the success category I would put the recruitment of several key deputies, including a new medical director, a new chief financial officer, and a new human resource director. At the top of my failure list I would put my inability to effect any changes on the board and my retention of some senior staff who undermined my various efforts. So, in the end, it may not be programs but rather people—and with the right people, change and programs are effected. Conversely, the wrong people represent stumbling blocks during the daylight and heartburn at night!

In the concluding sections of his book, Machiavelli notes that, despite all good warnings and plans, sometimes environmental factors over which the prince has quite limited control conspire against him and his plans go astray. These environmental factors could be anything from a natural disaster to broader political events affecting an organization. The horror of 9/11 impacted virtually every business, yet was for the most part totally unpredicted.

It may be asked whether any of Machiavelli's assertions have direct relevance to the operational problems of today's health care organization. What advice would Machiavelli give regarding an innovative hospital-based ambulatory care program that has been developed over the objections of a medical staff and perhaps a few trustees? He would probably say that a constituency should be developed for the program. This constituency might be a loose coalition of patients, staff, and physicians and could be built by services offered, interpersonal relations, personal diplomacy, organizational relations (e.g., staff conferences or participative management), and public relations activities such as newsletters and tours.

Second, he would say that enemies should be identified and neutralized. If the manager were powerful enough, enemies might be isolated, that is, excluded from the hospital. More commonly, innovators attempt to demonstrate that they are not a threat but can be helpful. In one situation, two physicians hostile to a program were neutralized in a way that was beneficial to both the physicians and their practice. One of the physicians was retiring, and the hospital arranged to buy his practice; the second physician wished to go into semiretirement and the hospital brought his patients into the group and hired him on a part-time basis. These former opponents became the most important supporters of the program.

Staying power and taking the long view is equally important. I am reminded of a group of physicians who in the early 1980s were so opposed to a local HMO that they hired a Washington lobbyist to block its application for federal funds for a new building. Now, two decades and several HMO owners later, there is little to no animosity toward the HMO in the medical community, and the building that was built with a federal loan still stands, now owned by a group practice with HMO contracts. The leaders of the opposition have retired, died, or been neutralized.

Next, Machiavelli would advise continual vigilance about what is happening in the environment and what the "competition" is doing. Strategic planning is critical in these unsettled times, even for a small hospital-based group practice. Finally, Machiavelli would suggest recruiting managers, leaders, and practitioners in order to succeed.

In sum, Machiavelli provides a good lesson in the "realpolitik" of complex organizations. Some of his ideas and concepts are, to say the least, distasteful; however, many are extremely useful for present-day health care management.

Case Study 9-1
THE ROAD TO THE TOP

In the fall of 20__, Eliot Van Buren was engaged as an independent consultant by the president of the board of the Gatesville Health system. Van Buren, a retired U.S. Public Health Service officer who had risen to the position of deputy surgeon general of the United States, was one of three partners in a boutique health care consulting firm.

(continues)

Case Study 9-1

The project at Gatesville involved a seven-day-per-month commitment to assist the board in straightening out a host of personnel, financial, and regulatory issues. For Van Buren, the project turned out to be both interesting and financially rewarding. Within three months he had become socially friendly with several members of the board, often dining with them on his visits to Gatesville.

One problem that Van Buren spotted was that of a lack of organizational leadership. Two years earlier, the board had fired Andy Jackson, who had served as CEO for nine years. Jackson was a well-known administrator who was caught up in a series of financial irregularities.

Rather than replace Jackson, the board opted to allow the organization to be managed by a committee, at the president's suggestion. Ten people were appointed to the committee: the deputy chief executive officer, the chief financial officer, the human resources director, the food services director, the director of the physical plant, the administrator of the extended care facility, the chief of the medical staff, the hospital director of nursing, the administrator of ambulatory care, and the director of development. Technically, the group was chaired by the board president (who rarely attended); in practice it was Calvin Pyle, the deputy CEO, who ran the meetings.

By the time Van Buren arrived, Pyle had been with the system for 15 years and had been promoted to his job several years earlier by Jackson. Many on the staff, including Pyle himself, had assumed that he would be promoted to the CEO position when Jackson was fired. Pyle was clearly disappointed, but in the following two years did everything he could to win the board president's confidence. Within weeks of arriving at Gatesville, it became evident to Van Buren that Pyle's sycophantic behavior toward the board president was part of his lobbying the president for the top

(continues)

Case Study 9-1

job. Van Buren quickly became convinced that the management team approach was a mistake. He proposed to the board that his consulting assignment should be expanded to include an executive search. The board agreed, and for the next five months Van Buren searched for appropriate candidates, several of whom were brought in for interviews. In each instance, the board's executive committee rejected the candidate.

Eight months after the consulting project began and subsequent to what he thought were visits from four candidates, Van Buren confronted the board with the difficulty in their selecting a CEO. Out of frustration he even suggested that Pyle be given the job. The board president responded to that suggestion by saying, "He is a decent number two, maybe the best, but as long as I'm board president he will never be the CEO." Van Buren was surprised by the president's statement and even more shocked by the president's next statement, "Eliot, I think we can't select anyone because we all agree that we simply want you to be our CEO. Name your deal! You can do anything you want—hire or fire anyone." Within a month Van Buren agreed to the proposal, resigning from the consulting firm and planning his move to Gatesville.

Based on his experiences with the system, Van Buren expected problems with Pyle. First, he recognized that Pyle had wanted the CEO job and did not get it. Second, he had heard through the grapevine that Pyle had been denigrating his experience and background and that Pyle thought that Van Buren would be a disaster. Shortly after accepting the job, Van Buren telephoned the board president and suggested that Pyle be terminated. The president rejected this proposal and told Van Buren that he wanted Pyle as number two in the organization and that he had just given Pyle a significant pay increase.

Van Buren is now having second thoughts about having taken the job.

DISCUSSION QUESTIONS

1. Assume Niccolo Machiavelli was Eliot Van Buren's personal consultant. What advice would Machiavelli give Van Buren if he chose to take the job?

2. Assuming Van Buren does take the job, what can he expect from Pyle?

3. What should Van Buren do?

CHAPTER 10

Structure and Staffing of Health Care Organizations

All organizations have a structure. Sometimes that structure is shown on an organization chart; other times the structure is unclear on first inspection. Regardless of the presumed structure, there are two major points to keep in mind. First, there is no magic in any given structure. A well-structured organization is no guarantee of success. A corollary of this is that no structure is sacrosanct. A structure that may work at one time might not work at a later time. The second major point is that a structure is similar to a road map. It gives an observer an idea about relationships and distance, but it does not provide an in-depth understanding of power, personalities, or functions.

Why bother to have an organizational structure? In one sense, there is an easy answer: It is unavoidable. Whether or not the structure is committed to a piece of paper and labeled as an organization chart, the organization has a structure. At the simplest level, there is the one-person organization, where all authority and responsibility are vested in a single individual. When the organization increases its size by 100% to two persons, some structure must be developed; otherwise, duplication of activities and perhaps conflict will result. Functions, responsibility, and authority must be delineated and assigned. As the organization expands and more staff are hired, more structure is imposed. Each step of structural development requires a clearer definition of organizational goals, responsibility, and authority. Structure, then, is a shorthand for identifying significant relationships. To a limited extent, it also provides information about the processes in the organizations.

People are socialized to organizational structure practically from birth. In families, parents serve as the top managers; there is division of labor, some delegation of responsibility, and, no doubt, conflict. Nursery schools, grade schools, and virtually any job introduce structured organizations to our lives.

The structure itself sets up certain expectations. For example, there is one person on top in a classic pyramid structure. Two people report to this person, several people report to these two people, and so forth. It is expected that communication up or down the organization will go through the specified chain of command. This is how the military functions, and going outside the chain is considered unacceptable organizational behavior. Thus, while a U.S. Navy captain and sailor, as citizens of the United States, have the right to correspond with their senator or representative, it would be frowned upon for either of these people to go to their elected official to register a complaint about how something was functioning in the naval service. Their recourse, it would be argued, is the next step up the chain of command; going to Congress would be jumping too many levels on the chain.

A final point on the notion of expectations is that the pyramid structure provides many people with a strong sense of security. It lets them know to whom they are responsible and for whom they are responsible; it tells them something about the path they must follow to reach any personal or professional goals. In organizations where this is unclear, it appears that individuals with a strong sense of personal direction are able to climb the illusory ladder faster than people who need greater direction and who tend to get stymied otherwise.

Most other organizational forms are simply variations on the pyramid. There recently has been more discussion about the ruling junta approach, or the office of the chief executive route. In this structure, a team at the top runs the organization, and teams may function at lower levels. Clearly though, team members have their own strengths and weaknesses, and thus the teams to some extent become pyramidal in a functional sense.

The matrix organization is a variation of the team approach in which a type of cooperative relationship is developed between the vertical and horizontal hierarchies involved in a particular function. For example, a typical hospital patient floor has people working from several different departmental areas, and the number of job titles and levels may exceed two dozen. Included are an attending physician, a resident from medicine, a chief resident from medicine, a consulting resident from surgery, a laboratory technician, a nurse supervisor, a staff nurse, an orderly, aides, volunteers, housekeepers and their supervisors, ward clerks, food services personnel and their supervisors, maintenance staff from the engineering department, respiratory therapists, and so on. A housekeeping supervisor is responsible for all the housekeepers, a food service director is responsible for the range of food service activities in the institution, and the director of nursing is responsible for everything from the nursery to the operating room. Conflict is almost inevitable when trying to coordinate the activities of all of these people in the best interest of the patients on the floor.

In the typical hierarchical organization, a problem, complaint, or change requires sending messages up the various chains of command and then having the middle managers (either the department heads or assistant administrators) coordinate their efforts, resolve the issue, and communicate the decision down their various command chains. The amount of communication involved carries a tremendous potential for distortion or incorrect interpretation. The matrix organization delegates large areas of responsibility and authority to an administrator on the unit, perhaps a nurse or a manager. The people on the unit are initially responsible to this administrator, who coordinates all disparate areas. The major criticism of this approach is that instead of one "boss," there are now two or three.

CENTRAL CONCEPTS

The traditional issues considered in discussions of structure are span of control, division of labor, departmentalization, and delegation.

Span of Control

Span of control is perhaps the most academic of all of these issues, since there is no clearly right answer. The basic question here is: How many persons can a given manager effectively manage? The answer depends on the skill of the manager, the intensity with which he or she wants to manage, the quality of the subordinates, the quality of the operating systems, and countless other factors. The condition of the physical plant may even have an impact. For example, if the health facility has a plant that is in excellent repair and does not need any major renovations or expansions, a manager will not have to deal with the myriad problems of a poor plant and frustrated maintenance staff and will be free to deal with other people or problems.

Discussions of span of control usually concern an industrial organization. In those instances, it is relatively easy to identify the number of contacts managers are likely to have outside of their line position. In health care organizations, the problems of managing a staff are compounded by the problems of managing a medical staff and a host of regulatory agencies. It should be clear to any health care manager that, regardless of what the organization chart states, it is the rare physician who walks into the manager's office with the idea of seeing the "boss."

The fundamental issue in health care organizational structure is that a major component of the organization, the medical staff, is effectively off the chart. Span of control, then, is a useful concept for certain portions of the administrative organization of most health care programs, but it is an unrealistic concept for many professional activities.

However, in vivo, organizational leaders must constantly examine and reexamine the span of control that individual managers have and readjust that control in light of changing circumstances. In one large health care organization a change in span of control was made four years after a new CEO took over. This change involved the CEO divesting himself of many day to day responsibilities so that he could concentrate more on strategic planning—but the change, while perhaps of significance, even earlier had to await the arrival of a new senior executive and a period of confidence building amongst the senior team. In essence then span of control is a delicate and well-tuned dance that, like many aspects of management, has its own internal clock.

Division of Labor

The second central concept in organizational structure is division of labor. Jobs are organized in such a way as to divide specific functions appropriately. The prime motivating force behind the division of labor into the most appropriate and manageable tasks should be logic. In industrial organizations, logic plays an important role; however, in the health care field, logic is somewhat constrained by licensure requirements, power relationships, and tradition. In nursing, for example, the registered nurse (RN) has the authority to administer certain medications under the physician's orders, while the licensed practical nurse (LPN) works under more restrictions. Years of experience, maturity, and skill will never allow the LPN to function as an RN. At the next step up the ladder, the RN cannot order, stop, or change a medication on pain of dismissal or worse. There are obviously standing orders and various ways around this situation, but the fact remains that even a person who has developed the skill and experience to function in a higher role will not be able to function formally in this role. Despite their skill and knowledge, nurse-midwives are never granted a franchise similar to that which the least experienced general practitioner has for the delivery of obstetrical services, and there is no way the administrator of a hospital in which she works under the direction of the medical staff can restructure the clinical services so that she can function exactly as an obstetrician. In the health field, the division of labor in many critical areas is more a function of tradition and licensure requirements than the logic of the system.

At a theoretical level, industrial engineers could come into the health care organizations, stopwatches in hand, and develop various schemes for maximizing the effectiveness and efficiency of the institution while minimizing the expenses. Their findings would likely involve reconstituting jobs and reorganizing relationships. The legal and social structure provides too many constraints about what could be reconstituted and thus reorganized, however.

In the best of all possible organizational worlds, a health care organization would be started from scratch. Jobs would be defined, people who met the specifications for the jobs would be hired, and the organization would be set up in a functional way to meet relatively clear goals. In the health care field, as noted in an earlier chapter, goals are a bit diffuse. When compounded by the constraints of labor division, this diffuseness presents problems in establishing theoretical departments. It is interesting to consider how frequently both private industry and government reorganize and reconstitute their various departments. In the late 1970s, Sears, Roebuck and Co. started emphasizing the importance of sales over profits, and the result was a massive selling effort by the various stores. A decline in profits resulted, since much discounting was taking place to spur sales. Each time Sears changed goals, a reorganization and rebalancing of the organization was required. Observers of both the federal and state health establishments will probably agree that these organizations have made reorganization their regular mode of operation.

Departmentalization

The third structural issue, departmentalization, takes place along traditional educational lines and, to a lesser extent, on professional functional lines. It should also be noted that some departmentalization takes place on purely political lines or, in some cases, economic lines. For example, one hospital studied had both a laboratory and a pathology department. These two departments in many respects had duplicate equipment and personnel, resulting in excessive laboratory and pathology costs for the patients. They were organized in this way primarily because of personality conflicts between the laboratory director and the pathologist. Further exacerbating the problem was the administration's interest in keeping tight control of the income in the laboratory, which was considered easier if the pathologist was not involved. From a general managerial perspective, the arrangement was senseless, but in terms of the politics of that organization, it was necessary.

Delegation

A fourth area for consideration is that of delegation, passing the authority and responsibility for a given operation to those at different levels of the organization's structure. The classic concept is that responsibility and authority should function in concert. An individual who has the responsibility for carrying out a job should also have the authority to finish the job. In the automobile production factory, this might be possible, but in the health setting with its myriad subspecialists, the situation is more complex. A respiratory therapist might be sent down to see a patient who is having difficulty breathing. At what stage in the patient's distress is the therapist in charge, or the nurse, or the physician (and which physician—the patient's family practitioner, surgeon, anesthesiologist, or psychiatrist)?

In general, health care organizations, most notably hospitals, manifest considerable confusion when it comes to organizational structure. They are typically organized along the axis of disease, age of patient, ambulatory status of patient, type of patient, and nature of supportive services. Hospitals usually have the following services: medicine, surgery, obstetrics, gynecology, and pediatrics. In more avant garde institutions, there is an ambulatory care service for the walk-in patient, which crosses all clinical barriers; an emergency service for the patient needing immediate care; and countless supporting services, ranging from the laboratory and X-ray to the laundry and cafeteria.

To say that the typical hospital organization chart is a hodgepodge is an understatement. It is a complete mess, full of dotted lines and direct lines of authority and responsibility that are meaningless. Who, for example, is responsible for the quality of professional care rendered by the respiratory therapist? The answer is simple: the head of respiratory therapy who, in turn, is responsible to a higher level of management, and eventually responsibility is traced up to the chief executive officer. The same chain can be followed to find who is responsible for the quality of lunch in the cafeteria. Now, who is responsible for the quality of surgical services delivered by Dr. Smith, a private practitioner who operates in the Jones Hospital seven times per week? The answers, despite all the organization charts, dotted and straight lines, become very fuzzy. It boils down to the fact that no one directs Smith for the most part; he is primarily responsible to himself. He certainly does not take orders from the elected chief of his service or the chief executive officer of the institution. He may negotiate with them, but views this as negotiations among equals.

The problem here, as with most other health care organizations, is that the organization's primary reason for being is not even on the organization chart. As an airline cannot function without pilots, a health care organization cannot function without physicians. While the airline does not have direct control over the minute-to-minute functioning of a pilot, there is no question in the pilots' mind that they work for the airline and that the airline has the authority and responsibility to schedule their activities, increase them (within limits), or change them. In other words, the airline has purchased their skill and time and can use them to meet its objectives. Of course, pilots retain the right to refuse and can attempt to sell their skill and time to another bidder.

For the most part, the voluntary hospital functions on stand-by, awaiting the utilization of its services by a theoretically undependable physician. *Undependable* means that physicians schedule their day, week, month, year, or professional career to meet their own needs, not the needs of the institution. How many physicians, for example, would be willing to reschedule their vacations and/or operating schedules in order to accommodate the low census problems of the local hospital? It is difficult for the institution, of course, to plan rationally when it cannot directly control its major component or, conversely, to develop extraorganization chart mechanisms that allow it indirect control over this component.

Other health care organizations, such as group practices or government hospitals, function differently, not because they are organized differently per se but rather because the nature of physician involvement is different. Physicians typically do not simply join a fee-for-service multispecialty group practice but are invited to join on the basis of what they are likely to contribute economically and professionally to the practice. No physician can free-float into the organization just by moving into the area. Second, expectations in terms of production are set either directly or indirectly for each new physician. In most cases, their incomes are a direct function of their gross input into the practice. Third, support services are developed to help the practitioner perform more efficient and effective medicine. As the practice grows, the management of the support services may become so complex that a business manager is hired, and this manager may also take the responsibility for managing the time and expertise of the clinicians for their best financial and professional interests.

Two points about this private group practice should be made clear: First, the manager is an employee of the physicians; second, sometimes the manager has a better understanding of the physicians' best interests than they do. In all instances, however, the manager's authority and responsibility are derived from the group's members, and the manager is theoretically involved in negotiating with them, not ordering them. The skills needed by a negotiator are quite different from those needed by someone whose authority comes from a line position. Negotiators must act from a base of expertise and hard data, and they must have the ability to persuade and inspire loyalty for themselves and their ideas. Finally, they must deliver, lest a poor performance undermine their expertise the next time. Thus, for the manager in the group practice situation the "track record" is all-important.

The nonprofessional components of the organization function according to the delineated structure, in which authority and responsibility are delegated to various people, and approvals for action are required up and down the line. Negotiation and leadership skills are replaced with directives and technical expertise on the job.

As noted earlier, the value of structure is that it gives some indications about the members of the organization and their general responsibility and authority. It does not reveal very much about the quality of their relationships or how well they do their jobs. Structure is also, at least in part, clear. Theoretical assumptions can be made. Since process is harder to deal with than structure, and outcome is even more difficult to deal with, there is a tendency to believe that changes in structure will inevitably lead to changes in process and outcome. This point is constantly illustrated in governmental organizations. Perhaps the best example of this was the establishment of the Department of Homeland Security. This "new" organization of 180,000 employees was basically a reshuffling of 22 agencies from various parts of government including the Departments of Treasury, Justice, and Agriculture. The new organization included the U.S. Secret Service, The U.S. Customs Service, The Immigration and Nationalization Service and the Animal and Plant Health Inspection Service.

VALUES OF ORGANIZATIONAL STRUCTURE

A clear value of a solid organizational structure is in the large multi-unit organizations in which it is imperative that response time be minimized. This organizational structure allows for policy development and policy interpretation but precludes continuous communication between the top levels and the operating levels of an organization. The written policy is a critical communication tool that is interrelated to the organizational structure, since it is dependent on the authority of someone in the chain of command.

Any health care organization has at least two structures: one is written on a piece of paper and is an artistic representation of what people believe happens, and the second is a nonwritten structure that actually represents the authority and responsibility centers of the organization. Further, despite what any chart states, a significant component group of those responsible, not only for the well being of the organization's constituents but also for the well being of the organization (perhaps its life) will not be on the chart. The "View of the World From 9th Avenue" is a well known and often imitated magazine cover drawn by Saul Steinberg for the March 29, 1976 edition of the *New Yorker*. In this drawing Steinberg shows Manhattan and the Hudson River covering most of America joined by a tiny wedge of land (the rest of America) and then the Pacific Ocean. And so it is oftentime in organizations—a larger than life personality, a CEO, a board chairperson, or a single physician, may so dominate an organization that no chart, other than one drawn by Steinberg, will give the chart justice.

A different and equally significant value of organizational structure is that the structure itself can be used as a medium for transmitting messages both inside and outside the organization. It is a means of emphasizing (or deemphasizing) functions and people, and it is also a way of establishing a person's authority over the organization and its events. For example, rarely does a senior-level executive or a new president come into an organization without almost ceremonially reorganizing. By reorganizing, a person is flexing organizational muscle; although in reality, little may have changed, the message has been sent that a new person is in charge.

A new structure has also become the mechanism for announcing a realignment of power or function in the organization. Hospital staff may be moved from a department head status to an assistant or full vice presidential status. There is a difference between being the director of planning, responsible to the vice president of operations, and being the vice president of planning, reporting to the executive vice president or the president. Restructuring is often a way of demoting someone without the actual embarrassment of moving that person down a notch. Everyone is moved up, but that person remains in the same place or is shifted laterally.

In sum, organizational structure has special value to any organization. However, structure is not static; it is clearly one of many important tools a manager can utilize in the quest for desired outcomes. Integral with the notions of organizational structure are those of staffing. An organization theoretically is built on the basis of goals, objectives, and concepts of outcomes. Managers are usually taught not to build their structure around people. People should be viewed as interchangeable, some urge. People are not interchangeable, however, particularly those valuable people who for whatever reason act as catalysts for the development and maintenance of an effective organization. Indeed, to satisfy these people, it is sometimes imperative that an organization be restructured to recognize their particular talents.

STAFFING

Staffing is perhaps the most critical function for which management is responsible. Through the type and quality of staff recruited, management can exert its greatest influence on the organization. Staffing includes several distinct phases:

- The identification of an organization's short-term and long-term manpower needs
- The definition of the jobs that are likely to be required
- The development of specifications for persons who will be suitable for these positions
- The recruitment of staff
- The development of staff
- The evaluation of staff

A question about organizational structure that must be resolved immediately is whether staffing functions shall be centralized or decentralized. A centralized model usually results in a personnel department that is most often viewed as a supportive service to the entire organization. In this model, the personnel department might coordinate all requests for personnel, in effect acting as a clearinghouse, and to some extent, as an adjunct for the chief executive. For example, during my CEO tenure I regularly met with my human resources department chief, considered him to be a key member of my executive staff, and worked with him on various organizational crises (including hiring freezes) to deal with fiscal problems.

In a totally decentralized model, all staffing decisions are made at lower organizational levels. In the medical center the ambulatory pediatric clinic might theoretically have the authority and responsibility for developing its own staffing patterns and then implementing them. The problem of course is that staff cost money. Despite the apparent needs of a unit, the funds may not be available to support the staff. In some instances funds from money-rich programs may be used to support a deficit operation—but this is likely only when there is a centralized system or a high level of understanding about the need for the various components to support the total system. Certain departments in the university are clear moneymakers while others are losers. However, as long as those revenue losers are central to the mission of the university they will also have the support of administration and the fiscally strong will subsidize the fiscally weak.

In the reality of health care organizations, there is a mixed central/decentralized model of authority and responsibility for staffing, despite the fact that most organization charts suggest that the structure is totally centralized. Typically, the planning for manpower needs goes on at a rather low organizational level, such as within a program or department.

Depending on the power of that unit—power being a function of its fiscal strength potential and its importance to the organization and/or personalities involved—the plan will either be implemented by central functionaries (for example, personnel) at the direction of the unit, or it will be implemented by the unit itself. The structure itself does not dictate how the decision process will flow, but the uncharted power relationships dictate the course of action.

The value of the decentralized approach is that the process can be streamlined and the response time to meet the needs of a unit can be minimized. On the other hand, decentralization precludes comprehensive staff planning and may result in higher costs because of problems, such as when a given program recruits a person at a salary that is out of line with those in other units. A centralized system provides guidelines within which each unit makes its own decisions. In certain situations in which operating divisions might be competing with each other, such staff decentralization would appear to be more sensible; however, in health care organizations, where careful articulation is almost mandatory, decentralization would appear to be a weaker approach.

Identification of Manpower Needs

In practice, a health care institution can either develop an organized and thematic method of evaluating its physician and manpower needs, or it can hope, pray, and muddle through. Most health care organizations choose the latter mode, unfortunately, which generally means that the decision to hire a new staff member may originate from any one of several places in the organization and for a variety of reasons. In one hospital, for example, the administration added a physician to the ambulatory care group because he was a prestigious medical staff member who was interested in scaling down his practice and the hospital wished to retain his patients. A "problem of success" then arose. The physician brought to the ambulatory care group enough patients for his scaled-down practice, as well as patients for the other group members. Indeed, shortly after he joined the group, another physician had to be added to handle the increased volume of business. The addition of one new person thus created the need for a second. However, whether the size of the group or the scope of its services actually reflected the needs of the community had never been addressed. In another case, a group of physicians decided to add a full-time physician because they "felt" that there was a two- to three-week wait for emergency treatment and that such a delay was excessive. The new person did fill a need, but several months after he arrived it was necessary for him to be discharged. What had occurred? First, the "clinical impression" of the two- to three-week waiting period, based on only a few shreds of evidence, was incorrect. Patients indeed waited that long to be admitted, but it was usually to accommodate their own schedule, not the physician's. Also, a demand for increased service was peaking in that community, which was something that analysis of past usage patterns could have disclosed and that demographic analysis could have explained.

Definition of Jobs

Both decentralized and centralized systems require a beginning point, and that is the definition of the job to be formed. This returns to the theoretical notions of structure. It is necessary to know exactly what jobs are required and, further, what persons working in those jobs are specifically going to do. The kind of physicians needed to develop a group practice depends on what the practice has as its objective. If they want to be a primary care group practice, physicians are needed who will provide first contact routine medical care to patients of all ages. Excluded from the practice will be surgery, other than the most minor types, and long-term psychiatric care. The job description thus explains the nature of the job and provides a general outline of the organization's expectations. It should also answer some fundamental questions: What are the duties to be performed in the job? How does this position relate to other positions in the organization? Who supervises the physician? Whom does the physician supervise? Together these reveal what the authority and responsibility of a job is. Theoretically, an organizational crossword puzzle can be made of all the job descriptions; if fitted together, they would generally indicate what the organization is actually about.

Job Specifications

The statement of job specifications emanates from the job description and, although it has similar components, it actually provides a list of qualifications that a suitable candidate should possess. For example, a job specification statement might include such obvious requirements as a license to practice in the state, along with more discriminating factors such as board certification or specialty. (Some job specifications identify needed value orientations or behaviors.) For a primary group practice, the kind of physician to be recruited obviously should be from one of the primary care specialties such as family practice, internal medicine, or pediatrics; a neurologist, dermatologist, or thoracic surgeon would be unsuitable. While the process of preparing and updating job descriptions and translating those descriptions into specifications can be time-consuming, sometimes tortuous, it can lead to a firmer understanding of the position for which someone is being recruited and a sharper focus on the type of person needed to fill the position.

Recruitment

Perhaps the most critical function in staffing is recruitment. The objective of any recruitment effort is to hire the person best suited for a position. Every organization has its own specifications for a given job; in order to maximize its potential for finding the "one person who fits," as broad a search as possible is usually suggested. This strategy is not universally accepted, however. Some believe that a narrower and more discreet recruitment effort has a higher payoff, both in terms of finding people and in terms of building the organization's image. By letting as many pre-targeted people as possible know that a search is underway and that all replies will be confidential, one can often identify candidates who were believed to be unavailable.

The various methods of recruitment that should be considered are in-house recruiting, colleague inquiries, employment agencies, and advertisements in professional journals and newspapers. The more clearly the job is defined, including the conditions of employment, the better the quality of the responses. For example, if an advertisement for an associate administrator in Florida states that compensation is dependent on experience and education, a pool of candidates will apply, ranging from recent graduates to senior administrators who are looking toward a financially viable retirement. Perhaps the advertisement should be for an associate administrator with five to seven years' experience with a clear starting salary.

In-house Recruiting

The logical first step in any search process is in-house recruiting. It essentially reviews the persons within the organization to ascertain whether one of them is qualified to fill the vacant slot. A second dimension of the process is that it allows the administration to keep the communication lines with the staff open. In this way, the recruitment process is not viewed as a threat, and information about available candidates can be exchanged. We have previously illustrated the importance of this approach with the example of the innovative manager. For example, when a veteran medical director of my organization retired I began by offering the associate medical direction a promotion to the top slot. This offer was declined because of the associate's other research and teaching interests as well as a disinterest in a senior administrative role. If I had not offered the job to this worthy person I suspect that he and perhaps other staff members would have carried a level of resentment toward me as well as the new medical director.

My in-house recruiting experience was positive because of the high quality of the associate medical director. But what happens when there is the case of a "Peter Principle" person who is potentially in line for the next level job? The Peter Principle posits, somewhat tongue-in-cheek, that people rise to their level of incompetence. Assuming that this is true, what happens when a medical director leaves, and the associate director is functioning at the lower level but unlikely to be able to handle the next level of responsibility? How is this problem handled? Some managers ignore the issues and simply go on with the outside recruiting efforts; others tell the associate flat out that he/she is not a candidate because they can't handle the job and then others search for a middle path. This path usually involves propounding the idea that the organization needs new perspectives that are most likely to come from outsiders. In my judgment these are delicate situations and kindness to long-term staff, while essential to organizational tranquility, must be balanced with the needs of both the organization and, most important, its patients.

Colleague Inquiries

One of the most popular search methods is writing letters to friends in the field and to other appropriate persons, such as university department chairs and staff of major hospitals. Responses to these letters vary from none to a deluge that includes the resumes of entire groups. If truly handled on a personal basis, the letter-writing process is time-consuming and expensive. It also tends to place a burden of increased correspondence on the recruiter, who may have to respond to requests for additional information or explain why a friend's choice was not selected.

Employment Agencies

A third strategy is the use of professional recruiting services. Organizations that provide such services include certain public accounting firms, national management consulting firms, and a host of executive search firms. In general, these firms secure candidates through the use of some advertising, a great many personal contacts, and files that have been developed over the years. The major advantage of these services is that they can identify and screen candidates fairly quietly, indeed sometimes anonymously. The primary disadvantage is that many of these organizations have limited experience and understanding of the health field, which affects their ability to evaluate candidates properly. Another unrelated but significant problem is that their fees can run as high as 35% of a year's salary. Overall, the major value of a good search firm is that they are the most likely source of candidates who are professionally successful and not actively searching for a job. Typically they find the people who are happy and secure in their jobs and not looking to leave—then they start marketing your job and organization, in a very real sense, enticing a successful practitioner from one organization to another.

A variation on the agency theme is the recruitment that is done by such professional organizations as the American Group Practice Association or the Medical Group Management Association. Somewhat like registries, these organizations attempt to provide candidates to institutions in search of a staff.

Advertising

Advertisements in professional journals are a popular and relatively inexpensive way of developing a candidate pool. There are two main types of journals that can be used: the classic professional journal, such as *Hospitals* or the *New England Journal of Medicine*, or the various controlled circulation journals. Although the cost of such advertisements is low and the readership is high, time lag is a problem. There are cases in which jobs are filled by candidates attracted via other media before the journal advertisement appears.

An alternative that is becoming increasingly popular is specialized newspaper advertising, particularly the health care opportunities section of the *Sunday New York Times*. Although these advertisements are not inexpensive, the response is generally quite good.

Basic Strategy

Persons considering a recruitment effort for professional level staff, either major or minor, might want to consider the following, somewhat eclectic, six-point strategy:

1. A mechanism for continuous assessment of the organization's professional manpower needs should be developed. This could be centralized in personnel or decentralized in units, with information provided to administration.

2. When a senior-level or critical vacancy is projected, a small search committee of three to five persons should be established to review or develop the job description and specifications. Basic questions to be considered are whether the job is still needed and where the position should be located in the organization.

3. After the job description and specifications are finalized, the search committee should engage an outside consultant as a reviewer for one day or a half day.

4. A staff recruitment coordinator should place advertisements and send letters in order to develop a pool of qualified candidates.

5. Initial review of applicants should be done either by the search committee or, in the case of technical positions, perhaps by a consultant. When the final group of candidates is selected, the search committee should interview and select.

6. After the selection has been made, the search committee and recruitment coordinator should evaluate the process and report on its effectiveness.

This six-point strategy is a general framework for thought. Recruitment is a time-consuming and expensive process that must be approached soberly and deliberately, as recruitment mistakes are costly.

Those involved in the search should feel that their recommendations are being taken seriously. Bypassing the recommendations of people who have spent a good deal of time recruiting a new staff member will be personally debilitating to those people and will have a negative ripple effect throughout the organization. Universities are frequently guilty of such behavior. With much fanfare, a search committee is appointed to find a person to fill a high position; many busy persons are tied up for days or weeks; finally, the administration selects the person it wanted in the first instance. The appointment of a search committee has accomplished several things. First, it has bought the administration valuable time to make or negotiate its decision; second, it has provided the necessary image of democratic process to assuage a sometimes hostile faculty and a busy "equal opportunity" officer; third, the committee occasionally identifies someone who might be appropriate to fill the job in question or some other job in the organization. Participation in the search committee ritual is a pastime some enjoy, whereas others dislike it intensely. In all cases, however, participants should feel that their time is not being wasted and that their efforts result in significant organizational contributions.

EVALUATION

Evaluation of structure or staffing assumes three key elements: (1) clear organizational goals, (2) identified production standards, and (3) objectivity on the part of those who are doing the evaluation and those being evaluated. Evaluation, then, is the art and science of organizational navigation. It is determining the organization's position in its chosen program area while simultaneously determining its efficiency and effectiveness. This is a rather tall order for the labor-intensive health care industry in which position, efficiency, and effectiveness are more likely to depend on the quality of staffing than on the quality of structure.

Can an excellent structure be effectively negated by a poor-quality staff or, conversely, can an excellent staff overcome the problems inherent in a poor structure? Countless examples can be cited in which a structure looks impressive on paper, but the organization itself simply does not function because the members of the staff are inadequate. For example, a few years ago, a university-based health services research organization failed completely despite the fact that its organizational design was based on one of the most successful research and development consulting firms in the United States. The organizational design was even translated architecturally to emphasize the equality of all staff and their functions. However, the research center was a total bust on virtually any indicator. Within four years of its inception, despite massive transfusions of foundation start-up capital, it was practically out of business. The research center had failed to generate any important research or funds for further operation. There was almost 100% staff turnover, and the quality of those coming in was considerably below that of those leaving. It was extremely difficult to attract researchers; overall morale was extremely low; finally, the research organization lost its credibility on the campus, thus making it even more difficult to secure funds from the university.

Why had this happened when a previously successful structure had been utilized? The success of the structure in the previous organization was a result of the clarity of its purpose and the quality of its staff. Structure itself does not generate quality, but quality may require major changes in structure. In many senses, the focus on structure in this new health services research organization was an example of the leadership's overconcern with form and insufficient concern with substance. Greater care was apparently taken in developing the structure and the conceptual mechanism for making the structure work, such as who will meet with whom and when, than with more important issues, such as what kind of research the organization will do, how it will provide its funding, and how it will attract top quality researchers.

When this organization was analyzed, it appeared that the top leadership considered high-quality researchers unimportant, since the structure was expected to generate better work because of the equality and cooperation required among junior-level people. The leadership was in no way malicious but, rather, naive. Although the leaders themselves were researchers, they apparently either understood little about how organizations functioned or were committed to concepts that simply could not function within a university environment. So there were two fatal flaws: a naïveness about goals and objectives, and a dogmatic commitment to a structure. The two flaws eventually brought the organization its problems: staffing.

Virtually everyone hired during the years of inception was expected, at least at the beginning, to express a belief in the organizational structure. Someone who didn't believe in the structure, with its countless meetings and, to an extent, intellectual insults from the organizational leadership, was to be considered an inappropriate candidate for a job. A genuine commitment to the structure sometimes soured after a while, and the person either left or became one of the mutterers. The top leaders, committed to the structure almost religiously, were unwilling to explore its cost/benefit ratio and thus provided themselves with a staff that was unable to meet the goals that the university had for it of financial self-sufficiency and high-quality professional publications.

Perhaps one of the more absurd examples of how this structure wasted the time and energy of the staff was an all-day meeting that was billed as an attempt to solve some of the research center's problems. All of the staff had been invited, since the structure dictated organizational equality despite financial inequality. The meeting was proceeding rather seriously, with several physician researchers venting their frustration with the way things had been progressing. One particularly promising person had just finished a rather emotional comment on his frustration with the center, his own inability to translate his energy into publications, and its implications for his future at the university. The leader responded by saying that he understood the points and needed time to think about them. Then, with the same seriousness of purpose, the leader asked a young staff member, a recent high-school graduate who ran the mimeograph machine, for his evaluation of the center. The young man replied that he felt the major problem was that lunch hours were scheduled at a bad time, since they did not coincide with those of his friends. In almost the same tone he had used earlier, the leader answered that he understood the seriousness of the point and needed time to think about it. The young researcher and some of his professional colleagues left the meeting at the next break and shortly thereafter resigned from the center. They considered the response to their problems within that structure inappropriate, and they believed the leadership was more concerned with the maintenance of the structure than with their own and hence the organization's development.

Evaluating either staff or an organizational structure must begin with identifying goals or objectives. Standards for performance can then be developed, and measurements can be made to determine how well the standard is being met. For example, the standard for a private airline probably is to make a profit. What is the standard for the airline's organizational structure? Probably, to maximize profit. Maximizing profit then can be translated into planes, pilots, routes, and schedules. The greatest planes in the world flown by the finest pilots are hardly important if an airline has poor routes and schedules. How many people are interested in flying on a 747 between Crowley, Louisiana, and El Paso, Texas? Assuming that the airline has good routes and schedules, it must next get the aircraft to fly efficiently and get passengers to fly on their aircraft. Is it worth the $250,000+ to get a top captain to man the controls of a multimillion-dollar 747? Considering the risk involved with the alternatives, not only is it worth the direct outlay for the salary and supporting staff, but it is also worth the continual investment in this person to ensure quality.

Health care organizations could learn some lessons from some segments of the airline industry. First, goals and objectives that are realistic and environmentally acceptable must be established. These goals are then translated into statements regarding the kind of people needed. Theoretically, these statements are turned into job descriptions and specifications, and then someone who can be evaluated on the basis of the job description and contributions toward the organization's goals is hired. The following companies used this strategy: Jet Blue, Southwest and Ryan Air in Europe—all companies with focused operations in all aspects of the business—and all companies with a solid bottom line. On the other hand we also have the bloated and confused airlines, American, United, US Air and countless European "flag" carriers that seem to spend considerable time with bankruptcy lawyers. In almost all instances it's people who made and make the difference!

To some extent, the acceptable or likely workload is unknown for some people, and this can cause an organizational structure to change. On one occasion, shortly after I had accepted administrative responsibility for a medical records department, I began to receive complaints about the slow turn-around time for patient summaries and the difficulty of getting records transcribed. It became apparent, after some investigation, that a centralized transcribing system for medical records was needed. During this investigation, inquiries about acceptable workload standards for medical record transcribers showed that, despite what appeared to be effective supervision, production varied by 100% within the department. Even the top producer was generating about 35% less than the norm for this job. Yet everyone looked busy; in fact, in the past few years, the supervisor had been given bonuses for her excellent supervision. Evidence now revealed, however, that this department was at least twice as big as it should have been and cost twice as much. With the new system, the department was restructured, and new standards became the basis for evaluation.

In some organizations, standards are so explicit that the standards themselves are part of the staffing process. For example, in one major university, faculty candidates are told during their interviews how many publications in which journals are necessary for contract renewal, promotion, or tenure. While at first glance that may seem rather arbitrary, it does set some rather clear expectations for the person considering the position. Further, it provides the standards for evaluation. There are many evaluation mechanisms and a great deal of literature on personnel evaluation, but the key to all of them is having a clear understanding of what is expected of the incumbent and how that person fits into the total organizational picture.

Eventually, each person who evaluates others is forced to rely on personal judgment; but to the extent that the evaluator understands what the organization is about and has empirical evidence on a given person, judgment can be refined and made most equitable.

In sum, then, organizational structures exist to facilitate decision making and to provide a road map to an organization. The structure itself should not be the goal, however, but rather the means for people within the organization to operate efficiently and effectively. The organizational structure may have to be redesigned, based on how well (or poorly) these people do their jobs.

Case Study 10-1
BARBARA JONES, RN

During the three years before her license to practice nursing was revoked, Barbara Jones had worked at the Clearview Nursing Center as a registered nurse. Some of the specific charges brought against Jones were that, for the three years she worked at Clearview, she had on 17 occasions failed to administer medication, treatment, and feedings to residents; 14 times she had made false entries into the residents' records concerning medications, feedings, and treatment; she had slept while on duty; she had removed residents' call bells so that she would not be called in the middle of the night; she had abused patients, including the forced feeding

(continues)

Case Study 10-1

of residents and hitting the stumps of two amputees against their bed rails; and she had failed to make rounds in accordance with the home's policies and the good practice of nursing.

After eight days of hearings, a hearing officer recommended that Ms. Jones's license to practice nursing be revoked. The State Board of Nursing agreed and revoked the license. Ms. Jones appealed the decision to the State Supreme Court, which upheld the decision.

A week after the State Supreme Court upheld the revocation, Ralph Robinson, the home's recently appointed administrator, was contacted by the administrator of a home in another state asking for a recommendation for Ms. Jones.

DISCUSSION QUESTIONS

1. What response should Mr. Robinson send to the nursing home that asked for a recommendation for Ms. Jones?

2. Why would the egregious behavior of Ms. Jones be tolerated for three years?

3. Is it possible that the behavior of Nurse Jones was unknown to her supervisor?

CHAPTER 11

Financial Management of Health Care Organizations

As I have attempted to emphasize both throughout this book and in my career, people are the heart and soul of an organization, but the reality is that money is the lifeblood of any organization. Whether you are running a small nursing home, a mega medical center or are simply "The Donald," you need money to operate the organization on a daily basis and you need money for capital upkeep and development.

Unfortunately, many managers in health care institutions have only limited training or education in the field of financial management. However, all managers need a basic understanding of the four major topics covered in this chapter: (1) the financial components of health care institutions and programs, (2) the elements of health finance, (3) special issues in health finance, and (4) the budgeting process.

FINANCIAL COMPONENTS OF HEALTH CARE INSTITUTIONS

Decision making regarding financial issues is handled in a variety of ways in any organization. While ultimate authority for financial decisions is in the hands of ownership or its representative, that is, the board, this top level of financial management may or may not actually be involved in the financial management of the organization, depending on the board's power. If it is powerful, that power most likely will be exercised through the purse strings. If it is not powerful, the board may simply act as a rubber stamp or may not be involved in the financial decisions at all. Quite often, boards take a middle-of-the-road position and act on annual budgets, any capital expenditure over a certain amount of money, or any major change in program that affects or risks the financial health of the organization. The daily management of finances is then delegated to the top managerial echelon which may delegate some of its responsibility and authority to others in the organization.

Within larger organizations and/or larger boards, the functions related to finance may be delegated to a finance committee. This committee may have limited direct authority, or it may simply be a fact-finding group for the entire board. There is, of course, no simple formula for how all this should work. The key point is that, in many organizations, the board is ultimately responsible and does indeed exercise that responsibility.

For publicly traded corporations, the early 21st century is surely the era of "Post–Sarbanes-Oxley." This federal law evolved as a response to eroding confidence in public corporations and developed a host of new financial reporting requirements, as well as emphasizing the role and responsibility (including the composition and qualifications) of audit committees. Sarbanes-Oxley is not directly applicable to most health care organizational managers, but it may well be a harbinger of the future.

It should be noted that while most boards are under no obligation to select only "financial experts" to serve on the finance committee or to be their guiding light on financial matters, it is certainly advisable to have people with enough expertise to communicate the board's needs to management as well as management's needs to the board. I have seen more than one board's finance committee composed of lawyers or businessmen who had no particular expertise in finance, much less health care finance, and had learned what they needed to know by experience. For example, in one hospital, the long-time board treasurer was the owner of a restaurant and catering business who had no knowledge of the intricacies of health care finance. On one hand, such a situation is helpful, in that the staff must make its case understandable to those who have only a general understanding of finance. On the other hand, the board is almost entirely dependent on staff for its information in such a situation and is, in a sense, a captive of its own employees.

The focus of financial activities within the health care organization or program is the chief financial officer, sometimes called vice president for finance or perhaps treasurer. Invariably these people are trained in accounting; sometimes they are certified public accountants, and occasionally they have special training in health care finance. In this day and age, it is imperative that the senior financial officer be literate in health finance and accounting, not merely general finance and accounting. At one point I was searching for a new CFO, and one of the board members suggested that I interview a friend of his who was a CPA and had at one time audited some hospitals in his community. The CPA was a pleasant and intelligent person but knew nothing about the current aspects of Medicare reimbursement or the local Medicaid situation. Additionally, his understanding and knowledge about the health care industry was spotty, at best. Despite the fact that he was likely a competent accountant, I simply couldn't afford the two to three years that would be required to get this man up to speed to be an effective CFO.

No position in the organization is more important to a CEO than that of his or her CFO. The CFO is responsible for developing and policing the systems that gather, analyze, and interpret financial and related operational data. If this data is correct and presented in a useful format, the CEO will have the proper evidence to make decisions or develop plans for the future. Inaccurate or indecipherable information will lead to disasters. Assuming the CEO does have a trusted CFO, they will undoubtedly become key partners in many of the important managerial decisions in the organization.

A major problem with an accounting and finance staff (and some might say their major value) is that they often lack experience in and perspective on health care operations. For example, most of the training programs in accounting and finance focus on the for-profit sector of the economy; entering the nonprofit sector with its slightly different systems, new nomenclature, and different objectives presents problems to a person trained in a different value system, and who possesses tools that are only useful when modified. To make up for the deficiencies, many organizations send promising individuals to special training programs and encourage them to enroll in the various health-related professional societies. Such educational and professional involvement serves two major purposes: It acquaints these people with the nature of health care organizations and their concerns, and it assists them in utilizing their professional skills to maximum effectiveness in the organization.

One major source of manpower for the accounting and finance team are the large public accounting firms. Until two decades ago, these firms were primarily involved in the auditing side of health care. However, they have now expanded their areas of interest and expertise by becoming involved in financial feasibility studies and a range of management consultant activities. In the late 1990s, for example, I used one of these firms to provide a financial feasibility study of a new assisted living center. Their product was a comprehensive analysis of the industry, the possibilities, the competition, and the probabilities of success (and failure). It was not merely an exercise in number crunching! Unfortunately for many people (and perhaps fortunately for health care organizations), the tight pyramidal structure of these accounting firms causes them to regularly jettison a significant number of their junior staff, thus providing a pool of experienced and well-trained personnel for the health industry.

Despite the expertise of the CFO, the CEO is held most closely accountable for the financial management of the organization. Administrators usually are not formally trained in finance or accounting but rather are trained in general management, which no doubt includes some background in accounting and finance. Typically, though, the board has delegated to both the CEO and the CFO considerable latitude in terms of financial expenditures. For example, in my organization, both the CFO and I had the authority to spend up to $25,000 at a time without seeking board approval. That, of course, did not mean that we could spend the money without accounting for it, but rather that each time an issue came up, we did not have to chase down the board and make a formal presentation on the expense. Thus, if a van broke down and needed a $5000 repair, it could simply be approved by the CFO. Or, as noted earlier, if a feasibility study needed to be commissioned, it could be ordered without reference back to the board. Obviously, the organization must have money in the budget for these items, but once the blanket authorization is provided, senior executives are empowered to use their judgment to make things happen.

Like most managers, however, administrators must depend on accounting and finance specialists for financial input into decision making. That is why trusting one's CFO is critical. In some ways, an administrator's lack of training in accounting and finance is an obvious limitation;

however, the administrator's primary value is in having a broad perspective on the institution's problems and opportunities. For example, one administrator pushed ahead on a money-losing geriatric program because she felt it was important to the long-range interests of the relationship between her hospital and the community. From a purely financial perspective, it might have been a bad decision; from a purely political perspective, it was certainly a reasonable choice.

Many others in a health care organization are important to its financial management. Among these people are business office staff, who are involved in the credit and collection systems of the organization; information systems people, who are involved in the systems that set up and record transactions; purchasing staff, whose decisions affect the cash flow and hence the financial health of the organization; the personnel department, which through its policies affects turnover, vacation substitutions, and a range of other activities that can be translated into dollars and cents. Indeed, the importance of information systems in the vitality of organizations is such that a new senior level profession of chief information officer (CIO) has emerged.

Essentially, then, any health care organization operates with a series of cash registers that, if properly utilized, take in (or ensure the receipt of) revenues and disburse money in a way that is organized and related to specific objectives. The nurse on the patient care floor of a hospital must ensure that the proper record is effected when the laboratory test is ordered or some product or drug is utilized; otherwise, the finance office does not bill the patient for the service. If the patient or insurer is not billed, then the organization has expended resources, such as the nurses' and laboratory technician's time, the machinery and supplies to perform the test, and all the overhead systems necessary to support the laboratory, without even the opportunity to be reimbursed. Clearly, everyone in an organization is part of the revenue-generating function. This was negatively demonstrated to me when I was on a consulting project at a health care facility where staff had bar-coded peel-off strips to record billable transactions. Because the nursing staff were so busy, they would frequently pull off the bar code label from the item and, instead of placing it in the proper place on the patient's billing form, they would merely place it on their uniforms. At the end of the shift I watched as these staff tried peeling the labels off their uniforms, tossed some of the wrinkled labels in the trash, tried to remember who should be charged for what, placed some on the correct form and others on incorrect forms, and finally, in frustration, tossed the rest. Money in the dumpster!

ELEMENTS OF HEALTH CARE FINANCE

Taxes

Health care organizations that are incorporated as for-profit organizations or are partnerships are taxed as any other corporation is taxed. Most hospitals and a number of other institutions and programs, however, are incorporated as nonprofit charitable organizations and, therefore, are exempt from a range of federal, state, and local taxes under Section 50l(c)(3) of the Internal Revenue Code. According to the Tax Code, they are "organized and operated exclusively for religious, charitable, scientific [or] educational purposes [and] no part of the net earnings of which inures to the benefit of any private shareholder or individual." This exemption does not preclude these organizations from making a profit or force them to operate at the break-even point, or even require them to lose money. Rather, it requires that any profit made by such an organization must not directly benefit any single person or group of stockholders.

The value of this exemption is enormous. First, the corporation is not required to pay federal income taxes. Second, most states and municipalities recognize this exemption and allow these organizations to be free of real estate and sales taxes. However, increasingly cash-strapped governmental units are now looking to 501(c)(3) organizations to either pay taxes or provide some type of payment in lieu of taxes.

In general, tax laws differentiate between related and unrelated income. Income from activities that are related to the operation and objectives of the organization, such as a profit-making cafeteria run by a large group practice for the convenience of the staff and patients, is tax-exempt. Clearly unrelated income would be taxable. For example, if a nonprofit organization owned a spaghetti factory, the profits from the spaghetti factory would be taxable before they could be transferred to the nonprofit organization. Farfetched example? Not really, since the Mueller Spaghetti Company was once owned by New York University's Law School. There is, as in most tax law, a gray area of questionably related income. For example, is the profit generated by a physician's office building taxable or not? What about separately incorporated businesses such as a hospital laundry or a kosher catering business? The general test is whether the activity has a substantial relationship to the parent charitable corporation. If it is substantially related and furthers the charitable mission of the parent, the courts tend to look favorably on it; otherwise, the tax may be due.

Philanthropy

Occasionally, a wealthy benefactor wills millions to a hospital or university. While that type of philanthropy is becoming rare, philanthropy on a smaller scale has continued for the past several decades; however, as a percentage of total revenue, it has declined. Philanthropy is important to an organization for spiritual as well as for financial reasons. Spiritually, it tells the organization that it has friends and supporters, and in today's often-hostile climate of management and regulation, such statements of support are comforting. From a financial perspective, philanthropy provides funds; however, many of the philanthropic gifts that health care organizations receive are specially targeted funds, that is, given for a single purpose, such as a building or a program endowment. When money is put into an endowment, the use of the principal is restricted, and the interest is available for the purposes of the endowment only.

A few of the problems facing health care organizations in terms of philanthropy include the source of the money, the restrictions placed on the money, the cost of getting the money, and baby boomers' sense of entitlement, rather than charity. In terms of source, despite the fact that there are over 50,000 family foundations, most foundations give away small amounts of money and the strings attached to that money are often burdensome. However, there are some exceptions. The Dorothy Rider Pool Health Care Trust and the Rider-Pool Foundation in Allentown, Pennsylvania, for example, focus their activities on health care in the Lehigh Valley and have had an enormous impact in that area. In 2002, for example, the Trust gave out $7.9 million; in 2003, it gave away another $4.0 million. Its record of gift-giving year appears to be 1998, when it provided $12.3 million to its community. The list of projects that this single trust has sponsored is truly remarkable—everything from endowed professorships to quality improvement programs, children's health initiatives, and programs for patients with AIDS. What is perhaps most impressive is how much impact one foundation can have on a community by its continuing commitment. In essence, this Trust has, over the years, become a veritable powerhouse for change in the Lehigh Valley of Pennsylvania. On a national basis, the Robert Wood Johnson Foundation has kept its focus on health care and has used its enormous leverage to develop a range of innovative programs, such as hospital-based group practices.

Throughout the country are many small foundations. One example is Miami's Blank Family Foundation, which provides small grants to organizations that become opportunities for innovation and change. Sometimes grants come from unlikely places. For example, I once obtained a grant from the Episcopal Church Foundation for research I was doing on Japanese hospitals; the Church owned one hospital in Japan and was interested in what was happening in that country. I received grants on two occasions from the Scholl Foundation (as in Dr. Scholl's foot products) for research and development activities about Alzheimer's disease. Unfortunately, while there are numerous sources of money, there are far more people in search of the funds, and over the years it has become increasingly difficult to snare even small grants.

A second issue is the strings attached to the money. When money is given, it appears to be transferred to the recipient in an unrestricted fashion less often than it was in the past. The problem with conditions on the money is that operational costs are rarely endowed; thus, for example, money may be provided for a new classroom and laboratory building at a hospital or university, but not for maintenance, heat, or cleaning the facility. These costs are sometimes quite high, but have little appeal to potential donors.

Development activities, although central to the finances of an organization, often function independently of the finance department. For example, in my organization, the development director, while not at the same organizational level as the CFO, nevertheless also reported directly to me as CEO. What is perhaps more important than organizational relationships is functional responsibilities. Typically, the development staff (in my case, nine full-time people plus an army of volunteers) are charged with the responsibility of developing and implementing a fund-raising plan involving annual giving, special appeals, membership drives, and capital gifts. There are many ways to go about this process, but the key is having staff that can make friends and can turn that friendship into raising money. While this may sound mercenary, it should be acknowledged that the purpose of fund-raising is assisting charitable organizations to reach their goals. Sometimes the best fund-raisers are also board members.

In one organization in which I worked, the chairman of the board was a masterful fund-raiser. He was careful to identify people of wealth whose family situations and other obligations were such that they would be likely candidates for major philanthropy. He would then befriend them very genuinely and warmly, treating them practically as if they were family. The donors or potential donors were always treated as VIPs at the organization and frequently feted. At some point in the relationship, they were expected to "pay the piper" with $50,000 to become an organizational donor. As they pledged or gave more money, they were feted in an even grander manner. Ego stroking paid off handsomely in these cases.

Another strategy that many sophisticated organizations use is the charitable remainder trust. This involves individuals giving stocks or other appreciated securities to a charitable organization in return for a guaranteed annual income. The value for the donor is tax deductions plus a guaranteed income, which is usually higher than could be received from conservative investments such as certificates of deposit. The money becomes available for investment for the organization, and upon the death of the donor there are no further financial obligations attached to the funds. Such trusts must be carefully managed and are subject to state regulation.

The point is that it takes considerable time and money to raise funds for any organization. Health care organizations must compete for limited charitable dollars with a range of other social programs that seem to materialize overnight. Success in the world of charitable fund-raising requires a program or service that people need, want, respect, or love; staff who can package and pitch the program or service; and attention to the details of the project and the relationships that are fostered. Despite the biblical injunction to tithe, it simply does not happen without the hard work of development staff.

Finally, all charitable organizations are facing what might be called the baby boomer-entitlement problem. Simply stated, the younger generation, Bill Gates excepted, is generally not very charitable. Despite the very respectable incomes of many professionals, they appear to spend money on their own luxuries to the exclusion of charity. Of all the support and fund-raising groups in my organization, the only one that consistently failed to break even and needed an annual subsidy was the support group of young (under 50) professionals. They were big on having organizationally subsidized parties but not generous with their own dollars. At one point, our organization had a 50th anniversary dinner, and as part of the fundraising for this event we prepared a journal. It fell to the director of development and me to solicit our medical staff for advertisements for the journal. The total collected from several dozen physicians, all baby boomers, some of whom made six-figure incomes thanks to our patients and residents, was $1,000 (one thousand dollars)! One of the specialists who claimed to not be able to afford a donation because of family expenses purchased the following year a 34-foot Intrepid fishing boat with twin 225 Yamaha 4-stroke engines—roughly $100,000.

Operating Finances

Revenues: General

Revenues to health care organizations can be broken down into two categories: operating and nonoperating. Operating revenues are generated by clients or patients who request the services that the organization is in business to offer. Nonoperating income is that which is generated independent of the patients in the organization, although it is directly related to the organization's existence and mission.

Operating income from patients may be financed by one of a variety of sources, including the government through Medicare or Medicaid; insurers, such as Blue Cross and Blue Shield; scores of other private carriers; managed care organization contracts; governmental uninsured patient care pools; and, in rare instances, patients themselves. Each of these different payers operates with a slightly different set of reimbursement rules for services, which translates into different billing and often different collection services. The income itself is generated by the patient who uses a hospital room, operating room, ancillary services (pharmacy, laboratory, X-ray), or professional services. In hospitals, because of differing agreements with the various payers, patients with similar diagnoses and treatment regimens being treated by the same physician in similar accommodations may, in fact, generate different revenues for the hospital. The same is often true in nursing homes or even ambulatory care settings. This is analogous to an airplane; despite the fact that all the passengers are flying between the same two cities, they are not all paying the same fare. Some are paying first-class fare; others are paying full tourist fare; others are paying a 14- to 21-day advance fare; others are paying a 45-day excursion fare; others are traveling on half-fare coupons; others on a tour-based fare; and so forth.

Nonoperating revenue comes from grants for projects or development, philanthropy, and other activities, such as parking lots, cafeterias, and gift shops. This income is important, particularly when operating revenues are tight, since funds generated from these sources can often provide the seed money for future development and thus help the organization maintain a competitive edge in its area.

Revenues: Medicare and Medicaid

For most health care organizations, Medicare and Medicaid are the two most significant sources of revenue. In the following discussion I shall clarify the distinctions between these two programs and, for illustrative purposes, provide some detail about the reimbursement in these programs within the long-term care industry.

Medicare and Medicaid are two programs with essential differences. Medicare is a federally funded health insurance program, primarily for persons 65 years of age and older. The Medicare program has a number of special provisions that provide care for younger people who are receiving Social Security disability payments or are in the categorical disease categories of end-stage renal disease. The original concept of Medicare was to pay for hospital stays. This concept in large measure still drives its system, which is really that of paying for hospital stays or alternatives to hospital stays. This conceptual understanding explains why other care, such as custodial nursing home services, are not provided by Medicare. (Medicaid is the state and federal partnership program that pays for services to the poor and medically indigent. This program, for example, does pay for custodial nursing home care. More details about Medicaid will be discussed shortly.) Reimbursement under the Medicare programs comes in two distinct parts, identified as Part A and Part B.

Part A essentially covers inpatient care: typically, inpatient services for hospitals, skilled nursing facilities, and certain other health care providers, as well as patients requiring daily professional skilled nursing and other rehabilitative care. Even where nursing home coverage is permitted, there are limits and qualifications, such as a requirement of medical necessity, a 100-day limit to the nursing home stay, and a required 3-day hospital stay before admittance to the skilled nursing home. Even then there is not full coverage for the stay in the nursing home.

Part B is supplemental coverage, for which the beneficiary must pay an additional premium. This section of Medicare provides reimbursement for physician services and other outpatient services, such as physical, occupational, speech therapy services, IV nutrition, certain medical items, and X-ray services received outside of a Part A–covered inpatient stay.

By way of illustrating the financial complexity of this reimbursement under Medicare, the next several pages will review the Medicare situation as it relates to skilled nursing facilities.

If a person is in a skilled nursing facility and the facility is being reimbursed under Part A Medicare, that reimbursement uses acuity levels. Acuity is determined by classifying the resident into 1 of 44 resource utilization group (RUG) categories, based upon the nature of the resident's condition and needed services. The U.S. Department of Health and Human Service's Centers for Medicare and Medicaid Services (CMS) adjusts the Medicare rates for the 44 RUG categories on October 1st of each year and inflates the RUGs' rates based upon an inflation factor referred to as the "market basket." Under Part B Medicare, the nursing facility is reimbursed based upon defined rates established by CMS.

Prior to October 1, 2002, the incremental Medicare relief packages received from the Balanced Budget Refinement Act and the Benefits Improvement and Protection Act provided a total of $2.7 billion in temporary Medicare funding enhancements to the long-term care industry. These funding enhancements fell into two categories. The first was "Legislative Add-ons," which included a 16.66% add-on to the nursing component of the Resource Utilization Group III rate and the 4% base adjustment. The second category was "RUGs Refinements," which involved an initial 20% add-on for 15 RUGs categories identified as having high-intensity, nontherapy ancillary services. The 20% add-on from three RUGs categories was subsequently redistributed to 14 rehabilitation categories at an add-on rate of 6.7% each.

The Legislative Add-ons expired on September 30, 2002 (referred to as the "Medicare Cliff"), resulting in a reduction of Medicare funding for skilled nursing facility operators of approximately $30 per day. The loss of this funding was partially offset by a 2.6% market basket increase in Medicare rates received by long-term care providers beginning on October 1, 2002. Effective October 1, 2003, CMS increased Medicare rates by 6.26%. This reflected (1) a cumulative forecast correction (Administrative Fix) that increased the federal base payment rates by 3.26%; and (2) the annual market basket increase of 3.0%. While these rate increases clearly provided additional revenues to nursing home providers, the funds simply did not flow to the bottom line because on the expense side, all operators were faced with higher labor and operating costs. Additionally, in October 2003, CMS published a notice to skilled nursing facilities that within future cost reports it would require confirmation that the Administrative Fix funding was spent on direct patient care and related expenses.

With respect to the RUGs Refinements, CMS announced in April 2002 that it would delay the refinement of the RUGs categories, thereby extending related funding enhancements until September 30, 2003. In May 2003, CMS released a rule to maintain the current RUGs classification until October 1, 2004. As should be obvious, any CMS decisions to discontinue all or part of the enhancements could have a significant adverse effect on providers of skilled nursing care. The ability of those providers to influence the decision-making process is clearly limited.

Outpatient therapy services under Part B present a different set of issues specifically related to caps on therapy services. As of January 1, 2003, the moratorium on implementing payment caps for outpatient Part B therapy services, which was scheduled to take effect on that date, was extended until September 1, 2003. The therapy caps were in effect from September 1, 2003, until December 8, 2003, when, as a result of the Medicare Prescription Drug, Improvement and Modernization Act of 2003, the moratorium was reinstated for a two-year period, until December 2005. The impact of a payment cap vary by facility and are difficult to estimate. But there is also the social cost; that is, it is unlikely that a person will receive an unreimbursed service when there are caps on payments. This was illustrated when one commentator noted that the caps on therapy reimbursement may mean that when a person comes into rehabilitation, they will be asked whether they want to walk or talk!

In another example of how the reimbursement and therefore revenue system works, in February 2003 CMS announced a plan to reduce its level of reimbursement for uncollectible Part A coinsurance. CMS did not implement the rule change as planned on October 1, 2003, and continues to review the proposed plan. Under current law, skilled nursing facilities are reimbursed 100% for any bad debts incurred. The plan was to reduce the reimbursement levels from the current 100% to 90% as of October 1, 2003; 80% as of October 2004; and 70% as of October 2005. This is consistent with the reimbursement policy applicable to hospitals. Perhaps the theory is that by reducing the uncollectible Part A coinsurance, the facilities will work harder to collect the money themselves.

Medicaid is a state-administered program financed by state funds and matching federal funds that provides health insurance coverage for certain persons in financial need, regardless of age, and that may supplement Medicare benefits for financially needy persons aged 65 or older. Medicaid reimbursement formulas are established by each state with the approval of the federal government and in accordance with federal guidelines. There is significant variation in the balance of federal and state money in the program, with each state's formula being calculated on the basis of the state's wealth. Further, while there is a baseline of services available throughout the country, some states offer additional services and programs, while others stick to the basic requirements. There are significant differences in how these programs are managed from state to state in terms of day-to-day administration, despite federal guidelines. In the past two decades, states with budgetary problems have typically looked to cut their Medicaid programs, often called "budget busters," as a first stop in saving money.

One way that states go about controlling costs and services under Medicaid is through their reimbursement strategies. Unlike Medicare, where a national RUGs strategy is employed, states are free to choose their systems. In the long-term care industry, two common strategies that demonstrate the complexity of the system are the cost-based systems and the price-based reimbursement systems. Under cost-based reimbursement systems, the facility is reimbursed for the reasonable direct and indirect allowable costs it incurs in providing routine resident care services as outlined by the program. Certain states provide efficiency incentives, and facilities may be subject to cost ceilings. Reasonable costs normally include some allowances for administrative and general costs as well as the cost of capital or investment in the facility, which may be transformed into a fair rental or cost of capital charge for property and equipment. The price-based or modified price-based systems pay a provider at a certain rate irrespective of the provider's cost to deliver the care. Price-based or modified price-based systems may use various methods, such as state averages tied to a specific base year, to determine the base cost, which could be subject to inflationary increases.

The reimbursement formulas employed by the state may be categorized as prospective or retrospective in nature. Under a prospective cost-based system, per diem rates are established based upon the historical cost of providing services during a prior year, adjusted to reflect factors such as inflation and any additional service required to be performed. Many of the prospective payment systems (PPS) contain an acuity measurement system, which adjusts rates based on the care needs of the resident. Retrospective systems operate similar to the pre-PPS Medicare program, in which nursing facilities are paid on an interim basis for services provided, subject to adjustments based on allowable costs, which are generally submitted on an annual basis.

The Revenue Cycle

Effective management of the revenue and accounts receivable cycle is key to the survival of a health care organization. No matter how good the service is, if the facility does not bill for the service and collect accounts receivable, it cannot stay in business for long. It sounds too simple, but many organizations take a significant loss due to unbilled charges through preventable omissions and errors, resulting in the ultimate noncollectibility of accounts. Long-term collection results will depend on effective systems and controls at every step of the way.

Intake and Admissions

A key element of the entire process is the presence of proper intake and admitting procedures. We will use a long-term nursing home facility as an example. This process starts with building an accurate and complete database from the time an inquiry for service is received by facility personnel. The persons taking inquiries should be well-trained in the financial aspects of the admission process as well as the marketing aspects. They must be capable of developing a preliminary assessment of a prospective resident's condition, needs, and financial resources while simultaneously marketing the facility to the prospective resident. The data gathered is evaluated, and a determination is made as to the appropriateness of the admission.

Verification of the prospective resident's third-party coverage should be an integral part of the admissions process. Additionally, because of the debilitated health status of most applicants, a visit to the hospital to meet with and evaluate the prospective resident may help avoid inappropriate placements. The need for and extent of these measures will depend on the relationship with the referral source. Ideally, the nursing home will build relationships of trust with referral sources over time, and they will be able to work together effectively to meet the needs of all parties involved.

If the applicant is admitted to the nursing home, the next step in the admission process is a review and execution of the admission agreement. Such agreements have become complex legal documents in their own right, with new requirements added every day. It is imperative that the new resident and his or her representative understand the obligations they are undertaking, as well as their rights as health care consumers. If the resident is deemed incompetent, a duly authorized representative who can legally act on behalf of the resident must be identified and assume the role of "responsible party."

When discussing payment, it is important that the resident or responsible party knows what is included in the facility's base rate, what is extra, and the possibility that, after proper notice, rates and payment arrangements might change. Likewise, care must be taken that the resident or representative understand what third-party coverage might be available, as well as the limitations of any such coverage. In some states, such as California, Medicaid requires that a "liability" be met by the resident before Medicaid coverage commences, a concept very much akin to a deductible in private insurance policies. Similarly, Medicare has certain deductibles and coinsurance that must be met by the resident or responsible party. If the resident is private pay, it is recommended that the facility collect a deposit equivalent to several months' charges at the time of admission, and the ground rules should be discussed as to when payment is expected on an ongoing basis. Generally, private-pay residents should pay in advance for the month upcoming.

One dilemma often facing the facility is how to deal with residents who have applied for Medicaid but have not yet been approved. These residents are commonly referred to as "Medicaid-pending" and present a risk to the facility inasmuch as it remains questionable whether the facility will be paid for its services. Where applicable, a deposit covering at least the first 30 days of care should be requested, and a thorough evaluation of the resident's Medicaid application performed. Here, too, the extent to which the family cooperates in the process and the known experience and accuracy of the referral source are factors that can minimize the facility's exposure.

Medicare admissions are among the most complex, since a number of additional steps must be performed. In addition to verifying the resident's Medicare coverage, a determination must be made as to whether the resident's condition meets Medicare's strict eligibility criteria from a level-of-care standpoint. This determination is based on a combination of the resident's diagnosis and the nature and extent of "skilled care" required. For this reason it is important to have the input of a qualified nurse who is well versed in the Medicare program. If it is determined that Medicare coverage is not applicable, the facility is required to issue to the resident or responsible party a "Medicare denial letter." The resident may challenge the facility's determination and request that an independent review be performed by the facility's Medicare intermediary. This can be done by requiring the facility to submit a "demand billing" to the intermediary and await its decision. The facility cannot request payment for services until a decision is made by the intermediary, which could have a negative impact on cash flow. However, in most cases, effective communication between the facility and the resident or responsible party will obviate many of these problems.

Medicare admissions also require screening other coverage such as HMO membership, since Medicare regulations mandate payment to be sought first from any other existing coverage. This screening is required under the regulations commonly known as the "Medicare secondary payer" rules. In fact, with the accelerating growth of HMO senior plans, in which Medicare participants sign over their benefits to the HMO in return for full medical coverage by the HMO, the facility should routinely check out other coverage for all admissions. Besides the fact that Medicare will not generally pay for the stay of residents enrolled in an HMO, most HMOs require the facility either to have a contract with their plan before authorizing services or at least to contact them for prior authorization of service.

Clearly, the best protection for avoiding problems in collection down the road is to have good policies and procedures up front during the admission process as well as well trained staff performing the intake and admission functions. It is the job of the staff to be sure that these policies are well explained to the resident, the family members, or the responsible party. A possible approach that provides additional protection to the facility against costly mistakes in this area is to have all admissions signed off on by a committee consisting of the administrator, director of nursing, and business office manager.

Billing for Services

Once again, having proper systems and procedures in place throughout the billing cycle is of paramount importance. Controls must exist that ensure that charges are generated and posted for all services and supplies that are considered chargeable. A complete "chargemaster," that is, a facility-specific comprehensive price list identifying these items and reflecting appropriate mark-ups over cost, is essential, as is the frequent monitoring of the nursing staff. In this regard, a central supply person who has the full backing and support of management is key to the program's success. Equally important is having proper documentation in the residents' records, such as physician orders and nursing notes detailing usage. One of the most effective ways of achieving control in this area is by utilizing a bar-code system.

The three major categories of revenue that we are concerned with are the following:

1. Basic care. This is also referred to as room and board. The key here is maintaining an accurate census at all times. It must be balanced daily and reflect all admissions, discharges, and transfers virtually immediately. This type of up-to-the-minute accuracy is essential for the efficient operation of intake and placement activities, as well as for controlling billing.

2. Ancillary review. This type of revenue includes physical, speech, and occupational therapy, laboratory and X-ray services, pharmaceuticals, and billable supplies. It represents an increasingly significant source of revenues, since patients are being transferred to nursing homes with higher acuity than ever before. A major portion of this revenue is covered by Medicare Part B, which has the

advantage that it is not subject to a specific cap, as is the "routine cost" associated with room and board under Part A.

3. Personal items. Revenue can be generated through such items as personal laundry, television rental, beauty shop, and so on. Policies vary from facility to facility as to how these items are charged, if at all. Given the cost of these items, they should not be overlooked as a potential source of revenue.

The key to maximizing revenue is to avoid lost charges that disappear through cracks in the system, often through staff indifference and lack of controls. A tight, fully integrated order entry and charging system is essential, as discussed earlier. Another significant control step with regard to ancillary charges is to tie the processing of the vendor invoices for contracted services or supplies to the billing cycle. Evidence that a charge has been posted to the revenue system should accompany the invoice sent to accounts payable for processing.

When the information generated from the census and the charging systems is posted to the resident's account, along with any cash receipts and adjustments, the facility is ready to bill. The concepts are the same whether the facility uses a computer for billing or a manual system. The key here from a cash-flow perspective is to condense the cycle as much as possible in order to get the bills out as quickly as possible. In addition, the following suggestions are offered as ways to speed up cash flow:

- Prebill private residents for the next month's room and board charges, mailing statements between the 20th and 25th of the month. Cut off charges for ancillary services and personal items on the 20th of the month, billing the charges from the 21st through the end of the month on the following month's statement.
- Consider "split-billing" Medicaid accounts, sending out two semi-monthly invoices instead of one monthly invoice (in those states that allow this). This will have the effect of evening out cash flow over the month.
- Process ancillary charges soon after month's end, so that Medicare bills can be mailed early in the month. Securing cooperation from outside vendors in furnishing their invoices soon after month's end is a very important step.

Follow-up and Control

The administrator should, as an integral part of his or her job, monitor the billing process on an ongoing basis, being alert to identifying possible bottlenecks or snags in the system. It is ultimately the administrator's responsibility to ensure that a bona fide source of payment exists for every resident who is admitted to the facility and that the systems for billing and collecting for services are in place and functioning properly. The administrator can be aided in this task by receiving, at a minimum, the following key reports:

- Monthly revenue and billing report. This report should indicate revenue by resident type (e.g., Medicare, Medicaid, private, etc.) and category (e.g., room and board, ancillary, personal items) actually billed. By comparing these data to the census and other indicators, the administrator will be able to identify and research any variances.
- Monthly un-billed report. Complementing the first report is a detailed listing of those accounts not billed, along with an explanation as to why each could not be billed, such as "awaiting Medicaid approval." It is critical that the administrator periodically follow up on these unbilled accounts and use this report as a control document.

In addition, the administrator should receive a monthly accounts receivable report, review it, and initiate appropriate follow-up billing and collection activity. Left unattended by the administrator, follow-up activities tend to take a back seat to current and ongoing activities in the business office. The result is that unresolved accounts get older and become progressively more difficult to collect. The simple fact is that the earlier a problem with an account is detected, the greater is the likelihood collection will be successful. Therefore, the facility should have a comprehensive collection policy that outlines the various actions to be taken at different times (e.g., a telephone call on the 5th of the month if no payment is received, followed by a letter on the 10th, etc.). Letters and calls should become progressively stronger, with the ultimate action being eviction or the filing of a lawsuit. The point is that the facility should pursue real collection efforts and should not be inhibited in asking for money it is entitled to for services rendered and for which the client has undertaken to pay.

Expenses

The other side of the financial equation is expenses. The major expense in most health care organizations is clearly salaries. Depending on the organization, anywhere between 40% to 70% of the expenditures will be in salaries and fringe benefits. Other expenses include cost of supplies, light, heat, malpractice insurance, bad debt allowances, maintenance of the physical facility, and so forth.

Capital Financing

The acquisition of money for capital projects, that is, for major expenditures that relate to purchasing, restoring, or expanding buildings, property, and major pieces of equipment, is a problem for a health care organization. Typical sources of capital financing have been philanthropy, taxable bonds, retained earnings, and tax-exempt bonds. Among these options for nonprofit entities, taxable bonds are not preferred because of the difficulty hospitals face in competing with private bonds and the high interest rate that they must offer in order to make their bonds marketable and attractive investments. Retained earnings are an attractive method, but it is hard for most health care organizations, particularly hospitals, to accumulate significant surpluses. Any surplus is usually fairly well wiped out by inflation, a new salary scale, or unanticipated expenditures, such as energy costs. Retained earnings are essentially the "profit" of the institution. Some argue that the depreciation costs passed on to patients through their insurers should, in fact, be placed aside for future capital expenditures and not be used for operating expenses. However, most organizations do not fund their depreciation.

The method of choice for most large health care organizations is the tax-exempt bond route, which allows the hospital to issue bonds either in its own name or through the auspices of a state bonding authority. The interest rate offered to the potential investor is lower than that on a taxable bond because the interest from the bond is exempt from state and federal taxes. To qualify for the bond market, the institution must undergo a level of scrutiny that is frequently quite rigorous. This scrutiny involves a time-consuming and expensive financial and marketing feasibility study that examines the present and probable future financial health of the organization. Elements of the investigation include the present and probable future demand for services, the nature of the organization, its financial health as manifested by its operating statements (including balance sheets and statements of revenue and expenses), and its operating history. These data are usually assembled for a package that is offered as a prospectus for potential investors. In many instances, an individual institution's offering is bundled together with offerings of other tax-exempt organizations, and the bond offering is sold as part of a larger tax-exempt package.

Lacking other sources of financing, an organization can simply turn to the private world of commercial banks and attempt to obtain money from them. When money is available, however, the interest rates are likely to be the highest. Also, as noted earlier, depending on the projects being considered, different states have unique arrangements for getting money, such as state dormitory or educational facilities money, and the federal government sometimes lends money through various development authorities. Aggressive and creative organizations have found money in rather unusual places.

Sometimes the source of money is organizational divesture; that is, selling off parts of the business in order to make other parts healthier. An interesting illustration of this occurred at the beginning of 2004 as this book was being written, when Tenet Healthcare Corporation announced it would sell 27 of its hospitals, 19 of which were in California: Tenet stated that these hospitals would require a $1.6 billion investment in order to meet California seismic standards and that such an investment was not justified in light of the lack of income generated by these hospitals. While the company could not forecast the dollars it would net from such a sale, it was clear that the sale would save it massive capital expenditures and stem some of the losses from these facilities, allowing it to concentrate on its other, more profitable institutions.

SPECIAL ISSUES

A variety of special issues and concerns face those involved in health care, particularly (but not limited to) those involved in hospital financing.

Cost of Regulation

One of the reactions to the barrage of new regulations that have hit the health field in the past decade has been criticism of the regulations themselves as the cause of (or at least a major contributor to) the problems they are supposed to solve. It is usually argued that regulations are developed to stem the sharp increase in health care costs, but industry spokesmen and politicians note that the regulations themselves are costly to implement and thus in turn drive up costs.

The cost of regulation can probably be categorized in three ways: recurring, capital, and investment. Recurring costs are those associated primarily with the workers who must be employed to provide the documentation necessary for compliance with regulations. Capital costs are usually one-time expenditures to bring a facility up to certain standards, such as meeting life safety code requirements. Investment costs are those regulatory expenditures associated with any project that would not exist but for the regulation and that add no particular value to the project, such as developing certificates of need or any steps in the planning process that might precede a certificate-of-need application. For health care organizations, many of these costs are recoverable from third-party insurers and do not present a significant internal management problem. However, there are other costs of regulation that are less clear, such as needed programs that were not launched or were delayed because of the regulatory process, finally being developed at a higher price than originally anticipated.

In general, discussions of costs center around the older regulatory programs such as rate setting and certificates of need or newer programs such as the Health Insurance Portability and Accountability Act of 1996 (HIPAA); one rarely finds cost-of-regulation discussions about the more established regulatory programs such as licensure or life safety codes. Debate on the cost issue will no doubt continue for many years; however, one should certainly balance this debate with a discussion of the benefits that will accrue to society as a result of regulation.

The costs of health regulation as well as its benefits remain unclear and are likely to remain so for the foreseeable future, both because the regulatory system is still developing and because the costs are difficult to ascertain. Perhaps in the future the health industry will behave like the trucking and airline industries with regard to regulation; after decades of regulation, they actively opposed deregulation that was proposed and implemented during the Carter administration. What they apparently had discovered was that the economic benefits of regulation outweighed the economic costs.

Cost Allocation

The trick for most health care organizations, particularly hospitals, is to maximize their revenue or reimbursements for the services they offer. As previously noted, patients, like airline passengers, each pay a different amount for the same service. Blue Cross, Medicare, and Medicaid pay the "reasonable costs" of services—but each of these three payers defines "reasonable" differently. Commercial insurers, on the other hand, tend to pay charges, and private, self-paying patients are effectively in the worst category (for themselves, not the organization) because they pay posted charges that are essentially what the traffic will bear. Indeed, it should be noted that even among the scores of Blue Cross plans, there is considerable variation as to what is paid for and what is disallowed.

All of this being the case, it is in the best interests of the institution to allocate costs in such a way as to maximize reimbursement. For example, if inpatient costs are more generously reimbursed than outpatient costs, as much overhead as possible may be allocated to the inpatient units. Within the commonly accepted principles of accounting and finance, there is considerable discretion for cost allocation to maximize reimbursement. In some instances, institutions have reorganized to take advantage of the reimbursement formulas. Caution should be used, however, because reimbursement strategy is one of the most complex and technical problems facing health care organizations. For that reason, the expenditures involved in utilizing specialized consultants' services are often worthwhile investments.

On the other hand, in today's environment of corporate compliance and Medicare and Medicaid fraud and abuse, it is imperative that all organizations behave in such a manner as to not invite investigation from any one of several branches of government. In essence, staying a mile or two under the speed limit is probably far smarter than running a few miles over the limit and thinking that you can talk your way out of the ticket (before or after the Miranda warning).

Cost Containment, Avoidance, and Reduction

Much of the regulatory activity, except HIPPA, that has occurred over the past few years in the health field has been intended to prevent further escalation in the costs of health care. In general, several strategies can be followed by organizations wishing to contain, avoid, and reduce costs.

These strategies include paperwork improvements, productivity improvements, scheduling, and training.

Typical of the problems faced by many health care organizations are cash shortages, overstaffing, poor utilization of present staff, low productivity, and equipment breakdown. With regard to cash shortages, an organization can establish a budgeting system that contains mechanisms for more accurate forecasting. In order to ensure appropriate cash flow billing and collection, systems must be developed and maintained. The key word is *systems*. It is always amazing to find out how poorly many health care organizations handle billing. Even a day's delay in sending out bills or asking for reimbursement is costly to an organization. Simple procedures such as electronic sweeps of cash accounts and overnight investing can sometimes provide useful cash infusions to organizations. For example, when my CFO implemented such a program in the organization where I was CEO, we were able to generate about $35,000 in cash per year for essentially zero expenditures.

Rare is the organization that does not have too many staff in certain departments and poorly utilized staff in others. Either situation is very costly and can be alleviated by better planning and coordination of personnel actions. It cannot be emphasized too strongly that in a labor-intensive industry such as health care it is imperative that all steps be taken to ensure the most efficient and effective utilization of staff. This, unfortunately, is not often done, and some institutions retain expensive anachronisms, such as doormen or pastry bakers, that are really throwbacks to a bygone era of, not so much amenities, but of cheap labor.

The related problem of low productivity could be a function of numerous factors. For example, low productivity may result from recruiting inappropriate staff, that is, people with poor skills or the wrong kind of skills. An emergency department that hires a recently retired psychiatrist from the state government system must expect a different level and type of productivity from this person than from a young physician who has just completed residency in family practice. Productivity problems, as noted in the earlier example involving medical records, are often the result of poorly developed expectations for workers, which can be solved by analysis of the jobs in question and related activities.

Sometimes low productivity is related neither to production standards nor to the caliber of staff but rather to the basic systems for getting the job completed. This can be seen most easily in any process that requires input or material from any other component of the organization before it can proceed with its workflow. On the Ford assembly line, each of the various functions must be carefully articulated with the previous ones, and materials must be readily available. Without the wheel assembly, the tires cannot be put on, and so forth. Even within health institutions there is a considerable amount of integration required: The operating room schedule can become bogged down because of a breakdown in central supply; the business office can be slowed down because information does not arrive from the ancillary service areas or other revenue-generating parts of a facility. Any of these breakdowns are expensive simply because they result in unproductive staff time that must be paid for.

Although it is considered unpatriotic, I have long advocated the outsourcing of certain organizational functions. Many back-office operations can be provided through central claims offices, information systems can often be purchased more cheaply through third parties, and in some large organizations it might be worth exploring the possibility of having some functions provided offshore. Obviously, all organizations have a responsibility to their present staff and the community, but in my judgment, the greater responsibility is to the patient and resident, and that responsibility may involve searching for and using alternatives that were not possible before high-speed data transfers were available.

Management of Working Capital

Working capital can be thought of as those assets of the organization that are essentially current, such as cash, accounts receivable, and inventory, as opposed to its fixed assets, which might include land and buildings. The basic idea of working capital management is to utilize the current assets to keep the organization in the strongest financial position. In considering this issue of management of working capital, there are three especially important areas of concern: inventory, accounts receivable, and accounts payable.

Inventory

The basic concern in inventory control is to balance the cost of not having enough with the cost of having too much. Inventory costs money to purchase, and this money is essentially out of circulation until the inventory is used and then converted back to cash. Inventory also costs money to store. A final problem is that some items have a limited life and must be destroyed if not used during their "shelf life." A typical question facing a health care manager is how many disposable syringes to buy at a time: a day's supply, a week's supply, a month's supply? It is not so very different from the question the consumer faces when the supermarket has a special on tuna fish. How many cans should the consumer buy? If the consumer uses all of his or her money for tuna, no money is left over for other needs. A second limitation is space, and a third limitation is shelf life; should tuna that was bought five years ago be used? So it is with the disposable syringes; all the money in central supply cannot be allocated to this item, even if it is bargain-priced and the cost is going to increase in the future, since central supply needs other items that of equal importance.

An additional factor in the inventory equation may be the likely availability of the product from suppliers. The reason most people do not carry large inventories of groceries is that large inventories are readily available in neighboring markets. One example is that of a hospital in Brooklyn, New York, that took this grocery-store approach with its oxygen systems. Since oxygen tank supplies were readily available, why should they use a more expensive (capital-wise) central system that required them to have a large storage tank on their premises? Rather, they reasoned, it would be better to buy tanks in small amounts and bring in new supplies a few times weekly. This worked well until a strike occurred and the oxygen tanks could not be found. Finally, an imminent disaster was averted when oxygen was located some 50 miles away in New Jersey. When things settled down, the hospital began work on its new central oxygen system. The experience of the institution changed its attitudes toward the cost/benefit ratios.

Today we live in a "JIT"; that is, Just In Time, concept of inventory. The idea is that organizations carry minimal inventory and get the deliveries they need on a daily basis. This obviously saves storage space and money as well as staff. When this works it is definitely the right route. But, as demonstrated with the oxygen—what happens when it does not work?

Accounts Receivable

Accounts receivable are an integral component of cash management, since they are the monies owed the organization for services rendered. Most health care organizations operate on a noncash basis; patients or their insurance companies are billed for services, and these bills take some period of time to collect. On the other hand, the organization has obligations to pay those staff who have rendered the services that generate the bills. A nurse is not told that she will be paid as soon as the insurer pays Mrs. Smith's bill. Rather, the nurse and the rest of the staff are paid on a periodic basis, even though a good deal of receivables do not come in on such a regular basis.

The key in accounts receivable is to set up an efficient billing and collection system so that bills are sent expeditiously with all the proper information (this is particularly important when dealing with the third-party reimbursers) and that follow-up takes place. One hospital in New York City got so far behind in its receivables that at one time it had over tens of millions of dollars in receivables. Over time, receivables can deteriorate to such a point that it becomes progressively more difficult to collect on them, particularly from private pay patients. There are no easy solutions to the accounts receivable problems, but the significance of organized systems must be emphasized. This includes use of credit cards for deductibles and copayments as well as time payment schemes for patients with significant and otherwise unpayable bills. Finally, it must be recognized that a dollar collected today is worth more than a dollar collected in two months, and therefore the investment in a good system has clear financial merits.

Accounts Payable

To some extent, accounts payable are the other side of the equation. They are monies the organization is paying out for services and supplies that it has acquired or is planning to acquire. The major account payable for most health care organizations is the payroll. From the organization's financial perspective, it is best if they can pay over the longest stretch possible. For example, they have a monthly payment of staff. This means 12 processings a year, and the organization has considerably more cash on hand during the month than under a weekly system in which 52 processings a year are required and, of course, are more costly.

In business, suppliers often offer incentives for rapid payment, such as a percentage discount if the bill is paid within 10 days. In one medical center, the working capital management was so poorly managed (some argued that it was actually good management) that the institution was several months behind in its payments. Some suppliers had cut off deliveries to the institution until old bills were cleared up, and thereafter they would supply the medical center only if cash were paid for the supplies. Again, the key is having an organized system for paying obligations, which must be integrated into the total working capital system. The total system is designed to ensure that money owed the organization is received as rapidly as possible and that funds are properly expended in inventory.

THE BUDGETARY PROCESS

A budget is essentially a planning statement of expected expenses and expected revenues over a certain period of time. Most organizations have some sort of budget and a process that arrives at that budget. Some organizations, such as hospitals, must meet requirements of the federal government and sometimes state governments for budgets of varying lengths. Indeed, some states, such as Connecticut, use the budget as a key regulatory device. Also, virtually every government-run or government financed program is required, at the least, to prepare a budget at its outset.

In theory, then, a budget is a financial timetable, a plan for the organization that has been translated into dollars and cents. A different way of viewing the budget is that it is fundamentally a political document that oftentimes involves a complicated bargaining process within the organization. Thus, forecasting, or in some cases educated guessing, becomes a key element in the entire budgeting process. Because of the political nature of budgeting and the control that management has when it makes decisions affecting department budgetary levels, the budget and the process can become very significant management tools.

For practical purposes, there are three general types of budgets many organizations use: cash, capital, and expense. The cash budget is concerned with cash receipts and disbursements; it is developed to ensure that the business of the organization proceeds at a smooth pace. The capital budget is concerned with capital acquisitions, such as buildings, land, or equipment. Finally, the major budget is the expense budget, which is essentially a statement of the planned operation for a subsequent period of time. The output, that is, the budgetary document, does not vary on the face of it from organization to organization, but the process to get to that document does vary. In the end, though, a financial document is prepared; some might be program-based, while others itemize each expense individually (hence are called line items). Regardless, each type can be translated into the other with minor effort.

The typical budgetary process has four stages: (1) dissemination of instructions, (2) preparation of initial budget, (3) review and adjustment, and (4) appeal. Dissemination of instructions is exactly that. The instructions to be followed in the preparation of next year's budget are sent to those people who have been designated as responsible for their section of the budget. This is, in reality, the beginning of management's political statement about the budget and its seriousness about the budget. The first question is: Who prepares the instructions? Is budget preparation by fiat from the management or finance department, or is the instruction rule-making process itself open for question and negotiation? The instructions must also contain some parameters and forecasts, which, again, is an opportunity for management to use its control. For example, in the instructions it might say, "Because of our tight fiscal situation, do not budget any new positions in your department or plan expense for consumable supplies at a level of 2.25% higher than last year." Effectively, management has sent a stark message to the department through the process itself.

Another way management makes an important statement about the budget is by its choice of staff to prepare it. In one large teaching hospital, the department secretaries were responsible for budget preparation, while in another it was the clinical chief of the service.

Having read through and digested the mechanics of the instructions, someone within the department is now ready to prepare the initial budget. Within a given component, the budgetary process may reflect the entire organization's approach or the management style of that department manager. For example, the department may have an open process where members of the department discuss their plans for the coming year and the money needed to translate those plans into action, or the manager may decide what should happen next year and plan accordingly. Sometimes there is no room in the budget for more than incremental financial plans for the future. Thus, ambulatory care, which had a budget of X dollars for Y number of patients, may expect an additional 10% next year based on the experiences of the past two years and may therefore request more money for supplies to meet this anticipated demand. Such a request is likely to be granted with no problem, but the request for the extra staff member to meet the extra demand may result in tough negotiation.

Negotiation takes place at the next stage, review and adjustment, at the next higher organizational level, perhaps the second level of management. Here requests are pruned and coordinated. Since the final budget must be adopted at the highest management level (in many organizations, the board level), it is in everyone's interest to make sure that the document is as defensible as possible when finally presented. A strong defense of requests is possible when the forecasts are good and the requests are reasonable. At this review level, it is important to see that each department has interpreted the forecasting data properly and is using assumptions similar to those of other departments. It is also an opportunity to ensure that there is no duplication.

The budget is then returned to the originating department. Depending on management's approach, a final appeal to top management is possible. If the department secretary has prepared the budget, there will be few appeals, since the secretary is not likely to be in a power position. By asking the secretary to prepare the budget, management also has said that they really consider the process just an academic exercise. On the other hand, if the process is serious and has consumed much energy of "powerful" department level personnel, an appeal process to override the decision of the coordinating managerial level may be necessary. Here, the case for an increase or change is again made, and the budget may be adjusted.

It should be remembered that the budget may be reviewed by the board's finance committee before it goes to the full board. At every one of these stages of review and negotiation, questions are asked; if clarifications are not forthcoming, the budget may not be adopted.

Negotiation is the key to this type of process. In many senses, top management and lower levels are negotiating. They are to a degree in adversarial positions; and, to the extent that each is operating at a high level of competence, the organization benefits by the challenge. For example, different groups may have different forecasts based on different interpretations of trends; it behooves the organization to analyze these interpretations before making a decision on the budget. In the closed and managerially dominant system, the opportunity for interaction and negotiation is limited and, this author believes, does not function in the best interests of the organization.

Even the timetable of the budgetary process is a statement of how serious and open management is about the process. Too short a timetable gives management total control of the process and the input data for decisions, while a reasonable timetable gives the individual departments the opportunity to analyze their own experiences and plans. A reasonable timetable also gives them opportunity to undertake negotiations in an atmosphere that is not pressurized.

The final budget should be an important and weighty document that presents management with a tool to evaluate department heads regarding their ability to meet expectations. Additionally, since the budget sets up the targets, variances from the budget act as flags alerting management of the need to investigate financial problems in a timely manner. Without timely intervention, financial problems simply get out of hand.

CONCLUSION

In sum, money is the fuel of all health care organizations. A wisely managed institution or program will use its economic resources well and plan for the future. A poorly run organization not only endangers its own fiscal viability but also compromises the health of its patients, residents, or clients.

Case 11-1
FINANCIAL CLOUDS OVER TEXAS

Consultants from the Washington-based accounting firm of Jefferson, Madison, and Associates were engaged by Dallas, Texas-based, nonprofit Hamilton-Burr Geriatric System's (HBGS) new CEO. HBGS is one of the oldest and most distinguished geriatric service providers in the Southwest with nursing homes, assisted living centers, adult day care centers, ambulatory care clinics, and independent living facilities in Texas (Dallas, Ft. Worth, Arlington, and Denton). HBGS owns five nursing homes (1,000 beds), three assisted living centers (190 units), one independent living building plus one under construction (eventually,

(continues)

Case Study 11-1

160 apartments), three ambulatory medical care centers, and three day care centers. Additionally, the HBGS Foundation raises money and holds a $50 million endowment for the system.

The consultants' report confirmed what the CEO had suspected; that is, the system was on shaky financial ground. This conclusion directly contradicted the position held by the board of directors and its chairman who had assured the new CEO that the system was financially sound and that any shortfalls could be covered by fund raising.

Excerpts from the consulting report are as follows:

- A review of the past three years of financial statements clearly demonstrates that but for transfers from the endowment fund and fortuitous fund raising opportunities the system would be running significant deficits.

- Based on our review of the financials we project a deficit of from $4–6.5 million in the next fiscal year.

- The likely causes of the deficit are a combination of low Medicaid reimbursement; a failure to attract a significant portion of Medicare residents; an increase in bad debts, slow collection procedures, overstaffing, excessive food service costs, and considerable long-term debt.

- The endowment income has been steadily declining and, in the past three years, has seen an erosion of the corpus of the endowment as money has been transferred to cover deficits.

- The current benefits package has resulted in excessive expenses in health benefits. It is anticipated that there will be in the present fiscal year close to $1 million in excess costs.

- Numerous programs are presently losing money. Most notably the three adult day care centers require a subsidy of close to $500,000 per year.

(continues)

Case Study 11-1

- Numerous programs are presently losing money. Most notably the three adult day care centers require a subsidy of close to $500,000 per year.
- The costs associated with the new independent living center are grossly out of line and represent almost 75% more in building costs than comparable facilities. Fees for housing are projected to be similar to that of other independent living units. The expectation is that this project will be another financial drain on the system.

The new CEO met with the board to discuss this report and was promptly chastised for spending $50,000 on a "useless piece of garbage." The board chairman said he wanted the system to "run the way I've been running it for 25 years and no bean counter is going to tell me who to hire or who to fire. And, I'll be dammed if the independent living building, which I'm naming in honor of my parents, will be anything other than the best facility in the world." The chairman finished his tirade by looking directly at the CEO and stating, "I hired you to run this place, not to change it. I'll raise the money, you just run it."

DISCUSSION QUESTIONS

1. What should be the CEO's next move?

2. How can the CEO make the necessary changes without offending the board?

3. How do mission and values impact financial planning?

4. How might this case provide guidance to similar organizations?

CHAPTER 12

Legal Imperatives for Health Care Administrators

Managers of health care organizations are often challenged by a perplexing range of legal issues that typically make them feel as if they need a telephone hotline to a multispecialty law practice. While the hotline is certainly one solution, it is expensive and simply not practical. An alternative, and the focus of this and the next three chapters, is the manager learning about law and the legal system. These next chapters are designed specifically to assist managers in learning about how the legal system analyzes legal problems. Understanding the contents of these chapters will pay off in an enhanced ability to communicate with lawyers, to read cases, statutes, and regulations with a far more critical eye, to understand the organization and functioning of the legal system, and finally to know some substantive law.

BACKGROUND

Prior to examining any substantive aspects of law, it is useful to consider the following questions: Where does law come from? What does law do? What is the theoretical model of law? How does law differ from ethics? And, finally, how does the legal analysis affect a given case?

When we consider where law comes from, there are generally three major answers. First, law comes from the federal and state constitutions. For example, the U.S Constitution has been the supreme law of the

United States since March of 1789. It states in Article II, Section 1 that no person other than a natural-born citizen of the United States shall be eligible to be president. Poor Arnold Schwarzenegger! In 1951, the XXII Amendment was ratified, limiting the presidential terms of office to two terms. These sections and amendments are relatively clear, and litigation over them is almost nonexistent. However, the cases over interpretation of the First Amendment, which deals with freedom of speech, could fill a library. Essentially, the primary source of our laws, the constitution, is somewhat problematic in that it is frequently ambiguous and, as a result, susceptible to changing political climates. It is, however, the source of last resort and the place where judges have found the rights that have struck down the concept of "separate but equal" that sanctioned racial segregation in this country and provided women with the right to legal abortions through the vehicle of the case of *Roe v. Wade*.

The second major source of our laws comes from the elected and sometimes appointed legislative bodies. Whether we are talking about the U.S. Congress, a state legislature, or a local board of health, we are generally speaking of laws that have some commonalities. In most cases, the laws emanating from these bodies are responsive to a perceived problem; they are usually comprehensive in design, tend to be prospective, and are a result of an open legislative process. Realistically, though, they are also the products of special interest lobbying and frequently are replete with ambiguities designed to appease different constituents. The Medicare drug legislation is a clear national example of this type of law. It came into being as a result of perceived problems and developed into such a comprehensive and confused bill that it took more than a year after passage for the elderly to realize how limited this highly publicized and praised bill truly was.

Another dimension of these legislatively enacted laws is that they most often require implementing regulations that are promulgated by administrative agencies. These regulations are typically developed by unelected governmental bureaucrats and follow adoption procedures outlined by the Federal Administrative Procedures Act. Although lobbyists and special interest groups can respond to the proposed regulations during mandatory time periods, the government is not obligated to listen to these views. What is perhaps most significant about many of these regulations is that the government agency not only writes the regulations but then also goes on to implement the regulations and interpret them through their own cadre of administrative law judges. The concept of separation of power is effectively absent in many parts of the statutory world.

The interplay of state law, federal law, and public policy is well demonstrated in Oregon's 1994 Death With Dignity Act. This state law, the only one of its kind in the United States, makes it legal for Oregonians who are within 6 months of dying from a terminal illness to take their own lives with the assistance of physicians who prescribe a lethal medication and pharmacists who fill the prescription. The law, passed by voter initiative, has been the focus of various political and lobbying assaults. National politics have also played a part in this bill's interesting history. During the Clinton administration, the U.S. attorney general refused to get involved in attempts to overrule this law, basically saying that the issue was a matter of state law. The Bush administration's attorney general, though, operating with a conservative philosophy, has actively pursued an agenda designed to nullify the Oregon law. Oregon has not taken the matter lying down, arguing in the federal appeals court that this was indeed a matter of state law—and winning. The court sided with the state in May 2004. This drama illustrates how the various interested parties get involved in a process and, depending on your political point of view, either move the process forward or else throw a monkey wrench in the machinery of progress.

The third major body of law is what we call the common law, that huge body of what we think of as judge-made law, based on cases and precedents. A confusion might set in here because judges often get involved in the interpretation of regulations and statutes as well as common law decision making. Unlike statutory law, the common law is developed like a giant jigsaw puzzle, one piece at a time. The essential building blocks of the common law are cases that establish precedents. Without an appropriate case, no piece is available. The common law is thus retrospective, that is, awaiting a case before a decision can be rendered to establish the law. Unlike laws that are established by legislative bodies, these laws are established by the judiciary, who may not be an elected body. For example, the U.S. Supreme Court is an appointed body, and historically many members of that court have not come from the judiciary. Warren Burger, a former Chief Justice, had been governor of California, and the present Chief Justice, William Rehnquist, was a private practicing lawyer for 16 years before becoming assistant U.S. attorney general for 3 years and then getting a seat on the Supreme Court.

Another and perhaps more complicated question is: What does law do? In many respects, its most significant value is that it orders relationships in six important ways. First, rights are recognized through the law. On May 17, 2004, hundreds of gay and lesbian couples throughout the Commonwealth of Massachusetts applied for and received marriage licenses. Until that date only heterosexual couples were permitted to receive licenses, but a judgment of the highest court in Massachusetts established a new right. It was the judgment of the courts that established the patients' right of informed consent in health care, meaning that a practitioner was required to get a patient's permission before undertaking any procedure on the patient.

Law also creates privileges. For example, someone can sit on a peer review committee and make negative judgments about a colleague. Thanks to the law, such judgments can be made without fear of personal liability. Similarly, the law creates power, as in the case of hospitals, which, if they follow appropriate procedures, have the right to deny an unqualified person staff privileges. Liabilities are also a creature of the law. Perhaps a good example known to many of us on April 15th each year is the subject of taxes. A for-profit corporation has tax liabilities, and those liabilities come from state and federal tax laws. The law also creates immunities. In many states there is a doctrine of charitable immunity, which allows charitable organizations to avoid or lessen their financial liability exposure because they are a charitable organization. For example, a state might have a law that limits charitable liability to $25,000 per incident. Finally, the law creates disabilities, as in the case of a minor who is disabled from the operation of the law because of his status as a minor.

From a theoretical perspective, what most of us probably want is somewhat contradictory: a legal system that is fair, unbiased, but with a heart (a bit unfair and a bit biased). This suggests we desire a system that is free of political or economic considerations and one in which the decisions would not vary from judge to judge. In many senses, then, we would like a computerized system of justice but with a heart, our heart! What we have instead is a very human system that is riddled with ambiguity for the consumer. We also have a system that has its own stylized dances and acceptable rules of intellectual and personal behavior, sometimes codified in procedural or evidentiary rules. Everyone seeks justice in the end, but when conflict exists, not everyone sees justice in the same way!

ROLES

Before examining some specific issues in law that health care managers might deal with in their daily activities, it is worthwhile to recognize the functions of lawyers, judges, and juries. The basic job of the lawyer is to represent the client or, as the old gangster movies put it, to be their "mouthpiece." The lawyers must understand the facts of the case, clarify the disputed legal issues, and research these issues and facts in order to present them in the light that is most favorable for their client. The judge is responsible for deciding issues of law and the rules that apply to a case; the jury is responsible for deciding issues of fact, essentially, whose side of the truth to accept. In the Martha Stewart case, we were presented with an example in which a judge decided to dismiss the most serious charge against the defendant. In dismissing this charge of securities fraud, Judge Miriam Cederbaum found that the prosecution had not presented enough evidence for a jury to make a finding of guilt beyond a reasonable doubt. Later in the trial, the jury failed to believe Stewart and found her guilty of the charges relating to obstruction of justice, conspiracy, and making false statements about her stock transactions.

One of the most famous trials of the late 1980s occurred in New Jersey and involved an infant known as Baby M. This trial pitted as adversaries the biological mother of the child, Mary Beth Whitehead, and William Stern, the biological father of the child, whose sperm was used to artificially inseminate Whitehead. The controversy revolved around a surrogacy contract between the two parties. Stern had agreed to pay Whitehead $10,000 in return for her having the baby and then forever giving up her parental rights so Stern's wife could adopt the baby. The case wound up in court when Whitehead decided after delivering the child that she did not want to give her up to the Sterns. In analyzing this case, the New Jersey courts struggled with classification of the case; that is, was it a family law or a contracts case? The significance of the classification is that different rules of law apply and the differing rules can impact the final decision. For example, if the Baby M case were to be classified as a custody battle, then the best interests of the child or even termination of parental rights might be the main legal issues. If the case were merely contractual in nature, then the legality of the contract or public policy considerations might be the rules of law. The Baby M case dealt with all of these issues at various times, and different rules resulted in slightly different results. In the end, the contract was invalidated because the judge said it was against the public policy of New Jersey. This left the door open to the state legislature to articulate policy on this matter through a new law. Custody of the child, however, was granted to Stern on the basis of the best interests of the child. A lower court ruling that terminated Whitehead's parental rights was voided, as was the adoption of Baby M by Stern's wife.

TORTS

In writing this chapter, I feel somewhat like the *Saturday Night Live* character Father Guido Sarducci, who would teach the most complex subject in less than a minute. Understanding the universe of torts could take a lifetime, and many scholars have made their careers on studying and writing about torts. The purpose of this section is merely to provide an introduction to and sensitivity about this crucial area of the law.

Torts are civil wrongs that utilize the judicial process to right the wrong. The basic idea behind tort law is that of making an innocent victim whole again (and much of the legal argument is often centered on how innocent the innocent victim really is). To make the victim whole, the system allocates blame and then uses economic damages as a way to right the situation. By placing the economic burden on the party who commits the wrong, that person, as well as other people in that class, will have an incentive (really a disincentive) to behave in a proper way. For example, if people could bang up other cars with abandon, such as happens at the demolition derbies, and not have to be concerned about repairing the other person's vehicle, I suspect we would have a lot more accidents and junkier-looking cars on the road.

The most significant tort affecting the health industry is malpractice, which is essentially medical or health care negligence. What exactly is negligence? Simply stated, it is behavior that does not meet a legal standard. Before discussing and illustrating the crucial elements in the malpractice equation, it is imperative that the distinction between a legally actionable tort and inappropriate ethical behavior be distinguished. Consider the following case. Mrs. Smith is at a public beach with Karen, her 16-year-old daughter, who decides to go swimming in the ocean despite the rough surf and lack of a lifeguard. Mrs. Smith, herself a non-swimmer, is keeping an eye on Karen just as Speedy Speedo, the 25-year-old three-time Olympic swimming champion, comes walking by. Speedy is well known at the beach, and Mrs. Smith recognizes him just at the instant that she sees Karen floundering in the water and yelling for help. Mrs. Smith runs over to Speedy and asks him to save Karen. He looks out at Karen and starts to take his three gold medals off his neck, but then asks Mrs. Smith how old Karen is. She replies, "16," at which point Speedy puts his medals back on, starts walking down the beach, and mutters under his breath, "I hate teenagers." Is Speedy negligent? The legal answer is "No." Why? More on that in the next pages. Is Speedy's behavior unethical? Is he a bum? Yes! But that does not make his behavior liable for damages!

The fundamental idea in negligence is that a person must act as a reasonable and prudent person would act under the same or similar circumstances. In terms of action, the courts are always looking for foreseeable or predictable behavior. Behavior or action that is outside of the realm of predictability is usually dubbed an accident and not negligence.

Almost all torts have something akin to a formula, that is, essential elements of proof. For example there is a tort labeled "intentional infliction of emotional distress." Claiming that someone was emotionally hurt by another's mere words is not enough to prove this tort. If this were the case, every time Donald Trump uttered the famous words "You're fired," he would be answering to a lawsuit. And so it is in negligence. There are essentially six elements in the formulation of this tort: duty, breach, causation, proximate cause, substantive defenses, and procedural defenses.

Many of the arguments that are heard in courts revolve around establishing the defendant's duty to act or to refrain from acting in the situation. In our fictional case, the argument is simply that Speedy had no duty to act. If that proves to be correct, then the case is over. In the world of malpractice, the next issue is what is the standard of care owed to the plaintiff by the defendant. Here is where the war of the experts generally comes into play. Each side typically has an expert witness who will present evidence that will likely make the case for their client. In the case of *Hall v. Hilbun*, 486So.2d 856 (1985), the argument about standard of care revolved around a concept called the locality rule. In this Mississippi case, a woman died, allegedly because she did not receive appropriate postoperative care from her surgeon who became the defendant. The plaintiff, perhaps because of the inability to find a local expert witness, brought an expert witness from Cleveland, Ohio. The expert's job was to establish the standard of care against which the defendant would be measured. Until the time of this case, Mississippi followed the locality rule, meaning that the standard of care would be the local standard, not the higher nationwide standard.

Once a standard of care is established, then the experts are asked to answer in a hypothetical way (this charade not being lost on the jury) whether the hypothetical doctor breached his duty by failing to meet the standard of care. Next there must be proof of actual causation, what lawyers like to call the "but for" cause: that is, but for the breach of duty by the doctor or hospital, the damages to the plaintiff would not have happened. There is simply no case without the damages associated with causation. Another facet of causation is what is called proximate cause, which is a policy consideration. The policy concern is about limiting liability to reasonably foreseeable consequences of a person's behavior. The concept of proximate cause is that the judicial goal of fundamental fairness to all involved parties is achieved by limiting liability to foreseeable consequences. An example to illustrate this concept is the following: Assume that a truck carrying explosives overturns and explodes. Someone a mile away hears the explosion and has a heart attack out of fear. Is the owner of the truck liable? Was it foreseeable that a person a mile away would become so frightened from the explosion that she would have a heart attack? If the answer is yes, what about two miles away? Three?

The problem of standard of care is not straightforward. My favorite case to teach is *Helling v. Carey*, 519 P. 2d 981 (1974). Despite its advanced age, it is an important case that is in many ways a hugely cautionary tale for everyone in the health care field. A young woman sustained serious damage to her eyes. For five years she had been complaining to her ophthalmologists about eye problems, but no one ever checked for glaucoma, which it eventually turned out she had. The argument the defendants made was that they were practicing ophthalmology just like everyone else and that virtually no other ophthalmologists would have done glaucoma testing. The court invoked an old formulation that in brief means if the cost of prevention is low and the cost of the potential injury is high, then the obligation is to act to prevent. Further, they noted most significantly that the standard is not what *is* but rather what *should be*. If one accepts this formulation, then it is in the organization's best interest to always be at the top of the standard of care curve. The problem is how does one know what the top of the curve is, and how does one afford to constantly stay on the top of the curve when the standard is a moving target? Answering this challenge is difficult, expensive, but not impossible! It requires a system of monitoring developments in the field to ensure that the organization is up to date in terms of the state of the art, whether practice guidelines for clinical care or merely equipment and procedures. Learning about developments in a given field requires constant attention to the literature as well as professional engagement through various associations and meetings.

Even in those instances where everything is up to snuff are instances of neglect that can be proven without expert witnesses. For example, there is a doctrine that lawyers can use to prove the breach of the duty, known in the Latin (we lawyers love to quote Latin) as *res ipsa loquitor* (the thing speaks for itself), such as when an instrument is left behind in the abdomen after the surgery. After all, the patient was anesthetized, and it is highly unlikely that he slipped the instrument into his abdomen himself. The courts are often left with figuring out which of the potential defendants should share in the liability. An example of another doctrine that might be utilized occurs when a physician violates a statute or law. For example, in the days before abortions were legalized, anyone performing an illegal abortion, no matter how professionally done, ran liability risks.

In the negligence equation, the next hurdle calls for developing the causal links between what happened to the patient and the actions or lack of actions by the defendant. Did the doctor fail to do the procedure properly? Did the hospital fail to monitor the patient? If the hospital had properly maintained the equipment, would the problem not have occurred? The scenarios are as endless as the imagination. This is why malpractice cases are both so intrinsically interesting to study, yet so alarming if one is the administrator of an organization.

Malpractice, though, is only one of many torts that an organization may have to deal with. As noted earlier, there are the emotional distress torts. Negligent or intentional infliction of emotional distress might occur because of someone's insensitivity to the needs of a staff member, patient, or their family. For example, in the case of *Ocasio v. Lehigh Valley Family Health Center*, 2003 U.S. Dist. LEXIS 3025, a Hispanic woman working as a medical assistant at a health center was terminated after two years' employment. Subsequent to her termination, she filed a lawsuit based on civil rights discrimination claims as well as intentional infliction of emotional distress. To prevail on such a claim, a plaintiff must meet a rather difficult standard by proving that the conduct of the defendant was extreme, outrageous, intentional, or reckless, that the conduct was the causal factor in the emotional distress, and that the distress that resulted from the conduct was severe. The emotional distress claims apparently were related to this plaintiff's feeling isolated in her job, receiving excessive discipline, and being "joked about" because of her ethnic background. This claim was dismissed at the district court level and not a matter of appeal (204 U.S. App. LEXIS 4711). Regardless for Lehigh Valley or any organization, such a claim is disturbing and expensive to defend.

Emotional distress claims can also come from the behavior of professionals toward their patients. In the Iowa case of *Oswald v. Legrand*, 453 N.W. 2d 634 (1990), a series of mishaps, perhaps negligence, and rude and offensive behavior on the part of hospital staff, including doctors, resulted in a complex lawsuit, with one claim being that of negligent infliction of emotional distress. The distressing incidents that formed the basis of the claim involved the rudeness of a nurse to Ms. Oswald upon her admission for delivery; a comment that if she miscarried it would not be a baby but rather a "big blob of blood"; an argument between the physicians about wanting to leave and not take responsibility for Ms. Oswald, which was overheard by the Oswalds; declaring that the newborn was a stillbirth, wrapping it in a towel, and putting it on an instrument tray, only for the father to find out 10 minutes later that the fetus was viable (it died 12 hours later). All in all, a total mess. Despite the trial court dismissing the claims, the appeals court in Iowa accepted the validity of most of the plaintiff's claims, including that of emotional distress, and sent the case back to the trial court.

Failure to obtain informed consent is a tort that is quite important in these litigious times. While the foundation of the informed consent action is battery, or the unwanted touching of another, the tort has been expanded to cover many other dimensions, such as the need for practitioners to explain alternatives and consequences. Several cases, each tragic in their own ways, demonstrate various dimensions of the informed consent issue. In the classic case of *Canterbury v. Spence*, 464 F. 2d 772 (1972), back surgery was proposed for a young man who was in significant pain. The young man as well as his mother agreed orally to the surgery. During the postoperative period he fell and was subsequently plagued with a range of problems, including paralysis, pain, medical expenses, and loss of his job. In an extensive discussion of the doctrine of informed consent, the court stated that the doctors failed to adequately inform the plaintiff of the risks and benefits of the treatment in a way so the patient and his mother could exercise their rights effectively. Although at the time this case occurred (1959) it was argued that most practitioners spoke to patients in generalities about surgery and medical care, the court dismissed that argument, basically saying that it is the right of the patient to knowingly grant consent, not the tradition or practice of the medical profession that shall trump this right.

In trying to ascertain the right standard for informed consent, the courts tend to rely on the basic concept of "Reasonable and Prudent Person Under the Same or Similar Circumstances" (RPPUSSC). (This was a mantra that my law students had to chant on a weekly basis.) The idea of this standard, while not perfect, is that the judge or jury must look at cases in an objective, not subjective, manner. Thus, when presented with the question of whether a practitioner provided the proper information about diagnosis, the type of treatment planned, the justification for the treatment, the various risks associated with the treatments, and what alternatives exist to the treatment, as well as their risks and benefits, the standard to be applied is whether a RPPUSSC would have agreed to or refused the treatment. The question is not what the plaintiff would have done. Obviously, they are arguing they would have done the opposite of what occurred; otherwise, why is there a case? By looking at a hypothetical RPPUSSC, the finder of fact uses an objective measure and not the subjective measure that would occur if one only looked at the plaintiff. In many ways we are merely asking the finders of fact to apply their common sense—although, strangely, common sense is not so common! This point is illustrated in the case of *Johnson v. Kokemoor*, 199 Wis. 2d 615, 545 N.W. 2d 495 (1996), where the plaintiff, long suffering from headaches, underwent neurosurgery to clip an aneurysm. This resulted in her becoming an incomplete quadriplegic with a range of other problems. It turned out that the surgeon had overstated his experience with these cases and had failed to explain the risks associated with the surgery. This case essentially established the significance of full disclosure for physicians. As noted earlier, the finders of fact are presented with a question of what the RPPUSSC would do if presented with this problem. In the case of Johnson, the added ingredients were her medical history, the diagnosis, the proposed surgery, and the risks and benefits. Certainly amongst the risks is the morbidity and mortality associated with the surgery and, in this case, the limited experience of the surgeon. With all that, the jury concluded that a person under those circumstances would not have consented to the surgery. What is learned from this case is that all significant variables in the equation must be disclosed to the patient and, indeed, disclosure must be in a manner that is clear and understandable.

Sometimes, a practitioner acting in what he or she sees is in the best interest of the patient deliberately fails to disclose information. This typically happens in cancer-related therapy. While this may be understandable, the courts have not found this paternalism acceptable (see *Arato v. Avedon*, 23 Cal. Rptr, 131, 858 P.2d 598 [1993]). I know from my own personal experience how painful it is to hear a physician speak of chemotherapy in statistical terms, yet it is also important to know what options are available and to go into therapy with a clearer understanding of what is ahead. Information and data can be delivered in a kind, sympathetic, and even hopeful manner (as was most often the case) or in a cold and even unkind way (and that was once the case). Regardless, the patient has the right to make a decision, and before that decision can be made, the patient has the right to know what he or she needs to know.

There are times when things go too far, in my opinion. The case of *Truman v. Thomas*, 165 Cal. Rptr. 308, 611 P.2d. 902 (1980), is such an instance. Fortunately this case only established limited precedent in California. A woman died of cervical cancer after refusing to get a recommended Pap smear. Over a period of several years, the doctor in this case advised the patient to get the test, but she simply refused. The court found that the doctor had essentially not been assertive enough in pushing the test by not clarifying the risks of foregoing the test. The single dissenting judge in this case reasoned that it would be an intolerable burden for practitioners to have to disclose the meaning of each diagnostic test and presumably the risks and benefits of each. On the one hand, I do not think that patients must be protected from their own inappropriate behavior, such as refusing a commonly understood test such as a Pap smear. On the other hand, practitioners could certainly use some serious lessons on effective communication with patients!

In a more recent case, *Gray v. Hoffman-LaRoche*, 2003 U.S. App. LEXIS 24321, the plaintiff sued the manufacturer of the drug Accutane, which is commonly used to treat acne. Ms. Gray used the drug for several years and suffered from major depression that she linked to Accutane usage. This drug is particularly interesting because, unlike for most medications, the patient is required to sign an informed consent agreement before it will be dispensed. In Ms. Gray's case, this agreement was changed during the course of her treatment, and she sought to introduce the development of the warnings, particularly about psychiatric risks associated with the drug, into evidence.

Informed consent often is merely one component of a larger lawsuit. This is demonstrated in the sad case of *Harnett v. O'Rourke*, 2003 U.S. App. LEXIS 14726 , where a 31-year-old woman went into a Colorado Springs, Colorado hospital for abdominal surgery. After the surgery, she had a massive abdominal bleed, followed by irreversible brain damage, followed by being placed on life support, from which she was later removed. While the central claim in this case was negligence on behalf of the surgeon, there was also a claim of lack of informed consent, perhaps as part of the negligence. Unfortunately, no part of the written opinion adds light to this aspect of the claim, yet it does represent another avenue for a plaintiff to follow.

Obviously there are many defenses to these torts, and it should never be assumed that just because a person has been sued that he or she is likely liable. There are more than a handful of lawyers who like to go on fishing expeditions, however, and they write demand letters without investigating. The U.S. medical malpractice system is based on lawsuits: aggrieved patients and their families on one side and practitioners and institutions on the other. Sometimes institutions can avoid or limit liability thanks to charitable immunity statutes, but the fates of practitioners are usually in the hands of their insurers. The insurers may choose to settle a suit rather than go through the expense of defending the claim. The decision to settle may make sense for the insurance company, but the settlement is a black mark for the practitioner, both in terms of his or her reputation and subsequent insurance premiums.

Here we see one of the three major differences between the system in the United States and the system of our Canadian neighbors. In Canada, the insurers are primarily the captives of the practitioners, and their decisions tend to be those of the practitioners. If a small claim comes in that might cost more to defend than it is worth, the Canadian insurer will fight it to preserve the doctor's reputation. By contrast, in the United States, the cost benefit from the insurer's perspective may be in settling the claim. A second difference is that U.S. trials are typically in front of juries who can be swayed by the theatrics of lawyers or by the sympathy factor associated with either party. In Canada, trials are in front of judge panels, who are usually in a better position to evaluate the evidence. The third difference is the general rule in Canada that the losing side pays the court costs. This is certainly a major disincentive to pursue frivolous claims.

Assuming the case is well beyond a fishing trip, there is a broad range of substantive defenses. The first and likely most significant is related to the standard of care. The argument here is pretty simple: The plaintiff claims through his or her expert witnesses that the standard of care was not met. The defense begins by trying to show that the plaintiff's expert does not know what he or she is talking about and then goes on to present his or her own expert witness to show that the defendant certainly met the standard of care. While it is well beyond this chapter to discuss every aspect of a defense, there are several interesting concepts well worth mentioning because each of these ideas demonstrate the human dimension of medical care.

The first of these is the respectable minority rule, which was articulated in the case of *Chumbler v. McClure*, 505 F. 2d 489 (1974). Mr. Chumbler was injured in an electrical explosion and subsequently suffered from cerebral vascular insufficiency. In treating Chumbler, Dr. McClure, a Nashville neurosurgeon, prescribed estrogen, which had the side effect of loss of libido and breast enlargement. What is significant here is that the testimony at trial established that Dr. McClure was the only neurosurgeon in the city to use this estrogen treatment for this condition, although there was a minority opinion in practice and literature that accepted this as a legitimate therapy. The court's analysis said that medical treatment is not the result of a plebiscite, but alternative minority approaches were not de facto breaches of the standard of care.

Where clinical innovation fits into the picture of standard of care was addressed in the case of *Brook v. St. John's*, 380 N.E. 2d 72 (1978). The problem in this instance involved a 23-month-old child who came into a hospital to get X-rays in order to confirm and treat a urological problem. Because of her size, the radiologist decided against using the traditional place for such injections (the buttocks) and instead injected the contrast dye into her calves. Several months later, the child had trouble with her right leg and subsequently needed surgery and, for a time, leg braces. In pursuing this legal action, the plaintiffs argued that the doctor had injected the medium into a site that was not delineated in the manufacturer's product insert nor that was used by other physicians. The court accepted the radiologist's reasoning: that he was acting so as to avoid sciatic damage to the child, a warning that was part of the accepted literature; that he had never read or heard of anything that suggested that the calf sites were inappropriate. The physician further stated that he had used the calf sites on other occasions with young children with successful outcomes. The court concluded that clinical innovation was in bounds in terms of a standard of care. Experimentation, on the other hand, presents a whole host of other problems, particularly in terms of informed consent—which truly should be drafted by attorneys!

Oftentimes it appears that patients, sometimes myself included, think that the standard is perfection! We all fail to recognize that practitioners and indeed health care institutions are human beings and human organizations—and humans make errors in judgment. Such was the case in *Ouellette v. Subak*, 391 N.W. 2d 810 (1986). In this case, a 20-year-old woman gave birth three weeks after her estimated delivery date. The baby girl, 9 pounds, 13 ounces, turned out to be profoundly retarded. The case itself turned on whether the "honest error in judgment" instruction was to be given or not. In Minnesota, where this case occurred, there is a jury instruction that states that a practitioner is "not a guarantor of a cure or a good result from his treatment and he is not responsible for an honest error in judgment in choosing between accepted methods of treatment."[1]

In practice, most health care organizations do not have on their staff full-time lawyers who can scrutinize every act of practitioners and staff for potential tort claims. It is imperative that there is a continual education program going on in the organization to sensitize people to potential legal actions and how to prevent them. Sometimes prevention involves recognizing problems and changing systems. Sometimes it involves changing personnel or clarifying roles, and sometimes it involves acknowledging reality and doing it better next time.

During my days as a CEO a number of problems came up, but there are two that stand out as illustrative of the issues that health care executives face. The first case came to my attention when my assistant Libby told me that Ms. Green was waiting to see me. Libby explained that Ms. Green was an active member of our volunteer group and that her father

---

[1]Minn. Dist. Judges Ass'n, Minn. Prac. JIG II, 425 G-S, 2d ed., 1974.

was a resident of one of our nursing homes. I welcomed Ms. Green and asked her how I could be of assistance. She proceeded to tell me a horrifying tale about the care her father was receiving at the nursing home.

Her father, an 88-year-old former businessman, had been a resident of the nursing home for almost two years. According to the daughter, the last several months had been a nightmare. Her father had lost a considerable amount of weight; he had developed serious pressure sores on his legs that had not been attended to; he had been hospitalized for the pressure sores; and one of his legs had required amputation. I was shocked by her story, particularly because I had always thought of this particular nursing home as the best within our system.

Ms. Green then went on to tell me that she did not intend to sue our organization, but she was telling me this because she wanted things to change. I assured her I would look into the situation immediately, which I did with two phone calls. First I called the administrator of the nursing home who assured me that everything was fine with Mr. Green and that his daughter had a shopping cart full of psychological problems. Next I called the nursing home's director of nursing and asked her what was going on. She, too, assured me that everything was all right and that the daughter was a chronic complainer. I asked both of these executives for a written memo reiterating their analysis of the situation.

The memos came the next day. I could have simply accepted their positions and gotten back to Ms. Green with a placating note or call that basically said, "We are right, you are wrong." If I had done that, I feel certain a lawsuit would have ensued, not necessarily to get money, but rather to get justice. My approach was different for two reasons. First, I wanted to send the message to the organization that I am in charge, I listen to complaints, I will investigate, and I will not accept BS. So, I asked that Mr. Green's records be brought to my office, and I sequestered myself with the records for 3 hours. I reviewed those records as I would have in the days I practiced law and concluded I had what we called a "slam dunk" case. The care that Mr. Green was receiving was outrageous. No one was paying attention. The charting was inaccurate. We had hung ourselves with our own records!

My next act was to call a meeting of all the staff involved in the incident: the two executives, the dieticians, and the supervisory nurses. All told, 15 people were at the meeting. And then I began. First I told of Ms. Green's accusations, and then I listened to everyone defend themselves.

When they finished, I presented the medical records and demonstrated to them how I could make an airtight case that would cost the institution a fortune. When I finished, I summarized by saying that I was less interested in the fact that we had been negligent than the fact that everyone was actively engaged in denial or covering up. I concluded by saying such behavior was unacceptable and that change needed to take place immediately.

Whether the changed behavior lasted beyond the contrition of that moment or the subsequent two years of my tenure is an open question. But I do believe health care executives must set the standards for their organizations and directly face and act to cure the diseases of lethargy, smugness, and blaming the victim.

On the other hand (lawyers just love to say that), there are times when "potential plaintiffs" can simply be outrageous! At this same nursing home there was a elderly noncommunicative woman, Mrs. Brown, who had a degenerative disease that pretty well kept her in front of her TV for hours a day. She had an old mechanical lounge chair that she sat in, and each morning the nurse's aide would set up the chair in a slightly reclined position so she could comfortably watch her TV in her room. One day the chair broke beyond repair. The nursing staff, who were quite fond of this woman, managed to convince someone in the storeroom to replace the chair with a new electrical one that had been ordered for someone else who had died. Every morning the staff would position the chair for TV watching and periodically check back to see how Mrs. Brown was doing. One day Mrs. Brown had a spasm. She accidentally hit one of the chair's buttons and ejected herself from the lounger, breaking both legs.

When I heard about this, I immediately did two things. First, I ordered around-the-clock aides in her room for a month and, second, I called her son, who lived 1000 miles away, to tell him of the incident. He seemed very understanding, and I thought that was that. About two weeks later I called him again to provide him with an update. Once again, we had a cordial conversation. Two weeks later Mrs. Brown was much improved, and after speaking with her orthopedist I made the decision to cut back on the 24-hour aides. Almost immediately I received a call from the son, who was irate that the aides had been cut back. After listening to his argument that she was still in casts, I relented and put the full complement back. Two weeks later the casts came off, and she was back to where she was before the accident.

Meanwhile, Mrs. Brown had grown accustomed to the company of the aides, who were no longer necessary and were quite costly. I decided to wean her off them and gradually began cutting their time. After two weeks the son called again, this time almost out of control and threatening me with lawsuits. I had prior to this learned that he had not visited once in the two months since his mother's injury, despite the fact that he had been in the city several weeks earlier. After listening to his threats, I reminded him that if his mother did sue us and win the suit, she would become a private pay resident, and a good chunk of her new-found wealth would merely go right back to us. Further, I explained that under Medicaid rules, she could not simply give him the money—so much for his windfall. Finally, I told him that since he seemed to be so concerned about his mother, I was finalizing arrangements to have his mother transferred at our expense to a first-class nursing home in his community so that he could be more actively engaged in her care. Suddenly his tone changed. We were great people, she loved us, he loved us, and "have a nice day." Sometimes you have to play hardball.

But all the time the organization must manage the risk. The following pages on risk management were written by George W. Pozgar and are excerpted from his book *Legal Aspects of Health Care Administration, 9th edition*.

RISK MANAGEMENT

Risk management is a systematic program designed to reduce preventable injuries and accidents and minimize the financial severity of claims. It involves the identification of potential accidents with an emphasis on claims prevention. In risk management, steps are taken on a team effort basis to improve the quality of care and eliminate or minimize the number of accidents that become potential lawsuits. Liability insurers have been strong proponents of risk management; in many cases, insurers have cut premiums for physicians and health care organizations that adopt sanctioned risk management practices.

Risk management must include a heightened sensitivity to providing a safe environment and addressing the emotional needs of patients. The input of the provider-patient relationship cannot be overemphasized when the provider-patient relationship is intense and inescapable. Individuals, not incidents, bring lawsuits. Good relationships with patients are very important in preventing malpractice suits. Public relations for health care professionals are a challenge. It is not only good medical practice but it is also at the very core of the problem of medical malpractice.

Increasing insurance costs and general financial constraints have pressured hospitals to assume leadership in the prevention of medically related injuries. Risk management programs should include the following components:

- A grievance or complaint mechanism designed to process and resolve as promptly and effectively as possible grievances by patients or their representatives
- A collection of data with respect to negative health care outcomes (whether or not they give rise to claims)
- Medical care evaluation mechanisms, which shall include a tissue committee or medical audit committee to periodically assess the quality of medical care being provided
- Education programs for staff personnel engaged in patient care activities dealing with patient safety, medical injury prevention, the legal aspects of patient care, problems of communication and rapport with patients, and other relevant factors known to influence malpractice claims and suits

Elements of a Risk Management Program

Valuable components of a risk management program include:

- Early intervention and sympathetic care after accidental injury to a patient
- Preparation of incident reports
- Prompt identification and investigation of specific incidents of patient injuries and, when possible, intervention
- Definition of the cause of each incident
- Generation and maintenance of a risk database from which hazardous trends and areas may be identified and corrected
- Evaluation of the frequency and severity of incident exposure
- Formulation and implementation of corrective actions to reduce risk and exposure to liability
- Training and education of employees and clinicians to assist in reducing exposure
- Continuing attention of a safety committee
- Use of a suggestion box
- A public relations program (employees should be trained in completing timely incident reports that document the facts and that are not used to cover up unfortunate incidents but to train personnel and identify problems)

Risk Management Committee

A risk management committee with representation from the organization's governing body, administration, and medical staff should be established. A person trained in medical audits and the risk management process should chair the committee. The risk manager should be responsible for the development and coordination of strategic prevention programs. Information from all committees (e.g., pharmacy, transfusion, infections, safety, audit, utilization, tissue, medical records, personnel, credentials, continuing education, product review, etc.) regarding potential liability hazards should be funneled into this committee for review, evaluation, and appropriate action. This committee serves to monitor all potential hazards. The organization's attorney should be readily available for legal counsel.

Because an organization's governing body has the ultimate responsibility for adequate patient care, that group's involvement in the risk management process is mandatory. The governing body must be just as concerned with reviewing the competence of the medical staff as it is with the financial aspects of institutional operations. Public expectations place a broad responsibility on organizations to ensure quality care, whether that care involves administrative, nursing, or physician activities.

CONTRACTS

It is astounding when organizations consider how many contracts they have. Using my earlier approach to teaching law, I shall once again take on the mantle of Father Guido Sarducci of *Saturday Night Live* fame and provide a one-minute overview of contracts.

Contracts are agreements between two or more parties to do something or to refrain from doing something. Like everything in law, there are requirements for contracts: Was there an offer? Was there an acceptance of the offer? Was there a meeting of the minds? Was there consideration? Was the consideration adequate? Were there reasons why the contract is not valid? There are countless cases, rules, and regulations for each of these questions and more. Suffice it to say that contracts are best if they do not follow the oral tradition, which inevitably leads to a conflict about who said what, but rather follow a written tradition, with the agreement being committed to paper.

Contracts permeate every sector of the health care organization. Formal employment contracts usually exist for some employees, and others often have contracts via employee handbooks. Contracts for health care benefits usually exist through master agreements with insurers. Contracts exist between patients and providers; the organization and suppliers; and even the organization and donors. Contract theory has been used in malpractice cases as a way of getting around some of the problems of tort law such as statutes of limitation (tort claim statutes typically are shorter than contract claim statutes). Another value of going the contract claim route is that it limits the need for expert witnesses, since the issues in the case would relate to whether there was a contract, whether the contract was breached, and what the appropriate damages are.

The oft-cited case of *Sullivan v. O'Connor*, 363 Mass. 579 (1973), involved a nightclub singer who went to a surgeon to get a nose job. When the bandages came off, her dreams of a ski-slope nose where shattered when she looked in the mirror and saw an uneven, bulbous nose. Her theory behind the suit was breach of contract, and she sought a contract remedy such as expectancy damages, meaning the money that she would have made had the nose job been done properly. The problem for most practitioners is finding the line between what the courts call optimistic coloring and promising specific results. The optimistic coloring is a signal of hope without the directness of a warranty. Crossing the line, such as saying, "This surgery will give you 20/20 vision," is an invitation to potential litigation.

Organizations seem to spend a great deal of their energy trying to avoid contractual liability through a variety of contract clauses that release them from liability. For example, in *Tunkl v. Regents of the University of California*, 383 F. 2d. 441 (1963), the UCLA Medical Center attempted to limit its negligence exposure by getting charity patients to sign a release from liability as a condition of their receiving care at the hospital. The court found the practice unacceptable and a violation of California's public policy. More recently, HMOs and other insurers have used their contracts to redirect potential litigation from the court system to alternative dispute resolution systems, such as arbitration. Indeed, much of what happens in managed care is about contracts and court interpretations of the ambiguities of the contract.

The significance of contracts is also illustrated by an arbitration case that I was involved with. The parties were a family and their HMO who were disputing benefits for a congenitally ill child. In the first two years of the child's life, the HMO provided an enormous amount of costly care to this child, including daily therapeutic services. In year three, the HMO notified the family that the group contract had been changed and that they were only eligible for a limited number of therapeutic services as per the contract. The family challenged the HMO, claiming that once they started receiving a certain amount and level of services, they were entitled to continue receiving the same services. The HMO argued that all their contracts explicitly stated that the service package was time limited and that the HMO could change the package on an annual basis. The decision, based on a clear reading of the contract, was in favor of the HMO. Fortunately, state-sponsored services were available to assist the family with their problems.

Employment-related issues form a major area of concern for all managers. At one level are the labor relations issues, which always require expert counsel. Another area that most likely requires outside counsel is discrimination law. In today's highly charged environment, it is imperative that, from the employment application to the termination procedures and all matters in between, everything pass a test to ensure that there is no discrimination on the basis of age, sex, race, sexual orientation, and even health status. The basic rule generally is that all employees are "at-will," meaning the employer can fire them unless there is a public policy exception, such as if there is a whistleblower protection law in the state and the employee is a whistleblower. Otherwise, the primary protection the employee has is through a specific employment contract or a labor relations contract.

An interesting case occurred during my management tenure when I decided to terminate a contentious and disruptive senior medical executive of the organization. The other members of the management team advised me that this physician did not have a contract and that he would not go quietly. Prior to meeting with the physician, I consulted with our outside labor counsel and was advised to say as little as possible and not to discuss his age or many years of service. It was to be the Donald Trump approach—"You're fired." I was uncomfortable with that level of cruelty, particularly in light of his many decades of service, even though the last several years had been a disaster. Before the meeting, I also insisted that one of my assistants review the two drawers full of files on this person to be certain that there was no contract. We struck gold when we found a 23-year-old contract that required a 30-day notice, did not require any reason for termination, and finally required the physician to pay $600 per month in rent for his office at the medical center. I immediately asked for an update on his rental payment, only to learn that he had dutifully paid it for 18 months and then had not paid for more than two decades. My simple calculation was that he owed the organization in excess of $150,000.

When I finally called him in to my office, with several witnesses present, I simply said, "In accordance with your contract, I have decided to terminate your services with our organization effective 30 days from today." He demanded to know why. I did not answer but rather repeated what soon became my mantra, "In accordance with your contract, I have decided to terminate your services with our organization 30 days from today." After listening to me saying this several more times, he turned and threatened me with a lawsuit for age discrimination and breach of contract. I looked him square in the eye and said that I would welcome a lawsuit because I would definitely want to enforce all the contract provisions, including the back rents he owed us. Suddenly there was silence. I made him an offer: If he would resign within 48 hours, I would forgive the back rent. If he wished to stay the 30 days, I would fire him and pursue him for the rent. Fortunately for all of us, an ugly lawsuit was avoided by his resignation the next day.

Unless administrators expect to have a hotline to a lawyer, it is essential that they sensitize themselves to legal issues. Professional journals typically carry law columns, and many newsletters for managers discuss legal issues. In larger organizations it is wise to have full time in-house counsel; smaller organizations might even consider part-time counsel. Administrators might also wish to avail themselves of legal continuing education courses, not only those offered to the health administration profession but also those provided to the legal profession, such as continuing education in health law. Finally, today's health care manager will not only be confronted by the traditional issues highlighted in this chapter but will be challenged as well by the corporate compliance issues to be analyzed in the next chapters.

Case 12-1

SEXUAL HARASSMENT

Shortly after Jane Robinson started her new job as an accountant in the business office of the Green Tree Valley Medical Center, she was approached by her supervisor, Bill Post, who asked whether she wanted to hear a joke. She agreed, and Post told a short but rather sexually explicit joke. Robinson laughed politely and then went on with her work. The following Friday, Post again approached Robinson and suggested that they have lunch together at a local restaurant. The luncheon conversation began with a discussion of the center's cash-flow problems and continued with more conversation about several financial issues related to the employee benefits program. As they were concluding lunch, Post reached across the table, touched Robinson's arm, and said, "How about continuing this conversation over dinner tonight and breakfast in the morning?"

Robinson said, "No, thanks. I have other plans."

Post got quite angry and responded, "Jane, I hope you understand that I run this department, and nobody is approved for a regular position unless I approve. I trust you remember that you are a probationary employee and that if you really want this job I need to give the word. So, let's not play games. You take care of my needs and I'll take great care of you."

Jane glared at Post, got up from the table, and walked out.

Over the weekend she thought more and more about the conversation with Bill Post and decided that it was important that she meet with Ms. Gail Page, the medical center's human resources director of 15 years. Ms. Page responded to Robinson's story by saying, "Look Jane, in this organization you have to learn to roll with the punches. Bill is a bit of a lecher, but he really is harmless and a terrific business manager. My best advice is just to ignore him and not go out to lunch with him any more."

(continues)

Case Study 12.1

Robinson said nothing to Page at that time, but as she left the HR office she decided that her situation in the medical center was simply untenable. However, she needed the work and enjoyed her coworkers, so she decided to stay and vowed to steer clear of Post. At the end of the three-month probationary period, she was terminated based on Post's evaluation that she was not competent to fulfill her duties.

Ms. Robinson has consulted an attorney who has contacted the medical center with an informal complaint.

EXHIBIT 12–1

Definition of Sexual Harassment from Code of Massachusetts Regulations (151 B CMR 1.8)

The term "sexual harassment" shall mean sexual advances, requests for sexual favors, and other verbal or physical conduct of a sexual nature when (a) submission to or rejection of such advances, requests or conduct is made either explicitly or implicitly a term or condition of employment or as a basis for employment decisions; (b) such advances, requests or conduct have the purpose or effect of unreasonably interfering with an individual's work performance by creating an intimidating, hostile, humiliating or sexually offensive work environment. Discrimination on the basis of sex shall include, but not be limited to, sexual harassment.

EXHIBIT 12-2

Code of Federal Regulations: §1604.11 (Sexual harassment)

(a) Harassment on the basis of sex is a violation of section 703 of title VII. Unwelcome sexual advances, requests for sexual favors, and other verbal or physical conduct of a sexual nature constitute sexual harassment when (1) submission to such conduct is made either explicitly or implicitly a term or condition of an individual's employment, (2) submission to or rejection of such conduct by an individual is used as the basis for employment decisions affecting such individual, or (3) such conduct has the purpose or effect of unreasonably interfering with an individual's work performance or creating an intimidating, hostile, or offensive working environment.

(b) In determining whether alleged conduct constitutes sexual harassment, the Commission [the Equal Employment Opportunity Commission] will look at the record as a whole and at the totality of the circumstances, such as the nature of the sexual advances and the context in which the alleged incidents occurred. The determination of the legality of a particular action will be made from the facts, on a case by case basis.

(c) Applying general title VII principles, an employer, employment agency, joint apprenticeship committee or labor organization (hereinafter collectively referred to as "employer") is responsible for its acts and those of its agents and supervisory employees with respect to sexual harassment regardless of whether the specific acts complained of were authorized or even forbidden by the employer and regardless of whether the employer knew or should have known of their occurrence. The Commission will examine the circumstances of the particular employment relationship and the job functions performed by the individual in determining whether an individual acts in either a supervisory or agency capacity.

(continues)

EXHIBIT 12-2

(d) With respect to conduct between fellow employees, an employer is responsible for acts of sexual harassment in the workplace where the employer (or its agents or supervisory employees) knows or should have known of the conduct, unless it can show that it took immediate and appropriate corrective action.

(e) An employer may also be responsible for the acts of non-employees, with respect to sexual harassment of employees in the workplace, where the employer (or its agents or supervisory employees) knows or should have known of the conduct and fails to take immediate and appropriate corrective action. In reviewing these cases the Commission will consider the extent of the employer's control and any other legal responsibility which the employer may have with respect to the conduct of such non-employees.

The principles involved here continue to apply to race, color, religion, or national origin.

DISCUSSION QUESTIONS

1. Does the action by Post constitute sexual harassment? (See Exhibits 12-1 and 12-2 for applicable regulations.)

2. What further actions can be expected from Robinson?

3. To what extent does Ms. Page's attitude affect sexual harassment in the organization?

4. If you were a consultant to the medical center, what would you propose the medical center do to become a sexual-harassment-free facility?

CHAPTER 13

Corporate Compliance: An Overview

More than 40 years ago, my family gathered with pride in the auditorium of the State University of New York's Downstate School of Medicine to watch as my older brother stood and recited the 2000-year-old Oath of Hippocrates as a part of the ritual prior to his being awarded the Doctor of Medicine degree. My brother, along with medical students throughout the country, swore by Apollo the physician and Asclepius and Health and All-Heal and all the gods and goddesses: "According to my ability and judgment, I will keep this oath and stipulation." The stipulation that they were to keep, and indeed almost all have kept, was, in the words of the oath, "Into whatever houses I will enter I will go into them for the benefit of the sick and will abstain from every voluntary act of mischief."

What went wrong? Why has this oath been dishonored by physicians and their administrative associates? Why has corruption in the health care field become such a big business? Is it merely because health care is where the money is, or is there a different explanation? In this and the following two chapters I shall explore this issue of corruption in health care, the kind of corruption that has the genteel and professional name of "corporate compliance." Call it what you may, it is simple dishonesty and greed. The results are fines, loss of reputation, and imprisonment. To be perfectly fair, we must recognize that corporate compliance is not a new idea. Indeed, it has clearly existed since biblical times, with Adam and Eve as the first noncompliant couple; their failure to follow clear rules about eating on the job led to denial of housing and other benefits.

In this chapter, I shall examine some of the background issues about corporate compliance and how this has become a front burner issue. It should be clear from the outset that corporate compliance is really nothing more than good business; that is, if problems are prevented, detected, and corrected, they are mitigated and the organization is protected to a greater degree. Corporate compliance is about ethically running integrity-oriented, honest organizations. In Chapter 14 I shall review some of the important court cases that have established the parameters of corporate compliance, and in Chapter 15 I shall look at how the government looks forward through the Office of Inspector General Advisory Opinions and other guidance designed to prevent problems.

FALSE CLAIMS ACT

The government today is deadly serious about corporate compliance in the health industry, specifically fraud and abuse, which is estimated to cost the government billions of dollars per year. To understand the roots of corporate compliance in health care, it is necessary to begin with a law passed in 1863 by President Abraham Lincoln. This law, known as the False Claims Act, evolved from the problems the Union Army was having with suppliers who were providing the soldiers with shoddy and defective goods. (Interestingly, the Confederacy had similar problems and also passed a false claims act law.)

The Act contained provisions for civil and criminal penalties and also introduced the idea of *qui tam,* which is a shorthand Latin phrase that in practice meant that citizens could bring actions against private individuals or companies on behalf of the government; if the government won, the citizen could collect 50% of the recovery. This essentially deputized each citizen as a private attorney general, giving them an incentive to go out and search for wrongdoers. During World War II the Act was amended, and it became extremely difficult to file and win a qui tam action. However, in 1986 the Act was again amended, and qui tam was back with potential recoveries for the private citizen of between 15% and 30%, depending on the government's involvement in the case.

The government recovered in excess of $12 billion under the False Claims Act between 1986 and 2003,[1] and in many cases there have been both civil and criminal actions under the Act. Out of the 25 companies that have had the largest civil and criminal fines under the Act, all but 6 have been in the health care industry. The largest penalty ever, $1.7 bil-

---

[1]Corporate Crime Reporter, "The Top 100 False Claim Act Settlements." A report released by Corporate Crime Report, December 30, 2003, National Press Club, Washington, DC, p. 7.

lion, was levied against HCA, which at various times has been called Hospital Corporation of America, Columbia, Columbia/HCA, and a variety of subsidies. The government's claims against HCA are a virtual encyclopedia of wrongdoing, including cooking the cost reports, false claims, paying kickbacks to physicians, and much more. The whistle-blowers in this case collected in excess of $151 million.[2]

Other health care operators in the top 25 include National Medical Enterprises, whose fines exceeded $324 million for their kickback and fraudulent behavior in inducing referrals;[3] First American Health Care of Georgia, fined $225 million, a home health company that over-billed and submitted false claims for a variety of personal expenses;[4] Beverly Enterprise, the largest nursing home chain, fined $170 million for filing false cost reports and mail fraud;[5] Vencor, another large nursing home chain, fined $104 million for filling false claims about patients and over-billing;[6] Quorum, a health care management company, fined $95 million for filing false cost reports.[7] Drug companies were also prominent in the list of top 25 fines. TAP Pharmaceuticals paid $559 million under the False Claims Act and another $316 million for claims under other government regulations for its activities involving fraud in the marketing and pricing of its drugs;[8] AstraZeneca ran into $266 million worth of trouble for its marketing activities for a prostate cancer drug sold as Zoladex;[9] Bayer's $257 million fine was related to a complex scheme involving discounts to HMOs and failure to properly provide required rebates to Medicaid;[10] finally, GlaxoSmithKline ran afoul of government regulations in a manner similar to Bayer and wound up with an $87 million fine.[11]

Clinical laboratories are another group that have had significant problems under the False Claims Act, typically for submitting false claims for unnecessary testing. Laboratory Corporation of America was hit for $182 million,[12] National Health Labs paid $100 million for its illegal

---

[2]Ibid., p. 4.
[3]Ibid., p. 13.
[4]Ibid., pp. 14–15.
[5]Ibid., pp. 16–17.
[6]Ibid., pp. 19–20.
[7]Ibid., pp. 20–26.
[8]Ibid., pp. 9–10.
[9]Ibid., p. 14.
[10]Ibid.
[11]Ibid., p. 22
[12]Ibid., pp. 15–16.

activities,[13] and Damon Clinical Laboratories had a total payout of $832 million.[14]

In addition to these large organizations and multimillion-dollar players, many "small fry" are caught up in the web of fraud and abuse. For example, of the more than 180,000 inmates of the Federal Bureau of Prisons, there are thousands who have been convicted and are doing time for white-collar crimes; almost 7,100 are incarcerated for extortion, bribery, and fraud, and another 600-plus are in the system for continuing criminal enterprises.[15] For individuals, this translated into a 27-month sentence for Helen Nwachuku, a nurse who was convicted under mail fraud statutes for conspiring to defraud the Social Security administration.[16] Thomas Sargeant, a California psychiatrist, stole over $100,000 from Medicare by billing for services he never delivered, netting him an 18-month prison sentence.[17]

Sometimes we see simple cases such as Sargeant. Other times we see complex schemes, such as the one in Florida that involved four people, Perla Martin Davis, Marta Morfa, Emilio Valdes, MD, and Elva Lamas, as well as 16 related companies and a scheme that solicited patients whose names and Medicare numbers were used for billing for expensive and extensive parenteral and enteral nutritional services. The penalties imposed on these convicted conspirators were staggering: Davis had to make restitution of $9.1 million plus serve 41 months in prison; Lamas had to make restitution of $8.1 million and serve 46 months behind bars; Morfa's restitution was $8.1 million and a sentence of 46 months; Valdes, the physician who signed the blank medical certifications, was given a 30-month sentence and had to reimburse the government $261,000.[18] In the First American Health Care of Georgia case, not only did the company pay, but its key executives Jack and Margie Mills were also criminally indicted and convicted of defrauding Medicare. Jack is serving a 90-month term and Margie was sentenced to 32 months. Their scheme involved paying for a host of personal expenses for themselves and family members through the company and then charging it to Medicare.[19] Obviously, crime does not pay!

---

[13]Ibid., p. 20.

[14]Ibid., pp. 23–24.

[15]Accessed (n.d.) from www.bop.gov/fact0598.html.

[16]*U.S. v. Irvine*, 1998 U.S. App. LEXIS 31781.

[17]Accessed (n.d.) from www.keepinformed.com/HHS/PR/1996/05/950513c.html, which is a "Fact Sheet" from the Department of Health and Human Services.

[18]*U.S. v. Mills*, 138 F. 3rd 928 (1998). See also Chapter 14, p. 306.

[19]Ibid., pp. 15–16.

A serious and developing problem for health care organizations is that governmental agencies are using the False Claims Act as the legal basis to litigate against organizations who fail to meet quality standards but nevertheless submit bills for service. The scenario goes something like this: A nursing home submits a bill to Medicaid for payment for a beneficiary, but during the month of care the home has had a state survey, which has found numerous deficiencies at the nursing home. The government then claims that the bill was submitted fraudulently because the assumption is that all the care was provided, but the survey indicates otherwise. And, if the bill was sent by mail, there is the additional problem tacked on of mail fraud. (Remember, the government nailed the gangster Al Capone on tax fraud, not murder.)

MEDICARE AND MEDICAID FRAUD AND ABUSE

Several weeks after I took my post as CEO, I received a call from my CFO informing me that there were two agents from the Federal Bureau of Investigation in her office with a court document, demanding that we produce for their review a year's worth of medical records and billing documents. The documents were "seized" by the government. A few months later I signed a consent degree that caused the organization to pay the government several hundred thousand dollars for Medicare over-billing. The whole story was more complicated. About three years prior to the FBI showing up, a company approached the organization and sold them on the idea that they could more aggressively bill Medicare for Part B charges and that the amounts received could be split. Initially, it sounded too good to be true, but the organization went along with the outside company.

As time passed, the finance staff became suspicious of the vendor, reviewed their work, fired them, and informed the fiscal intermediary of their suspicions. The health system even went on to take a second look at the work of the vendor and voluntarily reimbursed the government for overpayments that it had received. Nothing more was heard for two years until the FBI showed up at the door. If there is a moral to this story, it probably is: Do not assume anything in health care management!

The Medicare fraud and abuse legislation was designed as a zero tolerance program to ensure integrity and honesty in every aspect of the Medicare program. At various times, the program has developed catchy phrases such as Operation Restore Trust, and it has periodically focused on different parts of the health industry, such as durable medical equipment providers, mental health centers, and independent diagnostic testing laboratories. The primary way that the government scrutinizes the providers of care is through the billing systems. Basically, the government wants to be certain that it gets what it pays for and that beneficiaries are not receiving unnecessary services

In attempting to deal with these issues of fraud and abuse, the Department of Health and Human Service's Office of Inspector General (OIG) has developed a nationwide program of audits, inspections, and periodic investigations. In testimony before the House Budget Committee on July 9, 2003, Acting Principal Deputy Inspector General Dara Corrigan stated:

> The Office of Inspector General uncovers innocent errors, carelessness, mismanagement, exploitation of the programs, malfeasance, and outright fraud every day. Improper behaviors include providers billing for services not rendered, falsification of diagnosis, and unnecessary tests or services, abusing and neglecting beneficiaries and accepting kickbacks (p. 1).[20]

Corrigan then went on to identify a number of areas that are particularly vulnerable to fraud and abuse: prescription drugs, durable medical equipment, and the behavior of Medicare contractors, that is, fiscal intermediaries and their management of cancer treatments, lab tests, and durable medical equipment charges. With regard to the Medicaid programs, Corrigan evinced concern about prescription drugs and various hospital payment schemes. The issue of drug reimbursement under Medicaid is a complex one and the issue that led to many of the earlier mentioned huge judgments against pharmaceutical companies. In brief, the situation is that under Medicaid, states are by law entitled to pay a discounted wholesale price for drugs prescribed for eligible Medicaid beneficiaries. Overpricing thus falls into the category of false claims and fraud and abuse.

It is clear that in the past several years the government has been devoting significant resources to the issues of Medicare and Medicaid fraud and abuse. The results of such activities include prosecutions (568 successful cases in fiscal year 2002)[21] and other penalties, including fines and exclusion from participation in government programs. For example, in fiscal year 2002, almost 3500 individuals and corporate entities were excluded

[20]Accessed (n.d.) from www.oig.hhs.gov/testimony/docs/2003/070903fin.pdf.
[21]Ibid., p. 8.

from Medicare and Medicaid participation,[22] which means they were effectively put out of business. In some instances the decertification of one component of an organization can result in the decertification of the entire entity—a rather draconian remedy.

KICKBACKS, SELF-REFERRALS, AND STARK II

Among the central elements in the government's fight against fraud and abuse are the legislation, rules, and regulations of the Social Security Act that prohibit certain individual and organizational behavior. In November 1999, the Office of Inspector General of the Department of Health and Human Services issued a "Fact Sheet" on the anti-kickback law and safe harbor provisions, which provide a useful explanation of these issues. The following are excerpts from that document:

> Overview: On the books since 1972, the federal anti-kickback law's main purpose is to protect patients and the federal health care programs from fraud and abuse by curtailing the corrupting influence of money on health care decisions. Straightforward but broad, the law states that anyone who knowingly and willfully receives or pays anything of value to influence the referral of federal health care program business, including Medicare and Medicaid, can be held accountable for a felony. Violations of the law are punishable by up to five years in prison, criminal fines up to $25,000, administrative civil money penalties up to $50,000, and exclusion from participation in federal health care programs. . . .[23]

> Safe harbors immunize certain payment and business practices that are implicated by the ant-kickback statute from criminal and civil prosecution under the statute. To be protected by a safe harbor, an arrangement must fit squarely in the safe harbor. Failure to comply with a safe harbor provision does not mean that an arrangement is per se illegal. Compliance with safe harbors is voluntary, and arrangements that do not comply with a safe harbor must be analyzed on a case by case basis for compliance with the anti-kickback statute. . . .

In 1991 the government published a listing of arrangements that fell into the safe harbor provisions, including space rental, some small-scale

---

[22]Ibid., p. 8

[23]Office of Inspector General, Department of Health and Human Services, Fact Sheet (November 1999): "Federal Anti-Kickback Law and Regulatory Safe Harbors."

joint ventures, equipment rentals, certain types of personal services and management contracts, the selling of clinical practices by retiring physicians, and group purchasing arrangements. Periodically, new safe harbor issues are analyzed and new rules issued. For example, in 1993 and 1994, new rules were issued for physician investments in ambulatory surgical centers and for physician recruitment in underserved areas. My reading of these various safe harbors is that the government is genuinely concerned about securing medical care for covered populations, particularly in underserved areas, but they are also leery of schemes that might result in surreptitious payments to physicians for either referrals from themselves or others. To put it bluntly, the government is exercising considerable care to ensure that it is not ripped off!

Stark II

In 1989, Congressman Pete Stark, a Democrat from California, led the charge for the passage of the Ethics in Patient Referral Act, which later became known as the Stark bill. The initial issue that the bill and its subsequent regulations addressed was that of prohibiting physicians from referring Medicare patients to labs that those physicians either owned or had financial arrangements with, whereby they would receive a fee for referring a patient. The way the law worked was that it was okay to refer the patient to the lab but illegal to bill Medicare for the lab service and, indeed, Medicare was prohibited from paying for the service. Over the years, Stark has grown in complexity and now is the beneficiary of hundreds of pages of regulations covering far more than laboratories. The reach of Stark II is now into physician recruitment, leasing and personal service arrangements, group practice compensation plans, and even to such arcane areas such as professional courtesy arrangements.

In summary, the world of corporate compliance is like a deep, dark, and dense forest full of all manner of traps. Organizations and people sometimes fall into the traps because they simply are not paying enough attention. In general, though, most people and organizations manage to get through the woods relatively unscathed because, as in the fairy tale, they are good at heart, lacking evil intentions. On the other hand, there are those for whom the Medicare or Medicaid pot of gold is too tempting, and they use their positions of trust to attempt to beat the system. Some no doubt do so with petty crimes such as periodic upcoding, that is claiming charges for a slightly more expensive service than was provided. While I do not condone such behavior, these people pale in comparison to those who actively scheme to steal money from government programs. In the next chapter I shall review a number of cases that illuminate both the dark side of the health field and how the government responds to these problems.

CORPORATE COMPLIANCE CASE STUDIES

All cases for Chapters 13, 14, and 15 rely on the same basic organizational fact pattern and IRS (Internal Revenue Service) Code and Rulings as follows:

1. All the cases involve the same organization;

2. There appears to be no specific intent on the part of anyone in the organization to commit any illegal act;

3. The organization is the Northville Regional Health System (NRHS), which consists of 7 separate 501(c)(3) corporations. The best-known component of the system is the 147-bed acute care general hospital, named the Gideon Medical Center after its first family of philanthropy. The system also includes the 200-bed King's Park Nursing Home; the 80-bed Western Valley Assisted Living Community; the 75-bed Hightown Hospital Rehabilitation Center and the Bryna Home Health Agency; the 60-bed Isaac Louis Congregate Home; and the Northville Health Care Research Center.

   Financing for the system and its components comes from a combination of sources including Medicare, Medicaid, private pay, various managed care organizations and finally, a wide variety of health insurers.

4. The structure of the organization is as follows:
   a. The overall governance for the system is the responsibility of a self perpetuating 40-member board of trustees that also controls all of the subsidiary corporations. The chairman of the board is Robert Gideon, a lawyer by profession who served one term (3 decades earlier) in the state senate. Senator Gideon (as he likes to be called) has been involved with the NRHS for more than

30 years and for the past 20 has served as chairman of the board. Through his vision and hard work he has overseen its expansion from that of a small-town hospital to a regional health system. The board now is a personal reflection of his great influence and includes his three daughters, one son, his wife, his two brothers, and a bevy of friends. Board meetings occur 10 times each year and are primarily social dinners along with presentations of PR-type information. No financial reports are presented, and rarely is anything voted upon. In the past 10 years, every single vote has been unanimous with little discussion

b. The system is managed by a cadre of middle managers headed by a CEO who has been with the organization for nine years. An accountant with a MPH in health policy and management from the University of Massachusetts, Ms. Danielle Russo is an experienced administrator who has conceived and implemented many of the ideas that have led to the development and flourishing of the system. Ms. Russo has recently taken a graduate course in corporate compliance at the University of Massachusetts, and her sensitivity to these issues has been dramatically heightened. In pursuance of these concerns she has recently appointed you as the corporate compliance officer and asked your advice on a range of issues.

Please review each case and the attachments and evaluate all compliance issues. Your responsibility, unless otherwise indicated, is to assume you are the corporate compliance officer of the NRHS and must make a judgment in writing as to what is the organization's compliance exposure, why there is exposure, and what steps should be taken to minimize damage to the corporation. One of your current concerns is that of "Private Benefit and Inurement." Based on your research you have learned that section 501(c)(3) and IRS Treasury Regulation 1.501(c)(3)-1(c)(2) prohibits insiders in a tax-exempt organization from taking advantage of their status to get any type of private benefit. The penalties, you learn, are severe and may include forfeiture of an organization's tax-exempt status. You might want to do an online search for IRS Revenue Ruling 69-383.

Case Study 13-1

THE DONATION LETTERS

The chairman of the board of trustees has asked the CEO of the organization to send the following letter to one of the chairman's friends on the stationary of the NRHS. It has come to your attention that the chairman and his family regularly send out similar letters but never follow up on the letters with gifts. Russo once asked about this and was told the gifts are the time the Gideon family gives to the organization.

Northville Regional Health System
733 Red Road
Northville, MA 01060

Danielle Russo
Chief Executive Officer

May 14, 20—
Dr. John P. Jones
13 Ship-Shape Lane
Amherst, MA 01002

Dear Dr. Jones:

I am sure you will be pleased to know that Dana and Robert Gideon III and their children Tom and Jerry have made a lovely contribution to the Gideon Hospital in memory of your beloved mother, Tomasina Jones.

The Gideons' gift was most thoughtful and generous and I am sure reflects the friendship and affection they feel for you. We are honored that they have remembered our hospital in memorializing your mother. The entire family of the Northville Regional Health System wishes to express its deepest sympathy on her passing. If we may be of help to you in any way during this time of sadness, please do not hesitate to let us know.

With warmest wishes to you and your family.

Sincerely,

Danielle Stone
Chief Executive Officer

Case Study 13-2

MOTHER-IN-LAW DEAREST

The CEO has just learned of the following situation involving Mrs. Arlene Fox, who is the mother-in-law of Ira Lockman, a member of the board, a client of Senator Gideon, and a good friend of the Gideon family. Lockman's wealth is reputed to be in excess of $200 million, a part of which has been funnelled into his private nonprofit foundation, the Ira and Jessie Lockman Foundation. The facts of the situation that require your analysis and recommendations are as follows:

1. Three years ago, Mrs. Arlene Fox was admitted as a long-term resident of the King's Park Nursing Home. According to the admission documents, her daughter, Jessie Lockman, agreed to be financially responsible for the bill. No information on the admission form suggests that Mrs. Fox would be treated differently than any other full private pay resident.

2. Since her admission to the King's Park Nursing Home, Mrs. Fox's full charges have been written off on a monthly basis. These charges are for a private room as well as private duty aides. Her annual charges exceed $125,000, and to date she has incurred in excess of $350,000 in charges that have been written off.

3. Neither King's Park nor the system has a written "write-off" or "bill-canceling" policy.

4. There is no written authorization for the write-off of Mrs. Fox's bill; however, a memo exists from the comptroller to the accounts receivable supervisor indicating that Administration had authorized the write-offs.

5. Since the time of Mrs. Fox's admission, a monthly statement of the Fox account has been sent to the secretary of the Lockman Foundation. During the course of the past three years, the Lockman Foundation has sent checks that in the aggregate correspond to the amount of money written off. The statement of the Fox accounts include recognition of the Lockman receipts.

6. In response to the funds received from the Lockman Foundation, letters have been sent from NRHS indicating that a gift was made to the King's Park Nursing Home without benefit.

CHAPTER 14

Corporate Compliance: The Case Law

In the world of corporate compliance, the rubber hits the road when the organization or individual is hauled into court. Over the years there have been hundreds of documented cases of this. In this chapter I shall review a handful, selected to illustrate how the courts view the behavior of violators of the Medicare regulations. In some instances I shall provide my own comments or analyses and at other times, indicated by indented print, I shall allow the court to speak for itself in the actual words of the opinion. In all instances, my focus is not on the technical legal arguments or procedures but on the behavior of the defendants that brought them to court in the first instance. Unfortunately, as these cases illustrate, what may be deemed petty crimes can have terrible consequences.

FAHNER v. ALASKA, 591 F. SUPP. 794 (1984)

In this case a Chicago-area optometrist, Dr. St. Barth Alaska, was tried on charges that he had defrauded the State of Illinois Medicaid program (and thus the federal government as well). The evidence presented at trial demonstrated that Dr. Alaska had submitted 303 bills for exams he had never performed or eyeglasses that patients had never received. Dr. Alaska received $11,052.58 for these 303 bills. Additionally, Dr. Alaska submitted 248 bills totaling in excess of $8400.00 for services rendered before these particular forms of payment were authorized. The total dollar amount of Dr. Alaska's false claims was under $20,000, but the total number of false claims he made was 551. The rub for Dr. Alaska was that the federal false claims act as well as the comparable Illinois act provides for a $2,000 forfeiture for each false claim. (This amount has since been raised to between $5,000 and $10,000 for each act.) Here is what the court concluded:

> it is clearly consistent with the purposes of the Federal False Claims Act to impose forfeitures based on the number of false claims submitted by Dr. Alaska. The evidence adduced at trial established that Dr. Alaska knew he was submitting false claims . . . Applying the forfeiture of $2000 for each of these claims, the court has determined that Dr. Alaska's total forfeiture under the False Claims Act is $1,102,000.00.

> With respect to the double damage provision [the False Claims Act allows the government to recover double damages] the court finds that a total of $19,551.52 was paid out on Dr. Alaska's 551 false claims. Since the federal government and the State of Illinois each contributed one-half of this total payment, the federal government's actual damages were equal to one half of $19,551.52 or $9,775.76. Of course, section 231 provides for a doubling of the Government's actual damages, so the total damage award under the Federal False Claims Act for the false claims is $19,551.52.

In this case, Illinois had a treble damage provision, so its total award would be $1,131,327.28. For stealing less than $20,000 from the government, Dr. Alaska wound up with a judgment against him in excess of $2.25 million. Strangely enough, if he had merely defrauded the government of $20,000 on one bill, the total judgment would have been less than $55,000.

Clearly, repetitive schemes are fraught with serious economic danger despite the relatively meager value of the money achieved through the scheme. In a similar case from a punitive perspective, *United States of America v. Diamond*, 657 F. Supp, 1204 (1987), Dr. Richard Diamond, a New York physician, was found in 1985 to have submitted 39 false Medicare claims for an illegal benefit of $549.04. Using the False Claims Act formula enumerated in *Alaska*, the court awarded the plaintiff, that is, the U.S. government, $1,098.08 as the double damage penalty plus $78,000.00, which was arrived at by multiplying the $2,000 penalty by the 39 false claims. In total for a potential gain of $549.04, Dr. Diamond wound up paying the government $79,098.08, plus countless dollars to his attorneys.

THE *KATS* AND *GREBER* CASES

Two of the better-known cases in the world of Medicare fraud and abuse are those of the *U.S. v. Greber*, 760 F.2d 68 (3dCir. 1985), and *U.S. v. Kats*, 871 F. 2d 105 (9thCir. 1989). Greber was a cardiologist who owned a company that provided heart monitor services for referred patients. In addition to providing the monitors, Greber also interpreted the results of the testing. His company billed Medicare for the monitor and then turned around and gave the referring doctor a fee of 40% of the Medicare payment (but not more than $65 to the referring physician, who the government claimed did nothing but refer the patient). This the government alleged and the court agreed was a kickback in violation of the Medicare regulations. A key argument made by Greber on appeal was that he did indeed provide the service he charged Medicare for and therefore the services could not be a basis of a claim against him for fraud. This case, later reiterated in *Kats*, established a principle that even if one purpose of a payment is directed or intended to induce future referrals, the Medicare fraud statute is violated.

In *Kats*, the owner of a medical lab agreed to a 50% kickback to Total Health Care, a company that arranged with doctor's offices and clinics to collect the clinical specimens and send them to the lab, who in turn did the analysis and billed Medicare. If the lab wanted the business, they obviously were in a difficult position if they refused to make the kickback. Kats comes into the picture when he purchased a 25% interest in a community clinic and then went on to make a deal with the lab for a similar kickback. In the appeal, the defendant argued that the jury instruction under which he was found guilty was incorrect. This jury instruction, which the court upheld, stated the following:

> The government must prove beyond a reasonable doubt that one of the purposes for the solicitation of a remuneration was to obtain money for the referral of services which may be paid in whole or part out of Medicare funds. It is not a defense that there might have been other reasons for the solicitation of a remuneration by the defendants, if you find beyond reasonable doubt that one of the material purposes for the solicitation was to obtain money for the referral of services.

Yes, Dorothy, when it comes to Medicare, cleanliness is close to godliness!

U.S. v. LORENZO, 768 F. SUPP. 1127

This case is the story of an ambitious Philadelphia-based dentist who set up a company to do dental examination in Philadelphia-area nursing homes. Lorenzo ran afoul of Medicare when he switched from doing standard dental examinations that included an oral cancer screening component to doing oral cancer examinations on residents and then billing Medicare (who would not pay for the routine dental screening). Over time Lorenzo and his staff submitted a total of 3,683 claims to Medicare and received $130,719.10. The government's legal position was that Medicare payment is not authorized for oral cancer examinations unless the exam is a consultation requested by the resident's physician. The court's conclusion was that the bills were submitted although the defendant knew that Medicare did not cover the exams under the circumstances in which they were performed. This is clearly a complicated case because the defendant did not attempt to hide what he was doing and actually went ahead and solicited advice from the fiscal intermediary about payment for the services. Unfortunately for Lorenzo, the $130,000 he collected paled in comparison to the judgment against him under the False Claims Act of $18,415,000.

U.S. v. MILLS,
138 F. 3D 928 (11TH CIR. 1998)

In the previous chapter I introduced the Mills through the huge fine paid by their company, First American Health Care of Georgia. In fact the activities of the Mills family, their company First American, and its predecessor company ABC Home Health Care are so infamous that the General Accounting Office actually did a report on them (*ABC Home Health Care*, GAO/OSI 95-17). Many of the illegal activities of the Mills family reported on in the GAO report found their way into the comprehensive catalog of illegal behavior documented in the court opinion. The following pages provide a slightly edited version of the court's discussion of the seven schemes used by the Mills family to defraud the government.

The Mills Family Schemes

1. Personal Use of Medicare-Reimbursed Airplanes

First American owned, leased, or borrowed several airplanes, including a $2.8 million King Air jet that its executives used for business travel. Aetna [the fiscal intermediary] policies did not prohibit reimbursement of the corporate airplane costs. Aetna was skeptical, however, that corporate planes were a fiscally prudent way to fill First American's travel needs. In 1990, following the purchase of the King Air, Aetna agreed nonetheless to reimburse First American for its plane installment payments, provided that at least 90% of the plane's flight time was reimbursable, patient care–related travel. Aetna also consented to reimburse expenses such as maintenance and pilot salaries prorated to the percentage of time spent on business travel. In 1991, Aetna demanded and First American agreed to provide further documentation of the planes' use so that Aetna could measure the reimbursable use of the planes. That documentation included records of the purpose, passengers, length, and destination of every flight. [The case stated in a footnote that: The costs allocable to this personal use would not have been reimbursable, of course, under the arrangement with Aetna.] If this use rose over 10% of total flying time, moreover, it threatened reimbursement for the King Air payments. First American, at Jack's direction and with the cooperation of the chief pilot, Jim McManus, therefore undertook to disguise and conceal personal use. They used several methods. First, passengers with no business purpose for traveling would not appear on passenger manifests—so-called "ghost passengers." Second, pilots would pull a circuit breaker to prevent the planes' hour meter from adding the flight time during personal flights to the planes' total flight time; thus, these "breaker" or "ghost" flights would not lower the percentage of patient care–related flight time. Many breaker flights left no trace in company records, although First American employees would schedule the flights on Post-Its, some of which were in evidence, inserted in the airplane schedule book. Other breaker flights were listed in the company flight log with false or omitted destinations. Yet another method for concealment had pilots pad their Medicare-reimbursable expense reports with extra meals to recover expenses incurred during these "breaker" flights. . . .

During and after these discussions with Aetna, Jack and Margie [Mills] took First American planes on dozens of personal trips—twelve round trips alleged in the indictment, 72 total found by investigators—that included visiting their mothers, sunning in Cozumel, viewing prefab columns in Dallas that they wished to incorporate into their new mansion, and attending their high school reunions and sports events like Auburn University football games. They also transported non–First American related passengers, including their children, both Mills' mothers, then-Governor of Alabama Jim Folsom, Georgia Speaker of the House Tom Murphy, and University of Georgia football coach Vince Dooley.

2. Kickbacks on Aviation Fuel Purchases

First American purchased most of its fuel and leased hangar and office space from Golden Isles Aviation, Inc., on St. Simons Island. For some time, Golden Isles had discounted the fuel sold to First American because of the volume purchased. When First American leased new hangar and office space, however, the companies struck a new deal. Golden Isles would continue to charge less for the fuel First American purchased according to a volume-based stepped percentage. But the difference between retail and First American's price would go into a rebate account with Golden Isles. Golden Isles initially applied the rebate account to renovation costs for First American's hangar, but later the rebates went to pay other maintenance expenses. Jim McManus would typically present invoices to Golden Isles to be paid out of the rebate account, or he would charge bills on a credit card paid by Golden Isles out of the rebate account. Checks from this account also reimbursed Jack for fuel he bought for some personal flights; thus, although it would appear that Medicare was not fueling the flights, through the rebate mechanism it was.

First American and Jack never disclosed this arrangement to Aetna. Rather, First American reported the full fuel cost as part of its travel expenses. Thus, First American had the advantage of using the rebate money without having to justify the relation between the expenditures and patient care.

3. Lobbying Expenses

Medicare reimburses providers only their actual costs for patient care. Thus, Medicare providers cannot make a profit. A legislative proposal exists, however, that would change this system. Under the proposal, called the "prospective payment system," or "PPS," providers would receive a flat fee for patient care. Hence, an efficient provider—or one that successfully inflated the baseline costs on which the flat fee rested—could realize a profit. As Jack explained in a speech to First American employees, with PPS First American could go public and make lots of money.

For this reason, Jack hired lobbyists to promote PPS. Some were politicians such as former Georgia senator Mack Mattingly, whom First American hired as a "consultant" to introduce Jack to influential lawmakers and to exploit his connections for First American's benefit. Others were full-time, professional lobbyists. One of these was Paul Berry, a former roommate of President Clinton's. First American hired Berry, a federally registered lobbyist, in 1992 and 1993. Although nominally a "consultant,"

Berry in fact lobbied for First American. For example, he memoed Jack a recitation of his progress in persuading lawmakers of PPS's advantages. And Jack himself described Berry's job as help with the "project" of "getting prospective pay" so that First American could go public. Furthermore, Berry's functions included introducing the Millses to Capitol Hill staffers and members of President Clinton's newly formed health care task force. Another lobbyist was Steve Clark, a former attorney general of Arkansas and friend of President Clinton's, who was hired as a "vice president of managed care." Clark was well connected and succeeded in getting Jack into a foursome with Donna Shalala, Secretary of Health and Human Services, at a charity golf tournament in Texarkana.

In addition to exploiting their networks, Clark and Berry worked hand-in-glove with two Washington lobbying firms—one Democrat and one Republican—Global USA and the Borden Group. Together, they orchestrated a large First American campaign focused on changing certain proposed legislation. This campaign included television advertisements that were ostensibly for nurse recruitment, but were in fact intended to influence congressmen at home during recess. The drive also involved a mass distribution of a pro-PPS position paper to First American employees with the instruction for them to retype it and send it as a "letter to the editor" to their local papers. Some of this lobbying activity was nominally for the American Federation of Home Health Agencies, an organization that Jack claimed to control.

Lobbying costs are not reimbursable. First American's lobbying expenses were therefore reported on First American's cost reports as consulting expenses, which are reimbursable. There was no mistake here: Borden Group bills were indeed originally taken off First American's cost report by First American's reimbursement department. At Jack's direction, however, the bills were claimed on the report. And these misrepresentations were backed up by well-engineered paperwork. For instance, the check request generated to pay Mattingly's fee for introducing Jack to important politicians showed the purpose of the check as "consulting fee for matters relating to existing regulations"—an arguably reimbursable cost. All the contracts with the other lobbyists were couched in "consulting agreement" terms; Berry's contract in fact forbade him from lobbying.

4. Political Contributions

In June 1991, during a Georgia gubernatorial campaign, Jack pressured seven First American executives to attend a Zell Miller fundraiser. In fact, one executive, William Edwards, was called from vacation in the midst of home-moving and asked to attend the function. All seven executives made $500 contributions, which were then reimbursed by way of "bonuses" that were reported to Aetna as reimbursable salary expense. Jack testified that the contributions were purely coincidental to the bonuses, but there was no evidence that any executive who had not made a contribution received a $500 bonus at this time. When a similar scheme led to a federal indictment against another Medicare company, Jack told the worried executives that Georgia Attorney General Michael Bowers had provided First American immunity from prosecution for its actions. Bowers, who testified at trial, denied ever granting immunity to any First American–related person.

On two prior occasions, attempts to force lower-level employees to make campaign contributions were defeated by First American executives. In one, Jack sought to have First American's Florida employees contribute $100 apiece to the Lawton Chiles campaign, to be reimbursed by adding mileage to expense reports. Jack ultimately withdrew this request, persuaded by a Florida manager that it would get the company in trouble. Jack's demand of an Alabama manager to make campaign contributions, again to be reimbursed by padding expense reports, failed because First American's accounting department refused to approve the expense reports.

5. "Salaries" to Former Owners of Acquired Agencies

First American was growing rapidly during the late eighties and early nineties; in 1985, it operated only in Georgia, and by 1994 it was in 23 states. The company achieved this rapid expansion by acquiring local home health care providers, often those that were in financial difficulty. First American's cash-flow predicament, however, made it difficult for it to pay for even these ailing agencies. Medicare would not pay for First American's acquisition of other agencies' goodwill.

Jack solved this problem in a few cases by inducing the owners of acquired agencies to sell by putting them on First American's payroll to be "community relations" specialists or, as one was told, "vice president of smiles." Although the details differed from owner to owner, a common thread was that the jobs were sinecures that required a few hours of marketing work a week with no patient care–related responsibilities. Those who sought to do more were rebuffed. Many of these owners in fact pursued other enterprises, such as private health care work or real estate management. For instance, Catherine Brown, former owner of an agency in San Antonio, received $60,000 a year for five years as "salary." After an initial transition period, however, she performed almost no work for First American, working instead on her separate private-care business. Brown's secretary also received a First American salary while performing virtually no work for First American. In all these instances, First American was careful to maintain an appearance of employment, firing the former owners when—as in the case of one Michigan former owner who was imprisoned—they were patently unable to work. Blank time sheets, often signed by the owners, were also kept.

Another aspect of some of the agency acquisitions suggests that a purchase scheme motivated the sinecures' creation. First American avoided paying out of pocket more than a few thousand dollars for any agency, enough to cover the tangible assets such as furniture. Many of the owners had substantial liabilities, however, that they had guaranteed personally. Jack's solution to this problem was to encourage the agencies to delay reporting the purchase to the fiscal intermediary and to continue receiving periodic interim payments, which the owners would use as they pleased. Although the agency would owe those payments back to the government, the agency's sale of its assets to First American would prevent the government from ever collecting the money. Meanwhile, the liabilities would be paid, and the owner would walk away with a handsome employment contract.

The importance of this trick to First American's acquisition scheme is illustrated by two instances when owners balked at delaying report of the sale. In the case of one California agency, First American refused to honor the owner's employment contract, which prompted litigation that ended in a judgment in the owner's favor. A New Mexico agency owner refunded the interim payments rather than use them to payoff debts; First American then refused to a honor a contingent note intended to cover the agency's debts left over after the interim payments. Although several former owners independently testified to the existence of this strategy, Jack and current First American employees denied they ever proposed it.

6. Margie's Misrepresentations

The jury convicted Margie of only two acts of falsification. Both related to one trip in a First American plane. Margie filled out and signed two Aetna-mandated passenger manifests to report that she traveled in August 1992 from St. Simons, Georgia to San Antonio and back in connection with First American's acquisition of a home health care provider in Texas. In fact, Margie went to Mobile, Alabama, where the plane stopped en route, to attend her high school reunion. She did not return on the flight back from San Antonio.

7. Jack's Witness Tampering

During the grand jury investigation that led to the indictment in this case, a First American executive, William Edwards, was subpoenaed to testify concerning the campaign contributions that Jack had asked First American executives to make to the Zell Miller gubernatorial campaign and that were reimbursed as bogus bonuses. Edwards at that time had decided to resign from First American. Having obtained a copy of the subpoena, however, Jack offered Edwards about $100,000 to remain in First American's employ until after he had testified before the grand jury. Jack was concerned about the impression it would create for Edwards to resign so soon before testifying. Jack informed Edwards of the company line: that the bonuses were real bonuses, and that the use of the bonuses to make campaign contributions was merely encouraged, not coerced. Edwards refused the offer and resigned.

Obviously, after reviewing the schemes, it becomes clear why First American wound up with a $225 billion judgment against it.

In this chapter I have provided a mere sampling of fraud, abuse, and false claims cases. Many others exist, such as practitioners who billed for services never provided or who engaged in the process of upcoding, the psychiatrist who billed for almost 20 hours per day, and a company that used money postal drops for its shell rehabilitation business that had no employees.[1] There is the Florida case of Cape Coral Hospital, where administrators used hospital funds for personal matters, such as the purchase of a luxury home and a golfing trip. At this institution, one member of the board partook of this largess by using hospital funds for improvements to his business property. Another board member received free care at the hospital and then, with the cooperation of the hospital, filed an insurance claim.[2] In Kansas, there was the case against seven defendants who were associated with Baptist Medical Center and were engaged in efforts to refer nursing home patients to the hospital. In 2004 so far, the biggest potential case is against Healthsouth, the giant rehabilitation company, which has already seen 10 of its top executives convicted of criminal charges and its board disgraced. Although much of the concern with Healthsouth is about accounting fraud and related stock manipulation, Medicare fraud also plays a part in its drama, and as the government works through its process, it may be the string that unravels the company when pulled.

A final concern was highlighted by a GAO report to the distinguished senator from Maine, Susan Collins, about the involvement of organized crime in Medicare fraud. Summarizing their results, the GAO states the following:

---

[1]GAO/T-HEHS-95-157.
[2]*Wall Street Journal*, November 20, 1996, p. 1.

While the full extent of the problem remains unknown, we did determine that career criminal and organized criminal groups are involved in Medicare, Medicaid, and private insurance health care fraud or alleged fraud throughout the country. In the cases we reviewed, criminal groups varied in size from 2 or 3 participants to more than 20 participants and generally had one leader. Many group members had prior criminal histories for criminal activity unrelated to health care fraud, indicating that they moved from one field of criminal activity to another. The primary subjects in these cases had little or no known medical or health care education, training, or experience. At least two groups learned or were suspected of having learned how to commit health care fraud from others already engaged in such fraud. In some of the cases we reviewed, criminal-group members had relatives or associates in foreign countries who helped them transfer their ill-gotten health care proceeds.

These groups created as many as 160 sham medical entities—such as medical clinics, physician groups, diagnostic laboratories, and durable medical equipment (DME) companies, often using fictitious names or the names of others on paperwork—or used the names of uninvolved legitimate providers to bill for services and equipment not provided or not medically necessary. For the most part, these entities existed only on paper. Once the structure was in place, subjects used a variety of schemes to submit claims to Medicare, Medicaid, or private insurance companies.

One scheme used is sometimes referred to as "patient brokering" or "rent-a-patient." Under this scheme, which was used in one of the Medicare cases, the subjects used "recruiters" (also known as "runners") to organize and recruit beneficiaries (patients) who visited clinics owned or operated by such subjects for unnecessary diagnostic testing and/or medical services. Recruiters received a fee for each beneficiary brought in; hence they "rented" or "brokered" the beneficiary and/or identifying information to the subjects. In turn, recruiters paid a portion of their fee to each cooperating beneficiary. The beneficiaries' insurance was later billed for these and other services or equipment not provided. In addition to the beneficiaries, some physicians were willing to collaborate with subjects in exchange for money.

Another successful scheme is commonly referred to as "drop box" or "mail drop." In this scheme, which was used in six of the seven cases according to investigators, subjects rented private mailboxes or drop boxes, set up bogus corporations, and opened phony corporate bank accounts. Subjects then used stolen, purchased, or otherwise obtained beneficiary and provider information to bill insurance plans for medical services and equipment not provided. Members of the criminal groups retrieved insurance checks from the drop boxes and deposited them into controlled bank accounts. Once deposited, proceeds were quickly converted to cash or transferred to other accounts and moved out of the reach of authorities.

These activities sometimes continued even after subjects were indicted, arrested, or jailed.[3]

CORPORATE COMPLIANCE CASE STUDIES

All cases for Chapters 13, 14, and 15 rely on the same basic organizational fact pattern and IRS (Internal Revenue Service) Code and Rulings. (See Chapter 13, pp. 299–300.)

Case Study 14-1

FOOD FOR THOUGHT

Marcus Tyme is the president of the Good Tyme Wholesale Paper Corporation and a nephew by marriage of Senator Gideon. Tyme is also a member of the NRHS board and sells millions of dollars in paper goods to the various components of the system. A formal contract does not exist between Tyme and the organization. His prices are generally competitive, and at the moment neither Tyme nor any other board member has signed a conflict-of-interest statement with the organization.

---

[3]GAO/OSI-00 Criminal Groups in Health Care Fraud 10/5/99.

Case Study 14-2
PRIVATE DUTY AND PUBLIC ISSUES

It has come to your attention that many patients of the hospital and residents of the nursing home have private duty aides. The issue for consideration is that many of these private duty aides are in fact full-time employees of either Gideon Medical Center or King's Park Nursing Home. Although the aides perform their private duty services during their off hours, the NRHS, as a service to the families of the patients and residents, keeps track of their private duty work hours and issues checks for the hours spent as private duty aides. In turn, the families are billed without any additional service charge.

The checks issued to the aides are separate from their regular paychecks. No taxes are withheld, and no overtime rates are paid. The NRHS issues 1099 forms for the fees paid to the aides. Copies of the 1099 are properly filed with the Internal Revenue Service.

CHAPTER 15

Corporate Compliance: Guidance from the Government

Fortunately for the health care industry, the government does provide a modicum of guidance designed to explain complex regulations, answer questions, and generally assist organizations and individuals in not getting into trouble. As noted in Chapter 13, the Department of Health and Human Services has expended considerable efforts on its safe harbors program, which clarifies what arrangements are acceptable.

The Health and Human Services Office of Inspector General (OIG) periodically issues an open letter on potentially problematic issues. For example, a letter of November 20, 2001, primarily dealt with corporate integrity agreements and the power of the OIG in excluding providers from participation in government-funded programs. This letter makes clear that when determining remedies for fraudulent behavior, in particular the remedy of a corporate integrity agreement as well as what might be the substance of such an agreement, the OIG would be guided by whether and how well the wrongdoer fell on their sword. In this letter the OIG made it clear what it takes to get the most lenient penalty:

(1) whether the provider self-disclosed the alleged misconduct; (2) the monetary damage to the Federal health care programs; (3) whether the case involves successor liability; (4) whether the provider is still participating in the Federal health care programs or in the line of business that gave rise to the fraudulent conduct; (5) whether the alleged conduct is capable of repetition; (6) the age of the conduct; (7) whether the provider has an effective compliance program and would agree to limited compliance or integrity

measures and would annually certify such compliance to the DIG; and (8) other circumstances, as appropriate.[1]

Other guidance from the OIG comes in the form of periodic fraud alerts, bulletins, and general memo-type guidance documents. Illustrative of the guidance-type publication is a document issued on February 19, 2004 titled: "Hospital Discounts Offered to Patients Who Cannot Afford to Pay Their Hospital Bills." The problem analyzed in this alert is whether hospitals violate the federal anti-kickback statute when they offer discounts to uninsured or financially impoverished individuals. The answer, the OIG concludes, is that as long as the hospital is not using the discounts as a marketing strategy to attract business, discounts are not given as a matter of routine, and that the hospitals have a good faith method of determining whether someone is eligible for the discount, there is no violation of the statute.

Perhaps the most formal and legally binding type of document is the OIG Advisory Opinion, established in 1997 by rules implementing a section of HIPPA. Advisory Opinions are documents prepared by the OIG that answer specific questions posed by providers about business arrangements that might violate the anti-kickback legislation.

The process itself is voluntary; that is, there is no requirement for any organization to seek the OIG's review of a project. The process also costs money, since the OIG charges an hourly fee for its review (fees for this service are generally in the several-thousand-dollar range). If an organization chooses to have a review, then the OIG specifies the information needed about the potential business arrangement and proceeds to do its analysis. Its conclusions are binding upon the government. That is, if the OIG issues an opinion that an arrangement is not in violation of the statute and the organization proceeds with the project as initially stated in the documentation and is later accused by a governmental agency for wrongdoing, the opinion is a get-out-of-jail-free card (as long as the project has not changed).

The OIG does not review Stark issues (physician self-referral), theoretical questions, or straight-out Medicare fraud issues. Also, it stays away from any market determination issues or Internal Revenue Service Code questions. Finally, the opinions are published and available for review by

---

[1]Accessed (n.d.) from www.oig.hhs.gov/fraud/docs/openletters/openletter111901.htm.

anyone (the organizational and individual names are redacted), although they are only of legal authority for the organization that requested the opinion. This being the case, one might wonder, why bother reading the advisory opinions? In my judgment, they do represent useful guidance about the thinking of the government on the anti-kickback issue. If one becomes acquainted with their thinking, one is in a better position to make determinations for one's own organization without always searching for an official OIG opinion. In other words, they are models of excellent analysis and guidance for the profession.

Over the years I have read many of these opinions and have always made them a central part of my student's classroom work in my graduate course on corporate compliance. The opinions almost invariably follow a similar structure. The first several paragraphs state what the OIG has been asked to do and the following paragraph summarizes the OIG's findings, which are typically either that the proposed arrangement could potentially violate the statutes or would not generate a violation of the statute. The last paragraph of the section is a statement from the OIG that this opinion may not be relied upon by anyone other than the person or organization that requested the opinion. Next the advisory opinion goes on to state the factual background, followed by a legal analysis that reviews the applicable law, and applies the facts of the situation to the law. This leads to the next section, the conclusion, which is followed by a boiler-plate section on limitations, such as the aforementioned applicability only to the party who solicited the opinion. Where the OIG finds that the proposed arrangement is acceptable, there is typically a final paragraph that is almost contractual in nature, stating that the OIG will not proceed with any action against those that requested the opinion as long as they follow the proposed arrangement.

OIG ADVISORY OPINIONS

The following are examples of the type of issues dealt with by the OIG in their advisory opinions.

1. Opinion No. 03-01 Issued January 13, 2003

The story line in this opinion is of a dutifully cautious company trying to employ someone who may be a rainmaker but had better not make rain with federal dollars. The key players in this situation are a physician, who gave up his medical license after complaints were filed against him and was subsequently excluded from Medicare, Medicaid, and other federal health programs, and a for-profit company in the health care software business, which wishes to employ the doctor as a senior executive for business development. The problem is that the products that the company sells are in some respects used by government providers for reimbursement through the federal programs. The concern on the part of the company is whether their employment of this excluded physician will impact upon the physician; in other words, whether he would be in violation of his exclusion and whether that would put the company in jeopardy for administrative violation of government statutes.

The OIG analysis is that the company does not directly bill the government, although it is in the chain that does seek governmental reimbursement. The analysis also states that employment of excluded persons is allowed but under very restricted circumstances, and the circumstances outlined by the company do fit into that framework. Essentially, then, as long as the physician stays away from anything that smells like, looks like, or tastes like a federal program, the OIG thinks it is acceptable.

2. Opinion No. 03-14 Issued July 3, 2003

This may be a scratch-your-head opinion in that an organization doing the right thing for the right reason may be jeopardizing its future. In this case, a rural nonprofit hospital and a for-profit ambulance company are interested in making a deal to provide emergency transport services to trauma victims in a 17-county area. The deal they propose is that the ambulance company would buy, staff, and operate a fully equipped trauma helicopter. The hospital, for its part, would provide a landing pad next to the hospital and rest quarters for the helicopter and ambulance staffs (not restricted to the ambulance/helicopter company).

The conclusion reached by the OIG is that there is a possibility of statutory violations because there might be inducements or rewards for referrals. However, under the circumstances of this case, in particular the level of need in this rural area, the statewide support of this project by the statewide emergency medical services program, and the community benefits of this project, the OIG concludes that they will not impose sanctions.

3. Opinion No. 04-02 Issued March 1, 2004

This is another ambulance service–related opinion. In this situation, the ambulance services are provided by the city's fire department. The issue of concern is that the fire department wants to bill residents directly for their services to the extent of their insurance coverage. But the department is not planning on billing for copayments and deductibles. The question the OIG considered is whether the proposed policy of the fire department to collect insurance-only billings represents an anti-kickback violation. The reason this might be the case is that the government has looked harshly on organizations that routinely waive Medicare co-payments and deductibles without first examining the service recipient's ability to pay the extra costs. These routine waivers appear to be inducements to service and as such violate the statutes. Fortunately for this municipal ambulance service, there is an exception in Medicare rules for governmental services when the government itself provides the service (as opposed to the government contracting with an outside vendor). In this instance, then, the OIG finds that the fire department's planned billing practice is not a violation of anti-kickback statutes as long as the billing procedures extend only to city residents. It states rather critically, "Nothing in this advisory opinion would apply to cost-sharing waivers based on criteria other than residency."

4. Opinion No. 04-04 Issued May 26, 2004

In this case, a professional optometric association is proposing to implement a portion of the vision objectives of the Department of Health and Human Services' national policy, as found in their "Healthy People 2010" document. This portion calls for free vision screening of children between the ages of 6 and 12 months in an effort to detect a preventable condition called amblyobia (lazy eye). The project involves optometrists providing totally free screenings without any billing, even if the child is insured. Further, the project has no strings attached; that is, the free screening is not part of some package for which the optometrist charges. A final element of the project is that if amblyopia or any other problem is detected, the optometrist is obliged to offer the patient's family information about the freedom to choose any practitioner for care.

In their analysis of this situation, the OIG begins with a statement that there are provisions in the Social Security Act that generally prohibit practitioners from offering the type of incentive envisioned in this program. The idea is simple: Don't give "free" deals and attach other services to those deals that Medicare is then obliged to pay for. This sort of activity is viewed as an illegal inducement. However, the Social Security Act does have an exception when it comes to encouraging practitioners to provide preventive care, particularly prenatal and postnatal. The key in this analysis is the safeguard built into the program by the optometric association—in particular, the lack of overreaching by the optometrists: If a problem arises, the optometrists are obliged to inform the family of their right to freedom of choice and their options. All in all, this is a win-win situation for the patients, government, and optometrists, since the patients get free screenings, the optometrists are likely to generate legitimate business, and the government does not pay anything for the screening and potentially avoids more costly health problems in the future.

5. Opinion No. 04-09 Issued July 15, 2004

This is a complex arrangement with an interesting twist. A physician group practice specializing in geriatrics and nursing homes is proposing an arrangement whereby they pay primary care practitioners for consulting with them about the totality of the health situation of their former patients who are now residents of the nursing home. The ostensible reason for this arrangement is that the nursing home group claims that they have difficulty obtaining the necessary information on the patients in a timely fashion and the original primary care doctor could be helpful in their providing care. The finances of the arrangement involve a monthly consultation fee of $100 if the primary care practitioner has up to five patients with the group. If a practitioner has more than 20 patients with the group, the maximum he or she can receive is $750 per month (or $9,000 per year). To me, this surely looks like an arrangement that would induce primary care practitioners to transfer their patients to this group and henceforth become "consultants."

While this arrangement is generally a violation of the anti-kickback provision, there is a twist, in that the Internal Revenue Service ruled that the consulting primary care physicians are bona fide employees of the geriatric group. Because of their employment status, the conclusion is that there is no violation of the anti-kickback provisions because employer-employee arrangements are excepted under the anti-kickback provisions.

6. Opinion No. 04-08 Issued June 23, 2004

This advisory opinion is included in its entirety with no editing so that the reader can gain a clear picture of the type of analysis that is provided by the OIG when they publish an advisory opinion. We redact certain identifying information and certain potentially privileged, confidential, or proprietary information associated with the individual or entity, unless otherwise approved, by the requestor.

Issued: June 23, 2004
Posted: June 30, 2004
[name and address redacted]

Re: OIG Advisory Opinion No. 04-08

Dear [name redacted]:

We are writing in response to your request for an advisory opinion regarding a proposal by a physician group practice to develop and own a comprehensive physical therapy center and to lease the center's space, equipment, and personnel to physicians with patients requiring physical therapy services (the "Proposed Arrangement"). Specifically, you have inquired whether the Proposed Arrangement constitutes grounds for the imposition of sanctions under the exclusion authority at section 1128(b)(7) of the Social Security Act (the "Act") or the civil monetary penalty provision at section 1128A(a)(7) of the Act, as those sections relate to the commission of acts described in section 1128B(b) of the Act.

You have certified that all of the information provided in your request, including all supplementary letters, is true and correct and constitutes a complete description of the relevant facts and agreements among the parties.

In issuing this opinion, we have relied solely on the facts and information presented to us. We have not undertaken an independent investigation of such information. This opinion is limited to the facts presented. If material facts have not been disclosed or have been misrepresented, this opinion is without force and effect.

Based on the facts certified in your request for an advisory opinion and supplemental submissions, we conclude that the Proposed Arrangement could potentially generate prohibited remuneration under the anti-kickback statute and that the Office of Inspector General ("OIG") could potentially impose administrative sanctions on [name redacted] under sections 1128(b)(7) or 1128A(a)(7) of the Act (as those sections relate to the commission of acts described in section 1128B(b) of the Act) in connection with the Proposed Arrangement. Any definitive conclusion regarding the existence of an antikickback violation requires a determination of the parties' intent, which determination is beyond the scope of the advisory opinion process.

This opinion may not be relied on by any persons other than [name redacted], the requestor of this opinion, and is further qualified as set out in Part IV below and in 42 C.F.R. Part 1008.

1. FACTUAL BACKGROUND

[name redacted] (the "Physician Group") is a professional corporation comprised of five physicians, three of whom hold an ownership interest in the professional corporation. The physicians practice in various fields including neurology, psychiatry, and orthopedic medicine. The Physician Group proposes forming a limited liability company (the "LLC") for the purpose of establishing a comprehensive physical therapy center (the "Center"). The Center will lease space, equipment, and the services of a staff therapist to the physicians of the Physician Group and various other licensed physicians with patients requiring physical therapy services (collectively, the "Lessees").

The Center will serve physicians in multiple fields of medicine, including neurology, cardiology, orthopedics, and internal medicine. The Center will be located in the same building as the Physician Group and each of the intended lessees. The Center will be open six days a week for eight hours a day and will be available to the Lessees on an unlimited, first-come, first-served basis. The LLC will act strictly as the owner and landlord of the Center and will not bill Medicare, Medicaid, or any other third-party payor for services provided in the Center. Each Lessee will bill the appropriate health insurance provider for services rendered at the Center to their particular patients.

Each Lessee will enter into a one-year lease with the LLC and pay a monthly rental fee for unlimited use of the Center. Lessees utilizing the staff therapist will pay a higher monthly rental fee than those Lessees who provide their own therapist. The rental fee, excluding charges for the staff therapist, will be calculated at the beginning of the lease term by totaling the monthly rental value of all space, equipment, and administrative services provided in the Center and dividing by the total number of Lessees. Thus, each Lessee would pay the same amount regardless of actual usage. The Requestor has certified that the monthly rental value of all space, equipment, and personnel services will be verified and audited by an independent appraisal firm to ensure that it is consistent with fair market value.

II. LEGAL ANALYSIS

A. Law

The anti-kickback statute makes it a criminal offense knowingly and willfully to offer, pay, solicit, or receive any remuneration to induce or reward referrals of items or services reimbursable by a Federal health care program.

See section 1128B(b) of the Act. Where remuneration is paid purposefully to induce or reward referrals of items or services payable by a Federal health care program, the anti-kickback statute is violated. By its terms, the statute ascribes criminal liability to parties on both sides of an impermissible "kickback" transaction. For purposes of the anti-kickback statute, "remuneration" includes the transfer of anything of value, directly or indirectly, overtly or covertly, in cash or in kind.

The statute has been interpreted to cover any arrangement where one purpose of the remuneration was to obtain money for the referral of services or to induce further referrals. *United States v. Kats*, 871 F.2d 105 (9th Cir. 1989); *United States v. Greber*, 760 F.2d 68 (3d Cir.), cert. denied, 474 U.S. 988 (1985). Violation of the statute constitutes a felony punishable by a maximum fine of $25,000, imprisonment up to five years, or both. Conviction will also lead to automatic exclusion from Federal health care programs, including Medicare and Medicaid. Where a party commits an act described in section 1128B(b) of the Act, the OIG may initiate administrative proceedings to impose civil monetary penalties on such party under section 1128A(a)(7) of the Act. The OIG may also initiate administrative proceedings to exclude such party from the Federal health care programs under section 1128(b)(7) of the Act.

The Department of Health and Human Services has promulgated safe harbor regulations that define practices that are not subject to the anti-kickback statute because such practices would be unlikely to result in fraud or abuse. See 42 C.F.R. §1001.952. The safe harbors set forth specific conditions that, if met, assure entities involved of not being prosecuted or sanctioned for the arrangement qualifying for the safe harbor. However, safe harbor protection is afforded only to those arrangements that precisely meet all of the conditions set forth in the safe harbor.

The safe harbors for space, equipment, and personal services and management contracts, 42 C.F.R §1001.952(b), 42 C.F.R §1001.952(c), and 42 C.F.R §1001.952(d), respectively are potentially relevant to the Proposed Arrangement.

B. Analysis

The Physician Group and the Lessees are potential sources of referrals of Federal health care program business for one another. As such, the exchange of anything of value between them potentially implicates the anti-kickback statute.

As a threshold matter, safe harbor protection is not available for the Proposed Arrangement. In relevant part for purposes of this advisory opinion, the space, equipment, and personal services and management contracts safe harbors require that the aggregate compensation paid under the arrangement be set in advance and consistent with fair market value in an arms-length transaction. In addition, leases and arrangements that are for periodic intervals of time, rather than a full-time basis, must specify the exact intervals of use, precise length of intervals of use, and exact rent or charge for intervals of use.

The Physician Group has characterized the leases under the Proposed Arrangement as full-time leases; however, the Center is available to the Lessees only on an as-needed, first-come, first-served basis. As such, the Proposed Arrangement is more appropriately characterized as involving multiple, overlapping, and part-time leases. These leases do not meet the safe harbor requirements that periodic, sporadic, or part-time leases must specify precisely the timing and duration of the rental periods and the compensation charged for each rental period. In addition, as set forth below, the Proposed Arrangement raises significant concerns with respect to the issue of fair market value.[2]

While the absence of safe harbor protection is not fatal, several factors make the Proposed Arrangement susceptible to fraud and abuse. Accordingly, based on the facts presented we cannot conclude that the risk of fraud and abuse is acceptably low.

For purposes of the equipment rental safe harbor, "fair market value" means the value of the equipment when obtained from a manufacturer or professional distributor. 42 C.F.R. §1001.952(c). For purposes of the space rental safe harbor, "fair market value" means the value of the rental property for general commercial purposes. 42 C.F.R. §100 1.952(b). Both the equipment and rental safe harbor require that, when determining fair market value, the value not be adjusted to reflect the additional value that one party would attribute to the equipment or property as a result of its proximity or convenience to sources of referrals or business otherwise generated for which payment may be made in whole or in part under a Federal health care program.

The structure of the Proposed Arrangement, including the overlapping, as-needed aspect of the leases will make it difficult to monitor, assess, and document fair market value. Moreover, the Proposed Arrangement's structure increases the risk that at least some physicians will pay more or less than fair market value for the space, equipment, and administrative services actually used. Depending on the direction in which referrals flow between the Physician Group and the Lessees, there is a risk that these above or below fair market value payments could be remuneration for referrals.

Further, the Proposed Arrangement would appear to permit the LLC, and ultimately the Physician Group, to guarantee a desired maximum income stream from the Center by basing the rental payments from all Lessees on the total rental value of the equipment, space, and personnel

---

[2]We are precluded by statute from opining on whether fair market value shall be or was paid for goods, services, or property. See 42 D.S.C. §1320a-7d(b)(3)(A).

services of the Center, rather than the usage of the Center by the Lessees. There is a risk that this guaranteed income stream could be compensation in exchange for referrals.

Accordingly, based on the totality of facts and circumstances, we cannot conclude that the Proposed Arrangement poses a minimal risk of fraud and abuse.

III. CONCLUSION

Based on the facts certified in your request for an advisory opinion and supplemental submissions, we conclude that the Proposed Arrangement could potentially generate prohibited remuneration under the anti-kickback statute and that the OIG could potentially impose administrative sanctions on [name redacted] under sections 1128(b)(7) or 1128A(a)(7) of the Act (as those sections relate to the commission of acts described in section 1128B(b) of the Act) in connection with the Proposed Arrangement. Any definitive conclusion regarding the existence of an anti-kickback violation requires a determination of the parties' intent, which determination is beyond the scope of the advisory opinion process.

IV. LIMITATIONS

The limitations applicable to this opinion include the following:

- This advisory opinion is issued only to [name redacted], the requestor of this opinion. This advisory opinion has no application to, and cannot be relied upon by, any other individual or entity.
- This advisory opinion may not be introduced into evidence in any matter involving an entity or individual that is not a requestor of this opinion.
- This advisory opinion is applicable only to the statutory provisions specifically noted above. No opinion is expressed or implied herein with respect to the application of any other Federal, state, or local statute, rule, regulation, ordinance, or other law that may be applicable to the Proposed Arrangement, including, without limitation, the physician self-referral law, section 1877 of the Act.
- This advisory opinion will not bind or obligate any agency other than the U.S. Department of Health and Human Services.
- This advisory opinion is limited in scope to the specific arrangement described in this letter and has no applicability to other arrangements, even those which appear similar in nature or scope.
- No opinion is expressed herein regarding the liability of any party under the False Claims Act or other legal authorities for any improper billing, claims submission, cost reporting, or related conduct.

This opinion is also subject to any additional limitations set forth at 42 C.F.R. Part 1008. The OIG reserves the right to reconsider the questions and issues raised in this advisory opinion and, where the public interest requires, to rescind, modify, or terminate this Opinion.

Sincerely,

Lewis Morris
Chief Counsel to the Inspector General

MODEL COMPLIANCE PLANS

Fortunately, the government also provides guidance in the form of model compliance programs. Since 1998 they have been offering a number of model compliance programs for various organizations, including hospitals, clinical laboratories, home health agencies, third-party medical billing companies, parts of the durable medical equipment industry, hospices, Medicare-choice organizations, nursing facilities, the ambulance industry, small group practices, the pharmaceutical industry, and recipients of NIH research grants. While there are differences among the various programs, they all appear to focus on several key elements. First, there is a need for written policies. Compliance should not depend on an oral tradition. It is imperative that aspects of a compliance program be in writing and agreed upon by key staff and board. Along these lines, it is absolutely imperative that there be total organizational support for a compliance program. This means in plain language that the corporate boards and senior executives must be on board in both letter and spirit. Without this support, any program or document is merely air or paper, and it does not take long for the "paper tiger" to be recognized by everyone.

The designation of an individual to be the compliance officer is critical to the successful functioning of any program. In the best of situations, this person is a senior person who has the respect of the organization and can be counted on to act confidentially and judiciously. This must be a person who cannot be intimidated by others in the organization. In the worst-case scenario, the compliance officer is merely a pawn of those people in power who have the most to gain from a noncompliant organization. The compliance officer typically has some other function in the organization, often in the area of finance, such as CFO or perhaps internal auditor. In larger organizations, and indeed, in the best of situations, there is someone whose sole responsibility is CCO (chief compliance officer).

Training and educating all staff about corporate compliance is the next element. The training and education that goes on must be serious, recurrent, and certainly not perfunctory. For example, it must be part of the orientation programs as well as the continuing education programs. Any training and education must involve the entirety of the staff as well as others who might be involved in the compliance venture. What is essentially necessary is wall-to-wall education and training, so that there is full coverage with periodic updates to ensure that everyone knows about their responsibilities for corporate compliance.

The OIG then speaks to the need for internal monitoring and review. What they mean by this is that the programs should be reviewed on a regular basis and changed in order to be maximally effective. The next and perhaps most crucial element is that of open lines of communication. It is critical that "whistleblowers" have the opportunity to let the compliance officer and staff know what is going on in the organization. In practice, this means that there is an "800" number that is available 24/7 for people to report problems. It is imperative that all calls about compliance abuses be investigated expeditiously and thoroughly. It is equally imperative that all whistleblowers be protected from organizational retaliation. Without protection, people will simply be unwilling to report improprieties. Effective communication also means action and feedback. Problems must be addressed, and the organization must sense a willingness on the part of top management to make those changes that ensure a fully compliant organization. These latter two points are encompassed in the OIG's guidelines when they speak of "enforcing standards through well-publicized disciplinary guidelines" and "responding promptly to detected offenses and developing corrective action."

Essentially, then, an organization must begin with a serious and firm commitment to corporate compliance, develop the policies and procedures that are the structure of compliance, commit to an infrastructure that is the management of the compliance problems, and monitor the outcomes of the program with the objective of making those changes necessary for a more compliant organization.

In my experiences, the writing and implementation of a plan is an essential function of management today and is part and parcel of a healthy organization. For those organizations presently without plans, the starting point is reviewing OIG guidance documents, followed by reviewing plans from other organizations. The next step is simple: Just do it!

Some commentary based on my experiences working with various organizations interested in developing their own plans follows, which is based on model OIG offers. Clearly, the first step in any compliance plan is clarity of writing. The document should be part and parcel of every staff member's orientation, and in the best of situations every employee should have a copy of the corporate compliance document. Further, the organization should have every staff member sign a document stating that they have received and reviewed the document. Hopefully, somewhere along the line this means they would have actually been briefed about compliance and the essence of the document.

CORPORATE COMPLIANCE CASE STUDIES

All cases for Chapters 13, 14, and 15 rely on the same basic organizational fact pattern and IRS (Internal Revenue Service) Code and Rulings. (See Chapter 13, pp. 299–300.)

Case Study 15-1

THE AMBASSADORS

The NRHS is fortunate to have accumulated an endowment in excess of $30 million over the years. One way it generates money for its endowment is through a program called the Northville Ambassadors Fellowship (known as the NAF Program). To be an Ambassador, an individual must donate a total of $35,000 over a period of 5 years. The NAF Program has been the "baby" of Senator Gideon, and he has instituted a number of benefits for the Ambassadors. Some of these are monthly luncheons (at no charge). These luncheons are fairly lavish and often take place at the local country club or one of several restaurants. The typical cost to the system for each of these luncheons is approximately $40 per person. Other benefits include free parking at all of the system facilities, discounted meals at the Ambassador's

(continues)

Case Study 15-1

dining room located at Gideon Memorial Hospital, and free tickets to the system's Annual Ball (tickets cost non-Ambassadors $250 per person).

Internal Revenue Service Regulations require that a charitable organization (NRHS is such) that receives a quid pro contribution in excess of $75 must provide the donor with a good-faith estimate of the value of goods and services provided. Currently the NRHS provides Ambassadors with letters documenting their donations and stating that "this contribution provides no tickets, services, or any benefits that reduce its value for tax benefits."

Case Study 15-2
PRIVATE MATTERS

Approximately 10 years ago, Senator Gideon was asked by his good friend Maria Cook to be the sole trustee of the proceeds of her estate, which passed into the private Cook Foundation. Under the terms of the will and foundation documents, Senator Gideon is to receive a trustee's fee of $25,000 per year. For that, he is responsible for investing and monitoring the funds of the foundation and distributing the interest from the foundation corpus to any 501(c)3 charity he deems appropriate. Typically the distribution is in excess of $100,000 per year, with at least 90% of it going to the Northville Regional Medical Center.

Within the accounts of the Medical Center, Senator Gideon has established the Cook account, to which he directs all these donations. The Senator has directed that all

(continues)

Case Study 15-2

disbursements from that account be approved personally by him.

Several weeks ago, Senator Gideon ordered the financial office to prepare a check for $7,500 to Macy's to purchase furniture that was to be delivered to his grandson. A further check of the accounts indicated that over the past two years approximately $10,000 has been disbursed from that account to pay for presents that the Senator has provided to his wife, sister, and several friends. Approximately $2,000 of this went for items purchased at the hospital gift shop; $3,000 was for fund-raising activities involving the system (for example, he used this money to buy raffle tickets for himself and his family from the NRHS's Ladies Auxiliary), and the remainder of the disbursements were to pay for membership dues in the system and other related organizations for himself and other family members. Finally, there was a $3,700 disbursement that was used to pay for Senator Gideon and his wife to travel to San Francisco to attend the annual meeting of the American Hospital Association.

CHAPTER 16

Strategic Planning

INTRODUCTION

Strategic planning does not always work! The battlefield of business is littered with large, small, famous, and infamous failures. Sometimes there are product failures such as Ford's Edsel; other times there are business judgment failures that lead to spectacular bankruptcies of formerly successful businesses such as Penn Central, W. T. Grant, K-Mart, and United Airlines and the fiscal disasters of Lockheed, Chrysler, and Rolls Royce. Even America's favorite entrepreneur, Donald Trump, was forced to declare his Atlantic City casinos bankrupt in 2004.

In the health field, five of the eight largest publicly owned companies went into bankruptcy between September 1999 and June 2000. All of these corporations had in common good reputations and large organizations with seasoned executives and talented planners—but they all failed. They failed because the marketplace is so complex; matching the demand for services or products to needs while considering competition, availability, economic conditions, and myriad other factors requires almost perfect planning (if that exists). A slight miscalculation can spell organizational disaster.

In this chapter, I shall review two basic approaches to strategic planning. For lack of better terms, I shall label the first the "traditional method" (sometimes called the "SWOT approach") and the second the "balanced scorecard" approach. Both rely on similar data points in terms of environmental analysis as well as analyses of the world in which the organization operates and hopes to operate. The balanced scorecard is more "metrically" driven and seeks to find ways of identifying and measuring progress toward definable goals. It shall be discussed at the end of this chapter. I have participated in strategic planning efforts utilizing both approaches and generally am more persuaded that the traditional approach is less expensive and more likely to get organizational buy-in. The balanced scorecard is too consultant-driven and is, from my perspective, too measurement-based. So, while I am out of step with the Harvard Business School proponents of this approach, I do think that any strategic planning exercise is necessary if there is a commitment to follow-through. Without the commitment, it is a waste of time, energy, and money.

BACKGROUND

For the past several generations it has appeared that the demand for health care services and the money to finance those services have been unlimited. Controls on services were essentially unknown until relatively recently. For the most part, the free enterprise mentality still makes it difficult to provide comprehensive regulation in the health industry. Any surgeon, for example, can still simply begin to practice in any community without regard to the needs of that community for another surgeon. Critics of the U.S. health system attribute the high surgery rates throughout the United States to such situations and to the overabundance of surgeons.

How are hospital beds distributed? Who shall say when and where a new facility will be built? Perhaps the most glaring example of the lack of real control in this area occurred in the 1970s, when I was on the faculty of Tulane University in New Orleans. The federal government ignored its own planning agencies and alleged fiscal concerns and built a naval hospital in honor of the former head of the House Armed Forces Committee, Congressman F. Edwin Hebert. The hospital was built on a naval reserve facility that was practically closed, in a community where there were practically no naval or other armed forces activities. In fact, at the time the Navy was busy planning the hospital, the federal government was busy trying to close the neighboring U.S. Public Health Service hospital for a variety of reasons, one of which was underutilization. The naval hospital was eventually built at a cost in excess of $100 million, opened, and so underutilized that within a few years it was leased to a community hospital corporation.

The U.S. health system contrasts sharply with that of Great Britain, where centralized planning is a critical component of the National Health Service. For example, physicians cannot simply move into any community, set up practice, and receive payment from the government. They must move into an open area, essentially receiving authorization to practice in that community from the government before they can be reimbursed for National Health Service patients. Specialists must find an authorized post at an authorized hospital, or they will receive no fees from the government. Of course, British physicians who decide to be totally private entrepreneurs and not accept patients who do not pay privately can practice anywhere they choose, but this occurs in relatively few instances. Under the British scheme, physicians can be distributed according to the population's needs rather than the physicians' needs. In the United States, the distribution is made primarily on the basis of the physicians' needs.

On the other hand, one of the big issues in Canada is how difficult it is to get some services in certain areas. For example, there is a widespread perception that there are significant waits for procedures and that those waits have negative results in terms of health status. While some areas of Canada have addressed these problems by intensive management of waiting lists based on clinical criteria, through projects such as the Western Canada Waiting List Project and the Cardiac Care Network of Ontario, the problem still persists. In 2002, The Honourable Michael J.L. Kirby, Chair of Canada's Senate Committee on Social Affairs, Science and Technology issued a report on the health care situation in Canada. Perhaps the most interesting proposal the committee made for dealing with the perception of delayed access is a health care guarantee, whereby a maximum waiting time would be established for procedures and Canadians would be guaranteed that they would be seen and treated within the guaranteed times, if not within their home provinces, then elsewhere at the government's expense. The idea is simple: Offer the province incentives to provide the care. This is planning at a global level!

At an organizational level, strategic planning is primarily concerned with the organization's need to survive and flourish in a competitive, often quagmire-like environment. In one sense, strategic planning is a subset of general planning; but because of the "future shock" that most health care organizations are going through, with breathtaking, seemingly simultaneous breakthroughs in technology and regulation, strategic planning has come to occupy center stage for many health care organizations. All strategic planning begins with a clear statement of organizational mission. As noted earlier in this book, without a clear mission statement the organization is going 75 miles per hour but does not know where it is headed. A mission statement clarifies the objectives necessary to accomplish the goal. For example, if one has a plan to be a physician, one's objectives could be as broad as graduating from college and getting into medical school. More immediately, one's objectives could be passing biology and organic chemistry. Finally, strategic planning requires recognizing roadblocks, opportunities, and threats along the way and developing strategies to overcome those problems. Using the educational analogy one last time, a strategy might be to skip the party and study or perhaps hire a tutor to get through a critical course.

It should be emphasized that planning is an integral function of all management at all levels, not simply a function delegated to a special group of people labeled "planners." Theoretically, the higher a person is on the organizational chart, the more time he or she should spend in the strategic planning function. While this is likely accurate, the unfortunate reality is that even the most senior executives still spend a good chunk of their time involved in day-to-day organizational management. Hopefully, though, they are thinking more about preventing fires than merely putting them out.

Planning is an activity that requires a synthesis of virtually all the skills within an organization, and strategic planning involves a probing analysis of organizational objectives, strengths (most sensitively), and weaknesses. It also must address organizational opportunities and organizational threats.

There are inherent difficulties in the process of strategic planning. Problem number one is: Who does it? Theoretically, it ought to be an organizational effort. Since strategy and tactics are involved, however, the senior management staff (sometimes just the chief executive officer) often takes the responsibility for strategic planning. As noted earlier, it is easy to get caught up in the dynamics of the day-to-day running of the organization and not set aside the "ideal" planning time. In fact, a common criticism of strategic planning is that the senior executives do not give it sufficient thought, which leads to the second problem: continuity. To be successful, a strategy must have a certain element of continuity. Otherwise, the organization that is to implement the strategy is likely to provide more of a hindrance than help in the implementation.

Strategic planning requires an enormous amount of information and data. The subproblems here, of course, are the availability, timeliness, and quality of information. For example, how does an ambulatory care program determine the potential demand for its services? Census data are usually out-of-date, and it is difficult to get straight answers from physicians about their practices. Without actually undertaking an expensive and time-consuming survey, management is effectively forced to rely on informed guesses.

A final issue to be noted is: Who shall evaluate the strengths and weaknesses of the organization? Analyzing strengths is always a pleasant and usually self-serving job, but what about the weaknesses? How does management say that the institution is losing its patient base because of a move to the suburbs that had been vehemently opposed by the board chairman? In less dramatic terms, the issue might be phrased as: How many organizations ever sit back to analyze their success? Or, for that matter, to what extent do they understand what success is for their organizations? In business organizations, success usually refers to the "bottom line," or profit. An organization that cannot produce a profit is an organization that simply must leave the marketplace. In health care organizations, other than the few proprietary ones, the measure of success has never been profit. But what has it been? Prestige is one of the intangibles that health care organizations have striven toward, as is technical excellence. To some extent, survival has been a major goal in the last few years; although society is not asking many of its charitable organizations to make a profit, it certainly is saying, "Stop losing so much money." And, as noted at the beginning of this chapter, even publicly traded health care companies are not immune from organizational failure.

On the one hand, health care organizations must deal with a mystique about what they do; on the other hand, they must consider some realities, such as a payroll that must be met.

To complicate these basic considerations, health care organizations must also consider their role as socially responsible organizations. These responsibilities have many dimensions; for example, they have a responsibility toward the overall financial well-being of the nation; toward patients, medical staff, and personnel employed by the organization; and toward the community. At one time a hospital in a small upstate New

York town took upon itself an interesting social responsibility. For many years, it operated the only food service facility in the area that was open to the public 24 hours a day. In the early hours of the morning, not only were the late-night workers at the hospital, but also a range of others, including local police and late-night partygoers. According to the hospital's administrator at the time, the hospital felt a special responsibility toward their community, and the opening of their cafeteria was one way in which they met that responsibility.

A more dramatic example comes from a New Jersey hospital that was in the process of closing down patient rooms because of a decline in census. In the interest of good management, such cutbacks would normally result in staff layoffs. In this case, however, there were no layoffs because the hospital was concerned about the economic implications to its community if 100 people were unemployed. Here again can be seen the reality facing the health care organization; it is both a social organization with special responsibilities because of what it does as its daily work, and an economic organization with a vast influence on the total economic system because of the resources it commands. The point is emphasized by the fact that, in many parts of the United States, health services may be the largest industry in town.

An organization interested in strategic planning would have considered a range of basic issues in this case, such as its definition of success, its view of its social responsibility, and, most importantly, its objectives. In the business sense, this would answer the fundamental question: What business are we in, and why?

ENVIRONMENTAL ANALYSIS

The next step in management's strategic planning is to understand what is occurring in the environment around the organization and how that is likely to affect the organization. Environmental changes can be classified into broad categories, such as technological changes, social and political changes, and economic changes. The health field is one that has become particularly sensitive to technological change. Consider how drug therapy has affected the mental health field, literally emptying hospitals and restoring people to the community.

Perhaps an even more dramatic example is the essential elimination of the tuberculosis sanitarium and, for all practical purposes, the apparent elimination of tuberculosis itself until its reemergence in the last decade. But even that reemergence did not result in the reopening of huge TB institutions, since therapy today is easily provided in outpatient or office environments. Organizations dedicated to that disease, whether they were fund-raising or service delivery, needed to change their mission in order to survive. Some did; for example, the tuberculosis associations became lung associations. Others, such as the Will Rogers Sanitarium in Saranac Lake, New York, did not, and they closed.

In 2003, I visited one of those early TB sanatoriums, the world-renowned Trudeau Sanatorium, founded by Dr. Edmund Livingston Trudeau in Saranac Lake, New York. The Trudeau Sanatorium, under the direction of the Francis Trudeau, Jr., the grandson of the founder, shifted direction and became a distinguished research institution in the area of basic immunological and infectious diseases. Walking around their beautiful grounds and buildings, one sees scientists from many countries trying to develop solutions to the medical challenges of the 21st century. To the organization's credit, the elimination of the need for institutionalization of TB patients led to a redefinition of its mission within the context of its resources. If there were a Hall of Fame for strategic planning, the Trudeau Institute would be a member.

As any organization looks to the future, it is necessary and prudent to consider the research priorities and great financial investments being made, primarily by the government. Is it so unlikely that within the next 10 or 20 years cancer will be eliminated and heart disease and stroke will be controlled? What about the significance of stem cell research? What about control of Alzheimer's disease? Such changes would have a profound impact on virtually any health care organization—but how many have considered such eventualities?

The development of computers that allow for the storage and transmittal of vast amounts of information has had an equally significant effect on the health system. Telemedicine has evolved from being a mere experiment to an everyday aspect of some practices. Perhaps the physician distribution problem will be solved with television studios, telemetric equipment, and physicians on duty in emergency studios equipped with monitors and computers.

The technological developments of other fields find their way into the health system. For some procedures, surgeons have traded in their old steel scalpels for laser knives that "cut cleaner and faster." It was not so long ago that the glass syringe and needle that were sent to central supply for sharpening gave way to disposable plastic syringes and needles, which cut down the problem of cross-infection (and, some say, dull needles). Whether all of these changes are progress or not is probably a debatable point, but health care organizations must be sensitive to these possibilities. Who would have envisioned Lasik surgery? Or outpatient cataract surgery?

Most health care organizations greatly depend on people, both as patients and providers, and on the government as a source of financing. As a result, social and political changes have a strong effect on these organizations. For example, demographic trends, such as suburbanization, population mobility, and increased levels of education, all have an impact on the health system. It has been demonstrated in some research that population mobility has resulted in greater utilization of the emergency room by the physician-less patient. Some suggest that the depersonalization of our society has increased litigation. For the health field, this has resulted in an increase in malpractice claims and a subsequent rise in premiums, which eventually translate into higher fees. As one of the three largest employers in the United States, the health system is faced with hiring people who are significantly better educated than their parents and with offering them more challenging and different jobs.

Unionization in the health care field, not only among unskilled and skilled "hourly" workers but also among the professionals, can also be viewed as part of a social trend in labor relations that is part of a larger social movement of civil rights. The effect of social and political changes on the health system can be seen in the changes that began during the 1970s over the issue of abortion. For the first time in U.S. history, an abortion could be performed as a legal procedure. Some hospitals spent years delaying the offering of this service; others simply refused to offer it. At one time in western Massachusetts, the fact that one hospital offered abortion services was a key issue blocking a merger of two facilities. Subsequently, Medicaid payment for abortions affected the availability and distribution of services and manpower.

Today, consumers are realigning their entire relationship with the health system. Thanks to the Internet, many are becoming more knowledgeable about everything from their diagnosis to medications and the disciplinary history of their practitioner. It is possible to make your own diagnosis, decide on your prescription medication, and order it via the Internet. The traditional system has been eliminated.

The health system has been immersed in myriad changes for years now, often caused by changes in the broader economy. Whether inflation, stagnation, foreign competition, or a war in Iraq, the health system is affected. The health system must live in and be affected by the general economic climate.

In the last generation or so, traditional philanthropic sources for health facilities have dried up, and health care organizations have been forced to seek public and private funding for their operations. The notion of a hospital administrator on Wall Street signing a prospectus for a tax-exempt bond offering would have been absurd not too many years ago, but today it is a reality.

Taxes are another mechanism demonstrating how the total economic system affects the health system. Droves of practitioners have incorporated in the last few years in order to take advantage of a range of tax benefits available to the professional corporation but not to the private practitioner. Tax laws may be used as an inducement for certain practice situations, such as an inner-city or group practice. This is hardly farfetched in view of the financial incentives and disincentives Great Britain has used in order to make its system workable. Another area for concern is the occasional grumbling about the tax-exempt status of hospitals and other nonprofit facilities and organizations. Many of these institutions own considerable real estate and produce revenue from questionable activities. So far, judicial opinions have tended to favor the tax-exempt institutions in cases such as those concerning medical office buildings. The door has been opened to questions on the tax-exempt status for nonprofit health care organizations, however, and recent challenges suggest the development of a new paradigm for the 21st century; a paradigm that will hold nonprofits more fiscally responsible than they have been in the past.

The key to effective management in the face of such environmental changes is having a good early warning or scanning system. Such a system theoretically could cost the equivalent of a talented and expensive front office staff, which is considerably more than most organizations can afford. To a large extent, these scanning activities could be carried out by national, regional, and local trade and professional organizations.

Trends can be discerned by an organization that has made a commitment to be part of the larger economic and social picture in a region or community. Boards can be most helpful in pinpointing trends likely to affect an organization, but management must want to know what is happening; it must have an appetite for the future. Without this appetite, the organization will eventually find itself with problems that could have been avoided. Illustrative of this situation is one hospital that was located at the edge of the commuter belt of a metropolitan area. Although most members of the community were employed in the local areas, perhaps 30% of the workforce commuted the 45 miles into the city. A member of the hospital's board was the chief executive officer of the largest industry in the community, which employed over 5,000 people. Several years earlier his company had been taken over by a large conglomerate, and the plan was to move the plant to the South within the next few years. The administrator of the hospital never discussed the industry's business with its chief executive officer and had no idea that a move was in the works until it was announced in the local papers. An expansion being considered by the hospital was effectively scrapped, or at least put on hold, when the information about the impending transfer came to light. While it can be argued that the chief executive officer should have initiated talks with the administrator, it was the administrator who wanted to expand and should have been concerned about the environment. Or, to put it another way, it was the administrator's problem.

STRENGTHS AND WEAKNESSES ANALYSIS

The next step in the strategic planning process is perhaps the most difficult in that it requires the organization to identify its strengths and weaknesses. As noted earlier, the identification of strengths is psychologically easier than the identification of weaknesses. It is imperative, however, that those areas where the organization is vulnerable be identified; otherwise, the organization cannot be protected. A framework for considering strengths and weaknesses might be (1) demand for services; (2) capacity for delivering services; (3) competition, both present and projected; (4) market position; and (5) cost position.

Demand for Services

A consideration of demand for services could begin with an examination of the usefulness and/or substitutes for the "product" being offered. To an extent, health services are monopoly items, and consumers have little choice but to use health care practitioners and their organizations. However, change that can affect demand does indeed occur in the health care field. The optometric profession is one of those areas of significant change. In the early 1970s, only 22 states allowed optometrists to use diagnostic drugs to dilate the pupils, which results in a more effective eye examination. This expansion of the optometrists' scope of licensure had taken place in a heated arena, with ophthalmologists claiming that the dangers inherent in optometrists' using drugs were so great that it should not be allowed. But in 2004, every state allows optometrists to dilate pupils with medication. Today, every state except Massachusetts allows optometrists to treat glaucoma; this practice conflict revolves around the power of optometrists to prescribe antibiotics.

The past decades have brought extraordinary changes. As noted earlier, the legalization of first trimester abortions has resulted in a demand for services that were simply unavailable (legally) before the Supreme Court decisions. Safer and more convenient methods of family planning and changing public attitudes have resulted in a declining birth rate. Even Viagra has changed sexual behavior! New technology has given rise to organ transplants and a range of surgery that makes the notion of a "bionic person" not so unrealistic. On a long-term basis, all of this and more must be considered when the health care organization assesses its strengths and weaknesses. For example, is the mix of services being offered what is needed in the community? Does the demographic data in the area suggest that a different mix of services would be more appropriate today? Next year? In five years? Is today's success preventing the consideration of the formula needed to be successful two years from today?

Capacity for Delivering Services

The second area for consideration is the capacity for delivering services; in other words, to what extent does the present organization have the ability to deliver quality services at a competitive price? This is a function of a variety of factors, including the quality and price of the organization's labor force and its physical facilities. One hospital was extremely competitive because it had an old facility that had been totally depreciated and was in relatively good shape. A new facility at today's prices, however, would have made its cost of services two or three times higher than that of the best teaching hospital in the area.

Competition

For years, the notion that health care organizations competed with one another was avoided. Competition for physicians and patients does take place, however, albeit on a professional level and usually in subtle ways. Planners must consider both present and projected competition. In the case of a hospital-based group practice, competition might come from the private practitioners associated with the hospital, physicians practicing in a hospital-owned or hospital-operated office building, the emergency room in the hospital, other group practices in the community, or operating or planned health maintenance organizations.

Market Position and Cost Position

Once the sources of competition have been identified, it is necessary to assess the organization's market position. To what extent can it compete effectively with others offering similar services? Many factors come into play here, such as the organization's image, physical location, quality of facilities, reputation of practitioners, and cost. In the health care field, this last element may or may not be too significant, depending on the nature of the source of payment. If the organization is an ambulatory care program in which there is likely to be a fair degree of self-payment by the patient, cost might be an important element in the total market position.

Cost is related to a host of factors, such as efficiency of equipment, cost and productivity of labor, and the quality of the organization's operating systems. In considering cost, the opportunity cost to the patient of utilizing the program or facility should be analyzed, and ways of minimizing those costs should be sought. For example, what can an outstanding diagnostic center located in an out-of-the-way place, such as the Mayo Clinic or the Geisinger Clinic, do to make it easier for a patient to stay there for a few days for diagnostic tests? For example, it is relatively easy to get transportation from the Minneapolis International Airport to the Mayo Clinic in Rochester, Minnesota. The clinic is surrounded by hotels, and almost all of them connect via enclosed bridges or underground tunnels to the Clinic complex. This is quite important during the harsh Minnesota winters. The Clinic itself also has numerous educational opportunities for patients waiting for tests and appointments, including a library and Internet connections. Within its "underground city" are restaurants, gift shops, and a huge bookstore in a former movie theatre. Similarly, in Dallas, Texas, I visited Medical Cities, which is a complex that includes a hospital, parking garage, doctor's office building, and small shopping center where a person can do everything from shop for clothing to drop off dry cleaning. All of these are ideas that are designed to make the system more user-friendly for staff and consumers.

Now that this internal and external evaluation has been worked through, strategic planning next calls for the delineation of alternatives and the selection of the best strategy to meet these stated objectives within the constraints presented. When I was teaching a course at the Columbia University School of Business, a popular case that was used in strategic planning was that of the Head Ski Company; I used this company as an example also in Chapter 5. In the late 1950s and early 1960s, the Head Ski Company dominated the U.S. ski market, marketing a very small line of high-quality merchandise. Its main focus was the most technically advanced ski in the country, a metal laminated ski invented by Howard Head, the company's founder and chief executive. By the mid-1960s, the company lost ground to the new, lighter, and more colorful fiberglass skis arriving from Japan, and within a few years the company lost its leadership position in this rapidly expanding industry. Head is portrayed as an inventor more concerned with fine-tuning the edges of his skis than making a dollar in the marketplace; the world is portrayed as having an insatiable demand for high technology skis; and the Head Company is portrayed as being committed to only one technology, the metal laminate, and to one color, black. The question posed to the class is: What do you do?

There are many analogies to Head Ski in the health care field, and I present the following case of the Victoria Hills Geriatric Center to demonstrate how the aforementioned approach to strategic planning might look "in vivo."

Case Study 16-1

VICTORIA HILLS GERIATRIC CENTER:
An Illustration of Strategic Planning

Introduction

For more than six decades, the Victoria Hills Geriatric Center (VHGC) has been a premier provider of services to the elderly in South County, California. A snapshot of the organization on December 31, 2004, shows the 15-acre Victoria Hill campus with a 350-bed nursing home; a 108-bed subacute rehabilitation center; an 84-bed JCAHO-accredited geriatric hospital; a geriatric ambulatory medical clinic; two adult day care centers (one exclusively for Alzheimer's patients); and a 235-unit apartment complex that is used for both independent and assisted living. In rented space three blocks from the Victoria Hill campus, the Center operates a research institute in partnership with South County University.

This large enterprise represents a physical plant in excess of $100 million, a staff of almost 1,200 full-time employees, and an annual operating budget in excess of $87 million.

Resting on the laurels of being a premier organization is easy and attractive, but it is also dangerous because of the dynamism of the environment. On a global level, changes in Medicare and Medicaid funding, managed care, and private philanthropy (the backbone of the organization), as well as changes in terms of competition between providers all have an impact on the organization. On a regional level, the VHGC is finding itself having to establish new business lines in order to compete in a newer and more competitive marketplace and deal with the realities of an increasingly managed-care, organization-driven system.

Finally, as this organization looks toward the future, it must begin the process of transition to a new generation of

(continues)

Case Study 16-1

volunteers willing to lead the organization into the 21st century with the same vigor, vision, and commitment of those people who have spent the post–World War II years building its solid foundation.

The Strategic Plan is a major step in identifying and analyzing the Center's present strengths and weaknesses and in setting a course for its future, which, like all maps, often needs modification. As with all navigational tools, it establishes the goals and directions that are imperative for the success of the organization.

Mission

The mission of VHGC has been decided on by a consensus of staff with approval of the Board. The mission is to be the premier multicomponent, nonprofit, teaching-oriented, charitable geriatric health care system in the South County region, guided by traditional values, dedicated to effectively and efficiently serving a nonsectarian population of elderly, disabled, and chronically ill people with a broad range of the highest quality, institutionally based, community-based, and ambulatory care services.

Vision

The Victoria Hills Geriatric Center shall be an organization dedicated to excellence in the provision of care to the elderly and the chronically ill; to the education of health professionals; and to the provision of service to the community.

Values

The central value of the VHGC is the fifth Commandment of the Bible: "Honor thy father and thy mother." From this Commandment it derives its responsibility of providing a

(continues)

Case Study 16-1

quality and quantity of reverential and dignified care for the elderly of the community.

In the provision of care, the VHGC honors and supports the rights of residents and patients; in the area of education, it commits itself to the provision of teaching services by appropriately qualified professionals who are respectful of study; in the area of research, it commits itself to actively pursuing organizational-based research initiatives, as well as actively cooperating with researchers from other institutions.

Environmental Analysis

The Neighborhood: Victoria Hill is a neighborhood in transition. When the Center was built 60 years ago, Victoria Hill was a solidly middle-class community. Today it is a lower-class neighborhood with some of the worst crime and drug statistics in the county. While it is possible that the neighborhood is stabilizing and perhaps improving, there is still a long way to go before it attains its former comfortable status. Despite these problems, real estate in the area is expensive (in part due to the perception that the VHGC will pay anything it has to in order to expand). Because of the crime problem in the adjacent area, the Center expends significant funds for protective services.

South County: The county is in both political and financial turmoil. The political issues have resulted in the perception that the Center's formerly significant political clout in governmental issues is diminishing. The fiscal issues are likely to result in new county initiatives to increase revenues, such as proposed fire and rescue surcharges that could add $60,000 in expenses to the Center's budget.

There is a general perception that South County is losing its middle class. The "hot" growth areas appear to be

(continues)

Case Study 16-1

in the distant South County communities of DuMont, Brigham Hills, and Bialytsok—all at least 15 miles away from VHGC. There is a perception that much of the increase in the affluent communities is related to newcomers to California without any attachment to any traditional social service organizations such as VHGC. In each of these communities, new upscale nursing homes have been built, along with upscale assisted living facilities. Despite the fact that the VHGC owns 50 acres of land in DuMont, it has yet to develop that land, although plans for a 150-bed assisted living facility have been a subject of managerial and board discussion for more than five years.

Organizational Strengths

1. *Reputation:* On one hand, the VHGC name has been synonymous with quality for more than 60 years. Unfortunately, a South County University School of Business marketing survey in 2002 found that 45% of the studied population was not familiar with the Home.

2. *High Quality and Dedicated Staff:* The professional, senior executive, middle management, and operating staff of the organization is professionally trained, highly motivated, and sensitive to the needs of the VHGC clients. Many staff have been professionally recognized with extramural awards and positions on boards of other organizations and agencies.

3. *Strong Balance Sheet:* Because of their investments and fund-raising ability, the VHGC has been able to be fiscally sound and has utilized this strength to borrow funds for project development. Without the income from the endowment and fund-raising, the organization would be running a multimillion-dollar deficit.

(*continues*)

Case Study 16-1

4. *Lack of Bureaucratic Impediments:* Once organizational decisions are made, there are few bureaucratic impediments to their implementation.

5. *Continuum of Care:* In both the areas of geriatric services and mental health care, the VHGC has developed an almost seamless web of services that allows it to provide comprehensive services to its constituencies. This continuum also allows it to offer a broad range of services to the marketplace.

6. *Capacity to Meet New Demands:* The size and resources of VHGC allow it to effectively and efficiently meet new demands for services by temporarily deploying available resources until new ones can be developed.

7. *Tradition of Innovation:* All components of the organization have a tradition of being innovative and encouraging innovations. While innovation has a risk of potentially "wasting" resources, it also represents the benefit of being a leading organization that potentially captures market share and new resources.

Organizational Weaknesses

An appraisal of an organization's weaknesses is necessarily painful; however, such a careful analysis is also a prerequisite to organizational growth and development and should always be construed as organizational weaknesses, not personal weaknesses.

1. *Regulatory Environment:* All components of the organization perceive a more demanding regulatory environment in the future. Although a new corporate compliance plan has been developed, there is only limited support for this program from senior board members, who view the program as a governmental intrusion.

(*continues*)

Case Study 16-1

2. *Confusing Array of Products and Services:* The VHGC offers its products and services through nine separate corporations. While none of these directly compete with the others, it does result in the board of directors and outsiders being confused as to whether the Center is really a large nursing home or "something else."

3. *Name Recognition:* Much as the *South County Times* newspaper is known merely as the Times outside of South County, it is perceived that the Victoria Hills Geriatric Center name is a drawback outside of the local region.

4. *Lack of Coordinated Organizational Programming:* Departments often appear to be working at cross-purposes and are not aware of other programming going on. This results in conflicting policies that are confusing to the public as well as to the staff.

5. *Poor Organizational Communication:* There is poor or no communication within various departments of the nursing home and across different departments in the organization. As in number 4, this results in a confusing array of policies and procedures, and to some extent a sense of inequity.

6. *No Clear Measures of Expectations:* No processes are followed in decision making. Decisions appear to be a result of the desires of one or two board members, who in turn evaluate staff by whether the staff have been responsive to their individual needs.

7. *Board Needs Significant Restructuring:* There is a lack of a functioning board. Generally, there is an over-reliance on the deeply entrenched board leadership, who often make decisions based on their intuitive feel for a situation and tend to dismiss any analytical approach from management. Board leadership has a

(*continues*)

Case Study 16-1

deep distrust of all outside consultants. It is increasingly difficult to recruit new independent directors.

8. *Unfocused Budgeting:* There are no budgetary or "bottom-line" goals, making it difficult to develop administrative outcomes. There is a pervasive attitude that the budget can always be supplemented by fundraising, thus resulting in an over-dependence on fundraising activities.

9. *Location:* The location of the Center in a poor and crime-ridden community is thought to be a problem in terms of recruitment of residents for the nursing home and use of our ambulatory care services. Family members, particularly in the newly developing suburbs, are interested in finding facilities that are more convenient to their own homes. Staff recruitment also may be a problem, both because of the neighborhood and lack of public transportation. In order to have a secure campus, in excess of $1.5 million a year is spent on security. There is little that can be done to change this situation, other than to continue to work on making Victoria Hills a more secure and livable community.

10. *Slowness of New Ventures:* For a variety of reasons, the nursing home is slow to develop feeder beds from its other programs, such as its assisted living center and day care centers. The overall strategy of the skilled facility being the hub network of less skilled programming, i.e., day care centers, simply is not realized.

11. *Payer Mix:* At present, approximately 66% of the residents are covered by Medicaid, causing the Center significant losses each year. All efforts to increase the private pay census, including becoming a multilingual international referral center, have been unsuccessful.

Having gone down this analytical path, which took VHGC considerable preparation, countless person-hours of meetings, drafts, and redrafts of documents, the next step is to examine the opportunities for the future and make some decisions. Options include (1) "doing nothing," that is, allowing the organization to continue doing exactly what it has been doing, including potentially depleting its endowment corpus and losing ground to competitors; (2) going through a process of examining each of the components of the organization with an eye to both controlling expenses and generating new revenues; or (3) seriously considering a variety of merger options. Each of these options require their own analysis of strengths, weaknesses, opportunities, and threats, and then from this analytical model there will hopefully be a clearest path.

However, no path is without its challenges, and despite the finest and most careful due diligence, new issues always seem to emerge. For example, consider the now-bankrupt toy chain FAO Schwarz. At one point they were a prestigious money-making business, but they could not handle the competition from the high-volume business Toys R Us. Toys R Us, in turn, announced in the summer of 2004 that they were going bankrupt because they were having trouble competing with Wal-Mart. In the early 1990s, based on their positive experience and bottom line, Toys R Us probably never envisioned the day when Wal-Mart would drive them out of business, and the high-end FAO Schwarz probably never envisioned being driven to bankruptcy by a mass-market competitor.

Change is inevitable and often unpredictable, even in health care. Nevertheless, a strategic plan does help set direction and reviews progress on a periodic basis. Without a plan, the organization is merely drifting, always subject to winds and currents. With a plan, a better course is possible.

THE BALANCED SCORECARD APPROACH

Perhaps I should begin by stating that I am not a big fan of the balanced scorecard approach. I believe it tends to quantify the unquantifiable and, through its metrics, tends to be driven to measure what may not be central to an organization. On the other hand, any process that results in people sitting together to talk about the future of the organization is healthy in and of itself. By way of context, it should be recognized that every few years a new idea emerges that captures the attention of management. Forty years ago it was management by objectives, followed by strategic planning with the aforementioned SWOT analysis. More recently there has been a focus on Total Quality Improvement (TQI) or Continuous Quality Improvement (CQI). The latest entry, balanced scorecards, was developed by two Harvard Business School professors in the early 1990s. The balanced scorecard operates from the premise that traditional planning methods are backward-looking; that is, they measure performance that has already occurred, not those components of an organization that create its long-term value, such as its business processes, its customer satisfaction and loyalty, and its ability to change via learning and growth.

In 2003, I participated in a "Balanced Scorecard" project with a professional college's clinical division. While traditional strategic planning can be done by both internal staff and external consultants, balanced scorecard work needs the expertise of a specialist consultant to develop the project and educate the participants via a magnificent PowerPoint presentation. Prior to a retreat in which over 30 faculty and administrators participated, a faculty coordinator met with numerous faculty and staff to get input on various factors, and to solicit their involvement in the project. After hours of presentations, discussions, and small group work, a draft balanced scorecard with 30 bubbles was developed. At the highest level was the financial element. Its overall objective was to ensure financial viability in order to achieve the organization mission. Four other bubbles on that line related to that objective, including cost-control measures and revenue-generating measures. The retreat did not go any further on these issues but left it to management to come up with the numbers to measure success in these arenas.

The second component examined was that of "customers." Customers were defined as patients, the community, and the professional college's parent educational institution, which provides a service fee to the clinical division for educational expenses. Each of these constituencies has a variety of often differing goals, such as improved access to care for community members, increased donor or grantor support for the educational bubble, and improved affordability for patients.

Half of the bubbles on the chart were found in the "process" component. The four areas of concern in processes are product innovation, which is designed to make the organization a leader in the field; customer intimacy, designed to ensure that the organization and customer are in synch; operational excellence, a component that ensures the organization is operating at a "best practice" level; and finally regulatory and society, in which the organization focuses on meeting all regulatory requirements and even influencing developing regulations.

The final component in the scorecard is that of learning and growth. These bubbles focus on the organization's intellectual and communicative growth, clearly a noble objective.

At the end of the retreat, these ideas were spelled out. The next step was to operationalize them into measurable objectives and then evaluate how well these objectives were met over a predetermined period. While it is too early to tell whether the project in this organization will work, the Balanced Scorecard Collaborative points to successes at major companies such as Chemical Bank and AT&T Canada, and in the health field, Duke Children's Hospital and St. Mary's Duluth Clinic Health System are perhaps the leading organizations in this niche of the consulting industry.

In conclusion, strategic planning is imperative for any organization. Whether the organization does the planning itself or uses the help of outside consultants, whether it uses a SWOT analysis, a balanced scorecard approach, or any other process is, in my judgment, not as significant as the fact that organizational leadership and staff are engaged in a productive dialogue about the future of their organization. Equally important is a commitment that that dialog will lead to action and evaluation. Without a commitment to action and evaluation, the dialog is mere "hot air" that is debilitating to the organization. With commitment, though, a constituency of consumers and staff will exist who are dedicated to the organization's positive and prosperous future.

CHAPTER 17

Epilogue

MANAGEMENT AND PATIENTS

Throughout this volume, I have attempted to provide readers with a clear view of how to be an effective 21st-century health care manager. However, what I have not yet done is share a philosophical vision about what it means to do well and to do good! Somewhere along the line, many health care managers have either not learned or forgotten that their *raison d'être* is ensuring that patients receive health care that is accessible, high quality, and delivered in a cost-effective manner. Hospitals, HMOs, nursing homes, clinics, and other facilities and organizations exist for the benefit of the patients. The income and perquisites of employment generated by each enterprise for doctors, administrators, staff, owners, shareholders, and purveyors should be merely incidental to the organization's mission. Unfortunately, the message of the patient as central to the health of the organization has been lost in many cases.

One hypothesis is that this loss took place in the halls of academia during the years of transition between heath care administration education as essentially vocational training to the present day, where it is a respected academic discipline. From the 1930s through the 1960s, the directors of health administration (aka hospital administration) programs were academically oriented practitioners. In contrast, most of the founding fathers of the profession did not have doctorates but rather had experience. Gary Hartman at the University of Iowa distinguished himself as the director of the University of Iowa Hospitals and Clinics. Long after he retired, he was still a revered person on the medical campus; when I was visiting Iowa City, I was told that Hartman and the dean of the medical school breakfasted together and strategized every day for decades. At the University of Chicago, Ray Brown presided over both the graduate program and the University of Chicago clinics. I first met Brown in 1960 when I went out to Chicago to interview for graduate school. By then, Brown was a well-known author and leader in the field, but what impressed me was his hospitality and patient orientation. This was particularly interesting given that his program was situated in the business school.

John Thompson, a gruff-talking, warm-hearted, and humorous man, headed the Yale Program. Thompson was a nurse who later became an operating room supervisor at the Brooklyn Jewish Hospital. His lack of a doctorate hardly prevented him from becoming a beloved professor at Yale, an expert on health care architecture and quantitative methods, and one of the fathers of the DRG system. My own program director at Columbia University, Clement C. Clay, was one of the few physicians who went into the academic side of this fledgling field. Before taking his post at Columbia, Clay had been the director of the East Orange Medical Center in New Jersey. He brought into the classroom his experience in real-world management and his sensitivity to the needs of patients, as well as his expectations that we, as his students, would continue with a similar philosophy.

All of these men (unfortunately health care was a very sexist operation in those days) knew and understood patients and their centrality to organizational mission. Simply put, the patient aspect of management was second nature to them, and they passed that tradition down through their students.

Graduate programs today are high on intellectual prowess, PhDs, research, publications, and policy analysis. Lost in the educational equation is the patient. The days of the required one-year supervised field training have essentially disappeared, replaced by challenging coursework. Perhaps the greatest loss is that of the field preceptors, who truly mentored us young neophytes. My Obi-Wan Kenobi was Sydney Peimer who, like John Thompson, was an OR nurse. On the first day of my administrative residency, Peimer shocked me. I was just getting comfortable in a cushy leather chair when Peimer asked me into his office and proceeded to tell me that the first month of my residency would be spent delivering direct patient care as a nurse's aide. Within minutes I had changed out of my suit into the white uniform of an aide. For the next two days, I was tutored on the basics of being on the front lines of patient care, followed by a month on the wards—all shifts. I bathed patients, changed beds, helped people use bedpans and urinals, and then emptied and cleaned them. I transferred and transported patients and worked for a week in the operating room. What I learned in that exhaustive month provided me with an intense understanding and simpatico for front-line patient care staff, as well as the trauma associated with being a patient. Any distance or fear I may have felt for patients was forever erased, and to this day I am as comfortable with patients as I am with students or fellow executives.

The importance of the patient in the organization, and the role of management in that equation, were beautifully demonstrated to me in June 2004 when I visited a nursing home in Columbus, Ohio, that was owned by the EXTENDICARE corporation. This home sits in the downtown section of Columbus, adjacent to a Catholic-run community hospital. While visiting the home with other members of the EXTENDICARE board of directors, I learned of their Guardian Angel Program. This program assigns various staff members to be Guardian Angels to the residents in the home. In simple terms, nonpatient-care staff, such as the business office manager or someone in maintenance, is assigned to be a friend and essentially internal ombudsman to several residents. The responsibilities include regular visits, checking to see that the resident is being properly attended to, reporting any problems to the director of nursing or the administrator, and following up on problems. The result of this is a patient-centered organization and one in which everyone is engaged in the mission of providing quality care. The Guardian Angel Program has been so successful that it is being adopted throughout the company's facilities in Ohio and West Virginia, and is likely to be utilized through the entire organization.

The essence of this program and similar ones is an environment of kindness to patients. I have found some wonderful rewards as a result of getting to know patients over the course of my years in health care management. For example, I met a young man recovering from surgery who was completely confused about his career. It became clear after several conversations that hospital administration might be a good path for him. He went on to get a master's from Yale and a doctorate from Harvard and today is a well-known consultant.

A few years ago, I met a nursing home resident who turned out to be a famous Yiddish songwriter. He came to see me to complain about his room, and over the years of our friendship he became my guide to the history of Tin Pan Alley. From the many elderly patients I have known, I have learned about the preciousness of life and hope and the deliciousness and delicacy of relationships, particularly familial ones.

While working in a prison health system, I learned from inmates what could so easily and quickly go wrong, as well as how important human contact can be. I have also learned from these men about unlimited creativity, such as when inmates would feign illness for the sake of obtaining medications that were particularly valuable for resale to other inmates. And from the four Haitian nurse's aides who provided hospice care to my dying mother, I learned the boundlessness of human kindness, a kindness that clearly was unrelated to their low wages.

On the hospital ship REPOSE during the height of the Vietnam War, I sat through a painful group therapy with young Navy and Marine patients. I listened to their fear and heard them bare their psychic scars of war. Shortly after, I spent a couple of days in country at Chu Lai with the Third Marine Division and talked with patients injured with the physical scars of that war. In my 19-month tour at the naval hospital, Subic Bay, Philippines, I talked and worked with thousands of patients and hundreds of war casualties, some of whom I had to ship home dead. Decades later, I met the unfortunate who physically survived the battlefield but whose psychic wounds never healed, leaving them to a life in a VA psychiatric hospital in Northampton, Massachusetts. A sign for many years on the lawn of that hospital said it all: "Here the Price of Freedom Is Paid."

Unfortunately, the longest and most intense experiences I had were my five and a half years as the husband of a cancer patient. During those trying years, my late wife endured three major surgeries, several minor surgeries, over fifty hospital admissions, and countless office visits and telephone consultations. It often was the little things over which management had control that made a difference in our experiences. For example, the positive and helpful attitude of the parking attendants at the front door of Brigham and Women's Hospital simply set a good tone for the day. That fabulous hospital worked assiduously to ensure that each time my late wife was admitted she would be in the same room, in an attempt to cut down stress. The oncology floor had headsets and various educational and meditation tapes to assist people in getting through their awful journeys. At the Fox Chase Cancer Center in Northeast Philadelphia, the physical environment was itself soothing. At Baystate Medical Center in

Springfield, Massachusetts, staff seemed always available for an extra word that helped explain things or comfort us. On the hand, there were cancer centers that were cold, distant, and seemed to be so calculating that they could steal one's hope. In my opinion, it is management's job to position the environmental thermostat to a setting whereby no patient's self-esteem or his or her hope is diminished, whether by the place or the staff.

My two final stories are about Disney and L.L. Bean. A friend and his wife flew with their 12-year-old son to Disney World for a birthday trip several years ago. While sitting around the Disney hotel pool, the child was stung by a large insect, and it appeared that he was having a reaction to the sting. After consulting with a physician friend on the phone they decided to go to the nearest hospital, which was in the Disney development town of Celebration, Florida. They checked with the hotel's front desk about transportation (they did not have a car) and were informed that the best thing to do was to take a cab and keep the receipts, which would be deducted from their room charges! A few weeks after the trip, the boy wrote to Disney, saying how disappointed he was that he had spent an evening in the emergency room and had felt so badly the next day that he had missed out a day at Disney. He urged them to be more active about insect control and so forth. He received a profuse apology, as well as six tickets for future visits to Disney.

Story two involves the Maine-based clothing company L.L. Bean. I purchased a wool sweater from them one winter and hung it in my closet after the season. At the beginning of the following winter, I pulled the sweater off the hanger and discovered a moth hole. I called L.L. Bean and asked if they could reweave the sweater and what the cost would be. They replied that they would not reweave it, but if I mailed it back to them, they would send me a new sweater at no cost! Not only did they make me a customer for life, but I also became and still am a great promoter of the company.

Both these stories illustrate why these companies, as well as others such as Lands' End and Nordstrom's, have become legendary in the world of customer orientation and satisfaction. Health care managers must also strive to provide centers of clinical and spiritual excellence. In this way, we all fulfill our mission.

INDEX